Global Wealth Chains

Global Wealth Chains

Asset Strategies in the World Economy

Edited by

Leonard Seabrooke
Duncan Wigan

OXFORD
UNIVERSITY PRESS

Great Clarendon Street, Oxford, OX2 6DP,
United Kingdom

Oxford University Press is a department of the University of Oxford.
It furthers the University's objective of excellence in research, scholarship,
and education by publishing worldwide. Oxford is a registered trade mark of
Oxford University Press in the UK and in certain other countries

Published in the United States of America by Oxford University Press
198 Madison Avenue, New York, NY 10016, United States of America

British Library Cataloguing in Publication Data
Data available

Library of Congress Control Number: 2021952582

ISBN 978-0-19-883237-9

DOI: 10.1093/oso/9780198832379.001.0001

Printed and bound by
CPI Group (UK) Ltd, Croydon, CR0 4YY

Cover image: Torbjørn Vagstein

Links to third party websites are provided by Oxford in good faith and
for information only. Oxford disclaims any responsibility for the materials
contained in any third party website referenced in this work.

Acknowledgments

This book began with Sunday lunch. At that lunch we discussed how scholars had developed significant work on financialization, on how the 'offshore world' was becoming more important for corporations, and on how firms and corporations were becoming different things through processes of fragmenting, unbundling, decentering, and other terms that convey the sense that something that was coherent and whole is no longer. Conversations on these processes were taking place in economic geography, political economy, and management studies. Other conversations were taking place in sociology on the mechanisms through which elites and organizations changed finance, and in law on how indeterminacy permitted an international legal system to allow arbitrage on a massive scale. These conversations were taking place at these disciplines own tables, not across them, but they were all concerned with how actors used legal jurisdictions to create and protect wealth. At our lunch we asked: How could we possibly talk about how these processes are changing the world economy in a way that permitted a common conversation? We envied other discussions. Economic geographers, sociologists, and political economists had developed a common thread to discuss how production and commodity networks had internationalized through firms. It was possible to discuss how global value chains were constructed and maintained, and to codify types of transactions and how they assisted or impaired development. International organizations like the World Bank had readily adopted this language as well, providing a link between an interdisciplinary academic conversation and actual policy impact. Through the production of typologies it would be possible to build a series of cases from which development aims and corporate profitability could be pursued (Gereffi et al., 2005).

Such a conversation would be more difficult to create around wealth. After all, the normative aim of global value chains scholarship was to assist development by increasing transparency within the world economy. Firms involved in production could benefit from sharing information with them, as did international organizations and development agencies.

Those operating with global wealth chains had a strong interest in not revealing information. Firms and their corporate structures, as well as elites individuals, would have no particular interest in having researchers use typologies to build a series of cases in which sensitive information may be exposed. Still, the scholarly interest may gather momentum, in part because having a common conversation would allow us to talk about finance and taxation as drivers of global inequalities. Toward the end of the lunch we asked each other "why not global wealth chains?" Value and wealth, after all, were fundamentally different. They are the yin and yang of the modern firm and lead to different use of corporate forms. Both are required, but they are articulated in different ways. The purposes of creating multi-jurisdictional chains for value would differ strongly from those formed to create and protect wealth. Showing how the wealth chains were articulated and located would be interesting. It would require bringing together scholars from political economy, economic geography, sociology, accounting, management studies, anthropology, and law. All of these fields would be necessary to engage because looking into opaque structures requires light from many directions. We finished our lunch, quite happy with ourselves.

From then our plan was to build a research team and pilot project. The Norwegian Research Council generously funded the first push with the Systems of Tax Evasion and Laundering (STEAL) project (#212210/H30-STEAL). The team included scholars from political Economy, law, economic geography, management, and sociology. That group put together a series of cases, many of which have been published in journals. We then won a European Research Council Advanced project, led by STEAL team member Ronen Palan, on corporate arbitrage systems. This success permitted the second push. We assembled a new team of scholars, across all the fields mentioned above, and held a workshop near Exmouth Market in London to develop coherence around how some of the ideas in the global wealth chains typology, that we had developed to deliberately mirror the global value chain types from a decade prior (Gereffi et al., 2005), could be brought to life in original empirical material. The conversation worked. The anthropologist could talk to the political economist, the sociologist to the accountancy scholar, and so on. The focus was on different types of 'assets' used by firms and by professionals. We understood 'assets' as a legally binding document that provides differential claims on wealth—a legal affordance that, if defended by a jurisdiction and/or social group, would create or protect wealth for particular people or corporate entities.

This focus permitted the contributors to this volume to discuss how global wealth chains are constructed, knowing that the aim was to govern how assets were made to create and protect wealth.

For the initial workshop behind this book we thank the European Research Council (ERC) grant 'Corporate Arbitrage and CPL Maps' (#694943-CORPLINK), which has also supported our writing and editorial work for the volume. Our thanks also go to those who provided comments on draft chapters and the project as a whole, especially Glenn Morgan and Jason Sharman. Richard Murphy receives special thanks for his conversations with us on all the individual contributions. We also thank our excellent postgraduate students at the Copenhagen Business School, who ran ahead with ideas on how to trace wealth chains. Venja Wenche Birch and Sara Louise Synnevåg Nybø (on salmon), Riccardo Cavosi (on film), Mie Højris Dahl and Jam Kamb (on beer and drugs), Mads Godballe (also beer), and Saila Stausholm (on mining) deserve a special mention for thinking through how one can sensibly identify wealth chain corporate entities. For those who provided impetus and momentum to the project we thank Benjamin de Carvalho, John Christensen, Stine Haakonsson, John Humphrey, Helge Hveem, Stefano Ponte, Thomas Rixen, Helge Rynning, Eleni Tsingou, and Attiya Waris. For feedback on the framework we thank participants at seminars at RMIT Melbourne, University of Los Andes Bogota, Handelshøyskolen BI, the Independent Social Research Foundation, and the Norwegian Institute of International Affairs, as well as panels at the Society for the Advancement of Socio-Economics and the International Studies Association. Finally, we thank our contributors for our common conversation, and especially for their patience while we put the links in place.

Leonard Seabrooke
Duncan Wigan

Frederiksberg, Denmark

Contents

List of Figures   x
List of Tables   xi
Contributors   xii

1. **Asset Strategies in Global Wealth Chains**   1
   Leonard Seabrooke and Duncan Wigan

2. **Public Utilities**   30
   Colin Haslam, Adam Leaver, and Nick Tsitsianis

3. **Tax Treaties**   49
   Martin Hearson

4. **Advance Pricing Agreements**   68
   Matti Ylönen

5. **Intangible Capital**   89
   Dick Bryan, Michael Rafferty, and Duncan Wigan

6. **Private Equity**   114
   Jamie Morgan

7. **Beer and Pharmaceuticals**   133
   Mie Højris Dahl

8. **Food**   155
   Verónica Grondona and Martín Burgos

9. **Art**   182
   Oddný Helgadóttir

10. **Family Generations**   201
    Mariana Santos

11. **Transparency**   220
    Rasmus Corlin Christensen

12. **Mining**   242
    Saila Stausholm

13. **Legal Opinion**   262
    Clair Quentin

14. **Articulating Global Wealth Chains**   279
    Leonard Seabrooke and Duncan Wigan

Index   298

List of Figures

1.1 Typology of global wealth chains 11
1.2 Mapping contributions to global wealth chain types 14
2.1 Veolia Water UK assets and liabilities 42
2.2 Veolia Water UK reverse debt structure 43
3.1 Maximum withholding tax rates on dividends from direct investment permitted by sub-Saharan countries' tax treaties—average for selected treaty partners 52
4.1 Global wealth chains of advance pricing agreements 76
6.1 Key aspects of private equity firms 117
7.1 Selection of company cases based on firm size and geographical coverage 134
7.2 Number of corporate entities located in FSI/non-FSI countries for all case companies 137
7.3 Percentage of corporate entities located in FSI/non-FSI countries for all case companies 137
7.4 Number of VCEs, WCEs, MEs, and NEs for all case companies 139
7.5 Percentage of VCEs, WCEs, MEs, and NEs for all case companies 140
7.6 Corporate network of a large beer company 141
7.7 Corporate network of a mid-sized beer company 142
7.8 Corporate network of a small beer company 143
7.9 Corporate network of a large pharmaceutical company 145
7.10 Corporate network of a mid-sized pharmaceutical company 146
7.11 Corporate network of a small pharmaceutical company 147
8.1 Soybean meal—daily price difference, 2010/2013 173
8.2 Soybean oil—daily price difference, 2010/2013 173
8.3 Soybean—daily price difference, 2010/2013 174
8.4 Soybean oil—monthly US$ price difference, 2006/2016 176
11.1 Potential effects on wealth chain information asymmetries of transparency 224
11.2 Actual effects on wealth chain information asymmetries of transparency 228
11.3 Distribution of policy positions on tax transparency 230
12.1 Tax incentives by country 248
12.2 Tax incentives by category 249
12.3 Ownership structure of mining company 253
12.4 Number of incentives over time 257
14.1 Stylized representations of firm to corporate structure dynamics. 282
14.2 Linking micro-level actions to global wealth chain articulation 286
14.3 Distinguishing global value cChains from global wealth chains 290

List of Tables

2.1 UK/overseas ownership of UK water companies   35

3.1 Development of the role of tax treaties in value and wealth chain governance   54

5.1 Top 20 companies by total intangible value   94

8.1 Soybean exports as percentage of Argentine total exports   158

8.2 Companies share of Argentine soybean exports   158

8.3 Price differences in commodity exports by typical intermediaries and end clients found by the AFIP since 2009   163

8.4 Exporters, group membership and headquarters' location   164

8.5 Summary table with transfer pricing-related court decisions   166

8.6 Soybean Export under-pricing ($ and %)   172

8.7 Soybean Export over-pricing ($ and %)   172

8.8 Difference of prices of soybean meal exports. Argentina and the Netherlands. $ FOB per ton   178

9.1 Global art investment funds and assets under management (billions of $)   189

12.1 Number of contracts by country   246

12.2 Wealth-protection strategies in mining   254

Contributors

Dick Bryan is Professor Emeritus in the Department of Political Economy at the University of Sydney.

Martín Burgos is Coordinator of the Political Economy Department of the Centro Cultural de la Cooperación, Buenos Aires.

Rasmus Corlin Christensen is a Postdoctoral Fellow in the Department of Organization at the Copenhagen Business School.

Verónica Grondona is a Researcher in the Political Economy Department of the Centro Cultural de la Cooperación, Buenos Aires.

Mie Højris Dahl is a Crown Prince Frederik Fellow at the Harvard Kennedy School of Government.

Colin Haslam is Professor of Accounting and Finance at Queen Mary University of London.

Martin Hearson is a Research Fellow at the Institute of Development Studies, University of Sussex.

Oddný Helgadóttir is Associate Professor in International Political Economy in the Department of Organization at the Copenhagen Business School.

Adam Leaver is Professor in Accounting and Society in the Sheffield University Management School at the University of Sheffield, and Professor in the Department of Accounting at the Copenhagen Business School.

Jamie Morgan is Professor in the Leeds Business School at Leeds Beckett University.

Clair Quentin is Research Associate at the Policy Institute, King's College London.

Mike Rafferty is Associate Professor in the Department of Management at RMIT University, Melbourne.

Mariana Santos is a Post-Doctoral Researcher in the COSMOPOLIS, Center for Urban Research, at the Vrije Universiteit Brussel.

Leonard Seabrooke is Professor in International Political Economy and Economic Sociology in the Department of Organization at the Copenhagen Business School, and Research Professor at the Norwegian Institute of International Affairs.

Saila Stausholm is a Doctoral Fellow in the Department of Organization at the Copenhagen Business School.

Nick Tsitsianis is Senior Lecturer in Accounting at Queen Mary University of London.

Duncan Wigan is Professor MSO in International Political Economy in the Department of Organization at the Copenhagen Business School.

Matti Ylönen is a Lecturer in World Politics at the University of Helsinki.

1

Asset Strategies in Global Wealth Chains

Leonard Seabrooke and Duncan Wigan

The world economy operates around the production of value and the creation and protection of wealth. Firms and other actors use global value chains to make the most for the least cost, ideally also contributing to economic development. But production is not all that firms do. They also need locations to finance their operations, to book their profits, and to pay their taxes. Firms, individuals, and other actors use what we call "global wealth chains" to create and protect wealth. They strategically plan links in these chains across multiple legal jurisdictions to control how assets are evaluated and governed. Modern capitalism provides many opportunities for such planning, with high capital mobility and plenty of jurisdictions offering incentives to locate capital there rather than in high-tax, high-transparency locations or jurisdictions that do not offer the required legal affordances.

The outcomes from this planning are quite well known: increased income and wealth inequality within and between economies (Zucman, 2019), heightened pressures for firms to financialize (Morgan, 2014), and the spread of practices among elites to hide their wealth (Harrington, 2015; Beaverstock & Hall, 2016; Beckert, 2022). Less well known are the mechanisms through which this planning occurs. So while we know a great deal about global value chains (hereafter GVCs)—a body of scholarship that has not only produced an impressive range of cases but also had policy impact via international organizations (Gereffi et al., 2005; Gibbon et al., 2008; Gereffi, 2014; Neilson et al., 2014; Bair & Palpacuer, 2015)—we know much less about wealth chains. This book explores how global wealth chains (hereafter GWCs) are articulated, issues of regulatory liability, and how social relationships between clients and service providers are important for governance issues. Our contributors work in a range of

Leonard Seabrooke and Duncan Wigan, *Asset Strategies in Global Wealth Chains*. In: *Global Wealth Chains*.
Edited by Leonard Seabrooke and Duncan Wigan, Oxford University Press.
© Leonard Seabrooke and Duncan Wigan (2022). DOI: 10.1093/oso/9780198832379.003.0001

fields, including international political economy, sociology, accounting, geography, management studies, anthropology, and law. Drawing on approaches within and across these fields, they explore how assets are governed across a range of sectors such as public utilities, food, art, and pharmaceuticals, as well as in legal instruments like advance pricing agreements, tax treaties, regulatory standards, intellectual property, family trusts, and legal opinion.

The cases in this book concentrate on asset strategies, linking the treatment of assets to types of GWCs. Given the interdisciplinarity of this project, we have adopted what could be referred to as a "socio-legal" definition of asset; one that is inspired by John Commons (1924, 1936), Thorstein Veblen (1904, 1923), and others (Nitzan & Bichler, 2009; Pistor, 2019), that points to the importance of institutions and social norms in how property and legal contracts are considered and valued. Our conception of asset is a *legal affordance that provides differential claims on wealth*. That is, the key asset being traded, for firms and individuals, is normally a document providing rights and/or entitlements to the bearer, where affordances are supported by an interpretative community, including lawyers, judges, regulators, accountants, economists, entrepreneurs, and other professionals. The document or practice producing it may provide the beneficiary with access to returns that exceed the normal rate in any given sphere of economic activity. Firms and individuals organize to ensure that such assets are governed well through GWCs. They organize the location of their wealth across jurisdictions to maximize their claims to legal affordances, and support institutions and networks that maintain a common interpretation of these affordances (Grasten et al., 2021). These actors engage asset strategies to manage transacted forms of capital across multiple jurisdictions, with the aim of wealth creation and/or protection.

The contributions to this volume concentrate on wealth rather than value. It is also important to note that there are significant feedback effects between GVCs and GWCs. As others have recently commented, tracking "the 'onward journey' of value-added that accrues to firms across different tax regimes and jurisdictions is critical to understanding the socially and spatially uneven development impacts of global production networks" (Coe & Yeung, 2019, p. 786). We agree. We also suggest that understanding how wealth is managed as differentiated from value is important. Wealth is a different social phenomenon than value. While value requires effort and the transformation of physical states from raw material to product, or increases in the productivity of operations, wealth needs recognition of what can be legitimated, stored and traded. What is significant here is accepted legal assertions. This happens within interpretative communities, where agreements on legal affordances are secured. An important element is that within such communities wealth confers honor, where the accrual and transfer of wealth without productive effort is held in high esteem (Veblen, 1899).

Those at the top of the economic pyramid often eschew the art of making products to win on price and quality alone. Wealth accrues to manufacturers without factories, to financiers without credit facilities, to service firms that avowedly do not deliver and do not employ those delivering. Wealth chain operators navigate opportunity spaces provided by law for access to differential returns. Commons elaborated his legal theory of capitalism (1924) by pointing to how "goodwill" provided legally sanctioned outsized returns to those able to control access and derange the smooth flow of output. For Commons, distributional claims are made over the future wealth of society. The physical quantities of the production process are in the past, as products of spent labor, while differential distributional claims—wealth proper—are always invidious claims on the future. The concept of "futurity" denotes this (Commons, 1925). Futurity "indicates anticipation, or, literally, the act of seizing beforehand the limiting or strategic factors upon whose present control it is expected the outcome of the future may also be more or less controlled, provided there is security of expectations" (Commons, 1934, p. 58). Commons examines "reasonable value" in the formation of the large US trusts at the end of the nineteenth century (1924, pp. 1–65; 1934, pp. 649–875). Drawing from Veblen and hearings before the United States Industrial Commission, he shows the value of an entity is a function neither of its physical, corporeal property, nor of its incorporeal property, or debts due. Business valuation rests upon "intangible property." Andrew Carnegie's corporeal property in his omnipotent steel business was valued at $75 million, but he was paid $300 million in gold bonds by the holding company. While the corporeal property of the combination had been estimated to be worth $1 billion, its ultimate valuation stood at $2 billion. The excess, above historic cost, is a function of the owner's control over the industry, or of "Carnegie's threatening position in the market" (Commons, 1934, pp. 649–650). Both are "goodwill." Commons proposed a theory that eclipsed extant theories of value and wealth. We do not see an eclipse, but an invitation to engage with transformations in value and wealth.

To make the distinction between value and wealth in simple terms: value is accumulated often through actual physical transformation in production; wealth is from the recognition of a changed state through legal affordances and shared social norms. Raw gold may be physically transformed into a ring, giving the ring value. Recognition of who owns the gold ring bestows wealth upon the owner. An interpretative community provides this legal affordance to create and protect wealth. GWCs are composed of contracts and relationships across multiple jurisdictions where the recognition of wealth as a changed state is enabled and guarded.

A key means of guarding wealth is through the maintenance of information asymmetries between the parties involved in GWC transactions. In our framework these information asymmetries exist between suppliers, clients, and regulators (Seabrooke & Wigan 2017, pp. 13–16). All three parties have an interest in sharing or withholding information from others in this triad. In some cases suppliers can shield clients by expanding information asymmetries, increasing the knowledge gap between respective parties. Clients will often seek to hide or obscure information from regulators, especially on their fiscal and legal obligations. Suppliers may lengthen information asymmetries for similar reasons. The presence of information asymmetries heightens uncertainty for some parties in the triad, which can relate to both the actions and capacities of other parties, as well as one's own paths of action (Podolny 2010). The maintenance of such information asymmetries is important for the consistent articulation of GWCs (Christensen et al., 2021).

Our approach is built through a typology of GWCs, constructed around a series of ideal types based on assumptions of how actors align meaning and behavior through coordination. This introductory chapter first teases out the purpose of ideal typical forms in the GWC framework, and how it can help us identify asset strategies to control legal affordances in GWCs. We conclude by setting out key contributions in the volume.

How do we trace asset strategies?

We begin with a crucial question: how can we trace how corporations act if they are both agents and structures? What comprises the formal organization, and what form of organizing is important for providing a convincing analysis of corporate forms and tracing their activities? Understanding the forms of organizing within corporate structures is important if we seek to understand deviations from formal organization and how corporations as organizations are changing shape (Picciotto, 2011). Over thirty years ago,

Neil Fligstein (1990), argued that scholars of organizations were stuck in a specific conception of the firm and the corporation that obsessed over top managers of firms, focusing on their successes or failures. While there was much to gain from the focus on how managers could change their organizations to respond to external environments (Pfeffer & Salancik, 1978), more was needed. Fligstein stressed that what firms want is, above all, control over their internal and external environments. While other scholars understood this struggle between the firm and the environment in terms of generalist and specialist strategies within organizational ecologies, and how organizations sought to find niches within their population (Hannan & Freeman, 1977; Freeman & Hannan, 1983), Fligstein asserted that the means of control followed actions "determined by a legal framework and a self-conscious vision of the world that make both old and new courses of action possible and desirable" (Fligstein, 1990, p. 4). Understanding what types of legal frameworks and visions of the world are used to create GWCs is one purpose of this volume. If we want to trace corporate forms we have to distinguish some basic principles on what allows us to see how firms and corporations are agents and structures, how elites and professionals use them, what claims to actorhood can be made, how claims to authority can be understood, and what basic differences there are in types of formal organization and informal activity.

The first step here is to address a common confusion between the firm and the corporation. This error has been critically important for discussions of multinational firms as "decentered" (Desai, 2008), as well as how they are financialized (Morgan, 2014). It is important to clarify what is the firm and what is the corporation. Clearing up this confusion distinguishes what we can understand as "actorness" in corporate activity as well as the legal basis for what can be identified as structures. The idea here is that agency belongs in the firm and structure, the corporation. The conflation of what is the "firm" and what is the "corporation" is common in many fields. Jean-Philippe Robé (2011, p. 3) has been clearest on this argument in his dismantling of the role of agency in common theories of the firm. Robé points out that firms and corporations are confused in the literature, leading to the following assumptions. It is worth paraphrasing his key points at length:

1. Shareholders own shares issued by corporations, not firms. They do not own the firm or the corporation, which is legally structured to be owned by no one (see also Ireland 1999; Lan & Heracleous 2010).

2. Firm managers control assets owned by the corporation, not by shareholders. The legal personality of the corporation provides walls between asset control, dividends, and liabilities.

3. A firm is an organized economic activity, a corporation is a legal entity and personality that provides the firm with a legal structure. Firms and corporations are different things.

4. Corporations are not a "legal fiction" (Jensen & Meckling 1976), but important legal structures in societies that conduct business through contracts between legal persons and have property rights assigned to legal personalities.

5. Managers work on behalf of the corporation for the purposes of the firm; they are not agents of shareholders. They are empowered by being officers of the corporation.

6. To make decisions managers rely on the legal structure of the corporation, including the control of assets. Their decisions are singularly in the interests of their office, not taking into account all externalities affecting the firm.

7. Managers have fiduciary duties to those affected by their decisions which extend beyond the interests of shareholders because of the legal structures used to compose the corporation.

8. Corporate governance and firm governance are distinct. There is no real shareholder theory of corporate governance since managers are not agents of shareholders. Stakeholder theories of governance are imprecise or rely on magical thinking.

9. The concept of agency has led to the conflation of the firm and the corporation. Concentrating on fiduciary duties is more relevant to understanding the firm and the corporation, and how it responds to society's needs.

Given the absence of ownership, and concomitantly the absence of clear causal lines between structure and action, we identify corporate form as a product of actors seeking to meet the requirements established by fiduciary duties and normative principles within the given legal structure. Robé's (2011, 2020, 2021) vital contributions highlight that theories of agency should be replaced by analyses of the respective duties between those concerned with the firm, structuring the corporation, and those seeking external influence on how firms make decisions and how corporations are governed. His approach helps explain why there is so much "organized hypocrisy" from firms dealing with issues like corporate social responsibility, accountability reporting, and corporate wrongdoing (Archel et al., 2011; Cho et al., 2015; Gabbioneta et al., 2019). In sum, Robé points to the payoff for approaching corporate form as a function of the firm as "going concern" in the tradition of legal pragmatism and old institutionalism (Commons, 1934). Such an approach encourages seeing actors in firm ecologies making interstitial adjustments within legal structures provided by corporate forms that traverse jurisdictions, in a process described by some as "targeted touchdown" and "partial lift off" (Biggins, 2012).

Corporate forms exist in what Robé (2009) refers to as the "world wide web of contracts." Researchers tracing legal frameworks of corporate tax avoidance are right to focus on the structure (Cobham et al., 2015; Cobham & Janský, 2018; Fichtner, 2016), while also needing cases where fiduciary relationships are made clear. This is true too for those looking at regulatory frameworks (Palan & Wigan, 2014). Viewing corporate forms as an outcome of activity between legal jurisdictions and expert networks builds on a long line of work on the "offshore world" (Palan, 2002; Palan et al., 2010). The work in this collection on GWCs follows a similar idea. The GWCs framework offers a typology to be mixed and matched according to the international legal affordances provided, the types of capital available, and the interactions among professionals in structuring how wealth is created and stored across jurisdictions (Seabrooke & Wigan, 2017; Sharman, 2017; Finér & Ylönen, 2017; Quentin & Campling, 2018). As we clarify below, the purpose of the typology (market, modular, relational, captive, and hierarchy types of chains) is to provide a means of comparison that pushes the various insights from different disciplines into a case study focus. A key element of the GWCs approach is the implied regulatory liability, assuming that actors involved in coordination activities are knowledgeable about the types of activities taking place and where they have and lack information. This issue raises conceptual questions not only about actorhood but also about authority, which we now turn to.

One important issue in tracing corporate forms is the extent to which we can talk about the actorness of firms and corporations. As Robé argues, it is more fruitful to think about duties and obligations from interactions between parties than it is to think of firms' agency, especially the role of shareholders. In considering how firms and corporations assert authority, scholars like Sol Picciotto (2007, 2011, 2015) have long demonstrated how authority over firms' activities and their corporate governance structures is constructed by claims to legal position, and the political economic significance of this authority.

Claims to authority from officers of the corporation rely on contracts within legal structures. As these structures are determined not only by contracts but also through standards and regulations, much work on claims to authority over corporate form has looked at how networks of experts are important influences on standards and regulations. This has included cases such as international banking standards (Tsingou, 2010; Young, 2012), the OECD's base erosion and profit-shifting action plans (Büttner & Thiemann, 2017; Christensen, 2021), and expert conflicts through international organizations (Eskelinen & Ylönen, 2017; Kentikelenis & Seabrooke, 2017). Work looking more at claims to authority from market positions has included theories of rhetorical legitimation in how dominant corporate forms claim hyper rents from the world economy (Suddaby & Greenwood, 2005; Murphy et al., 2019), as well as forms of professional closure tied to the globalization of corporate forms (Boussard, 2018). The fiscal consequences of claims to authority are the dynamics that have been studied by scholars of the offshore world (Palan, 2002; Palan et al., 2010; Fichtner, 2016), as well as those interested in how tax professionals respond to moral outrage following scandals (Radcliffe et al., 2018). The importance of delineating such claims to authority is to establish not only the relationships that need investigation but also the need to imagine how such an order could be unsettled (Genschel & Rixen, 2015; Hearson, 2018) and recomposed (Rixen, 2016; Christensen & Hearson, 2019).

Tracing asset strategies via ideal types

Tracing asset strategies is a task that can be conducted in a number of ways. Recent advances in network analysis have permitted the mapping of multiple corporate units within network structures via intra-firm ownership stakes (Heemskerk et al., 2016, Buch-Hansen & Henriksen, 2019). Here research has found key "sink" and "conduit" jurisdictions, and a range of jurisdiction-specific sector-based specializations (Garcia-Bernardo et al., 2017). Macroeconomic data has also identified distinct regional agglomerations of foreign direct investment flows (Haberly & Wójcik, 2015), permitting the identification and characterization of "global financial networks" (Haberly & Wójcik, 2021). Our work is complementary, adding a focus on corporate forms with attention to interactions that are reflective of relationships and duties among actors in corporate networks. We suggest tracing corporate form through thick case description and an approach informed by classic Weberian sociology as well as drawing from insights from the fields noted above: institutional economics, international political economy, law, accounting, and sociology.

Our use of ideal types here sticks to the conventional Weberian usage— ideal types are heuristics to be used to interpret and analyze empirical information. Ideal types should be used as models to be modified and reformed in relief against empirical evidence rather than treated as descriptions of reality (Parker, 2013, pp. 136–137). An ideal type is not shorthand for the abstraction of a general phenomenon (Swedberg, 2018, p. 195). Ideal types are "emergency safe havens until one has learned to find one's bearings while navigating the immense sea of empirical facts" (Weber, 2012, p. 133). They are useful for studying how empirical phenomena have a relationship to meaning. As such, they are constructed by the researcher from elements of observed phenomena, but the ideal types are nowhere to be found in the real world. It is nonsensical to compare ideal types to "real types" (Kristensen, 1996). Rather, the ideal type is to provide clarity in what the researcher is observing, where its "unreality and one-sidedness will not only guarantee its sharpness, but should also preserve it from the danger of hypostatization" (Bruun, 2001, p. 156). Ideal types are not to be reified, but built up and then broken down as learning progresses.

Weberian ideal types start from artificial assumptions about meaning and behavior from an actor; that they act rationally, have complete information, are totally aware of what they are doing, and do not make mistakes (Weber, 1978, pp. 21–22). Richard Swedberg (2018, p. 189) outlines how social scientists should develop ideal types according to the Weberian model, focusing on the following five steps:

1. Establish the meaning toward which the actor invests in her or his behavior.
2. Check that meanings and actions are aligned to satisfy step 1. If so,
3. Assume that the actor acts in a rational manner, acts with full knowledge of the situation (this is unrealistic but useful to consider), is aware of what is being done, and that the typical actor does not make mistakes with intended actions.
4. Check that there is causal adequacy, that meaning plus behavior can have the intended effect.
5. Confront the ideal type with a concrete empirical example of the phenomena being investigated.

Our conception of types of GWCs follows these steps. They are unrealistic theoretical types of how transactions are structured within relationships among suppliers, clients, and regulators, varying in the degree of explicit coordination required by these actors.

Global wealth chains as ideal types

Our established framework explains how GWCs are created, maintained, and governed (Seabrooke & Wigan 2014, 2017). Just as readers can imagine the production lines and logistics trucks and vans involved in global value chains, we seek to make the movement of assets, use of legal affordances, and conditioning of corporate form in global wealth chains legible.

In their framework on global value chains, Gereffi, Humphrey, and Sturgeon (2005, pp. 83–84) delineate value chain governance to five ideal types; market, modular, relational, captive, and hierarchy value chains. *Market* value chains are characterized by low levels of information and asset complexity. There is little need for complex communication channels between suppliers and buyers and asset maintenance is minimal. *Modular* value chains provide differentiated and modified options to buyers on the basis of generic product. *Relational* value chains are where coordination increases and interactions are repeated, with transactions more tailored to circumstance and demand. *Captive* value chains involve large buyer dominance from lead firms over smaller firms. *Hierarchy* value chains are vertical and integrated; here, complexity is heightened and difficulties in codification acute. These types of value chain governance have generated a huge body of case work which has readily traversed lines between science and policy arenas. The GVC approach has been picked up by a range of international economic organizations, including the World Bank, OECD, IMF, UNCTAD, and EU. GWC research complements value chain research with added focus on finance, law, accounting, and tax, and shares its concern with policy relevance. By allusion, value chains follow the commodity and wealth chains follow the capital.

Our conception of GWCs deliberately mirrors Gereffi, Humphrey, and Sturgeon's (2005) typology of GVCs, but is distinct in ways that matter. Gereffi and co-authors base a theory of value chain governance on three factors: (1) the complexity of information to sustain transactions, (2) the ability to codify transactions, and (3) the capabilities of potential suppliers to meet the requirements of the transaction (Gereffi et al., 2005, p. 85).

When identifying GWCs we follow the value chain framework on two factors, and differ on one. While the capacity to codify a transaction in GVCs determines coordination requirements, in GWCs corporate form and asset strategy is often instrumentalized to lower the ability to codify. More important in wealth chains is the regulatory liability attached to an asset. Suppliers offer products that are variously exposed to the regulator, and client and supplier relations differ according to the regulatory shield provided. Corporate form and change in GWCs are therefore a function of: (1) transaction complexity, (2) regulatory liability, and (3) supplier capacity on product offer and development. The variables allow for identification of the range of GWCs depicted in Figure 1.1.

Assets in market chains may be relatively simple and readily available. These assets, which include shell companies and simple trust structures, are protected from regulators by tax and fiduciary law on one hand, and administrative capacity and practice on the other, which in these instances may impede the flow of information on ownership. At the other end of the scale are hierarchy chains, where highly complex products may be tailor-made for clients or developed in-house by the firm (Bryan et al., 2017; Bryan et al., Chapter 5 in this volume). Regulators have low levels of traction on these types of assets, including structured financial assets and the spatio-legal organization of leading multinational firms, where information asymmetries can be extremely high, such as with Apple (Seabrooke & Wigan, 2014). Between these extremes are products that are relatively simple but modulated according to market and client characteristics, and

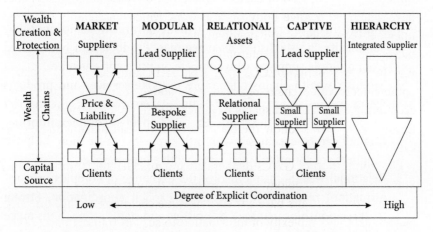

Fig. 1.1 Typology of global wealth chains
Source: Seabrooke & Wigan, 2017, p. 12, adapted from Gereffi et al., 2005, p. 89.

assets that require carefully cultivated relational work. Expatriate banking services and private wealth management for the ultra-wealthy are exemplary in respect to each of these (Harrington, 2015; Beaverstock & Hall, 2016; de Carvalho & Seabrooke, 2016). Figure 1.1, above, shows the five types of GWCs. We see the input of the source of wealth from clients and its management and augmentation by suppliers before it flows back. There are sometimes lead suppliers who provide services through secondary suppliers who may adapt the service or simply represent a channel to clients. As we proceed from left to right of the figure, coordination requirements heighten as transactions become more complex and the management of regulatory liability more exacting.

As noted, our wealth chains are ideal types and should be treated as such. Application requires following the steps outlined above, to relate meaning and behavior based on assumptions that actors behave in rational ways, that actors are informed, that behavior relates to the intended meaning, and that mistakes are not being made. As the GWCs are ideal types they are theoretical constructs that should be broken down and reconfigured in the process of investigating cases. For example, regulatory interventions may produce movement from one chain to another (Sharman, 2017). Components of one chain may be combined with components of another to create hybrids, understanding that these are not "real types" but reflected against elements of the ideal types presented. Alternatively, distinct chains may act to reinforce or undermine each other. For clarity we provide definitions of the five ideal typical wealth chains (see Seabrooke & Wigan 2017, pp. 10–11):

1. Market linkages occur through arm's-length relationships with low complexity in established legal regimes. Products can be accessed from multiple suppliers who compete on price and capacity.
2. Modular wealth chains offer more bespoke services and products within well-established financial and legal environments that restrict supplier and client flexibility. Products involve complex information but can be exchanged with little explicit coordination. Bespoke suppliers are commonly associated with a lead supplier.
3. Relational wealth chains involve the exchange of complex tacit information, requiring high levels of explicit coordination. Strong trust relationships managed by prestige and status interactions make switching costs high.

4. Captive wealth chains occur when lead suppliers dominate smaller suppliers by controlling the legal apparatus and financial technology. Such control is maintained by lead firms and apex professional groups. Clients' options are limited by the scope of what can be provided by small suppliers and, in turn, lead suppliers.

5. Hierarchy wealth chains are vertically integrated. A high degree of control is exercised by senior management, such as a chief financial officer. Clients and suppliers are highly integrated and coordinate on complex transactions.

Asset management and interaction between suppliers, regulators, and clients has been the focus in cases on GWCs developed by researchers. This work has the aim of highlighting how assets are used in corporate forms, be they in the area of financial services (Bryan et al., 2016; 2017, and Bryan et al., Chapter 5 in this volume), art (Helgadóttir, Chapter 9 in this volume), mining (Stausholm, Chapter 12 in this volume), transparency (Christensen, Chapter 11 in this volume), money laundering (Waris, 2018), utilities (Haslam et al., Chapter 2 in this volume), corporate tax avoidance (Morgan, 2021), housing (McKenzie & Atkinson, 2020), and others. It includes the strategic deployment of elite barrister legal opinion (Quentin, Chapter 13 in this volume), the management of family wealth via cultivated control on intergenerational wealth transfers (Santos, Chapter 10 in this volume), and wealth extraction from firms by private equity (Morgan, Chapter 6 in this volume).

Global wealth chain types and hybrids

We have proposed that the ideal types of global wealth chains provide a useful heuristic framework for identifying and studying these forms, and providing some order to the interpretative process. We now briefly introduce some examples of global wealth chains, drawing on scholars' work from this volume.

Figure 1.2 shows the links between the contributors' cases and the wealth chain types. We work through our contributors' cases to highlight diversity in GWCs, noting that this is the editors' interpretation of the cases in this volume. The authors were not explicitly asked to identify the types, given that this volume is an interdisciplinary conversation that requires freedom to explore outside of our own bossy rules. As discussed above,

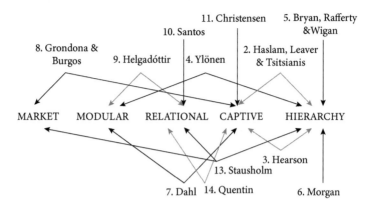

Fig. 1.2 Mapping contributions to global wealth chain types

our GWC types can be mixed when compared with empirical examples. Figure 1.2 shows the extent of this in our contributors' chapters, with Bryan et al. (Chapter 5), Morgan (Chapter 6), Santos (Chapter 10), and Christensen (Chapter 11) identified with a single type. The material in other chapters is understood, by us, as a combination of the types. We are fine with this, given that the purpose of typology is not to match one to one, but to discover how case content can be best explained (on modular theory building for GVCs see Ponte & Sturgeon, 2014). Stausholm (Chapter 12), for example, places her attention on how mining companies strategically exploit different types of wealth chain depending on the legal affordances and professional networks available to them.

Moving from left to right, legal opinion is an important source of corporate form determination in GWCs. Chapter 13 provides an example of a case that can be characterized as a mix between market and relational types within wealth chains. Clair Quentin's work specifies how the supply of legal opinion by a small coterie of Queen's Counsel to shield declared tax positions from regulator intervention occurs in rarefied markets. The resulting corporate form and tax position are produced by exploiting the potential bifurcation between legal argument and forensic outcome. Queen's Counsel are positioned to offer this bifurcation with authority, essentially selling deliberately false legal opinions at a huge premium. This position is a function of institutionalized claims to status within the UK legal market and Queen's Counsel collectively enacting norms of distinction to fortify privileged market position. Legal opinion reflects a kind of "virtual offshore," yielding potentially huge tax savings and the opportunity to recognize tax avoidance as a form of "risk mining." The magnitude of resulting tax savings is a function of how far the client and supplier are willing to climb the high wire of risk and return. At the extreme end of deliberately false legal opinion, the key information asymmetry is with regard to the fact that the risk mining is occurring at all, since it will be expected to fail in challenges from the tax authority. In the plainer vanilla cases, the key information asymmetry is with regard to the extent to which tax risk is successfully managed, since the likelihood of regulatory challenge depends on the tax authority's assessment of its own risk in challenging the position. In such cases, there is an open market for legal opinion for those with deep pockets, and affective foundations to chain maintenance. For those with high status and the appropriate social ties, the chain is relational in being bound to a status–trust network. Unraveling activity in what can be understood as a captive-relational wealth chain requires the dissection of legal opinion from close reading and content analysis, as well as from elite interviews and participant observation.

Capital flight via transfer mispricing can take multiple forms, including export under-pricing, import over-pricing, royalties over-pricing, and business restructurings. Verónica Grondona and Martín Burgos (Chapter 8) explore mispricing in Argentine soybean exports as an example of a national value chain, with dispersed entities trading at arm's length. Formally, this system is a market wealth chain, but Grondona and Burgos demonstrate how in practice it has evolved along with the expansion of the sector into a captive GWC. With soybean exports accounting for 24 percent of all Argentine exports the fiscal impact of export mispricing, where reported prices are below market prices and detract from the tax base, is significant. The eight exporters subject to analysis in this chapter accounted for more than 48 percent of the soybean exports and more than 67 percent of soybean oil and meal exports in 2013. Concentration in the market is high and provides the opportunity spaces necessary for coordination of export prices between related entities. This is a clear example of the going concern coordinating wealth via corporate structures that span multiple jurisdictions, with major exporters executing the wealth strategy via entities in Bermuda, the Netherlands, Singapore, and Switzerland. The "sixth method" in transfer pricing is sanctioned in Argentinian law and applied to commodities with readily observable prices. Here, the price of an internal transaction is compared to the price of the same commodity on a recognized international exchange. By comparing the average prices of soybean exports reported in daily customs registrations with the daily price on the Gulf of Mexico the chapter demonstrates systematic underpricing of exports in the Argentine soybean sector.

Beer and pharmaceuticals are the focus in Mie Højris Dahl's contribution (Chapter 7), which explores how sector and firm size impact the way multinational firms manage wealth. A combination of modular and captive chains are prevalent here. Valuation in the pharmaceutical sector rests in large part on intangible assets, which often account for more than 90 percent of firm value. As noted by Bryan et al. (Chapter 5) intangible assets are easy to move and difficult to value, providing ample opportunity for strategic placement and pricing. Beer, in contrast, is a commodity and a simple physical product. By comparison of large global firms, mid-sized multiregional firms, and smaller regional firms in both sectors, the role of firm size and product complexity in the articulation of GWCs is identified. Drawing on Orbis data, Dahl maps corporate structures to delineate wealth and value chain entities. Interviews complement this analysis. For corporate entities located in jurisdictions with a high financial secrecy score on the Tax Justice Network's index, the number of employees is identified and profit per head calculated as an indication of whether the entity is engaged in wealth chain activities. Dahl reveals that size is a significant factor in conditioning firm reliance on GWCs. Somewhat counterintuitively, however, Danish pharmaceutical firms do not rely upon wealth chains more than firms in the beer sector.

Recent investigations of wealth chains containing markets for high-value art show how ideal types can be mixed to present a more accurate understanding of phenomena. High-value art markets can be characterized as in part modular and in part relational. Oddný Helgadottír (Chapter 9) demonstrates how art is being stored for tax-avoidance purposes in a bespoke system of freeports, reflecting a modular type of wealth chain. While the establishment of the trade is from more opaque trust-based networks that we theorize as prominent in relational wealth chains, freeport services are modular in their low complexity. Since 2000 the market for high-value art has witnessed growth of 600 percent, reaching a total value of $1 trillion. While auction prices are known, approximately 70 percent of the market operates privately and no data on sales and prices are available. Further, a "true value" is difficult to ascertain. This valuation difficulty is the distinctive feature of this asset when deployed in GWCs, leaving lots of room for price fixing, tax avoidance, and money laundering. That prices are highly elastic and concertedly contrived in sense-making processes between chain participants means that substantial relational work is required to secure that prices remain high and that confidentiality and shared norms convert into wealth creation and protection (Helgadóttir, 2020). Here suppliers cultivate prestige and status in embedding markets in elaborate non-market activities, where strong norms about deportment and standards of behavior, and even forms of entertainment, are maintained. The value of the assets is almost entirely construed in these ways. The wealth associated with the art is in turn protected by legal structure and the use of specialized storage facilities such as the Geneva Free Port, which shield the asset behind a veil of secrecy and Switzerland's network of tax treaties. Close relationships between suppliers and clients ensure effective coordination and stable prices, placing this asset in the relational wealth chain type where status and prestige are decisive. Here the regulator in multijurisdictional space is not unified, with regulators split between criminal activity, such as INTERPOL, and transgovernmental groups working on tax-evasion and money-laundering issues (Levi et al., 2018; Tsingou, 2018). Fragmentation inhibits regulatory traction in these markets. Notably, since there is no income stream attached to the asset, ownership is predicated on the effect of increasing inequality on art prices. Ethnographic approaches to market formation and valuation practices involve participant observation at events and a focus on everyday practices in high-value art markets.

Advance tax rulings (ATRs) are agreements between tax authorities and the taxpayer determining the application of the tax law regarding transactions, investments, or corporate structures. Since the 1980s, ATRs have been applied to tax rulings on prices for intra-firm trade in advance pricing agreements. The pre-emptive fixing of a future tax liability provides surety for firms going forward, reducing the mutual uncertainty that surrounds the determination of a corporation's tax position and intra-firm prices that in part determine this position. In Chapter 4, Matti Ylönen provides a delineation of ATRs on the basis of whether rulings pertain to the national or international and the chains are modular or hierarchy. In hierarchy chains, states (as suppliers) unilaterally provide rulings to clients directly. In international hierarchy chains two states may provide a bilateral ruling to a corporation and multiple states may provide a ruling for a corporate client. However, often tax advisory firms may intermediate this process, negotiating with the tax authority an agreement deployed in a national/modular chain and/or with multiple tax authorities, an agreement deployed in international/modular chains. Here advisory firms including, as revealed in the Luxleaks scandal, Deloitte, E&Y, KPMG, and PwC, act as interpretative authorities able to legitimately assert in negotiation with tax authorities, in the terminology of John Commons, "reasonable value." Given the intrinsic ambiguity of prices for intra-firm trade, the authority to adjudicate is paramount. The resulting agreements can be modulated according to various client requirements.

In relational wealth chains a great deal of stock is placed in high-trust status-based relationships between clients and suppliers. These relationships are fostered to ensure client continuity and that clients are protected from oversight by regulators. Mariana Santos (Chapter 10) explores what is clearly a relational case in which wealth managers carefully cultivate close relationships with ultra-high-net-worth individuals to maintain client relationships over generations, and where 500 individuals will pass over $2.1 trillion to heirs over the next 20 years. A crucial dimension of transgenerational wealth protection is the preparation of children for inheritance. Relational work fosters necessary intimacy and trust between ultra-high-net-worth clients and suppliers, the private banking and wealth management industry. Affective work securing emotional and financial commitment includes providing tutelage on managing investment accounts gifted from parent to child or advice to parents on appropriate choices regarding the children's education. Santos suggests that if the GWC types are not to be taken as silos then it is necessary to explore how the types are governed, maintained, and combined in everyday practice. Drawing on ethnographic research with 30 wealth managers in Lisbon, London, Geneva, and Zurich, the chapter demonstrates the intensity and affective content of relational work in supplier attempts to ensure that a relationship with a client persists beyond the death of that client. In sum, the chapter traces the careful cultivation of affective bonds between suppliers in private banks and wealth management firms with ultra-high-net-worth clients and their heirs (see also Santos 2021).

Similarly, Saila Stausholm (Chapter 12) explores how a mix of market, relational, and hierarchy wealth chains are articulated in the mining industry, in which firms actively use GWCs to lower their tax exposures. Stausholm sifts through 100+ mining contracts, from 21 developing economies, to identify the contractual and multijurisdictional structures they use to minimize taxes. What emerges from this reading are the power asymmetries present between mining firms and developing economy governments. Stausholm identifies common tax advantages obtained by mining companies in developing countries. A market system works where mining companies simply adopt what is available in national law. However, many mining companies use relational work to tip the scales in their favor. A common scenario here is close relationships involving a small number of professionals who coordinate and negotiate mining contracts. The analysis highlights the range of incentives given to mining firms and how the affordances in contract provisions extend far beyond what is offered in standard law. This includes tax holidays, accelerated depreciation of assets, multiple tax exemptions, lower taxes on property, withholding charges and licensing fees, longer loss carry-forward periods, and others. The chapter argues how these tax advantages form a captive wealth chain in which governments are pressured to provide favorable tax treatment. Additionally, the chapter provides a case study of how mining wealth is further protected through hierarchical wealth chains involving multijurisdictional schemes, such as the establishment of multiple corporate entities in offshore jurisdictions like the British Virgin Islands.

Rasmus Corlin Christensen's (Chapter 11) work provides a great example of relationship dynamics within what can be described as captive wealth chains. Christensen investigates how regulatory institutions develop rules governing the taxation of cross-border economic activity on ostensible grounds of rational responses to stimuli perceived to exist in the environment. Recent efforts by the OECD to upgrade international rules (nationally adopted) in the base erosion and profit shifting (BEPS) initiative were premised on a recognition that tax rules had become less useful in the face of corporate forms that can readily deploy international tax arbitrage (Ylönen & Teivainen, 2018). Regulatory responses, however, are less a function of rational response than shared norms amongst actors in regulatory networks as to what is considered legitimate and which authorities can be considered valid. Leading providers of accounting, tax, and financial expertise are positioned to capture both private and public imagination of what is acceptable and possible, especially the Big Four accountancy firms (Suddaby & Greenwood, 2005; Murphy et al., 2019). Given that the ideas and technologies circulating in expert networks are constrained, efforts to upgrade transfer pricing rules in the OECD BEPS process have followed this logic with transfer pricing experts coalescing on the boundaries of the acceptable in terms of regulatory intervention (Christensen, 2021). While concerns as to rule inadequacy had led to the consideration of radical solutions in initial discussions, such as public country-by-country reporting (and even a shift to a system of unitary taxation), norms corralled these considerations so that eventual rule change stayed within the boundaries set by established practice. The BEPS process brought stakeholders with various levels of investment in GWCs to the table, contesting the proposed regulatory changes. Christensen's argument is that technicization of the BEPS policy process constrained the post-crisis political momentum for expanded transparency of corporate form in hierarchy and captive wealth chains. Technicization is the process of embedding highly political discussions in a specialized, knowledge-intensive policy context. Such settings mask politics as "technical" or "neutral," favoring expertise and technical efficiency, as opposed to public politicized policy settings where explicit political interests dominate. Constraints on a broadly established post-crisis political momentum for expansive corporate tax transparency are constructed through three key processes: policy insulation, re-framing, and appropriateness judgments. These processes of technicization influenced the views of experts and policymakers on key policy issues and solutions, effectively shaping policy outcomes (Christensen & Hearson, 2019). Evidence for this wealth chain is drawn from qualitative content analysis of the policy debates surrounding BEPS, as well as extensive interviews with select informants involved in the policy process.

Tax treaties can provide important links in what can be characterized as a connection between captive and hierarchy wealth chains. A network of around 3,000 such treaties limits the extent to which the cross-border transactions at each stage of the chain can be taxed in the countries between which earnings flow. Originally created to remove the tax disadvantages of multinational-firm cross-border investments by reducing the threat of double taxation, tax treaties soon became a source of tax advantage (Hearson, 2021). In Chapter 3, Martin Hearson suggests that tax treaties as GWC assets have undergone a further metamorphosis, with the "Big Four" professional services firms providing tax planning based on corporate restructuring, in which the value chain is restructured around wealth chain structures premised on tax treaties and other such assets. Treaties had been used to funnel income from the value chain to entities strategically registered in low-tax jurisdictions and which had little role in the "real economic activities" of the firm. The emergence of "tax-efficient supply chain management" involves the allocation of significant economic functions and risks to hub companies that accumulate fees and other income streams from related entities for supply chain management services. Hearson points to the catalytic role of the OECD's BEPS initiative in driving this shift, as efforts to remerge value creation and wealth allocation have generated an outcome where value follows wealth rather than wealth following value. As noted above, GWCs will mutate under pressure of regulatory intervention.

A mix of captive and hierarchy chains can enable complex internal organization to also assert control externally over technologies and knowledge to dominate smaller suppliers. Colin Haslam, Adam Leaver, and Nick Tsitsianis (Chapter 2) use the seemingly mundane case of assets such as public utilities to show how the firm is increasingly being treated as an integrated financial and productive asset. With regulation providing a floor to prices (and clear profit-making opportunities), state guarantees for foundational activities are translated into outsized opportunities for private wealth appropriation. In the case of the multinational French firm Veolia and its UK-centered wealth chain, the provision of water and waste services has been organized through subsidiaries in such a way that the subsidiary makes little profit but is subject to financial predation from the French parent. The wealth chain is primarily hierarchy but also captive in that firms linked to Veolia are tied into relationships in which the lead firm, the lead supplier, dominates. This is an accounting story about redistribution where the corporation becomes a rehypothecable financial asset for the firm; a source of collateral to back extended chains of financial engineering. Such hierarchical chains are tightly coordinated and here the supplier and client are only separated by legal boundaries between related corporate entities. The regulator is distant to this extraction process as it relies on accepted corporate and investment law. Any intervention would require not only changes in domestic regulation but multilateral coordination. The regulator of the water sector in the UK acts as co-creator of the asset by establishing floors to market prices that undergird the process of rehypothecation. At one point in chain formation the regulator is more supplier to the corporate client, and at another, later stage, it is the representative of a construed public interest. Tracing this corporate form tells us about the creation of complex webs of contracts and the socially constrained enactment of duties (Tischer et al., 2019).

In hierarchy wealth chains, firm managers, and sometimes large advisory and financial firms, construct elaborate chains of control via networks of corporations, where the wealth accrued is a function of success in extracting cash flows from entities down the chain that may be internal or external to the firm. In a singular hierarchy type, high-tech firms operating in the digital economy construct networks of corporations that disaggregate activities and assets so the legal structure of the firm in corporate forms is clearly distinguishable from its economic activity and sources of wealth. As Dick Bryan, Michael Rafferty, and Duncan Wigan demonstrate (Chapter 5), firms operating platform economies organize to exploit discrepancies between rules built on concepts of substance and presence more applicable to tangible economies. Derivative markets have long exploited these relationships (Wigan, 2008). A further clear example here is intellectual property, where tax rules based on ready valuation by comparison, accrual concepts of liabilities and assets, and a physical tie between legal jurisdictions and asset have been transcended. Companies such as Apple have been at the forefront of these developments (Bryan et al., 2017). Information asymmetries between the regulator and client/supplier are large as they are a product not only of multijurisdictional strategies deployed by firms within corporate structures but also of the fact that regulatory tools are based on outmoded concepts.

Jamie Morgan (Chapter 6) interrogates what can be understood as another hierarchy type in the execution of leveraged buyouts by private equity firms. In this case, the private equity firm deploys solicited funds to take a target firm, or acquisition, into private ownership. Debt disproportionately finances the buyout so that returns to now concentrated equity (ownership) are accelerated and inflated. From the perspective of private equity, the acquisition is a financial rather than productive asset, providing the grounds for the capture and concentration of wealth. In the case of the 2007 leveraged buyout of Alliance Boots in the UK, Stefano Pessina, a board member with a 15 percent stake in the firm, and KKR, one of the giants of the private equity industry, each secured 30 percent of returns from, and 50 percent of the control of, a £11 billion asset. Pessina and KKR each contributed £1.02 billion to the buyout. Taxable income in the UK was subject to the enlarged debt-servicing costs the acquisition was now obliged to meet which are deductible against tax charges. Returns flowed out of the UK via the tax-optimized structure of the acquisition (placed in Switzerland in 2008) and corporate entities owned by KKR and Pessina and located in jurisdictions such as Luxembourg, the Caymans, Monaco, and Gibraltar. Returns to the private equity fund, as opposed to fund investors, take the form of carried interest, typically set at 20 percent of returns above a set performance threshold. Carried interest is taxed as a capital gain in the UK and therefore returns to the private equity partners, despite the fact that management work justifies these returns, circumvent the higher income tax. Private equity leveraged buyouts provide access to the financialized logic that imbues GWCs (Morgan & Nasir, 2021).

Finally, we conclude this volume (Chapter 14) by reflecting on how the GWC framework leads us to consider the importance of legal affordances, how firms and corporations act and differ, how professional strategies play out in interpretative communities to select GWCs, and the future research agenda.

Conclusion

This volume provides a tour of GWCs, making a strong claim that how wealth is created and protected across multiple jurisdictions should be viewed through the allocation of legal affordances, including the capacity of the firm and the corporation to act differently, and the ability of elites and professionals to manipulate both (Christensen et al., 2021). Our contributors explore a range of cases where wealth is being created and protected, providing original research that allows us to consider how asset strategies are articulated in different ways. Given the inadequacy of theories of the firm which rely on the agency of the firm or the corporation (often conflated), in this introduction we have proposed using a heuristic device of ideal types. Reflecting on how empirical phenomena compare against these types is important in illuminating how asset strategies are articulated in the world economy. It is important in revealing more information about the "offshore world" and about global sources of economic inequality. This volume represents a call to arms for those intent on understanding distributional outcomes from global economic processes.

References

Archel, P., Husillos, J., & Spence, C. (2011). The institutionalisation of unaccountability: loading the dice of corporate social responsibility discourse. *Accounting, Organizations and Society*, 36(6), 327–343.

Bair, J. & Palpacuer, F. (2015). CSR beyond the corporation: Contested governance in global value chains. *Global Networks*, 15(s1), S1–S19.

Beaverstock, J. V. & Hall, S. (2016). Super-rich capitalism: Managing and preserving private wealth management in the offshore world. In I. Hay and J. V. Beaverstock (eds.), *Handbook on Wealth and the Super-Rich*. Edward Elgar, 401–421.

Beckert, J. (2022). Durable Wealth: Institutions, Mechanisms, and Practices of Wealth Perpetuation. Annual Review of Sociology, 48(1).

Biggins, J. (2012). Targeted touchdown and partial liftoff: post-crisis dispute resolution in the OTC derivatives markets and the challenges for ISDA. *German Law Journal*, 13(12), 1297–1328.

Boussard, V. (2018). Professional closure regimes in the global age: The boundary work of professional services specialised in mergers and acquisitions, *Journal of Professions and Organization*, 5(3), 279–296.

Bruun H. H. (2001). Weber on Rickert: From value relations to ideal type. *Max Weber Studies* 1(2): 138–160.

Bryan, D., Rafferty, M., & Wigan, D. (2016). Politics, time and space in the era of shadow banking. *Review of International Political Economy*, 23(6), 941–966.

Bryan, D., Rafferty, M., & Wigan, D. (2017). Capital unchained: finance, intangible assets and the double life of capital in the offshore world. *Review of International Political Economy*, 24(1), 56–86.

Buch-Hansen, H. & Henriksen, L. F. (2019). Toxic ties: Corporate networks of market control in the European chemical industry, 1960–2000. *Social Networks*, 58, 24–36.

Büttner, T. & Thiemann, M. (2017). Breaking regime stability? The politicization of expertise in the OECD/G20 process on BEPS and the potential transformation of international taxation. *Accounting, Economics, and Law: A Convivium*, 7(1).

Cho, C. H., Laine, M., Roberts, R. W., & Rodrigue, M. (2015). Organized hypocrisy, organizational façades, and sustainability reporting. *Accounting, Organizations and Society*, 40, 78–94.

Christensen, R. C. (2021). Elite professionals in transnational tax governance. *Global Networks*, 21(2), 265–293.

Christensen, R. C. & Hearson, M. (2019). The new politics of global tax governance: Taking stock a decade after the financial crisis. *Review of International Political Economy*, 26(5), 1068–1088.

Christensen, R. C., Seabrooke, L., & Wigan, D. (2021). Professional action in global wealth chains. *Regulation & Governance*. Advance online publication. https://doi.org/10.1111/rego.12370.

Cobham, A. & Janský, P. (2018). Global distribution of revenue loss from corporate tax avoidance: re-estimation and country results. *Journal of International Development*, 30(2), 206–232.

Cobham, A., Janský, P., & Meinzer, M. (2015). The financial secrecy index: Shedding new light on the geography of secrecy. *Economic Geography*, 91(3), 281–303.

Coe, N. M. & Yeung, H. W. (2019). Global production networks: Mapping recent conceptual developments. *Journal of Economic Geography* 19(4), 775–801.

Commons, J. R. (1924). *The Legal Foundations of Capitalism*. Macmillan Company.

Commons, J. R. (1925). Law and economics. *Yale Law Journal*, 34, 371–382.

Commons, J. R. (1934). *Institutional Economics: Its Place in Political Economy*. University of Wisconsin Press.

Commons, J. R. (1936). Institutional economics. *American Economic Review*, 26(1), 237–249.

de Carvalho, B. & Seabrooke, L. (2016). Expatriates in global wealth chains. *NUPI Policy Brief 16–6*. Norwegian Institute of International Affairs.

Desai, M. (2008). The decentering of the global firm, *Working Paper 09-054*. Harvard Business School.

Eskelinen, T. & Ylönen, M. (2017). Panama and the WTO: New constitutionalism of trade policy and global tax governance. *Review of International Political Economy*, 24(4), 629–656.

Fichtner, J. (2016). The anatomy of the Cayman Islands offshore financial center: Anglo-America, Japan, and the role of hedge funds. *Review of International Political Economy*, 23(6), 1034–1063.

Finér, L. & Ylönen, M. (2017). Tax-driven wealth chains: A multiple case study of tax avoidance in the Finnish mining sector. *Critical Perspectives on Accounting*, 48, 53–81.

Fligstein, N. (1990). *The Transformation of Corporate Control*. Harvard University Press.

Freeman, J. & Hannan, M. T. (1983). Niche width and the dynamics of organizational populations. *American Journal of Sociology*, 88(6), 1116–1145.

Gabbioneta, C., Faulconbridge, J. R., Currie, G., Dinovitzer, R., & Muzio, D. (2019). Inserting professionals and professional organizations in studies of wrongdoing: The nature, antecedents and consequences of professional misconduct. *Human Relations*, 72(11), 1707–1725.

Garcia-Bernardo, J., Fichtner, J., Takes, F. W., & Heemskerk, E. M. (2017). Uncovering offshore financial centers: Conduits and sinks in the global corporate ownership network. *Scientific Reports*, 7(1), 6246.

Genschel, P. & Rixen, T. (2015). Settling and unsettling the transnational legal order of international taxation. In: T. C. Halliday and G. Shaffer (eds.), *Transnational Legal Orders*. Cambridge University Press, 154–184.

Gereffi, G. (2014). Global value chains in a post-Washington Consensus world. *Review of International Political Economy*, 21(1), 9–37.

Gereffi, G., Humphrey, J., & Sturgeon, T. (2005). The governance of global value chains. *Review of International Political Economy*, 12(1), 78–104.

Gibbon, P., Bair, J., & Ponte, S. (2008). Governing global value chains: An introduction. *Economy and Society*, 37(3), 315–338.

Grasten, M., Seabrooke, L., & Wigan, D. (2021). Legal affordances in global wealth chains: How platform firms use legal and spatial scaling. *Environment and Planning A: Economy and Space*, DOI: 10.1177/0308518X211057131.

Haberly, D. & Wójcik, D. (2015). Regional blocks and imperial legacies: Mapping the global offshore FDI network. *Economic Geography* 91, 251–280.

Haberly, D. & Wójcik, D. (eds.), (2021). *Global Financial Networks: What They Are and Where They Come From*. Oxford University Press.

Hannan, M. T. & Freeman, J. (1977). The population ecology of organizations. *American Journal of Sociology*, 82(5), 929–964

Harrington, B. (2015). Going global: Professionals and the micro-foundations of institutional change. *Journal of Professions and Organization*, 2(2), 103–121.

Hearson, M. (2018). Transnational expertise and the expansion of the international tax regime: Imposing "acceptable" standards. *Review of International Political Economy*, 25(5), 647–671.

Hearson, M. (2021). *Imposing Standards: The North-South Dimension to Global Tax Politics*. Cornell University Press.

Heemskerk, E. M., Fennema, M., & Carroll, W. K. (2016). The global corporate elite after the financial crisis: Evidence from the transnational network of interlocking directorates. *Global Networks* 16(1), 68–88.

Helgadóttir, O. (2020). The new luxury freeports: Offshore storage, tax avoidance, and 'invisible' art. *Environment and Planning A: Economy and Space*, Advance online publication. https://doi.org/10.1177/0308518X20972712.

Ireland, P. (1999). Law and the myth of shareholder ownership. *Modern Law Review*, 62(1), 32–57.

Jensen, M. C. & Meckling, W. H. (1976). Theory of the firm: Managerial behavior, agency costs and ownership structure. *Journal of Financial Economics*, 3(4), 305–360.

Kentikelenis, A. E. & Seabrooke, L. (2017). The politics of world polity: Scriptwriting in international organizations. *American Sociological Review*, 82(5), 1065–1092.

Kristensen, P. H. (1996). Variations in the nature of the firm in Europe. In R. Whitley and P. H. Kristensen (eds.), *The Changing European Firm: Limits to Convergence*. Routledge, 1–36.

Lan, L. L. & Heracleous, L. (2010). Rethinking agency theory: The view from law. *Academy of Management Review*, 35(2), 294–314.

Levi, M., Reuter, P., & Halliday, T. (2018). Can the AML system be evaluated without better data? *Crime, Law and Social Change*, 69(2), 307–328.

McKenzie, R. & Atkinson, R. (2020). Anchoring capital in place: The grounded impact of international wealth chains on housing markets in London. *Urban Studies*, 57(1), 21–38.

Morgan, G. (2014). Financialization and the multinational corporation. *Transfer: European Review of Labour and Research*, 20(2), 183–197.

Morgan, J. (2021). A critique of the Laffer theorem's macro-narrative consequences for corporate tax avoidance from a global wealth chain perspective. *Globalizations*, 18(2), 174–194.

Morgan, J. & Nasir, M. A. (2021). Financialised private equity finance and the debt gamble: The case of Toys R Us. *New Political Economy*, 26(3), 455–471.

Murphy, R., Seabrooke, L., & Stausholm, S. (2019). A Tax Map of Global Professional Service Firms: Where Expert Services are Located and Why. COFFERS Working Paper D4.6, February.

Neilson, J., Pritchard, B., & Yeung, H. W. C. (2014). Global value chains and global production networks in the changing international political economy: An introduction. *Review of International Political Economy*, 21(1), 1–8.

Nitzan, J. & Bichler, S. (2009) *Capital as Power: A Study of Order and Creorder*. Routledge.

Palan, R. (2002). Tax havens and the commercialization of state sovereignty. *International Organization*, 56(1), 151–176.

Palan, R., Murphy, R., & Chavagneux, C. (2010). *Tax Havens: How Globalization Really Works*. Cornell University Press.

Palan, R. & Wigan, D. (2014). Herding cats and taming tax havens: The US strategy of "not in my backyard." *Global Policy*, 5(3), 334–343.

Parker, M. (2013). Beyond justification: Dietrologic and the sociology of critique. In P. Du Gay and G. Morgan (eds.), *New Spirits of Capitalism*. Oxford University Press, 124–141.

Pfeffer, J. & Salancik, G. R. (1978). *The External Control of Organizations: A Resource Dependence Perspective*. Stanford University Press.

Picciotto, S. (2007). Constructing compliance: Game playing, tax law, and the regulatory state. *Law & Policy*, 29(1), 11–30.

Picciotto, S. (2011). *Regulating Global Corporate Capitalism*. Cambridge University Press.

Picciotto, S. (2015). Indeterminacy, complexity, technocracy and the reform of international corporate taxation. *Social & Legal Studies*, 24(2), 165–184.

Pistor, K. (2019). *The Code of Capital: How the Law Creates Wealth and Inequality*. Princeton University Press.

Podolny, Joel M. (2010) *Status Signals: A Sociological Study of Market Competition*. Princeton University Press.

Ponte, S. & Sturgeon, T. (2014). Explaining governance in global value chains: A modular theory-building effort. *Review of International Political Economy*, 21(1), 195–223.

Quentin, D. & Campling, L. (2018). Global inequality chains: Integrating mechanisms of value distribution into analyses of global production. *Global Networks*, 18(1), 33–56.

Radcliffe, V. S., Spence, C., Stein, M., & Wilkinson, B. (2018). Professional repositioning during times of institutional change: The case of tax practitioners and changing moral boundaries. *Accounting, Organizations and Society*, 66, 45–59.

Rixen, T. (2016). Institutional reform of global tax governance: A proposal. In P. Dietsch and T. Rixen (eds.), *Global Tax Governance. What is Wrong with It and How to Fix It*. ECPR Press, 325–350.

Robé, J. P. (2009). Conflicting sovereignties in the world wide web of contracts–property rights and the globalization of the power system. In G.-P. Calliess, A. Fischer-Lescano, D. Wielsch, and P. Zumbansen (eds.), *Soziologische Jurisprudenz: Festschrift für Gunther Teubner zum 65. Geburtstag*. De Gruyter Recht, 691–703.

Robé, J. P. (2011). The legal structure of the firm. *Accounting, Economics, and Law*, 1(1), 2152–2820.

Robé, J. P. (2020). The shareholder value mess (and how to clean it up). *Accounting, Economics, and Law*, 10(3), https://doi.org/10.1515/ael-2019-0039.

Robé, J. P. (2021). Property, Power and Politics. Why We Need to Rethink the World Power System. Bristol University Press.

Santos, M. (2021). High net-worth attachments: emotional labour, relational work, and financial subjectivities in private wealth management. *Journal of Cultural Economy*, 14(6), 750–764.

Seabrooke, L. & Wigan, D. (2014). Global wealth chains in the international political economy. *Review of International Political Economy*, 21(1), 257–263.

Seabrooke, L. & Wigan, D. (2017). The governance of global wealth chains. *Review of International Political Economy*, 24(1), 1–29.

Sharman, J. C. (2017). Illicit global wealth chains after the financial crisis: microstates and an unusual suspect. *Review of International Political Economy*, 24(1), 30–55.

Suddaby, R. & Greenwood, R. (2005). Rhetorical strategies of legitimacy. *Administrative Science Quarterly*, 50(1), 35–67.

Swedberg, R. (2018). How to use Max Weber's ideal type in sociological analysis. *Journal of Classical Sociology*, 18(3), 181–196

Tischer, D., Maurer, B., & Leaver, A. (2019). Finance as "bizarre bazaar": Using documents as a source of ethnographic knowledge. *Organization*, 26(4), 553–577.

Tsingou, E. (2010). Transnational governance networks in the regulation of finance—The making of global regulation and supervision standards in the banking industry. In M. Ougaard and A. Leander (eds.), *Theoretical Perspectives on Business and Global Governance: Bridging Theoretical Divides*. Routledge, 138–155.

Tsingou, E. (2018). New governors on the block: The rise of anti-money laundering professionals. *Crime, Law and Social Change*, 69(2), 191–205.

Veblen, T. (1899). *The Theory of the Leisure Class*. MacMillan.

Veblen, T. (1904). *The Theory of Business Enterprise*. Charles Scribner's Sons.

Veblen, T. (1923). *Absentee Ownership and Business Enterprise in Recent Times: The Case of America*. B. W. Huebsch.

Waris, A. (2018). Creating and building a post-conflict fiscal state through global wealth chains: A case study of Somaliland. *Journal of Money Laundering Control*, 21(2), 171–188.

Weber, M. (1978). *Economy and Society: An Outline of Interpretive Sociology* (vols. 1 and 2). University of California Press.

Weber, M. (2012). The "objectivity" of knowledge in social science and social policy. In H. H. Bruun and S. Whimster (eds.), *Max Weber: Collected Methodological Essays*, translated by H. H. Bruun. Routledge, 100–138.

Wigan, D. (2008). A global political economy of derivatives: Risk, property and the artifice of indifference (Doctoral dissertation, University of Sussex).

Ylönen, M. & Teivainen, T. (2018). Politics of intra-firm trade: Corporate price planning and the double role of the arm's length principle. *New Political Economy*, 23(4), 441–457.

Young, K. L. (2012). Transnational regulatory capture? An empirical examination of the transnational lobbying of the Basel Committee on Banking Supervision. *Review of International Political Economy*, 19(4), 663–688.

Zucman, G. (2019). Global wealth inequality. *Annual Review of Economics*, 11, 109–138.

2

Public Utilities

Colin Haslam, Adam Leaver, and Nick Tsitsianis

Introduction

There are many ways to understand the coordinating role of lead firms in markets—as transaction cost managers engaged in make-or-buy decisions (Coase, 1937), as information brokers building collaboration (Spekman et al., 1998), or as strategic pivots and governance agents in increasingly complex markets (Gereffi et al., 2005). This chapter argues that because firms perform operational and financial reporting activities, they are articulated in both value chains and global wealth chains. Understanding this dual identity has implications for our understanding of firm strategy. In reporting terms, if firms are conceived as a bundle of separable assets, wealth may be created and hoarded through the "legal affordances" granted to asset owners through forms of financial engineering. Taking UK water companies as our case study, this chapter explores how utility firms responded to regulatory price-setting changes by innovating around these legal affordances and accounting arrangements to capitalize on new private wealth appropriation opportunities. In the case of the multinational French firm Veolia, the secure income streams generated through the provision of water and waste services collateralized the debt-loading of subsidiaries who remitted returns back to the French parent. Asset revaluations, intercompany debt, and special dividends were used to concentrate a greater share of wealth within the corporate network and evict the claims of other stakeholders such as the UK state.

This case illustrates how the firm has become a conduit between debt markets and investor returns and a site that backs extended chains of financial engineering. In utilities we argue that these global wealth chains are a hybrid of captive and hierarchy—the regulator is close during the price-setting phase, but kept at a distance as client and supplier coordinate tightly to seek extractive opportunities from the new regulatory arrangements and

Colin Haslam, Adam Leaver, and Nick Tsitsianis, *Public Utilities*. In: *Global Wealth Chains*.
Edited by Leonard Seabrooke and Duncan Wigan, Oxford University Press.
© Colin Haslam, Adam Leaver, and Nick Tsitsianis (2022). DOI: 10.1093/oso/9780198832379.003.0002

are separated only by legal boundaries between related corporate entities. Any intervention would therefore require not only changes in domestic regulation but multilateral coordination.

Conceptualizing lead organization relations in a supply chain or network

How might we begin to conceptualize the relations around lead organizations in the governance of supply chains like water or waste? Since Coase's (1937) seminal work on the role of transaction costs in make-or-buy decisions, two influential approaches have emerged within academic writing on this issue. The first is the literature on supply chain management (SCM), rooted in operations management and consulting, which emphasizes the role of lead firms in embedding coordination and trust in supply networks within innovative markets. A second set of literatures which emerges from world systems theory is the research on global value chains (GVC), which emphasizes the role of firms as strategic pivots and key governance agents. Both have revealed the emergence of new network forms of coordination, but also tend to emphasize operational governance relations which can downplay wealth chain governance in a mundane, financialized business like water.

Supply chain management

According to the SCM approach, lead firms increasingly perform the role of "information brokers" rather than transaction managers in modern supply chains (Spekman et al., 1998). The background to this claim is a broader perception that the sources of competitive advantage have changed fundamentally after globalization. Specifically, lead firms have become central to the organization of looser networks of firms, allowing for both cost-cutting and value-adding advantages (Miles & Snow, 2007). This coordinating role has been facilitated by new, sophisticated information systems which improve the efficiency of logistics and other functions and allow for a more modular form of production and service provision (Carter & Price, 1993). This facilitated lead firms' access to smaller, more specialized firms whose skills would allow them to meet changing, more refined consumer preferences (Dale et al., 1994; Harland, 1996). Out of necessity this led to alternative modes of contracting, such as outsourcing (Willcocks et al., 1995) and the emergence of temporary, project-based organizational forms (MacBeth & Ferguson, 1994) to allow for such flexibility.

For SCM authors, lead firms' competitive advantage depends less on their ability to manage their internal processes and more on their ability to manage the performance of the total supply chain (Chen & Pulraj, 2004; Harland, 1996). According to Stadtler (2015, p. 10) "no single organizational unit now is solely responsible for the competitiveness of its products and services in the eyes of the ultimate customer . . . competition has shifted from single companies to supply chains." This means lead firms have had to manage the broader integration and coordination processes across organizations (Monczka & Morgan, 1997), to foster cooperation, collaboration, and partnerships within the whole chain to secure long-term competitive advantage for all participants (Carr, 1999; Hammer, 2001; Balakrishan, 2004; Azadegan, 2011; Hartmann & De Grahl, 2011; Paulraj, 2011).

The supply chain management literature on the water industry is minimal, and those references which do exist tend to focus on the narrower, though related, concept of sustainable SCM (see Seuring & Muller, 2008 for an overview). This work develops the themes of SCM to emphasize, for example, the importance of collaborative benchmarking and transparency (Braadbart, 2007) or the forms of information and coordination required to meet the challenges of water scarcity (Grant et al., 2015). The representation of lead firms as information brokers continues.

Global value chains

Whilst accepting some of the contextual background discussed by SCM authors, the GVC approach differs significantly in its view of lead firms—particularly around the theorization of lead firm power and the coordination and governance of the networks within which they are embedded. GVC authors focus on the different governance arrangements of, and the uneven appropriation of value within, a network. This differs markedly from SCM's emphasis on mutual gains, goal congruence, and the marginalization of opportunism (see Storey et al., 2006 for an overview).

In terms of power, GVC authors are less inclined to discuss lead firms' "legitimate power," as is discussed in some SCM analysis (see e.g. Benton & Maloni, 2005), and instead view power as something not always exercised consensually. This was central to the original work of Gereffi and Korzeniewicz (1994) on buyer-driven and producer-driven global commodity chains (GCCs), which broke down the financial value embedded in a product and traced its unequal distribution across the supply chain (Dedrick et al., 2010). This inequality was linked to firms' structural sources of power (market power) and power over the dominant normative conventions of the network—such as the qualification of specific products—which allowed them to govern supply chains in ways that served their interests (Ponte & Gibbon, 2005).

More recent GVC work has emphasized the technical and economic aspects of governance at the expense of the more political questions around distributional outcomes (Palpacuer, 2008). This research has centered on how lead firms make strategic selections to optimize gains from new organizational and governance arrangements, against the backdrop of fragmenting market structures and the vertical disintegration of the multinational firm. For example, Gereffi et al. (2005) in their later work move beyond the dichotomy of buyer- versus producer-driven chains to outline five governance patterns in GVCs—market, modular, relational, captive, and hierarchy—to better understand the different organizational and governance structures emerging in new technology sectors. Each suggests a different role for lead firms: transaction-based governance in market structures; codification of complex information in modular chains; outsourcing to access core competences in relational networks; locking in suppliers in captive networks; and the exchange of tacit knowledge internally, logistics development, and the management of intellectual property in hierarchical systems (Gereffi et al. 2005, pp. 86–87). This differs from SCM's singular and occasionally prescriptive approach to governance by emphasizing the multiple ways lead firms reorganize and govern production in increasingly complex markets. However, GVC scholarship on the water industry is also scant.

Financialization and global wealth chains

Both SCM and GVC do provide useful insights into the changing shape of global production and service provision. But the more recent emphasis on complex, innovative goods has tended to ignore important but mundane sectors like water which generate significant employment and provide essential services. Water is an interesting case because the mundane features of its activity contrast with the increasingly international and fund-based character of its ownership (Table 2.1) and the attendant financial innovations that have facilitated the global movement of wealth within—and out of—the industry. These "financialized" developments have become an object of interest within GVC scholarship in particular (Milberg, 2008; Palpacuer, 2008; Ponte & Gibbon, 2005). Understanding water as a financialized business therefore has the capacity to change the way we conceptualize the relevant governance arrangements within which water companies are embedded.

After financialization, firms have become sites of financial transformation—a relay between debt markets and investor distributions as much as productive, value-adding nodes in a supply chain or network. This financial transformation can take a number of forms. First, as Fligstein (2005) noted, the corporation has become understood as a collection of separable assets which can be divested, sold and leased back, secured against debt, securitized, and put to many other financialized uses in the interest of maximizing shareholder returns.[1] At the same time, the rising value of financial assets relative to total assets gives companies the incentives and capacity to shift these asset-related profits across borders (Morgan, 2014). Second, after the fair value revolution, the accounting treatment of assets can be used to create wealth, illustrating the constructivist character of profit as an artifact of accounting and law (Mitchell & Sikka, 2011; Riles, 2011). Growing practices like transfer pricing, intellectual property management, and the use of special dividends have been used to recognize or direct income to areas of lowest regulatory costs (Sikka & Wilmott, 2010; Shaxson, 2012). Similarly an array of complex corporate arrangements, including the use of tax havens and other quasi-legal, under-the-radar practices, have been used to hoard that wealth more efficiently within the corporate network (Palan et al., 2010). This illustrates the Jekyll and Hyde quality of modern governance relations. Trust, information sharing, collaboration, and cooperation may well characterize some systems of governance on the productive side (though this too may be overstated—see Brooks et al., 2017), but on the financial side, opportunism, gaming, obfuscation, and nondisclosure characterize relations with users of financial reports.

---

[1] We should recognize that Fligstein (2005) believed the Enron debacle marked the end of the shareholder value conception of control. Our view is that Fligstein's conclusion was premature.

Table 2.1 UK/overseas ownership of UK water companies

Water company	UK or overseas ownership	Owner
Affinity Water (formerly Veolia Water Central, Veolia Water East, Veolia Water Southeast)	UK & overseas	Allianz Group, HICL Infrastructure Company Ltd, DIF
Anglian Water (includes Hartlepool Water)	UK & overseas	Osprey Acquisitions Limited—a consortium of several companies based in the UK, Australia, and Canada.
Bristol Water	UK & overseas	iCON Infrastructure Partners III L.P., iCON Infrastructure Partners III (Bristol) L.P., and Itochu Corporation of Japan
Cholderton and District Water	UK	Independent water company
Dwr Cymru Welsh Water	UK	UK-based Glas Cymru
Northern Ireland Water	UK	Government-owned company
Northumbrian Water (including Essex & Suffolk Water)	Overseas	Hong Kong-based CK Hutchison Holdings Ltd
Portsmouth Water	UK	UK-based SD Parent Ltd
Scottish Water	UK	Government-owned company
Severn Trent Water (including Dee Valley Water)	UK	Severn Trent plc
South East Water	UK & overseas	Utilities Trust of Australia, RBS Pension Trustee Ltd, Desjardins Entities (RRMD, Certasm DFS)
South Staffordshire Water (including Cambridge Water)	Overseas	US-based KKR & Co L.P. and Mitsubishi Corporation
South West Water (including Bournemouth Water)	UK	UK-based Pennon Group plc
Southern Water	UK & overseas	UBS Asset Management, JP Morgan Asset Management, Whitehelm Capital, Hermes Infrastructure Funds
Sutton and East Surrey Water	Overseas	Japanese companies Sumitomo Corporation and Osaka Gas
Thames Water	UK & overseas	Kemble Water Holdings Ltd, a consortium of investors
United Utilities	UK	United Utilities Group plc
Wessex Water	Overseas	Malaysia-based YTL Power International
Yorkshire Water	Overseas	Kelda Group, which is owned by a consortium, including Deutsche Asset Management and private equity fund Corsair Capital

Source: Company accounts, correct at the time of writing.

Corporate strategy in listed firms has thus drifted toward the less conventional financial engineering and creative reporting practices of alternative investment funds where the goal is levering financial assets for cash extraction as much as levering productive assets for value creation (Froud et al., 2007; Erturk et al., 2010; and Morgan, Chapter 6 in this volume). Here the firm itself has become a kind of mutable, rehypothecatable asset to be pledged in the interest of shareholder value creation. With that move toward alternative investment strategies, capital has become more mobile and assets more mutable so that there is a growing disconnect between the location of value creation and the geographical allocation of profits and wealth (see Bryan et al., Chapter 5 in this volume for insight on the spatio-temporal character of contemporary capital). If we are to understand this process, we must engage with the organization of financial flows which shape the geographic footprint of capital. This is the start point for Seabrooke and Wigan's (2017) concept of global wealth chains—a kind of vertical analogue to Gereffi et al.'s (2005) horizontal global value chain.

The GWC aim is to map "transacted forms of capital operating multi-jurisdictionally for the purposes of wealth creation and protection." This may involve an interactive relation between the organization of the financial and operating activities—financialized pressures may, as Falcounbridge and Muzio (2009) recognize, feed back into corporate and public organizational forms and discourses, altering systems of governance within, and the geography of, production chains. The GWC approach therefore has the capacity to shed light on the organization and governance of global financial flows in unfashionable sheltered sectors like utilities. Understanding these sections of the economy is important when activities like water, gas, electricity, public sector operations, etc. still employ upwards of 10 million people in the UK or approximately 35 percent of the national workforce (Bowman et al., 2014), yet so little is written about the governance of those networks and their financialized character. We will now explore some of these themes with the example of UK water.

Regulating water in the UK: Close but distant

The organization and governance of global wealth chains are influenced by three key variables: (1) regulatory liability, (2) the innovative capacities of product suppliers in wealth chains, and (3) the complexity of transactions (Seabrooke & Wigan, 2017). We will deal with the first concern, before exploring the other two variables in subsequent sections.

The nature of the relation between the regulator and regulated enti-ties in the UK is temporally contingent. Relations are closer during the price-setting phase, whilst the regulator is held at a distance during the AMP5[2] phase. These relations reflect the relatively unique characteristics of the activity and a very particular regulatory history post-privatization.

UK water provision was privatized in 1989 under the Thatcher govern-ment and the particular regulatory regime that emerged in the UK reflected an ongoing attempt to resolve a central tension evident from the outset: that water provision, due to its requirement for large capital outlays, is a natural monopoly and thus resistant to the kind of market logics en-visaged in the privatization programme. The regulatory framework that therefore emerged was complex and multi-layered in an attempt to simu-late market forces in the absence of consumer switching power. The Water Services Regulatory Authority or "Ofwat" is the economic regulator of the water and sewerage sectors, tasked with promoting competition to pro-tect consumers, monitoring water companies' productive and financial performance against a set of benchmarks and a broader "sustainable devel-opment" remit. The Department for Environment, Food and Rural Affairs (DEFRA) sets the overall water and sewerage policy framework in England, including the setting of core legislation and standards, as well as creating special permits such as drought orders. Much of the same activities are governed by the Welsh Government in Wales. The Environment Agency advises government on the environment and thus has a role in regulating the water and sewerage sector, for example in seeking to avoid flood risk. There is a Drinking Water Inspectorate which checks that water companies meet the standards set in the Water Quality Regulations. The Consumer Council for Water acts as consumer advocate and investigates consumer complaints, whilst Natural England advises government on certain en-vironmental aspects of water supply and preservation. In addition to all that, there are European water, wastewater, and environmental standards set by the European Union, which are still relevant even in a post-Brexit context.

From a GWC perspective, Ofwat is the most relevant regulatory actor be-cause it deals with economic practice in the sector. But Ofwat has always had a conflicted regulatory role. In the absence of competition Ofwat is tasked with simulating market effects by setting price limits on the whole-sale water and sewerage business every five years. But at the heart of this

---

[2] The AMP5 is the asset management plan for the next five years.

price-setting remit lies a balance between the need to incentivize capital investment over the long term and the goal of empowering consumers and stimulating efficiency (Ogden, 1997). This manifests in a tension between keeping prices low enough to justify Ofwat's consumer protection remit and preventing them falling so low that they compromise the supplying entities' ability to meet investment and sustainability targets. Ofwat is therefore simultaneously close to the industry in the negotiation of key metrics which feed into the pricing review, with informal, cooperative relations present between regulators and the regulated (Willman et al., 2003), and also held at a distance by industry players as they draw on law and accounting expertise to aid them in maximising distributions from the activity over the five-year period after prices are set, ensuring they also meet (or appear to meet) their obligations on service provision, investment, and so on. The water industry might therefore be thought of as a form of either captive or hierarchy chain, or a hybrid of both within the GWC schema (see Figure 1.2 in Chapter 1 of this volume), depending on the period of time observed.

To understand this unusual client–regulator relation it is worth examining the price-setting mechanism more closely to grasp how shareholder distribution strategies are built in response to it. Ofwat's remit is to ensure that water companies can finance their activities. This means that the central goal of the pricing methodology is to guarantee a return on the capital invested in the business, effectively putting a floor under the price whilst also underwriting water company profits. This is done by imputing a "regulatory capital value" (RCV), which includes the costs of capital and is indexed to inflation, both of which are forecasted for the subsequent five years during the price review (Ofwat, 1992). Adjustments to the RCV are then made, based on the expected capital expenditure required to enhance and maintain the network, whilst deducting capital grants and other contributions to the cost of the new assets. Current cost depreciation on a replacement cost basis is also deducted from the RCV (Ofwat, 2017). Companies are then encouraged to outperform these regulatory assumptions and are allowed to retain any efficiency gains made on a rolling basis. There are no restrictions on dividend payouts, which were abolished by the 1989 Water Act.

A calculation this complex creates opportunities to innovate around the legal affordances granted to water industry firms. The history of water regulation has been a cat-and-mouse game as each price-setting review encourages industry reporting practices which try to arbitrage the new regulations. Gaming goes back to the very first days of privatization when newly privatized companies set up holding companies with multiple subsidiaries to relocate various activities outside of the realm of Ofwat's reach (Ogden & Glaister, 1996). Similarly, companies soon realized that "outperforming" (underspending) early in the price review period allowed them to keep the benefits of the cost-saving efficiencies for longer (Ofwat, 2017). Firms also discovered ways of bringing in new sources of income not well captured by the RCV calculations—such as the selling of land and other assets—which the 2015 review tried to address. With each new regulatory intervention, a new set of practices have emerged on the blind side of the regulator. Arguably the most important of these, in recent years, has been the debt-loading of water companies, which has coincided with high levels of shareholder distributions.

Innovative capacities: Firms as financial conduits

The GWC approach allows us to understand firms like water companies differently—as a kind of conduit between debt markets and equity holders. Alternatively, these firms can be understood as a portal, which alters the temporal allocation of income and costs so that it is entirely possible for investors to take out distributions over and above the firm-generated cash residual, whilst leaving the corporate entity with the present costs of the future debt-based liabilities.

Not all firms can be put to this kind of use, but public utilities are particularly attractive as a conduit asset, because of the security and predictability of income streams. This may explain the appeal of public utilities to private equity funds where there is a strong preference for investments with strong and secure cashflows to finance the levered nature of the acquisition (see Morgan, Chapter 6 in this volume, on private equity GWCs). Water companies have little demand risk because they provide an essential service. The income stream is linked to RPI and the return on capital is underwritten by the regulator, so there is no innate inflation or interest rate risk. There is no commodity price risk because water companies do not "own" the product they distribute, and there is minimal competition risk because the activity is a natural monopoly. These characteristics are highly appealing to alternative investment funds because asset-heavy, cashflow positive, secure industries give funds multiple "outs" and financial innovation opportunities. The firm, when compared to other asset classes, has a mutability rooted in its limited liability status, which makes it amenable to financialized practices.

In the case of water, the central opportunity has been to increase leverage and pay out dividends—a product of the original 1989 Water Act which lifted restrictions on both. Water companies notoriously distribute very high levels of dividends to investors, and—it is argued—in recent years much of this has been funded by debt issue (Financial Times, 2015). Ofwat first became aware of the dividend issue in the mid 1990s when companies claimed that they did not need to invest as much in the future network because of their capital efficiency savings, which justified higher dividend payouts (Lobina & Hall, 2008). The early 2000s were then characterized by underinvestment as water companies pared back capex in order to increase distributions: between 2000 and 2005 the investment underspend was estimated to be around £1.7 billion or 9 percent of Owfat projections, whilst companies paid out £3.4 billion in dividends (Ofwat, 2006). This worsened in 2006 when the capital underspend reached £1 billion in a single year—22 percent lower than the level assumed by Ofwat when setting the price limits (Lobina & Hall, 2008). By 2009 the industry paid out almost twice its free cash flow before interest in dividends, funded by debt as gearing ratios rose from 46 percent in 2000 to 72 percent by 2009 (Armitage, 2012). Ofwat did respond amidst a public backlash against dividend payouts: regulated companies (i.e. the regulated operating subsidiaries) were required to report dividends paid to their parent company and to explain the basis of the dividend; firms were also reminded that dividend payouts should not impair the ability to finance the regulated businesses and that dividends should only reward efficiency and the management of economic risk. But in reality, the latter was difficult to measure and thus enforce, and the former was always susceptible to hold-up risk when firms' inability to deliver on investment promises would be viewed at least in part as an indictment of Ofwat itself given its responsibilities to underwrite the financing of those firms; the temptation to lower expenditure targets[3] or revise pricing arrangements[4] was high and not unprecedented. Cox (2013, p. 10) found that little had changed: subsidiary distributions to parent companies continued so that "at the top end of the range, companies have been paying out close to 25% of their equity asset base ('equity RAV') to their holding companies in each year."

---

[3] For example, in Ofwat's 2004 review it recommended that Thames Water cut its expenditure on fixing leaky pipes by 27 percent (Armitage, 2012).

[4] In some cases shortfalls in revenues are recoverable through the revenue-correction mechanism (RCM) at the next price review. The RCM is designed to compensate water companies for lower-than-anticipated consumption by "tariff basket" (largely household and smaller commercial) customers.

The stretching of accounting rules and aggressive financial engineering have been important features of this period of debt-loading and high levels of shareholder distributions. Research has highlighted that the costing methodology is flawed and open to too much discretion in the accounting of unit costs (External Stakeholder Survey, 2005, p. 38). Similarly, others have noted that profits are exceptionally sensitive to the method of valuing the assets and the rules regarding depreciation (Armitage, 2012). Below-the-line innovations to reduce tax costs have also proliferated. Water companies have levered up to depress corporate tax receipts (Financial Times, 2015). They have also booked large deferred tax allowances against future investments. Government estimates are that water, electricity, and gas companies denied the Treasury up to £1 billion through complex and aggressive forms of tax avoidance (Kavanaugh, 2013). Securitization in the case of Welsh Water's deal with RBS and Yorkshire, and Southern Water's use of derivatives like index-linked swaps, show there is also an appetite for more exotic forms of financial innovation.

The complexity of these financial reporting interventions means accounting and law professionals play a prominent role in the governance relations of water company GWCs. The governance relations that underpin these extractive strategies are closer to hierarchy (Figure 1.1 in Chapter 1 of this volume). They are more likely to be bespoke than off the peg because their goal is something quite specific to water companies—to maximize extractions from the AMP5 period where prices have already been set and there is a certain confidence in a margin-positive but low-ROCE future. There is also significant divergence in practice and levels of debt across the water companies (Armitage, 2012; Ofwat, 2015), suggesting the services are firm-specific and work with an integrated supplier–client relation due to the complexity of information and knowledge transfer. This may also be shaped by the specificity of clients' requirements, which are always shaped by the different domiciles and thus tax regimes within which parent organizations are based. To explore the role of accounting and law expertise and how it influences practice, we now look at the case of Veolia Water.

Veolia and complex transactions

Veolia Environnement SA is a French utilities company which had a UK subsidiary, Veolia Water UK plc/Ltd[5]—then its main operating entity in the

---

[5] The subsidiary was named Veolia Water UK plc until 2012; it became Veolia Water UK Ltd thereafter.

UK water utility sector. Veolia Water UK was often held up as an exemplar of good practice in a sector where high gearing ratios and complex corporate structures were the norm (see Allen & Pryke, 2013). But whatever its operational achievements, the story of Veolia Water UK is also one of financial engineering, specifically the use of intercompany debt and special dividends to move wealth around within an international corporate structure.

The backdrop to the story is the Eurozone crisis which forced Veolia Environnement SA to assess its position in a number of global markets, including its water businesses (Boxell, 2012). This was in part forced upon it due to large losses from its financing activities. Veolia's senior management therefore sought a €5–6-billion divestment programme focusing mainly on foreign assets to reduce corporate debt (Veolia Environnement SA, 2011). But this accumulation of corporate debt at the consolidated group level must be understood within the context of the relations between French parent and UK subsidiary.

The financial engineering in this particular example began in 2010 when Veolia Water UK revalued its tangible fixed assets from historic cost methods to fair value methods, following accounting rule FRS15. This had a profound effect on the balance sheet as Veolia Water UK PLC revised the value of some of its tangible assets up by £436.6 million. This, through the double-entry effect, directly increased reserves on the liability side by the same amount (see Figure 2.1 below). Even though this innocuous accounting exercise had added close to half a billion pounds to its reserves, this was still only a paper gain and non-distributable because it was recorded in the revaluation reserve as the 2006 Companies Act and prevailing accounting rules dictate. To make distributions from that new value created, Veolia

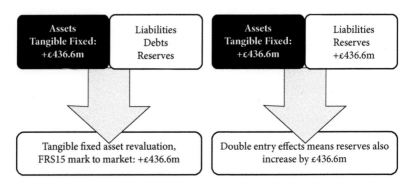

Fig. 2.1 Veolia Water UK assets and liabilities

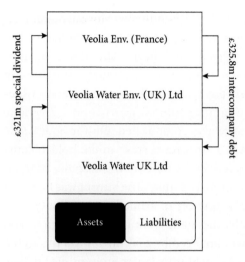

Fig. 2.2 Veolia Water UK reverse debt structure

Water UK PLC group first cancelled some capital, freeing up £251,829 from the revaluation reserve to the "distributable" profit and loss reserve. The entities that comprise the consolidated group of Veolia Water UK plc were then loaded with £325.8 million of new long and short term debt from group undertakings. This intergroup financing provided at least some of the cash to pay £321 million in dividends back up the corporate structure to the French parent (Figure 2.2). The French parent then increased its own dividend payout to €735.6 million in 2010 from €434 million in 2009—a sum similar to the special dividend paid to it by its UK subsidiary.

The use of intercompany debt and special dividends provided Veolia with an additional benefit: the higher interest payments resulted in a lower post-interest profit, which reduced the tax burden. Debt-loading therefore helped to limit the claims of the UK tax authorities on the surpluses of the UK subsidiary; surpluses effectively underwritten by the regulator, and which could have been redirected into socially useful capital investment.

At the consolidated level the intercompany debt balances out. But by 2011 the French parent wanted to exit the UK water business (at least in part) to raise money to pay down debt. Veolia Water Ltd was sold in 2012 to a consortium of investors. This was a complex arrangement: the separate licenses of Veolia Water Central Ltd (VCE), Veolia Water Southeast Ltd (VSE), and Veolia Water East Ltd (VEA) were unified and held by a holding company: Veolia Water Capital Funds Limited (Ofwat, 2012a). Veolia Water Capital Funds Limited was then sold to a consortium led by Infracapital Partners (part of the M&G investment group, Prudential's investment arm), Beryl Datura Investment Ltd (BDIL) Equity, and Morgan Stanley Infrastructure Partners. The takeover vehicle was given the moniker of Rift Acquisitions (Investments) Ltd (Ofwat, 2012b), but later became Affinity Water Acquisitions (Investments) Ltd. A holdco, midco, and another subsidiary were then inserted between it and the bought-out Veolia Water Capital Funds Limited.

The financing arrangements were also complicated. On the equity side Veolia Water UK Limited retained a 10 percent stake in the holdco company, with the remaining 90 percent stake held by Infracapital, Morgan Stanley Infrastructure Partners, and BDIL Equity. The buyout was financed with shareholder loans and £552 million of bank loans (Affinity Water, 2013); but within five months the loans were repaid through a new £572.9-million intercompany loan, financed by a securitization through a new Cayman Islands registered vehicle: Affinity Water Programme Finance Limited. A further £200 million from an existing bond facility was provided by Affinity Water Finance to Affinity Water Limited acting as the guarantor (Affinity Water, 2014). The complexity of the deal perhaps obscured some sizeable extractions. Veolia were paid an additional £60 million in dividends from the UK subsidiary in July 2012 just as it was sold. Upon handover and in the same financial year, Affinity then paid its investors £95.2 million from the operating entity it had just bought (Affinity Water Capital Funds Limited, 2013).

Conclusion

The complexity of the reporting strategies above requires persistent rather than periodic engagement between client and suppliers of accounting and law advice. Much of this coordination takes place on the blind side of regulators who either become aware of or obtain a position to respond to these practices three or four years after they occur at the next price-setting review. Water companies therefore operate as a hybrid of captive and hierarchy in global wealth chains: the regulator is close to the client during the price-setting phase, but kept at a distance as client and supplier coordinate tightly to seek extractive opportunities from the new regulatory arrangements once the pricing criteria have been set.

This emphasis on the governance of wealth rather than production casts an altogether different light on the water industry. Its mundane activity characteristics stand in contrast to the complex financial maneuverings that take place within the corporate network. This might also open up the analysis of global value chains to processes of financialization as water companies become treated increasingly like a conduit or syphon between debt markets and investor returns.

References

Affinity Water (2013). Our Business Plan for 2015–2020, December 2013. https://www.affinitywater.co.uk/docs/corporate/plans/2015-2020/AW-summary-business-plan-2015-2020.pdf

Affinity Water (2014). Affinity Water Investor Presentation, July 2014. https://www.affinitywater.co.uk/docs/financial/listing-presentation/investor-presentation.pdf Affinity Water Capital Funds Limited (2013). Annual Report & Financial Statements For The Year Ended 31 March 2013. https://www.affinitywater.co.uk/docs/financial/limited/annual-report/affinity-water-limited-2013.pdf

Allen, J. & Pryke, M. (2013). Financialising household water: Thames Water, MEIF, and "ring-fenced" politics.' *Cambridge Journal of Regions, Economy and Society* 6, 419–439.

Armitage, S. (2012). Demand for dividends: the case of UK water companies. *Journal of Business Finance & Accounting*, 39, 464–499.

Azadegan, A. (2011). Benefiting from supplier operational innovativeness: the influence of supplier evaluations and absorptive capacity. *Journal of Supply Chain Management* 47(2), 49–64.

Balakrishan, A. (2004). Collaboration and coordination in supply chain management and e-commerce. *Production and Operations Management*, 13(1), 1–2.

Benton, W. & Maloni, M. (2005). The influence of power driven buyer/seller relationships on supply chain satisfaction. *Journal of Operations Management*, 23(1), 1–22.

Bowman, A., Froud, J., Johal, S., & Law, J. (2014). *The End of the Experiment?: From Competition to the Foundational Economy*. Oxford University Press.

Boxell, J. (2012). Veolia aims to cut debt as operating profits fall 25%. *Financial Times*, 8 November 8.

Braadbaart, O. (2007). Collaborative benchmarking, transparency and performance: Evidence from the Netherlands water supply industry. *Benchmarking*, 14, 677–692.

Brooks, S., Leaver, A., Spence, M., Elliott, C., & Dean, M. (2017). Pragmatic engagement in a low trust supply chain: Beef farmers' perceptions of power, trust and agency. *Competition & Change*, 21(2), 114–131.

Carr, A. S. (1999). Strategically managed buyer–supplier relationships and performance outcomes. *Journal of Operations Management*, 17, 497–519.

Carter, J. R. & Price, P. M. (1993). *Integrated Materials Management*, Pitman.

Chen, I. J. & Paulraj, A. (2004). Understanding supply chain management: critical research and a theoretical framework. *International Journal of Production Research*, 42(1), 131–163.

Coase, R. H. (1937). The nature of the firm. *Economica*, 4, 386–405.

Cox, J. (2013). Observations on the regulation of the water sector. Royal Academy of Engineering, March 5.

Dale, B. G., Lascelles, D. M., & Lloyd, A. (1994). Supply chain management and development. In D. G. Dale (ed.), *Managing Quality*, Prentice-Hall, 292–315.

Dedrick, J., Kraemer, K. L., & Linden, G. (2010). Who profits from innovation in global value chains?: A study of the iPod and notebook PCs. *Industrial and Corporate Change*, 19(1), 81–116.

Erturk, I., Froud, J., Johal, S., Leaver, A., & Williams, K. (2010). Ownership matters: Private equity and the political division of ownership. *Organization*, 17(5), 543–561.

Faulconbridge, J. R. & Muzio, D. (2009). The financialization of large law firms: situated discourses and practices of reorganization. *Journal of Economic Geography*, 9(5), 641–661.

Financial Times (2015). Ofwat should tighten the spigot on water profits. *Financial Times*, October 20.

Fligstein, N. (2005). The end of (shareholder value) ideology? In D. E. Davis (ed.), *Political Power and Social Theory, Political Power and Social Theory*, Emerald Group Publishing Ltd, 223–228.

Froud, J., Leaver, A., & Williams, K. (2007). New actors in a financialised economy and the remaking of capitalism. *New Political Economy*, 12(3), 339–347.

Gereffi, G., Humphrey, J., & Sturgeon, T. (2005). The governance of global value chains. *Review of International Political Economy*, 12(1), 78–104.

Gereffi, G. & Korzeniewicz, M. (1994). *Commodity Chains and Global Capitalism*. Praeger Publishers.

Grant, D. B., Trautrims, A., & Wong, C. Y. (2015). *Sustainable Logistics and Supply Chain Management* (revised edition). Kogan Page.

Hammer, M. (2001). The superefficient company. *Harvard Business Review*, 79(8), 82–93.

Harland, C. M. (1996). Supply chain management: relationships, chains and networks. *British Journal of Management*, 7(s1), S63–S80.

Hartmann, E. & De Grahl, A. (2011). The flexibility of logistics service providers and its impact on customer loyalty: An empirical study. *Journal of Supply Chain Management*, 47(3), 63–85.

Kavanagh, M. (2013). Water groups open coffers amid regulatory push to share profits. *Financial Times*, July 14.

Lobina, E. & Hall, D. (2008). The illusions of competition in the water sector: A UNISON Response to the Cave Review of Competition and Innovation in Water Markets. UNISON.

Macbeth, D. K. & Ferguson N. (1994). *Partnership Sourcing: An Integrated Supply Chain Approach*. Pitman.

Milberg, W. (2008). Shifting sources and uses of profits: Sustaining US financialization with global value chains. *Economy and Society* 37(3), 420–451.

Miles, R. E., & Snow, C. C. (2007). Organization theory and supply chain management: An evolving research perspective. Journal of Operations Management, 25(2), 459–463.

Mitchell, A. V. & Sikka, P. (2011). The pin-stripe mafia: how accountancy firms destroy societies. Association for Accountancy & Business Affairs.

Monczka R. M. & Morgan, J. (1997). What's wrong with supply chain management. *Purchasing*, 122(1), 69–73.

Morgan, G. (2014). Financialization and the multinational corporation. *Transfer: European Review of Labour and Research*, 20(2), 183–197.

Ofwat (1992). Assessing Capital Values at the Periodic Review: a Consultation Paper on the Framework for Reflecting Reasonable Returns on Capital in Price Limits. Office of Water Services.

Ofwat (2006). Financial Performance and Expenditure of the Water Companies in England and Wales, 2005–06 report. Office of Water Services.

Ofwat (2012a). Variation and Modification of Veolia Water Central Limited's Instrument of Appointment as a Water Undertaker. Office of Water Services.

Ofwat (2012b). The Completed Acquisition of Veolia Water Capital Funds Limited by Rift Acquisitions (Investments) Limited. Office of Water Services.

Ofwat (2015). The Development of the Water Industry in England and Wales. Office of Water Services.

Ofwat (2017). RD 04/10: Regulatory Capital Values 2010–15. Office of Water Services.

Ogden, S. & Glaister, K. W. (1996). The cautious monopolists—Strategies of Britain's privatized water companies. *Long Range Planning*, 29(5), 663–674.

Ogden, S. G. (1997). Accounting for organizational performance: The construction of the customer in the privatized water industry. *Accounting, Organizations and Society*, 22(6), 529–556.

Palan, R., Murphy, R., & Chavagneux, C. (2010). *Tax Havens: How Globalization Really Works*. Cornell University Press.

Palpacuer, F. (2008). Bringing the social context back in: Governance and wealth distribution in global commodity chains. *Economy and Society* 37(3), 393–419.

Paulraj A. (2011). Understanding the relationships between internal resources and capabilities, sustainable supply management and organizational sustainability. *Journal of Supply Chain Management*, 47(1), 19–37.

Ponte, S. & Gibbon, P. (2005). Quality standards, conventions and the governance of global value chains. *Economy and Society*, 34(1), 1–31.

Riles, A. (2011). *Collateral Knowledge: Legal Reasoning in the Global Financial Markets*. University of Chicago Press.

Seabrooke, L. & Wigan, D. (2017). The governance of global wealth chains. *Review of International Political Economy*, 24(1), 1–29.

Seuring, S. & Müller, M. (2008). From a literature review to a conceptual framework for sustainable supply chain management. *Journal of Cleaner Production*, 16(15), 1699–1710.

Shaxson, N. (2012). *Treasure Islands: Tax Havens and the Men Who Stole the World*, Vintage.

Sikka, P. & Willmott, H. (2010). The dark side of transfer pricing: Its role in tax avoidance and wealth retentiveness. *Critical Perspectives on Accounting*, 21(4), 342–356.

Spekman, R., Kamauff Jr, J. W., & Myhr, N. (1998). An empirical investigation into supply chain management. *International Journal of Physical Distribution & Logistics Management*, 28 (8), 630–650.

Stadtler, H. (2015). Supply chain management: An overview. In *Supply Chain Management and Advanced Planning*. Springer, 3–28.

Storey, J., Emberson, C., Godsell, J., & Harrison, A. (2006). Supply chain management: Theory, practice and future challenges. *International Journal of Operations & Production Management*, 26(7), 754–774.

Veolia Environnement SA, (2011). Presentation for Investor Day. https://www.veolia.com/en/veolia-group/finance/analysts-and-investors/investor-day

Willcocks, L., Lacity, M., & Fitzgerald, G. (1995). Information technology outsourcing in Europe and the USA: Assessment issues. *International Journal of Information Management*, 15(5), 333–351.

Willman, P., Coen, D., Currie, D., & Siner, M. (2003). The evolution of regulatory relationships: Regulatory institutions and firm behaviour in privatized industries. *Industrial and Corporate Change*, 12(1), 69–89.

3

Tax Treaties

Martin Hearson

To realize the profits made within "hierarchical" global value chains (GVCs), multinational firms need to construct parallel global wealth chains (GWCs). These chains extract earnings from the operating country in which value chain activity takes place and repatriate them to the country from which the capital investment originated, or move them to an offshore centre where the profits are sheltered. Global wealth chains are indeed "the yin to the yang of value chains" (Seabrooke & Wigan, 2017), but the relationship between the two has changed over time. Tax treaties, the subject of this chapter, were originally a pragmatic legal tool created by states at the request of multinationals to help them expand their GVCs by resolving the cross-border tax impediments to the accompanying GWCs (Hearson, 2021). Successive waves of competitive emulation and innovation turned tax treaties into tax arbitrage tools and, turning the position upside down, the management of GVCs themselves is now used in the construction of multinational firms' GWCs.

Bilateral tax treaties are the links in multinationals' GWCs. A network of around 3,000 such treaties limits the extent to which the cross-border transactions at each stage of the chain can be taxed in the countries between which earnings are flowing. In a GWC, the typical supplier provides a product operating across borders that enables its clients to create and protect pecuniary wealth. In this chapter, such products are tax planning structures derived from real cross-border trade and investment transactions, and clients are companies that invest or conduct business across borders. While it might seem odd to categorize a class of intergovernmental agreements as *assets*, they are indeed used by the suppliers of multinationals' GWCs to create these products. The treaties themselves originate from a transnational policy community (Tsingou, 2014) comprising tax officials from governments, multinational companies, and professional services firms—in GWC parlance, by regulators, suppliers, and clients.

Martin Hearson, *Tax Treaties*. In: *Global Wealth Chains*. Edited by Leonard Seabrooke and Duncan Wigan, Oxford University Press. © Martin Hearson (2022). DOI: 10.1093/oso/9780198832379.003.0003

Historically, tax treaties were highly specific assets that enabled firms to expand their integrated GVCs abroad, removing the disadvantages arising from international double taxation; they, and the products created with them, were also based on a high degree of standardization. They were initially developed by multinational firms—acting as supplier-clients in treaty-based GWCs—and governments acting in concert. Over time, tax treaties came to be used for tax competition, through which they conferred locational and ownership advantages on multinational firms. The next change came as new classes of suppliers came: a tax profession based in advisory firms independent from their multinational clients, and certain jurisdictions that developed a network of tax treaties to attract GWCs. The resulting growth of complex international tax structuring made tax treaties less geographically specific, because access to the benefits they provided was not limited to firms from the two signatories: multinationals from third countries could take advantage of any treaty through "treaty shopping." It also increased the complexity of products made with them. Most recently, the "Big Four" professional services firms have begun to provide a new type of product, highly bespoke tax planning based on corporate restructuring, in which the value chain is restructured around tax structures premised on tax treaties and other such "assets." The tail now wags the dog.

Tax treaties as assets

A tax treaty is an agreement between two countries that clarifies where and how cross-border economic activity will be taxed. It does this by allocating the "rights" to tax particular forms of income to either the country of source (in which income is earned) or the country of residence (in which the taxpayer resides).[1] Consider the stylized example of a British tour operator with a subsidiary that operates safaris in Zambia. In the absence of a tax treaty, both Britain and Zambia would have the right to tax the income earned from the safari tours: Zambia on the grounds that they were earned in Zambia (the source principle), and Britain that they were earned by a British firm (the residence principle). In practice, the core conflict between the two is resolved by the British tax system, which would historically have

---

[1] For example, the term "taxing rights" appears 11 times in a special issue of the *Bulletin for International Taxation*, the house journal of tax treaty specialists, introducing the 2011 update to the United Nations model treaty (UN Model 2011 Special Issue 2012).

offered a credit against UK tax amounting to the tax paid in Zambia, and since 2005 would have exempted the firm's overseas profits from UK tax altogether.[2] With a treaty, however, Zambia's capacity to levy taxes on the safari operations would be constrained. For example, absent the treaty (the case for, say, an Australian-owned tour operator), Zambia would impose a 15 percent withholding tax on dividend payments from the Zambian subsidiary to its parent. The UK–Zambia treaty, however, restricts Zambia's "taxing right" to a rate of 5 percent. Because there is no further tax to pay in the UK, the lower tax cost allows the British-owned tour operator to increase its profit margin, or to undercut its Australian-owned competitor's prices while earning the same post-tax profit.

The classic Gereffi et al. (2005) framework from which Seabrooke and Wigan draw inspiration is concerned with the different modes of GVC governance. It argues that the selection of a particular mode is a function of asset specificity: if the supplier needs to purchase highly specific assets in order to make a product, this will result in a high degree of coordination along the value chain. The same applies to suppliers within GWCs. Tax treaties are bespoke assets insofar as they, and the products made with them, are highly geographically specific, and tailored to their signatory countries' tax systems as well as to the business models of investors from those countries. At the same time, because these assets are all derived from a common model treaty, the degree of standardization within the GWC is high. Tax treaties are not "bought" by the suppliers of tax planning structures, they are provided by governments and exploited by the private sector. But they do entail costs for these suppliers, in the form of lobbying expenditure, participation in negotiations and consultations, and technical input into the development of models and eventual treaties. The insight that acquiring highly specific assets shapes wealth chain governance is therefore pertinent.

To understand the geographical specificity of tax treaties, consider the example given above. The treaty between the United Kingdom and Zambia is only valuable to British residents earning income in Zambia (or, in principle, vice versa) and in principle it provides no benefit to Australian-resident multinationals. As subsequent sections of this chapter illustrate, many countries' pursuit of tax treaties with others is driven by the desire to supply these assets to potential investors, in order to stimulate greater

---

[2] Zambia may have foregone some of its rights by offering the British company a tax incentive (see Stausholm, Chapter 12 in this volume).

investment. Some treaties also provide benefits tailored to particular in-vestors who lobbied for them, although once in force they take the form of a public good that can be accessed by any firm present in one of the two signatory countries.

Geographical specificity is, however, a flexible concept in the world of global wealth chains, which have a unique geography all of their own (see Bryan et al., Chapter 5 in this volume). More complex forms of GWC have grown up specifically to exploit the commercialized sovereignty provided by "treaty havens" such as the Netherlands and Mauritius, which offer an attractive cocktail of advantageous tax treatment, a certain amount of opac-ity, and a network of tax treaties. In the example above, the Australian firm could reduce the withholding tax rate on its dividend payments to 5 percent, the same as the British firm, by using an intermediate holding company in Mauritius or the Netherlands, both of which have treaties re-stricting Zambia's taxing right over dividends to this amount. As Figure 3.1 shows, the tax treaties that restrict taxing rights over dividends most in sub-Saharan countries such as Zambia are not those with outward-investing countries, such as Canada, France, Germany, and the UK, but those with offshore financial centres such as Mauritius, the Netherlands, and the Seychelles.

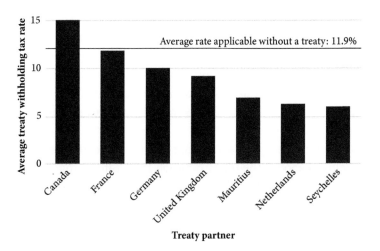

Fig. 3.1 Maximum withholding tax rates on dividends from direct investment permitted by sub-Saharan countries' tax treaties—average for selected treaty partners
Source: The ActionAid Tax Treaties Dataset (Hearson, 2016)

The Netherlands, the Seychelles and Mauritius have acquired assets that enable them to supply a form of "commercialized sovereignty," making it attractive for a wealth chain to pass through them, borrowing a nationality that becomes advantageous because of its tax treaties (Palan, 2002). To conceive of these "treaty havens" as purely "offshore" jurisdictions would, however, be to underestimate the sophistication of tax planning structures and the capacity of GWCs to distort real-world economic incentives. As Seabrooke and Wigan state,

> while conceptualizing the practices and relationships we explore as constitutive of an offshore world has been helpful in emphasizing the bifurcation of sovereignty, it deflects attention to the pervasive and systemic presence of GWCs. The cartographic imaginary of "offshore–onshore" alludes to a spatial demarcation that is not tenable.
>
> (Seabrooke & Wigan, 2014, p. 13)

As the final section of this chapter explains, recent developments in international tax planning involve the merging of multinational firms' "offshore" wealth chains with their "onshore" value chain activity.

Tax treaties as forms of advantage

Typically, global wealth chains that leverage tax treaties are designed to extract the profits generated in operating companies that are part of global supply chains. In the stylized example above, this wealth extraction took place through dividend payments from subsidiary to parent, although it could also take place through various other internal transactions. Because of this, this chapter is concerned with the interaction between the two. That is, the wealth chains that multinational businesses create using tax treaties confer on them certain advantages that in turn lead to the adoption of an "integrated" structure of value chain governance. The nature of these advantages has changed over time, as multinationals have evolved, a process that we can consider using John Dunning's "eclectic" paradigm, in which investment decisions by multinational firms are the product of ownership, location, and internalization advantages (Dunning, 2001). In brief, tax treaties were originally created to help overcome the tax *disadvantages* of multinational integration, whereby multiple states' overlapping claims to taxation placed on firms operating across national borders a greater tax

Table 3.1 Development of the role of tax treaties in value and wealth chain governance

Role of tax treaties	Form of advantage	Driver	Wealth chain governance form
Elimination of double taxation	Removal of disadvantage	Value chain	Hierarchy
Tax competition	Location and ownership	Value and wealth chains	Hierarchy
Tax treaty shopping	Internalization	Wealth chain	Hierarchy–captive
Tax-efficient supply chain management	Internalization	Value and wealth chains	Captive

burden than their national competitors. By the 1970s, however, tax treaties had come to be seen as conferring ownership and location advantages on multinational firms. A British firm operating in Zambia had an *ownership* advantage because the Zambia–UK treaty reduced its tax costs below those faced by its competitors; it also obtained a *location* advantage through the combination of tax incentives and a generous tax treaty, which reduced the tax costs for British firms choosing to operate in Zambia (Hearson, 2018). The next development came as firms began to recognize the *internalization* advantages of tax treaties: the multinational form allowed them to structure internal transactions in such a way as to turn tax treaties into assets from which independent firms would not be able to benefit. In the final stage of the evolution, firms have begun to integrate decisions about the structure of their supply chains and wealth chains through the process of "tax-efficient supply chain management" (see Table 3.1).

Stage 1: Removing disadvantages

The introduction of taxes on business income at the beginning of the twentieth century created a potential problem for individuals and businesses who earned income in more than one country. If each country imposed a tax on income, they might each lay claim to taxing the same income. Specifically, the taxpayer's country of residence (in particular, where a business was headquartered) might expect to tax its worldwide income, while the countries that were the source of its income (where it earned money) might also expect to tax a portion of that income. Without some international agreement, such instances of "double taxation" placed multinational firms at a stark disadvantage to national firms, whose income was all earned in the same country and so could only be taxed once.

Although a handful of treaties dealing with this issue had been negotiated before, it was through the League of Nations that the modern tax treaty network came into being, beginning in the 1920s with a series of reports published for the League of Nations that set out the broad principles on which an international tax regime would develop over the subsequent century. One of the original League of Nations reports articulates the concern expressed by international businesses:

> Double taxation . . . imposes on such taxpayers burdens which, in many cases, seem truly excessive, if not intolerable. It tends to paralyse their activity and to discourage initiative, and thus constitutes a serious obstacle to the development of international relations and world production.
>
> (League of Nations, 1927, p. 8)

The modern-day successor to that report, the OECD model tax treaty, adds that "It is scarcely necessary to stress the importance of removing the obstacles that double taxation presents to the development of economic relations between countries" (OECD, 2014a, p. 7).

What was being developed was a set of technical specifications for the creation of highly standardized tax treaties, which would in turn standardize the tax planning products created with them. From this very early stage, the creation of these assets was characterized by a high degree of coordination between multinational firms and governments, through a transnational policy community centered around the League of Nations and the newly created International Chambers of Commerce, which had taken up the problem of international double taxation at its founding in 1920 (Picciotto, 1992, p. 15). National chambers of commerce lobbied their governments, while the ICC began to develop terminology and concepts that would eventually underpin the League of Nations' own work. According to Graetz & O'Hear (1997, pp. 1070, 1073), the ICC "exercised primary leadership in the movement against international double taxation," and according to one observer they cite, resolutions passed by the ICC were "used as the firm basis on which draft conventions have been built or actual treaties adopted." The ICC's influence came about in part because of the overlapping memberships of the ICC's Double Taxation Committee (representing businesses), and the League's Technical Expert Committee (representing governments). For example, Thomas Adams, the

US-appointed member of the League committee, chaired a committee for the US Chambers of Commerce as well as participating in the ICC's work; his successor, Mitchell Carroll, was a lawyer advising multinational firms on their tax affairs, as well as working on behalf of the US at the League (Carroll, 1978).

The consolidation of a transnational policy community led to a sense of optimism that national interests would melt away. Sol Picciotto cites the chairman of the ICC's committee on double taxation, in a report to the ICC Congress in 1923, as follows:

> If only the principle that the same income should only be taxed once is recog-
> nised, the difficulty is solved, or very nearly so. It only remains then to decide
> what constitutes the right of one country to tax the income of a taxpayer in pref-
> erence to any other country. It does not seem probable that there would be any
> serious difference on the matter.
>
> (Picciotto, 1992, pp. 15–16)

One of the participants in the early League of Nations work, Edwin Selig-man, observed that, while at first the technical experts' "concern was primarily to enter into some arrangement which would be politically agreeable to their respective countries,"

> when they learned to know each other more intimately; and especially in pro-
> portion as they were subjected to the indefinable but friendly atmosphere of
> the League of Nations, their whole attitude changed. Suspicion was converted
> into confidence; doubt was resolved by the feeling of certainty of accomplish-
> ment; and aloofness gave way to warm personal friendship which contributed
> materially to smoothing out the difficulties.
>
> (Seligman, 1928, pp. 143–144)

There were, in fact, dramatic differences between countries, principally over the relative emphasis on "source" and "residence" taxation (Graetz & O'Hear, 1997; Jogarajan, 2018). The compromise hammered out within the policy community at the ICC and the League sets the broad parameters of an agreement, incorporating concepts such as the idea that countries of source cannot tax the profits of a branch if it does not constitute a "permanent establishment," that is, if its activity does not reach a certain threshold. The precise details, such as the forms of business and length of time that constitute a permanent establishment, were left to a network of now over 3,000 bilateral agreements. The League's expert committee recognized that a multilateral agreement on all these points would provide a more comprehensive solution to the problem, but also that such an agreement would be very challenging to reach (Picciotto, 1992). Even the limited consensus provided by the OECD model bilateral agreement took decades to arrive at, and only represents a de facto agreement, without explicit endorsement from states beyond the relatively homogeneous OECD membership.

A tax treaty regime thus came into being that allowed firms to internationalize—forming integrated global value chains—without facing a fiscal disadvantage relative to national firms. They could construct wealth chains that allowed them to extract profits from operating countries without facing onerous double taxation, but only if home and host country had a tax treaty in place. The tax planning products on which the GWCs were based were bespoke, negotiated bilaterally, but they were highly standardized, thanks to the work of the international policy community's technical experts. Naturally, having secured the creation of this piecemeal international regime, the community turned its attention to creating the assets needed to protect individual wealth chains from incurring double taxation. By the 1970s, however, firms and governments came to realize that a tax treaty could provide more than just relief from the disadvantages of double taxation: it could provide positive benefits too.

Stage 2: Treaties and tax competition

The 1970s saw a step change in the number of tax treaties concluded between states, as the network expanded beyond its core OECD constituents. By this point, however, most major capital-exporting nations had adopted unilateral measures to eliminate double taxation, so a treaty was often largely unnecessary for this, its formal, stated purpose (a point made by Dagan, 2000). Instead, governments and investors came to understand that tax treaties conferred geographically specific advantages, available only to multinationals investing between the two signatories (Hearson, 2018). They provided the capital-importing country with a location advantage, which made operating through a subsidiary there more cost-effective, and they provided the capital exporter with an ownership advantage, which lowered costs in the developing country market relative to its competitors. At this stage, tax planning structures within multinational firms were opportunistic and relatively simple, because complex "treaty shopping" structures had yet to become widespread. Tax treaties were primarily assets to be leveraged within the GWCs that grew up naturally around the expanding GVCs of multinational firms.

One of the main drivers of asset creation was the large number of recently independent developing countries keen to attract foreign direct investment into industries necessary for their import substitution industrialization (ISI) policies (see e.g. Seidman, 1974). They offered generous tax incentives to these investors, but found them to be of limited use because most investors were headquartered in countries that prevented double taxation on their multinationals by giving them a credit against their home tax. A lower tax bill abroad because of a tax incentive meant a lower credit, and hence a higher tax bill at home, rather than lower tax costs overall.

Consider Uganda, whose Minister for Finance, Planning and Economic Development announced in 1993 that the country would "embark on negotiating double taxation agreements with identified major trading partners" (Mr. J. Mayanja Nkangi, quoted in "Uganda parliamentary debate," 1993). Uganda was seeking "tax-sparing" clauses, provisions through which multinationals' home states agreed to treat their foreign income as if it had been fully taxed, even if that tax had been reduced or eliminated through a tax incentive. As Nkangi explained, the purpose of the treaties was to "ensure that the effectiveness of current incentives is not eroded by the absence of complementary tax credits" because "in the absence of any complementary tax holidays with the home countries of foreign investors, the revenue foregone by reducing a company's tax liability in Uganda represents a revenue gain by the Ministry of Finance in the home country" with no benefit to the company concerned. Consequently, Uganda's subsequent treaties with the UK, South Africa, Mauritius, and Italy all included tax-sparing provisions.

Twenty years earlier, Zambia had also embarked on a major tax treaty negotiating programme with the aim of securing tax-sparing credits. All the 11 treaties it signed with OECD member countries during the 1970s and 1980s provided explicitly for them, or else contained provisions that had the same effect. A formal letter sent by Zambia to the UK in 1969, requesting that negotiations be opened, began with the request that "Zambia would, in particular, wish to discuss matters arising from the operation of the Zambian Pioneer Industries (Relief from Income Tax) Act" (quoted in Hearson, 2017, p. 371).

For developing countries, then, tax treaties offered a kind of location advantage. They allowed the government to reduce the tax costs of foreign investors in sectors where it was keen to attract foreign capital and expertise through investment. Developing countries were already engaged in a "race to the bottom" to attract foreign multinational investors (Swank, 2016), and tax treaties became a part of that dynamic (Baistrocchi, 2008; Barthel & Neumayer, 2012).

Because the advantages conferred by each tax treaty were selective, applicable only to investors originating from a particular country, their impact was also seen through the lens of ownership advantages: to obtain those benefits, one had to be a multinational company headquartered in the treaty partner. This was the main reason why private and public sector members of the transnational policy community in Britain, for example, pursued tax treaties so avidly. Businesses lobbied their government for tax treaties with certain key developing countries such as Brazil and India, expressing concern at "forfeited opportunities for investment" in countries with which the competitor firms' home states had treaties (Hearson, 2017). The UK became an enthusiastic supporter of tax-sparing clauses, as illustrated in a speaking note drafted for a meeting of Commonwealth finance ministers in August 1973: "We have taken the opportunity to offer matching credit for pioneer reliefs to all the developing countries with whom we have double taxation agreements. We also offer matching credit to any developing countries with which we enter into negotiations for the first time" (quoted in Hearson, 2017).

This continued until 1998, when the OECD published "Tax Sparing: A Reconsideration," which highlighted the potential negative impacts of tax-sparing arrangements in tax treaties, in particular that they could potentially be abused, and that they created an incentive to repatriate profits quickly, rather than reinvest them in the developing country (OECD, 1998).

Nonetheless, tax treaties continue to confer several other selective advantages on investors, especially as home states move increasingly towards exempting foreign source profits from tax altogether (PwC, 2013). They reduce the withholding taxes that investors face on cross-border transactions, such as dividend and royalty payments, between the signatory states, which allows the repatriation of wealth more cost-effectively. They shield the investor from some taxes, such as those on capital gains, altogether. They provide the investor with a guarantee that they will not be taxed more aggressively than permitted within OECD standards, enforced through increasingly stringent dispute-resolution measures, including binding arbitration clauses (Christians, 2011). Each of these benefits increases the risk-adjusted return on investment that a multinational firm can expect to make, but is only available to firms originating in the treaty partner. Hence, it constitutes an ownership advantage.

Since the 1970s, then, tax treaties have become assets that can be exploited to derive unique forms of selective tax incentive, available only to multinational firms investing between the two signatory countries. They allowed firms to repatriate their profits at a lower tax cost—indeed, they incentivized the repatriation of profits over reinvestment in the developing country. Tax treaties therefore facilitated the creation of GWCs aligned closely with GVCs, enabling the expansion of the latter. As forms of corporate organization became more complex, however, and as tax treaty networks grew, these selected advantages have been eclipsed by the use of tax treaties to create new wealth chains as ends in themselves: tax avoidance.

Stage 3: Tax treaty shopping

A multinational corporate structure creates many opportunities for tax avoidance, including moving taxable income from a country where it will be taxed to one where it will not, and creating the legal fiction of nationality to qualify for special treatment (Sharman, 2010). Such tax planning structures were first adopted by pharmaceutical companies during the 1950s, following the increase in value of their intellectual property, an intangible asset that they could situate in a tax haven in order to shift profits there (Durst, 2016; see also Bryan et al., Chapter 5 in this volume). The global proliferation and, perhaps, normalization of such base-erosion and profit-shifting (BEPS) activities has been a more recent phenomenon, and has occurred in tandem with the formation of a dedicated tax profession within law and accountancy firms that created a new cohort of suppliers independent of multinational clients (Frecknall-Hughes & McKerchar, 2013). It is now law firms such as Baker McKenzie, and accountancy firms such as Ernst & Young, who invest resources in influencing the development of tax treaty networks to provide assets they can exploit, as much if not more than their clients.

The explosion in BEPS is due in no small part to the consequent growth in the network of tax treaties, which are often the key enabling characteristic that holds together tax-avoidance structures (Hearson & Brooks,

2010; Lewis, 2013; OECD, 2013). Tax treaties prevent the country in which real economic activity takes place from taxing it, by binding that country into using definitions that can be exploited, imposing limits on tax rates or outright prohibitions on certain forms of taxation, and crucially by occupying a higher legal status than domestic law, preventing countries from simply changing their tax laws to catch the investor. These are necessary characteristics of a tool designed to prevent double taxation, but they also provide ample room for multinational firms to use them in ways that were not intended—tax "treaty shopping."

During the tax competition phase, treaties had been created by government actors, as members of a transnational policy elite, in response to demand from multinational firms that already had part of their GVC within their borders, or planned to do so. The tax treaty shopping phase, however, entails the provision of tax treaties by other jurisdictions as facets of "commercialized sovereignty" to attract intermediate stages of GWCs without any expectation that the GVC would move as well. "Treaty-rich" jurisdictions such as the Netherlands, Switzerland, and, later, Mauritius have come to be the jurisdictions of choice for GWCs that rely on the availability of a tax treaty network.

For example, Uganda and the Netherlands are currently in dispute over $85 million of capital gains tax from the sale of Celtel Uganda Ltd from Kuwait-based Zain Telecom, and India-based Bahti Airtel (Gupta, 2016; Hearson & Kangave, 2016). The dispute, which follows a court ruling in the Uganda Revenue Authority's (URA's) favour on a procedural point, involves the Netherlands because the sale took place via a network of holding companies in the Netherlands. The URA maintains that Ugandan law permits it to tax the sale of Celtel Uganda even though what changed hands was technically a Dutch holding company. Zain maintains that the Uganda–Netherlands tax treaty allocates the right to tax this transaction to the Netherlands, with no anti-abuse provision for Uganda to fall back on.

Another example is the case of Zambia Sugar, a Zambian subsidiary of Associated British Foods (ABF). In this case, the Zambian firm took a loan from a UK-based bank via an Irish intermediary, also part of ABF, to take advantage of the zero rate of withholding taxes on interest payments specified by the Zambia–Ireland treaty, instead of the 10 percent prescribed by the Zambia–UK tax treaty (Lewis, 2013). Even more perverse is the case of the India–Mauritius tax treaty, which had the effect of making Mauritius the main source of foreign investment into India, on paper at least, because Indian domestic investors took advantage of the treaty provision preventing India from taxing capital gains made by Mauritian investors in

India, even if those Mauritian investors were merely tax-avoidance vehicles established by Indian investors (Norwegian Government Commission on Capital Flight from Poor Countries, 2009). Both these treaties have now been amended to prevent such avoidance, partly as a result of the attention shone on these examples, but there are many more. The contentious tax structures of Google, Apple, Amazon, and Starbucks, for example, all rely in part on tax treaties between the countries involved. There is now a global effort to reduce the opportunities for treaty shopping led by the OECD (2014b), though it is unlikely to fully succeed.

Each of the examples above is a global wealth chain created to transport income of one form or another from the country in which it is earned, through one or more intermediary jurisdictions, to its ultimate beneficiary, without paying the tax that governments intended to be paid on that income. In an increasingly popular tax terminology, the profits created by such internalization advantages constitute "stateless income," which the multinational can choose to locate in the most tax-efficient jurisdiction. These tax planning strategies use tax treaties, assets that in this case are created by the base jurisdiction to attract the GWC. Just as in the example of Apple discussed by Seabrooke and Wigan (2017), much of the expertise used to supply this tax structure is internal to the firm, which is both client and supplier. This is because the highly standardized nature of tax treaties reduces the need for a highly specialized supplier, while the bespoke nature of the firm's needs increases the incentive to internalize. Where geographically specific knowledge is needed, such as if the firm is entering a new market or structuring its ownership across a region, it is likely to need a supplier with knowledge of sensitive aspects of its corporate structure and tax position, and this will be a captive wealth chain in which the tax advice is supplied by one of a small number of global professional services or law firms.

Stage 4: Tax-efficient supply chain management

The tax planning described above entails the establishment of a "base" company in a low-tax jurisdiction to which mobile profits can be attributed for tax purposes. The base company generally exists on paper only, and plays little role in the real-world value chain. The "state of the art" in tax planning, especially in the aftermath of OECD-led efforts to minimize the potential for base erosion and profit-shifting (BEPS), instead involves the creation of "hub" or "principal" companies in low-tax jurisdictions (Durst, 2016). These companies take on real high-value business functions and risks, including typically the management of the supply chain and the procurement of goods and services. In contrast to "base" company tax avoidance, which has little connection to the firm's tangible activities, "hub" company structures, such as promoted by "tax-efficient supply chain management" (TESCM), are the leveraging of the value chain in order to create a wealth chain. As an article in a tax industry magazine explains, "Because production involves company employees performing labour-intensive activities, supply chain management, through buying agents, contains the economic substance necessary to support tax planning in a post-BEPS era" (Patton & Burakoff, 2015).

Because it entails a substantial restructuring of the way value and wealth chains work within a firm, as well as very sophisticated tax planning involving dozens of countries, "suppliers" of TESCM must possess professional expertise across a wide geographical area and a range of competences. This needs highly bespoke advice, and is difficult to implement in-house, so it falls to only the largest professional services firms to deliver it. In 2010, the professional services firm PwC pitched a TESCM project to the Dutch beer company Heineken, in a 125-page PowerPoint document that was made available online (PwC, 2010). The pitch quoted a cost in the region of £25 million. In an annexed list of similar projects, PwC claimed a similar restructuring of a "UK parented global food group" had generated "1% to 2% effective tax rate (ETR) savings" (PwC, 2010, p. 71).

The Heineken document explains that the goal is simultaneously to improve the efficiency of the group's procurement system and to benefit from "tax arbitrage." It discusses TESCM structures in evolutionary terms. In the first, "centre-led," stage, a hub company in a low-tax jurisdiction with a "core team" of staff sets procurement strategy and policy, and establishes framework agreements with suppliers, for which it charges a fee to the group's operating companies. The tax advantage comes from these fees, which shift profits from operating countries to the hub, but which may be challenged by tax authorities. The second stage of the evolution is the creation of a principal company in the low-tax jurisdiction, which can obtain greater tax advantages and reduce the risk of tax authority challenges because it assumes real ownership of the products, and hence real responsibilities and risks: "Core team physically co-located. In addition to centre led responsibilities, centre takes title of goods and services and sells onto OpCo [operating company]—so has responsibility for contracting, inventory management, price, demand, supply, commodity price and FX [foreign exchange] risks" (PwC, 2010, p. 10).

Promotional materials from other companies online confirm the aims of TESCM. According to an article placed by KPMG in *Financial Director* magazine,

> The fundamental premise of TESCM is that including tax arbitrage in supply chain structures by locating key functions, assets and risks in a low-tax environment brings more benefits than conventional operational savings alone. These benefits, however, are not derived from setting up a shell company in a low-tax country like Switzerland, but by relocating a large part of the business.[3]

A 2008 presentation by a KPMG staff member to an International Fiscal Association conference explains that, while for operating companies in jurisdictions with normal rates of tax the "profit level can be controlled" so that they "receive a stable and relatively low profit level," the hub entity in a low-tax jurisdiction would be entitled to the "residual (entrepreneurial)" profits, the "stateless income" mentioned earlier.[4]

As with tax treaty shopping, the selection of a low-tax jurisdiction for the hub company entails a tax treaty network that will ensure the withholding taxes on any fees paid to the hub are kept low, and that the operating company's tax authorities are obliged to follow international tax standards. This is therefore a similar type of GWC to the treaty shopping type, but it entails redesigning the way the value chain works.

Conclusion

Narratives about the growth of international tax avoidance often focus on how an international tax regime based on bilateral tax treaties, designed to alleviate double taxation, has design features that in themselves leave it vulnerable to "double non-taxation" (OECD 2013; Rixen 2008). A GWC approach to this problem allows us to see a more agent-centered perspective, in which changes in the pattern of asset provision, and in the governance structure of GWCs, are as much a part of the story as the path dependency in international tax institutions. As Ronen Palan (1998) has suggested, what begins as a pragmatic attempt by states to resolve a conflict between national law and international capital mobility (here,

---

[3] See http://www.the-financedirector.com/features/featurefde-kpmg-tax-efficient-supply-chain/.
[4] Presentation on file with the author.

the double-taxation problem) can become a full-fledged part of the off-shore world, as the initial step is elaborated through legal innovations, which in turn fuel competitive emulation between states (Christensen & Hearson, 2019).

Tax treaties are highly standardized assets lending themselves to the production of standardized wealth chains, because they all derive from the OECD model tax treaty. But they are also highly bespoke in the sense that they are highly geographically specific. It is this specificity that fuelled a process of competitive emulation, which led the transition from GWCs based on double taxation avoidance to those based on tax competition. The choice by certain jurisdictions to become "treaty rich" as part of a strategy of commercialized sovereignty paved the way for the explosion in "treaty shopping." The appearance of a tax profession in advisory firms, in part a product of the growth in demand for more complex international tax planning, created a group of suppliers independent of clients, shifting away from the hierarchical form that had dominated tax treaty GWCs. That shift finds its apotheosis in the complex corporate restructuring for tax optimization that the Big Four professional services firms now provide to clients under the banner of "tax-efficient supply chain management." This is a captive GWC controlled by the transnational tax policy community in its purest expression—the Big Four. In the earlier stages of tax treaty-exploiting GWC development, the GWC either served the interests of the underlying GVC, or else was independent of it. In this latest evolution, however, the value chain has begun to serve the interests of the wealth chain, not the other way round.

References

Baistrocchi, E. (2008). The use and interpretation of tax treaties in the emerging world: theory and implications. *British Tax Review*, *28*(4), 352.

Barthel, F. & Neumayer, E. (2012). Competing for scarce foreign capital: Spatial dependence in the diffusion of double taxation treaties. *International Studies Quarterly*, 56(4), 645–660.

Carroll, M. B. (1978). *Global Perspectives of an International Tax Lawyer*. Exposition Press.

Christensen, R. C. & Hearson, M. (2019). The new politics of global tax governance: Taking stock a decade after the financial crisis. *Review of International Political Economy*, 26(5), 1068–1088.

Christians, A. (2011). How nations share. *Indiana Law Journal*, 87(4), 1407–1453.

Dagan, T. (2000). The tax treaties myth. *New York University Journal of International Law and Politics*, 32, 939–996.

Dunning, J. H. (2001). The eclectic (OLI) paradigm of international production: Past, present and future. *International Journal of the Economics of Business*, 8(2), 173–190.

Durst, M. C. (2016). Self-help and altruism: Protecting developing countries' tax revenues. In, T. Pogge & K. Mehta (eds.), *Global Tax Fairness*. Oxford University Press, 316–338.

Frecknall-Hughes, J. & McKerchar, M. (2013). Historical perspectives on the emergence of the tax profession: Australia and the UK. *Australian Tax Forum*, 28(2), 276–288.

Gereffi, G., Humphrey, J., & Sturgeon, T. (2005). The governance of global value chains. *Review of International Political Economy*, 12(1), 78–104.

Graetz, M. J. & O'Hear, M. M. (1997). The "original intent" of US international taxation. *Duke Law Journal*, 46(5), 1020–1109.

Gupta, A. (2016). Channeling Vodafone in Africa, *Tax Notes International*, 630–633, May 16.

Hearson, M. (2016). Measuring tax treaty negotiation outcomes: the ActionAid Tax Treaties Dataset. ICTD Working Paper No. 47. Institute of Development Studies.

Hearson, M. (2017). The UK's tax treaties with developing countries during the 1970s. In, P. Harris & D. Cogan (eds.), *Studies in the History of Tax Law* (volume 8). Hart Publishing, 363–382.

Hearson, M. (2018). Transnational expertise and the expansion of the international tax regime: Imposing "acceptable" standards. *Review of International Political Economy* 25(5), 647–671.

Hearson, M. (2021). *Imposing Standards: The North-South Dimension to Global Tax Politics*. Cornell University Press.

Hearson, M. & Brooks, R. (2010). *Calling Time: Why SABMiller Should Stop Dodging Taxes in Africa*. ActionAid UK.

Hearson, M. & Kangave, J. (2016). *A Review of Uganda's Tax Treaties and Recommendations for Action*. International Centre for Tax and Development Working Paper No. 50. Institute of Development Studies.

Jogarajan, S. (2018). *Double Taxation and the League of Nations*. Cambridge University Press.

League of Nations (1927). *Double Taxation and Tax Evasion*. Committee of Technical Experts on Double Taxation and Tax Evasion. Geneva.

Lewis, M. (2013). *Sweet Nothings: The Human Cost of a British Sugar Giant Avoiding Taxes in Southern Africa*. ActionAid UK.

Norwegian Government Commission on Capital Flight from Poor Countries (2009). *Tax Havens and Development: Status, Analyses and Measures*. Oslo.

OECD (1998) *Tax Sparing: A Reconsideration*. Organisation for Economic Co-operation and Development.

OECD (2013). *Addressing Base Erosion and Profit Shifting*. OECD Publishing.

OECD (2014a). *Model Tax Convention on Income and on Capital*. OECD Publishing.

OECD (2014b). *Preventing the Granting of Treaty Benefits in Inappropriate Circumstances*. OECD Publishing.

Palan, R. (1998). Trying to have your cake and eating it: How and why the state system has created offshore. *International Studies Quarterly* 42(4), 625–643.

Palan, R. (2002). Tax havens and the commercialization of state sovereignty. *International Organization*, 56(1), 151–176.

Patton, M. & Burakoff, O. (2015). Supply chain planning in the post-BEPS era. *International Tax Review*, March 26.

Picciotto, S. (1992). *International Business Taxation: A Study in the Internationalization of Business Regulation*. Weidenfeld & Nicolson.

PwC (2010). *Heineken GPCo*. Document on file with the author.

PwC (2013). *Evolution of Territorial Tax Systems in the OECD*. Prepared for the Technology CEO Council. Washington, DC.

Rixen, T. (2008). *The Political Economy of International Tax Governance*. Palgrave Macmillan.

Seabrooke, L. & Wigan, D. (2014). *The Governance of Global Wealth Chains*. NUPI Working Paper 839. Norwegian Institute of International Affairs.

Seabrooke, L. & Wigan, D. (2017). The governance of global wealth chains. *Review of International Political Economy*, 24(1), 1–29.

Seidman, A. (1974). The Distorted Growth of Import-Substitution Industry: The Zambian Case. *The Journal of Modern African Studies*, 12(4), 601–631.

Seligman, E. R. (1928). *Double Taxation and International Fiscal Cooperation: Being a Series of Lectures Delivered at the Académie de Droit International de la Haye*. Macmillan.

Sharman, J. (2010). Offshore and the new international political economy. *Review of International Political Economy*, 17(1), 1–19.

Swank, D. (2016). The new political economy of taxation in the developing world. *Review of International Political Economy*, 23(2), 185–207.

Tsingou, E. (2014). Club governance and the making of global financial rules. *Review of International Political Economy*, 22(2), 225–256.

Uganda parliamentary debate (1993). Mayanja Nkangi, Speech to the National Resistance Council of Uganda, reported in Hansard, June 25, 1993.

4

Advance Pricing Agreements

Matti Ylönen

Introduction

Once familiar only to a handful of tax professionals, advance tax rulings (ATRs) and advance pricing agreements (APAs) entered the limelight of international tax policy discussions in the mid 2010s. In late 2014, a former employee of the Big Four company PwC, Antoine Deltour, leaked 28,000 pages of APA documents to the International Consortium of Investigative Journalists. A major international scandal ensued. The LuxLeaks scandal centered on Luxembourg, but it is not the only country offering tax-driven pricing agreements. For decades, multinational enterprises (MNEs) have sought tax benefits by acquiring APAs from the Netherlands, Belgium, and other countries. The few studies on this topic have mostly been published within legal sciences, and this chapter expands the understanding on the role of ATRs and APAs in the contemporary political economy.

ATRs are agreements between tax authorities and the taxpayer determining the application of the tax law regarding transactions, investments, or corporate structures. ATRs are useful for example in situations in which the applicable tax law is subject to interpretation, and can be applied for a single transaction or a series of transactions (Markham, 2012, p. 78). While there is no consensus on the exact definition, the European Commission has defined an ATR as "any communication or any other instrument or action with similar effects, by or on behalf of the Member State regarding the interpretation or application of tax laws" (quoted in European Parliament, 2015, p. 7). The Organisation for Economic Co-operation and Development (OECD) (2015, p. 47) defines rulings as "any advice, information, or undertaking provided by a tax authority to a specific taxpayer or group of taxpayers concerning their tax situation and on which they are entitled to rely." ATRs are typically used for determining corporate income taxes,

Matti Ylönen, *Advance Pricing Agreements*. In: *Global Wealth Chains*. Edited by Leonard Seabrooke and Duncan Wigan, Oxford University Press. © Matti Ylönen (2022). DOI: 10.1093/oso/9780198832379.003.0004 but they can also be requested for various other taxes, depending on the jurisdiction.

In the 1980s and 1990s, many countries expanded their rulings systems to include advance rulings on the prices used in intra-firm trade, commonly referred to as advance pricing agreements (APAs). There is no single established definition of an APA. However, the OECD's influential 1995 Transfer Pricing Guidelines defined an APA as "an arrangement that determines, in advance of controlled transactions, an appropriate set of criteria . . . for the determination of the transfer pricing for those transactions over a fixed period of time" (OECD, 1995, p. 54). In addition, the OECD's (2010, p. 336) transfer pricing guidelines have differentiated APAs from ATRs, stating that APAs differ from the classic ruling procedure because they require "the detailed review and to the extent appropriate, verification of the factual assumptions on which the determination of legal consequences is based, before any such determinations can be made." Furthermore, the OECD notes, "the APA provides for a continual monitoring of whether the factual assumptions remain valid throughout the course of the APA period" (ibid.). From a legal standpoint, APAs are exceptional cases of ATRs. Some ATRs deal with intra-company transfer prices, and some APAs include elements commonly associated with ATRs. The emergence of APAs added an important international dimension to the advance rulings, as aggressive intra-firm pricing in one state can have major impacts on the tax revenues of other states (see Christensen, Chapter 11 in this volume).

This chapter analyzes the role of APAs in global wealth chains (GWCs). APAs play a central and, from a social scientific viewpoint, thus far neglected role in confounding expectations for "market-based" prices in intra-firm GWCs. The growing importance of APAs also reflects the failure of international tax governance to create well-functioning models for international business taxation. I draw three kinds of conclusions from the empirical evidence. The first and most obvious consequence of the increasing importance of APAs is that they concentrate disproportionate amounts of the intra-firm financial flows in the few jurisdictions that maintain aggressive APA regimes. This alone necessitates analyzing intra-firm GWCs as distinct from traditional value chains or production networks. Second, APAs transform the relationship between states, large enterprises, and private tax advisory companies in ways that extend the common frameworks of "private governance"; hence, aggressive APA regimes represent a significant extension of the commercialization of sovereignty. Third,

APAs are the latest step in a decades-long development in which corporations have attempted to restrict the application of market mechanisms in intra-firm trade.

The article proceeds as follows. In the second section, the chapter provides a history of ATRs and APAs. The third section focuses on the role of APAs in global wealth chains. In the fourth, penultimate section, I discuss the implications of APAs for analyses of power in the global economy. The final section provides policy recommendations and directions for future research.

The emergence and uses of APAs and ATRs

The decades following the Second World War have witnessed phenomenal growth in intra-firm trade. While corporate secrecy makes it difficult to accurately estimate the exact share of intra-firm transactions in world trade, international organizations and researchers have made various estimates. Depending on the set of countries and sectors, these studies show that as much as 30–60 percent of international trade takes place within large multinational enterprises (UNCTAD, 1996; OECD, 2002; UNCTAD, 2004; Lanz & Miroudot, 2011). Yet the international rules that dictate the determination and distribution of tax revenues from this trade are based on flawed models developed a century ago. Since the 1960s, the OECD's Transfer Pricing Guidelines have provided the main source of rules for determining prices used in intra-firm transactions. These guidelines rely on the arm's-length principle (ALP), developed prior to the First World War by the International Chamber of Commerce and institutionalized by the League of Nations in the 1930s (Avi-Yonah, 1995; OECD, 2005; Eden, 2016). Debates on partially abandoning the ALP have gained prominence only very recently in discussions associated with the OECD (Ylönen & Finér, 2021).

According to the ALP, entities belonging to the same corporate structure should trade as if they were at "arm's length," implying that firms should use market-based prices in intra-firm trade. However, determining correct market-based prices is either extremely difficult or downright impossible (Avi-Yonah, 1995; Rixen, 2008; Rixen, 2010; May, 2015; Bryan et al., 2017). In consequence, authorities began to abandon the ideal of market-based prices as early as the 1960s by allowing companies to use an increasing number of formulary or "other" methods for determining intra-firm prices (Avi-Yonah, 1995; Durst & Culbertson, 2003). The current OECD transfer pricing guidelines allow for the use of several different pricing methods including cost-plus, comparable uncontrolled price, and resale price methods (OECD, 2012). The complexity of international tax regulation has provided MNEs with ample opportunities to exploit the system. There are valid reasons to question whether much of this trade should even be analyzed using market-based concepts (Ylönen & Teivainen, 2018). As argued below, in contrast to established definitions of markets (Lazonick, 1991; Aspers, 2011), intra-firm trade does not take place between unrelated parties and at prices that fluctuate according to the forces of supply and demand. Using only market-based concepts to analyze intra-firm trade fails to account for the key mechanisms driving it.

The ALP is closely connected with another key feature of international tax regulation: the separate entity principle (Picciotto, 1992). According to this principle, companies belonging to the same corporate group are treated as separate entities for tax purposes (Biondi et al., 2007; Biondi, 2013). This poorly reflects reality, where large, centrally managed enterprises plan their corporate structure and transactions as a single enterprise. This discrepancy provides MNEs with a wide range of tools for planning in which countries they want to allocate how much profit (Finér & Ylönen, 2017). These decisions are typically at least partly tax-driven. The inadequacies of the ALP and the separate entity principle lie behind many of the difficulties that states face in taxing multinational corporations (see e.g. Robé, 2011; Ting, 2014).

APAs can be an attractive tool both for MNEs and states (albeit for different reasons) because they reduce or eliminate the mutual uncertainty that surrounds the determination of intra-firm prices, replacing it with substantial scope for negotiation. Limits on the scope of negotiation vary from one jurisdiction to another. The International Fiscal Association (IFA) notes this by reporting that "an attempt to establish basic statistics failed because of the wide diversity. Each country is specific, and within many countries the rules differ according to the nature of the question raised, the tax, and/or the region" (International Fiscal Association, 1999, p. 21).

National ATRs have a long history. Several countries issued letter-ruling systems after the Second World War, and Sweden issued its first ATRs as early as 1911 (Romano, 2002, pp. 16–17). Arguably the most famous practice was developed by the Netherlands, where the Ministry of Finance aimed to soothe investor fears amidst the dramatic uncertainty of the post-war years (Romano, 2002, p. 23). The new ruling system addressed a wide number of issues, including transfer pricing (ibid., p. 28). Since then, the Dutch ruling system has evolved through administrative act and legal change. In the 1970s, harmonization efforts led to the centralization of rulings activities in the Tax Office for Large Enterprises in Rotterdam. This put an end to a widespread practice in which companies sought rulings from several tax offices in order to reach the most advantageous conclusion; a form of rulings shopping (Romano, 2002, pp. 26, 35; see also Hearson, Chapter 3 in this volume, on "treaty shopping").

Many states followed the Dutch example, as the post-Second World War years witnessed a steady growth in international trade and investment flows, resulting in an increasing number of disputes over the taxation of corporate profits. From early on, many tax professionals held high hopes that the introduction of ATRs would remedy these problems (Romano, 2002, pp. 16–17). In the United States, the letter-ruling system began to evolve in the 1950s, and requests for rulings exploded in the 1970s and the 1980s. In 1987, the Internal Revenue Service (IRS) was granted the right to charge user fees for its services. In its 1996 revenue procedure, the IRS introduced an APA process which was "designed to be a flexible problem-solving process, based on cooperative and principled negotiations between taxpayers and the [IRS]" (Rev. Proc. 96–53, quoted in Hickman, 1998, p. 177).

Typically, APAs run from two to five years and can span hundreds of pages (European Commission 2015a, pp. 7–8). The legal status, level of publicity, and other details of APAs and ATRs differ from country to country. ATRs should be considered one-directional statements from tax authorities (Markham, 2012, p. 135). In contrast, APAs are generally regarded as agreements, especially in countries with aggressive APA regimes. However, both APAs and ATRs aim to bring certainty to transactions the legal admissibility of which the tax authorities might otherwise challenge. Taxpayers seeking an APA approach tax authorities before engaging in a transaction and provide detailed information to an authority regarding activities, plans, competitors, and so on. Following discussions and negotiations, the parties may reach agreement on a transfer pricing methodology and enter into an advance pricing agreement (International Fiscal Association, 1999, p. 48). The agreement can cover all of a corporation's operations, but is more commonly focused on a particular market or product niche (Hickman, 1998, p. 178).

More recent years witnessed a significant increase in the use of bilateral and multilateral APAs. While the world's first genuine bilateral APA was granted in the early 1990s, some important developments took place before that. In the 1980s, General Motors (GM) sought written agreements from several European countries, requesting they respect the company's pricing model. Reportedly, 16 out of 17 countries that GM approached entered into unilateral agreements with the company (Eliot, 1991 quoted in Ring, 2000, p. 163). However, this was an ad hoc event. The formalization of bilateral APAs began in 1986, when United States tax officials organized a meeting to consider an advance resolution process for transfer pricing issues as a means of reducing controversies. This was motivated by a series of failed transfer pricing cases against taxpayers (Ring, 2000, p. 156). Companies and industry groups also lobbied intensely for the establishment of bilateral APAs (Romano, 2002, p. 24; Markham, 2012, p. 2).

Together, the IRS and the Australian Tax Office developed the idea of a bilateral rulings approach (Romano, 2002, p. 24). Eventually, the United States announced a draft IRS Revenue Procedure for Advance Determination Rulings in the early 1990s, opening the possibility of negotiating multilateral agreements. Consequently, in 1991, Apple Computer Australia Pty. Ltd. announced that a historic transfer pricing agreement had been reached between Apple, the Australian Taxation Office, and the United States IRS (Ring, 2000, p. 159; Markham, 2012, p. xvii; Romano, 2002, p. 24). This agreement constituted the world's first bilateral APA. In the years since, both unilateral and bilateral APA regimes have evolved significantly and many countries have implemented similar programs. Today, there is a wide variety of APAs from unilateral to bilateral and even multilateral agreements, though the latter are not common (Borkowski, 2000, pp. 3–5).

Recently, APAs have become a widely utilized practice for resolving actual or potential transfer pricing disputes (Markham, 2012, p. xvii). Already at the turn of the millennium, 75 percent of 187 APA requests in the United States were for a bilateral or multilateral APA (Ring, 2000, p. 193). However, the APA regimes of most European countries still rely predominantly on unilateral APAs. In 2019, bilateral and multilateral APAs accounted for less than 18 percent of all the APAs in force in EU countries in 2019 (calculated from European Commission, 2021). The institutionalization of APAs took place in the context of "a consensus that traditional mechanisms for administering the law and resolving disputes have virtually collapsed in the area of transfer pricing"

(Ring, 2000, p. 145). Tax arrangements were becoming increasingly complex and deviations from the transfer pricing rules had become commonplace. In 2007, the OECD's *Manual on Effective Mutual Agreement Procedures* (MEMAP) described APA programs as "best practice" followed by most OECD countries because they "reduce the number of international tax disputes and provide taxpayers and tax administrations with greater tax certainty" (Markham, 2012, p. 23).[1]

Existing (mostly legal) research on APAs and ATRs has focused predominantly on the pecuniary and administrative gains they create for the MNEs and states engaging in these kinds of tax wars (Christensen & Shaxson, 2016). Legal researchers have noted how "judicial mechanisms such as litigation are also not an optimal way to resolve transfer pricing disputes," as "entering into adversarial litigation proceedings with one or more revenue authority is an expensive and protracted process" (Markham, 2012). OECD guidelines take a similar view, stating that APAs "may prevent costly and time-consuming examinations and litigation of major transfer pricing issues for taxpayers and tax administration" (OECD, 2010, p. 132). Litigation is commonly seen as costly, time-consuming, and—interestingly—a "very public" option (Klotsche, quoted in Markham, 2012, p. 19).[2]

An additional factor behind the growth and increasing sophistication of APAs has been pressure coming from private sector advocacy groups and financial intermediaries. In 1965, the IFA decided to use its annual congress as a venue for discussing advance tax rulings. In its resolution, the IFA identified the lack of ATR legislation as a major weakness of international tax governance. The organization issued a bold call to tax administrations to establish binding advance rulings in tax matters. This call for action was a major driver of the growth of ATR regimes. By the 1980s, five of the 20 countries that the IFA surveyed had answered the call for ATRs and developed comprehensive systems for issuing advance rulings (Romano, 2002, pp. vii–x).

In subsequent decades, the Big Four accounting firms (Deloitte, PwC, E&Y, and KPMG) have been instrumental in the development and marketing of APAs. Together, these firms act as gatekeepers for APAs, as they design and market tax planning arrangements whose certainty before the

---

[1] Bearing in mind that many ATRs also include APA-like provisions, I speak of APAs in the rest of this chapter for the sake of simplicity, unless there is a specific reason to address ATRs separately.

[2] Paradoxically, however, unilateral APAs may sometimes lead to potential double taxation in non-participating countries, increased risk of audits for years not covered by the APA, and a drain of the tax authority's resources (Borkowski, 1996, p. 26).

law APAs then help to secure. This development has taken place in a wider context in which the sale of various tax-avoidance-related services and arrangements has become a major industry (Sikka and Hampton, 2005; Sikka, 2013; Addison & Mueller, 2015; Sikka, 2017). As the United States senate subcommittee noted in 2005, "The sale of potentially abusive and illegal tax shelters is a lucrative business in the United States, and some professional firms such as accounting firms, banks, law firms, and investment advisory firms have been major participants in the development" (United States Senate, 2005, p. 6). Subsequently, the size and importance of the tax planning industry has grown further, as revealed by the LuxLeaks scandal (Marian, 2016).

The role of APAs in global wealth chains

The previous section discussed how supposedly "market-based" intra-firm trade is grounded on assumptions that have very little in common with market ideals. The contrast between the planned prices used in intra-firm trade and the market-based assumptions underlying rules ostensibly guiding intra-firm pricing becomes clear on comparison of intra-firm transactions with established definitions of markets. Patrik Aspers (2011, p. 4) defines the market structure as "constituted by two roles, buyer and seller, each standing on one side of the market, facing the other." Elsewhere, William Lazonick (1991, p. 59) noted that the "definitional social characteristic of a market is the impersonal relation between buyer and seller." These characteristics are not applicable to intra-firm trade. Corporate planning surpasses markets by setting prices not according to market-based prices (which are typically nowhere to be found), but through strategic planning conducted in the headquarters of an MNE.

Another feature that distinguishes intra-firm trade from market transactions is the temporal fixing of prices. Textbook definitions of markets assume that the prices used in markets respond immediately to price signals. Lazonick notes that, "by definition, the existence of market exchange requires that buyers have *equal access* to the resources of sellers," which means that, "a long-term contract, once entered into, ostensibly precludes market exchange for the duration of the term" (1991, pp. 59–60, emphasis in original). Although few researchers or policymakers would assume that markets function like this all the time, the idea of prices that react to supply and demand carries strong appeal.

However, prices used in intra-firm trade are often fixed for some period and adjusted periodically, making it easier for MNEs to administer prices and internal wealth flows (Deloitte, 2013, p. 5). However, for an MNE, long-term certainty in internal pricing can sometimes result in increased risk of disputes with tax authorities. Keeping intra-firm prices constant for a long period may create grounds for tax authorities to argue that these prices do not adhere to "market-based" pricing where there is evidence of price fluctuation. Moreover, if tax authorities successfully challenge the prices an MNE uses internally over a longer period, penalties may also be applied retroactively.

APAs can help MNEs in adding a layer of certainty to intra-firm pricing models. Whereas in normal situations, fixing intra-firm prices may create a heightened risk of tax audits, APAs help to turn price-fixing into an advantage, also from a legal standpoint. Recalling that GWCs are "transacted forms of capital operating multijurisdictionally for the purposes of wealth creation and protection" (Seabrooke and Wigan, 2017, p. 2). APAs further distance wealth chains from the underlying value chains by fixing terms for intra-firm flows of wealth according to the terms agreed upon in an APA. APAs fall into several categories in the GWC typology: hierarchy/national, modular/national, hierarchy/international, and modular/international. In addition, there are also borderline cases that do not fit neatly into these categories (see Figure 4.1). I discuss each of these GWC types in turn.

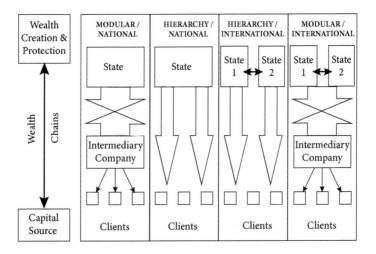

Fig. 4.1 Global wealth chains of advance pricing agreements

Most traditional ATRs are issued in the form of an administrative act rather than a contract (Romano, 2002, p. 77). This creates a hierarchical relationship between the tax authority and the clients (enterprises). The company applies for an ATR from the state, which gives a unilateral ruling on the taxation of a particular type of income. This ruling binds the state when it imposes taxes on that enterprise. While these rulings or agreements can be partially or entirely tax-driven, the administrative nature of the ruling creates less space for intermediary companies to commercialize them. As such, these agreements are "tailor-made." In Figure 4.1, these ATRs constitute a hierarchy/national wealth chain.

Depending on jurisdiction, APAs can also resemble ATRs in being more or less unilateral. However, intermediary companies and especially the Big Four accounting firms have a much greater role, especially in aggressive APA regimes. Recalling that APAs are typically agreements between one or more tax authority and a taxpayer (Romano, 2002, p. 135), the contractual nature of APAs allows a greater role for intermediaries such as the Big Four companies in these wealth chains. The intermediaries can act as suppliers that both design and market APAs granted by the state (lead supplier) to the clients (the MNEs). In Figure 4.1, this is nominated as modular/national wealth chain.

Luxembourg is a key example of an APA regime fitting the modular wealth chain type. The LuxLeaks scandal demonstrated the significant role of the Big Four as conduit companies that help MNEs to benefit from the aggressive pricing agreements granted by Luxembourg (Marian, 2016). The agreements revealed in the LuxLeaks scandal typically consist of a one-page letter issued by the Luxemburg authorities to the tax advisory firm PwC, with a statement such as "I find the contents of said letter to be in compliance with current tax legislation and administrative practice" (Government of Luxembourg, 2010). After this short letter of consent, the Big Four accounting firm, in this case PwC, drafts the rest of the ruling. The ruling itself begins with an accompanying letter from the "bespoke supplier" that underlines its role as the de facto authority behind the ruling. For example, a 2010 letter from PwC to one client began as follows:

LSP Holding S.á.r.l.—Tax Number 2010 24 24 361
    Dear Mr. Kohl,
    In our capacity of tax consultant of the above-mentioned company, we discussed in our meeting held on 25 August 2010 the tax treatment applicable to the transaction implemented by our client. This letter aims at confirming

the conclusions reached during this meeting and will serve as a basis for the preparation of the tax returns of the Luxembourg company involved.

(PwC in Government of Luxembourg, 2010)

This demonstrates the near absence of information asymmetries between lead suppliers, bespoke suppliers, and clients; a typical feature of modular wealth chains. However, foreign tax authorities and the public are completely excluded from obtaining any information on these APAs, and secrecy is a major factor for companies wanting to avoid publicity regarding their tax planning arrangements. As the IFA notes, "there are few issues where the position in the reporting countries is more deeply divided than on the question of whether advance rulings should be accessible to persons other than the applicant" (International Fiscal Association, 1999, p. 34). What is more, some jurisdictions allow applications on behalf of a class of (anonymous) applicants. This is convenient especially for "product rulings" that determine how persons who invest in a particular type of financial product will be taxed (ibid., p. 32). These types highlight the various ways in which APA-driven wealth chains are distinct from other intra-company wealth chains, and, often by definition, the underlying value chains. Finally, bilateral and multilateral APAs can be characterized either as hierarchy/international or modular/international, depending on the role of the Big Four companies or other intermediaries in the negotiation process.

APAs, commercialized sovereignty, and the power of MNEs

While scholars were already voicing calls for studies on the societal power of corporations in the early 1970s (Ylönen, 2018; Ylönen, 2019), and there is an even longer history of these questions in evolutionary economics (Galbraith, 1973), much of the emerging body of research on so-called private regulation has analyzed private political power within the context of private political associations and self-regulatory bodies (see e.g. Büthe, 2010). In other words, studies in international political economy (IPE) often focus on the use of power with *forms* of organization and decision-making, and pay less attention to the ways corporations exert power directly over states (for exceptions, see May, 2015; Baars & Spicer, 2017; Babic et al., 2017; Mikler, 2018; Ylönen & Teivainen, 2018). The GWC framework is one attempt to question and problematize this divide by suggesting that corporate activities traditionally associated with the private, economic sphere may have important societal effects.

More specifically, the power relations that APAs create and sustain have important implications for IPE. One concept that transcends simplistic public/private divisions in world politics is commercialized sovereignty, which refers to the ability of states to tailor their domestic laws to lure disproportionate amounts of capital from other countries, effectively poaching their tax bases (Palan, 2003; cf. Baker & Murphy, 2019). The contractual nature of APAs enables states to commercialize sovereignty in unprecedented ways, often in collaboration with the Big Four accounting firms.[3] In a way, states that offer aggressive APA regimes commercialize the power to decide on the prices that determine taxes levied in intra-company trade. Consequently, aggressive APA regimes represent a new frontier in the commercialization of sovereignty, which has typically been associated with secrecy laws, immaterial rights regimes, and so on (Palan, 2003; Christensen, 2012). As the OECD states, "APAs should not be viewed as a means for increasing tax revenue," as they are "primarily aimed at providing some certainty to taxpayers" (OECD, 2012). The contractual nature of APAs allows states and intermediary companies to transform pricing models and decisions into tax products that bespoke suppliers can market to clients. Modular chains are typically national as they operate by "ring-fencing" companies from tax obligations in other jurisdictions.

APAs also impact GWCs by influencing the division of tax income *between* certain jurisdictions. Essentially, most bilateral and multilateral APAs ensure that a particular income is taxed at least once, while, depending on the case at hand, the actual tax rate may be low. However, these contractual agreements may impact third states as well. For example, two or more states could agree on a pricing agreement of an immaterial income that, in principle, could be legitimately taxed in a third country. This fact has important consequences. Usually, international negotiations in tax and trade law have been associated with disputes and agreements over the *principles* that dictate the rules of the global economy. The material consequences, when they occur, have been only indirect and have followed after the treaties or organizations have been initiated. APAs significantly alter this dynamic. Instead of negotiating the rules addressing international

---

[3] Again, great variety among the countries that issue APAs should be noted. This commercialization of APA regimes is mostly relevant to states such as Luxembourg and the Netherlands.

economic activity, states directly negotiate a division of tax revenues. This is another way in which APAs extend the sphere of commercialized sovereignty.

A typical example of "traditional" commercialization of sovereignty is a situation where a tax haven country issues special legislation allowing corporations to derive income from intellectual property rights that they have transferred to a group company registered in that country. This traditional model enables MNEs to calculate what kinds of monetary benefits and potential risks are entailed in transferring patents, trademarks, or other intellectual property rights to a holding company registered in that particular jurisdiction. However, given that APAs are negotiated between MNEs and states, issuing an APA is only a starting point for a process that involves negotiations between MNEs, states, and intermediaries. This phenomenon could be termed the contractualization of commercialized sovereignty.

For corporations, APAs are essentially derivative assets. Given that derivatives are contracts that derive their value from the performance of an underlying entity or asset, APAs perform this function for corporations. Though APAs are not tradable in the way that financial derivatives are, they nevertheless fix the pricing mechanism applied to a particular trade for a given period of time, as well as taxes levied from these trading activities over the same period. Consequently, the pricing mechanism significantly affects expected profits from future trade. The profits generated under the APA are derivative of the volume of trade the MNE manages to generate. This "fixing" of prices undermines traditional conceptions of markets as arenas where buyers and sellers respond to the pressures of the price mechanism.[4]

Above it was suggested that APAs may challenge some of the established conceptions of private governance. Most existing research on "private governance" addresses how private bodies have become increasingly engaged in rule-making areas previously regulated by states and intergovernmental organizations. This idea of private governance is rooted in the established division between public and private spheres. However, the derivative nature of APAs underlines the problems behind these kinds of liberal-democratic approaches to the contemporary global economy. The

---

[4] Interestingly, companies that use market-based and negotiated transfer pricing methods have been less likely to participate in US APA programs than companies using cost-based and other formulary methods for determining their transfer prices. This is not surprising, however, since MNEs using market-based or negotiated methods are less likely to have transfer-pricing related problems with authorities (Borkowski, 1996, pp. 32–33).

private governance of modular APAs is worth highlighting here. In modular APAs, the state (e.g. Luxembourg) first commercializes its sovereignty by effectively granting the Big Four tax advisory companies the right to grant APAs to MNEs on its behalf. The Big Four tax advisory companies can then use this right to sell derivative assets solely based on this commercialized sovereignty. This process takes place simultaneously in the "political" and "economic" spheres and therefore belies established conceptions of "public" and "private."

This might seem merely semantic. However, one of the main assumptions that legitimizes and reproduces corporate power is the idea that democratic norms are only valid within the political and not the economic sphere (Teivainen, 2002). Therefore, understanding the nature of APAs opens up possibilities for new ways to regulate both MNEs and the states that build and maintain aggressive APA regimes. This is clear on comparing the normative aspects of APAs to those present in regular intra-firm trade that does not rely on APAs. Whereas the significant non-market planning element in intra-firm trade offers the possibility to see corporations as political agents (Ylönen & Teivainen, 2018), the modular wealth chains of APAs open up new ways to conceptualize tax advisory companies as political entities. By effectively selling APAs on behalf of Luxembourg and other states that offer aggressive APA regimes, the Big Four companies exert political power much more clearly than in some other tax planning activities.

In practical terms, recognizing the political nature of the large tax advisory firms constitutes grounds for stricter separation of their tax planning services from other consultancy work they perform. Previous research on the societal role of the Big Four argued that internal "Chinese walls" do not prevent the firms from selling tax-avoidance schemes to audit clients and then claiming to independently attest the resulting transactions" (Sikka & Hampton, 2005, p. 339). However, the problems and conflicts of interest related to the Big Four go deeper than this. All of the major tax advisory firms participate in public procurement tenders for background studies that governments commission when they are revising their tax laws or other legislation (House of Commons, 2013, p. 5). All of these firms also offer consultancy on matters related to corporate social responsibility. The fact that the Big Four exert political power in global wealth chains highlights the urgency of breaking these companies into parts to reduce the risk of such conflicts of interest.

Current and future developments

In the very recent time, the political standpoints of Member States have changed radically with respect to tax practices and in particular concerning tax rulings. Where in the past unilateral tax rulings appear to have been accepted as a characteristic of tax competition, not least the LuxLeaks have made public that the lack of transparency in this area fosters aggressive tax planning on a grand scale, leading to massive base erosion.

(European Commission, 2015a, p. 5)

Policymakers have recently focused on enhancing the regulation and transparency of APAs and ATRs. In early 2014, the OECD began the base erosion profit-shifting process (BEPS), addressing base erosion caused by MNE profit shifting. The process was completed in October 2015 (Markham, 2015). One of the action points (#5) in the BEPS process addressed harmful tax practices. This included APAs and ATRs. Moreover, action point 14 included seeking new ways of enhancing dispute-resolution mechanisms in international tax matters. In 2014, the OECD's Forum on Harmful Tax Practices decided to develop a framework for compulsory spontaneous information exchange in respect to rulings related to preferential regimes (OECD, 2015). As a second step, the OECD addressed the ruling regimes in OECD and associate countries. The BEPS outcome document stated that "the requirement to undertake compulsory spontaneous information exchange should generally cover all instances in which the absence of exchange of a ruling may give rise to BEPS concerns" (ibid., p. 45).

The OECD has also developed a general best practice framework for the design and operation of ruling regimes (ibid., p. 46). Here, the OECD relied on a "soft law" approach, issuing general guidelines and promoting only spontaneous exchange of information instead of automatic, compulsory information exchange. More recently, the Paris-based organization has continued to develop new rules for international corporate taxation in its "BEPS 2.0" process, which seeks to develop new ways for taxing digital and online trading businesses and addresses a global minimum corporate tax rate. Improving dispute resolutions and addressing problems related to APAs have also featured in these discussions. The background document of Pillar 1 of the BEPS 2.0 negotiations highlights the need to improve access to bilateral and multilateral APAs, noting that the proposed new taxing formulas should not supersede APAs agreed before their implementation

(OECD, 2020a). Moreover, the *Guidance on the transfer pricing implications of the COVID-19 pandemic* that the OECD (2020b) published in December 2020 further clarified the conditions related to implementing APAs in the exceptional pandemic situation.

In the European Union, the Directive on Administrative Cooperation in the Field of Taxation came into force at the beginning of 2013. This provided for the exchange of information that is of "foreseeable relevance" to the administration and the enforcement of Member States' tax laws, including all taxes except VAT (European Commission, 2015b, pp. 9–10). However, the formulation was ambiguous with regard to the definition of "foreseeable relevance." Consequently, in the tax transparency package of March 2015, the Commission required that, every three months, national tax authorities must send a short report to all other Member States on all advanced cross-border tax rulings and advanced transfer pricing arrangements issued. According to the Commission, "the automatic exchange of information on tax rulings will enable Member States to detect certain abusive tax practices by companies and take the necessary action in response." Moreover, the system allows Member States to request more information on a particular ruling if needed (European Commission, 2015b). Member States agreed on the new rules in October 2015, and they came into effect in January 2017. It remains to be seen how this information exchange will work in practice and how effective it will be.

In the European Parliament, the LuxLeaks scandal provoked the assembly of an ad hoc committee on Tax Rulings and Other Measures Similar in Nature or Effect (TAXE) and its follow-up committee TAXE 2. While these committees suffered from insufficient access to information and from the refusal of many of the major corporations to attend hearings, they have increased pressure to tackle harmful tax practices within the EU. Currently, the main venue for discussing harmful tax practices has been the Code of Conduct (CoC) for Business Taxation. Originally formed in 1998, the CoC group has a mandate to assess business tax measures that may fall within the scope of harmful conduct. While not a legal instrument, this nonetheless reflects the political commitment of Member States. One criterion the group uses for measuring harmful practices is a lack of transparency. There have been calls for an upgrade of the CoC group to give more weight to its decisions, but these have faced fierce resistance in the European Parliament as well as from certain Member States.

By way of conclusion, all major regulatory efforts have aimed at increasing the transparency of APAs and ATRs. If successful, increased transparency would potentially damage APA-driven corporate wealth chains, not least because wealth chains are often articulated to avoid regulatory scrutiny (see Chapter 1 in this volume). However, the first steps toward greater transparency have been either half-hearted (the spontaneous exchange of information in the OECD) or limited in geographical coverage (the EU's automatic information exchange). It is difficult to foresee any ground-breaking substantive changes in the immediate future. The EU's automatic information exchange may help to tackle APA-related wealth chains in the EU, but its impact in third countries will remain limited. Therefore, it is likely that the new EU rules will transform the geography of APA-related wealth chains, but the underlying problems will remain.

The EU's automatic information exchange will not be a panacea even within the Union. The information exchanged will be accessible only to authorities and not the wider public. Moreover, while transparency can help foreign tax authorities challenge some arrangements, information exchange alone does not prevent states from establishing and promoting aggressive APA regimes. In order to achieve this, states would need to agree on common guidelines for APAs or abandon the separate entity principle in favor of taxing MNEs as single-enterprise entities based on a commonly agreed-upon formula—as the BEPS 2.0 process has envisioned in regards to selected groups of companies (Siu et al., 2015; Picciotto 2016; Finér & Ylönen, 2021). However, the current OECD proposals clearly fall short of genuinely addressing the underlying problems, and both theoretical and policy-related issues surrounding APAs discussed in this chapter remain highly relevant in the foreseeable future.

References

Addison, S. & Mueller, F. (2015). The dark side of professions: The big four and tax avoidance. *Accounting, Auditing & Accountability Journal*, 28(8), 1263–1290.

Aspers, P. (2011). *Markets*. Polity Press.

Avi-Yonah, R. (1995). The rise and fall of arm's length: A study in the evolution of US international taxation. *Virginia Tax Review*, 15(89), 89–159.

Baars, G. & Spicer, A. (2017). *The Corporation: A Critical, Multi-Disciplinary Handbook*. Cambridge University Press.

Babic, M., Fichtner, J., & Heemskerk, E. M. (2017). States versus corporations: Rethinking the power of business in international politics. *Italian Journal of International Affairs*, 52(4), 20–43.

Baker, A. & Murphy, R. (2019). The political economy of "tax spillover": A new multilateral framework. *Global Policy*, 10, 178–192.

Biondi, Y. (2013). The governance and disclosure of the firm as an enterprise entity. *Seattle University Law Review*, 36, 391–416.

Biondi, Y., Canziani, A., & Kirat, T. (2007). *The Firm as an Entity: Implications for Economics, Accounting and the Law*. Routledge.

Borkowski, S. C. (1996). Advance pricing (dis)agreements: Differences in TAX AUTHORITY and transnational corporation opinions. *International Tax Journal*, 22(23), 23–34.

Borkowski, S. C. (2000). Transfer pricing agreements: Current status by country. *International Tax Journal*, 26(1), 1–16.

Bryan, D., Rafferty, M., and Wigan, D. (2017). Capital unchained: finance, intangible assets and the double life of capital in the offshore world. *Review of International Political Economy*, 24(1), 56–86.

Büthe, T. (2010). Private regulation in the global economy—A (p)review. *Business and Politics*, 12(3), 1–38.

Christensen, J. (2012). The hidden trillions: Secrecy, corruption, and the offshore interface. *Crime, Law and Social Change*, 57(3), 325–343.

Christensen, J. & Shaxson, N. (2016). Tax competitiveness—A dangerous obsession. In T. Pogge and K. Mehta (eds.), *Global Tax Fairness*. Oxford University Press, 265–298.

Deloitte (2013). *Operational Transfer Pricing: Enhancing Insight and Process Management through Technology*. Deloitte Tax LLP.

Durst, M. C. & Culbertson, R. E. (2003). Clearing away the sand: Retrospective methods and prospective documentation in transfer pricing today. *Tax Law Review* 57, 37–84.

Eden, L. (2016). The arm's length standard: Making it work in a 21st-century world of multinationals and nation states. In, T. Pogge and K. Mehta (eds.), *Global Tax Fairness*. Oxford University Press, 153–172.

European Commission, (2015a). *Technical analysis of focus and scope of the legal proposal Accompanying the document Proposal for a Council Directive amending Directive 2011/16/EU as regards exchange of information in the field of taxation*. Commission Staff Working Document SWD 2015(60), final, 18 March, European Commission.

European Commission (2015b). "Tax Transparency Package." https://ec.europa. eu/taxation_customs/tax-transparency-package_en.

European Commission (2021). *Statistic on APAs (Advance Pricing Agreements) in the EU at the End of 2019*. European Commission.

European Parliament (2015). *Draft Report on Tax Rulings and other Measures Similar in Nature or Effect*. 2015/2066(INI). Special Committee on Tax Rulings and Other Measures Similar in Nature or Effect.

Finér, L. & Ylönen, M. (2017). Tax-driven wealth chains: A multiple case study of tax avoidance in the Finnish mining sector. *Critical Perspectives on Accounting*, 48(2017), 53–81.

Galbraith, J. K. (1973). *Economics and the Public Purpose*. Houghton Mifflin.

Government of Luxembourg (2010). *For the attention of Fiona Monsen. A tax ruling regarding LSP Holding S.á.r.l.*, 29 September.

Hickman, Kristin E. (1998). Should advance pricing agreements be published? *Northwestern Journal of International Law & Business*, 19(1), 171–194.

House of Commons (2013). *Tax Avoidance: The Role of Large Accountancy Firms*. House of Commons, Committee of Public Accounts. Fourth-fourth Report of Session 2012–2013. House of Commons.

International Fiscal Association (1999). *General Report*. International Fiscal Association.

Lanz, R. & Miroudot, S. (2011). Intra-firm trade: Patterns, determinants and policy implications. *OECD Trade Policy Papers*, No. 114. OECD.

Lazonick, W. (1991). *Business Organization and the Myth of the Market Economy*. Cambridge University Press.

Marian, O. (2016). Is something rotten in the Grand Duchy of Luxembourg? *Tax Notes International*, 84, 281–293.

Markham, M. (2012). *Advance Pricing Agreements: Past, Present and Future*. Kluwer Law International.

Markham, M. (2015). New developments in dispute resolution in international tax. *Revenue Law Journal*, 25(1), 1–28.

May, C. (2015). *Global Corporations in Global Governance*. Routledge.

Mikler, J. (2018). *The Political Power of Global Corporations*. Polity.

OECD (1995). *Transfer Pricing for Multinational Enterprises and Tax Administrators*. Draft Text of Part II, Commission of Fiscal Affairs. OECD.

OECD (2002). *Economic Outlook*. OECD.

OECD (2005). *E-commerce: Transfer Pricing and Business Profits Taxation*. OECD.

OECD (2010) *OECD Transfer Pricing Guidelines for Multinational Enterprises and Tax Administrations 2010*. OECD Publishing.

OECD (2012). *Advance Pricing Arrangements: Approaches to Legislation: Pilot version for comments*. Tax & Development. OECD.

OECD (2015). *Countering Harmful Tax Practices More Effectively, Taking into Account Transparency and Substance*. OECD Publishing.

OECD (2020a). *Tax Challenges Arising from Digitalisation—Report on Pillar One Blueprint*. OECD.

OECD (2020b). *Guidance on the Transfer Pricing Implications of the COVID-19 Pandemic*. OECD.

Palan, R. (2003). *The Offshore World: Sovereign Markets, Virtual Places, and Nomad Millionaires*. Cornell University Press.

Picciotto, S. (1992). *International Business Taxation: A Study in the Internationalization of Business Regulation*. Cambridge University Press.

Picciotto, S. (2016). Towards unitary taxation. In T. Pogge and K. Mehta (eds.), *Global Tax Fairness*. Oxford University Press, 221–237.

Ring, D. M. (2000). On the frontier of procedural innovation: Advance pricing agreements and the struggle to allocate income for cross-border taxation. *Michigan Journal of International Law*, 21, 143–234.

Rixen, T. (2008). *The Political Economy of International Tax Governance*. Palgrave Macmillan.

Rixen, T. (2010). From double tax avoidance to tax competition: Explaining the institutional trajectory of international tax governance. *Review of International Political Economy*, 18(2), 197–227.

Robé, J.-P. (2011). The legal structure of the firm. *Accounting, Economics, and Law*, 1(1), 1–85.

Romano, C. (2002). *Advance Tax Rulings and Principles of Law*. IBFD Publications BV.

Seabrooke, L. & Wigan, D. (2017). The governance of global wealth chains. *Review of International Political Economy*, 24(1), 1–29.

Sikka, P. (2013). Smoke and mirrors: Corporate social responsibility and tax avoidance—a reply to Hasseldine and Morris. *Accounting Forum*, 37(1), 15–28.

Sikka, P. (2017). Accounting and taxation: Conjoined twins or separate siblings? *Accounting Forum*, 41(4), 390–405.

Sikka, P. and Hampton, M. (2005). The role of accountancy firms in tax avoidance: Some evidence and issues. *Accounting Forum*, 29(3), 325–343.

Siu, E., Picciotto, S., Mintz J., & Sawyer, A. (2015). *Unitary taxation in the extractive industry sector*. ICTD Working Paper 41. Institute of Development Studies.

Teivainen, T. (2002). *Enter Economism, Exit Politics: Experts, Economic Policy and the Damage to Democracy*. Zed Books.

Ting, A. (2014). iTax—Apple's international tax structure and the double non-taxation issue. *British Tax Review*, 1, 40–71.

UNCTAD (1996). *World Investment Report 1996: Investment, Trade and International Policy Arrangements*. UNCTAD.

UNCTAD (2004). *World Investment Report 2004: The Shift towards Services*. UNCTAD.

United States Senate (2005). *The Role of Professional Firms in the US Tax Shelter Industry*. Report Prepared by the Permanent Subcommittee on Investigations of the Committee on Homeland Security and Governmental Affairs. United States Senate.

Ylönen, M. (2018). *Planned Economies? Corporations, Tax Avoidance and World Politics*. PhD thesis. Publications of the Faculty of Social Sciences, 79/2018. Available at: https://helda.helsinki.fi/handle/10138/234809. University of Helsinki.

Ylönen, M. (2019). Who's to blame for the money drain? Corporate power and corruption as competing narratives for lost resources. In P. G. Alston. & N. Reisch (eds.), *Tax, Inequality and Human Rights*. Oxford University Press.

Ylönen, M. & Finér, L. (2021). Global tax governance. In A. Garcia, C. Scherrer, & J. Wullweber (eds.), *Handbook on Critical Political Economy and Public Policy*. Edward Elgar.

Ylönen, M. & Teivainen, T. (2018). Politics of intra-firm trade: Corporate price planning and the double role of the arm's-length principle. *New Political Economy*, 23(4), 441–457.

5

Intangible Capital

Dick Bryan, Michael Rafferty, and Duncan Wigan

Over the last three decades, and with increasing current significance, a historic transformation has been occurring in both the value composition and the institutional and organizational forms of global capital. The rise of intangible capital as a frontier form of global capital and source of accumulation is one such transformation, and is the focus of this chapter. From a small and residual category in corporate balance sheets (then called "goodwill"), intangible capital, like patents, trademarks, brand names, and platforms, now dominates the valuations of leading global corporations. According to a 2019 estimate by UK Treasury economist Charles Price, "the world's five most valuable companies are worth £3.5 trillion together, but their balance sheets report just £172 billion of tangible assets. *95% of their value is in the form of intangible assets*" (Price, 2019, emphasis added).

Intangible capital is not only large in value terms, it is also changing the nature of production, exchange, and consumption, and relationships between state and capital. The rise of intangible capital has clearly been historic, and it is presenting significant empirical and analytical challenges across a range of disciplinary areas from accounting and finance to law and economics. For instance, how are expenditures and investments in intangible capital accounted for, and how is intangible value measured and capitalized? Many forms of intangible value accrue from activities that exceed the formal factories of the Fordist era, raising the questions of "where" and even "how" intangible value is produced.

A question that immediately arises is how to understand intangible capital within existing conceptual approaches. Recent analytical categories like global production networks (GPN) and global value chains (GVC) were developed when the capital being analyzed was the increasingly internationally unbundled and fluid production of physical commodities, like coffee (on coffee, see recently Grabs & Ponte, 2019). While concepts such as GVC and GPN have provided new and significant insights into

Dick Bryan, Michael Rafferty and Duncan Wigan, *Intangible Capital*. In: *Global Wealth Chains*.
Edited by Leonard Seabrooke and Duncan Wigan, Oxford University Press.
© Dick Bryan, Michael Rafferty, and Duncan Wigan (2022). DOI: 10.1093/oso/9780198832379.003.0005

global production, trade, and investment (Gereffi & Korzeniewicz, 1994; Henderson et al., 2002; Humphrey & Schmitz, 2002; Gereffi et al., 2005; Kaplinsky, 2005; Coe & Yeung, 2015), they have not been without their critics. Two weaknesses of GVC/GPN are important for our purposes here. First, these paradigms are based largely on what in an earlier series of debates about the international development of capitalism was characterized as neo-Smithian (Brenner, 1977; Weeks, 1979). Consequently they focus on internationalization largely in terms of a trade-based division of labour, and an expansion of international relations of (unequal) exchange, to the neglect of relations of production and work (Bernstein & Campling, 2006; Bair & Werner, 2011; Selwyn, 2018). Second, internationalization in GVC and GPN is limited and partial. These paradigms focus on internationalization as the actual movement of commodities and MNCs. A more inclusive concept of internationalization includes the movement of commodities *and* money (i.e. capital). Indeed, even actual cross-border movement may be limited because it needs to include the spatial scope of activity that is *subject to* international mobility, even where that movement may remain within the nation (Bryan, 1995; Bryan & Rafferty, 2006). As Bryan notes, "Internationalisation is defined with reference to the space in which capital is free to circulate; it is not a characteristic attributed *ex post* to an individual commodity" (1995, p. 428).

For our purposes here, notions of linear cross-border flows of commodities and networks of exchange between MNCs may be appropriate for linking the growing spatial disaggregation of physical commodity production and the blurring of boundaries between inside and outside of corporations, as well as some aspects of the relations of power across those chains and networks. But these are eclectic frameworks based largely around some stylized and limited facts of internationalization of trade and exchange in the 1980s and 1990s.

Intangible capital presents a different order of empirical and conceptual challenge, in part at least because it involves more abstract and non-linear forms of movement, and in part because it demands an integration of capital in the commodity and money form. One of the propositions developed in this chapter is that integrating intangible capital into many existing frameworks remains an ongoing challenge. While GVC and GPN have led to many of the most significant innovations in the analysis of the growing fluidity of the organization of production on a global scale, these new abstract and intangible forms of capital present as a stark contrast. The implications of intangible capital are still working their way through international political economy (IPE) research (see Dedrick & Kraemer, 2017; Durand & Milberg, 2020; Schwartz, 2021), and as they do so they are likely to change IPE's conceptual frameworks in some important ways.

To consider the empirical and conceptual challenges of intangible capital for IPE and the GWC framework, and to set that analysis in motion, the next section introduces some background on the changing organization and institutions of international capital before considering the key developments in intangible capital. The chapter does not seek to find conceptual consensus where none exists, but rather lays out the key developments in intangible capital, and the challenges they pose, as a way of scoping out some opportunities for GWC research. The chapter then opens up some of the empirical and conceptual challenges posed by intangible capital, illustrating how they play out in wealth chains articulated for tax minimization. We conclude with reflection on the implications of global intangible capital for trade and exchange focused frameworks such as GVC and GPN, and for the project of global wealth chains.

Fordist MNCs to post-industrial factoryless goods producers and platforms

It is well established that the period from the 1990s to the present has been a historically (and conceptually) transformative one, especially in the spatial unbundling and organizational decentring and fragmentation of global production (Desai, 2008; Baldwin, 2011, 2016). For many years, globalization was widely understood to be driven by, and owned and organized through, the multinational corporation (MNC). The MNC was widely conceptualized as the key ontological and institutional unit of global capital, despite the fact that internationalization in the nineteenth and early twentieth centuries was advanced differently (mercantile family firms and partnerships) (Jones, 1987). But in the 1960s, in the first significant phase of MNC expansion, the MNC was seen largely as "new" and something of an exception, initially an expression of national attributes, or unique ownership attributes, particularly associated with the rise of industrially sophisticated MNCs from the United States. FDI was conceived as a new form of national capital export, and MNCs as a form of national competitive expansion (Servan-Schrieber, 1968; Hymer, 1970, 1976; Knickerbocker, 1973). It is also true in part that attributes of the MNC—especially the size of these firms, their technological advantages, and the market structure of the industries (oligopoly)—were seen to be crucial determinants of MNC advance.

But by the 1970s and 1980s, as MNCs expanded from many more countries and industries, it also came to be understood that a wider range of attributes were now driving the international expansion of firms. The ownership of production assets and the scale of that production (global Fordism), internal efficiency, as well as market concentration (oligopolistic markets) were seen as key to the international advance of MNCs (Hymer, 1976; Dunning, 1977). The core concepts that bound these approaches to globalization together were the ontological primacy of the MNC as the unit of the global organization of production (these approaches literally were theories *of* the MNC) and the key "advantages" of MNCs being their ownership of production or marketing assets.

Since the 1990s, a different sort of globalization can be observed, with direct implications for the way MNCs are conceptualized. Two of the key developments associated with this phase of globalization have been the much more extended spatial "unbundling" and "fragmentation" of production and the "decentring" of the corporation as the ownership unit of global production (Hagel & Singer, 2000; Desai, 2008; Baldwin 2011). The growth of global production has been extended beyond MNCs setting up new factories or acquiring and expanding existing ones. There is now an extensive use of arrangements such as subcontracting, strategic alliances, and franchising. This has transformed the way global production and trade are organized and how MNCs are integrated into that process. Importantly, it has meant that MNCs often do not need to own many (or any) stages of physical production, but instead locate their activities at key points or nodes in the networks and chains of production, notably in R&D, design, marketing, and after-sales service (Baldwin et al., 2014).

In 1989, Richard Walker presciently forecast the imminent demise of corporate geography, and implicitly all similarly MNC-centric approaches (Walker, 1989). He noted that capital was outgrowing the corporation, with the division of labour increasingly organized across extended spatial processes and new organizational means (virtual across-the-board improvements in the integrative capability of production, facilitating global alliances, joint ventures, subcontracting, and the like), as well as beyond the confines of individual industries.

The GVC and GPN paradigms emerged as important conceptual innovations to understand this growing fluidity and spatial spread of production and trade, and the governance structures that developed to organize them (Gereffi, 1994; Henderson et al., 2002; Gereffi et al., 2005; Gibbon et al.,

2008; Coe et al., 2008; Coe & Yeung, 2015). In their eclectic framings they have permitted an understanding of global capital in terms of flows and networks rather than the institutional fixity and thingness of earlier MNC-centric theories. These frameworks provided researchers with concepts more responsive to the changing roles and importance of nation states and corporations, but set within broader globalized industrial contexts and processes, where firms play a range of coordinating (governance) roles in production chains and networks without necessarily owning production, logistics, or trade activities, and where states attempt to attract and retain. GVC and GPN approaches have been particularly useful in analyzing developments in agricultural, mining, and manufacturing sectors, where physical commodities are produced and traded. With the development of a range of forms of organizing international production and trade, including subcontracting, joint ventures, franchising, licensing, and even factoryless goods producers, firms are now opened up and situated in fluid relations along chains and in networks.

The rise of intangible capital

Sometime in the early 2000s, in the United States and some other developed countries, investment in intangible assets outgrew investment in tangible assets (Nakamura, 2008). By then also, the value of intangible capital stock had outstripped tangible capital stock in the majority of developed countries, and the growth rate of intangible capital had eclipsed that of tangible capital (Corrado et al., 2016, pp. 10, 19). Between 1975 and 2020 the proportion of market value on the US S&P comprised of intangible capital grew from 17 percent to 90 percent (Ocean Tomo, 2020, p. 2). While the US S&P is an intangible-capital-heavy index, other capital markets show similar growth patterns. With the quantitative increase in the value of intangible capital have come changes in the industrial/sectoral composition of capital. Internet and software, cosmetics and personal care, aerospace and defence, pharma, and healthcare occupy the first five places in a ranking of top industry sectors by total intangible value (Brand Finance, 2020, p. 16). A clearer picture of the current structure of corporate intangible capital and corporate structures can be seen in Table 5.1 showing the top 20 global companies by intangible capital.

The growth of intangible capital has also contributed to changes in the world's leading firms, notably with the increasing prominence in the top firms by market capitalization of those with very high levels of intangible

Table 5.1 Top 20 companies by total intangible value

Rank (and 2018 position)	Company	Intangible value ($bn)	Total Intangible value/enterprise value (%)
1 (2)	Microsoft Corp.	904	90%
2 (1)	Amazon	839	93%
3 (3)	Apple Inc.	675	77%
4 (4)	Alphabet Inc.	521	65%
5 (6)	Facebook Inc.	409	79%
6 (9)	AT&T Inc.	371	84%
7 (7)	Tencent Holdings Ltd	365	88%
8 (8)	Johnson & Johnson	361	101%
9 (11)	Visa Inc.	348	100%
10 (5)	Alibaba Group Holding	344	86%
11 (17)	Nestlé SA	313	89%
12 (19)	Proctor & Gamble Co.	305	101%
13 (10)	Anheuser-Busch InBev	304	99%
14 (12)	Verizon Communications Inc.	300	83%
15 (22)	Comcast Corp.	276	92%
16 (20)	Mastercard Inc.	259	99%
17 (29)	Novartis AG	252	101%
18 (-)	Walmart	252	68%
19 (13)	UnitedHealth Group Inc.	245	94%
20 (14)	Pfizer Inc.	235	98%

Source: Brand Finance, 2020, p. 20.

capital. While in the 1970s, there were large firms like IBM and Proctor & Gamble with intangible capital, the proportion of firm value accounted for by it was relatively small (20 percent of firm value), and the largest firms included industrial conglomerates like GE and extractive industry companies like ExxonMobil. By 2018, the largest firms by market capitalization were all intangible-capital-heavy companies; Apple and Microsoft, and even post-industrial firms like Facebook and Amazon (where *tangible* capital comprises 20 percent and less of firm value) (Ponemon Institute, 2019, p. 1).

There are of course at least two ways of accumulating intangible capital: to invest in R&D, marketing, and brand management, or acquiring those assets from developments occurring elsewhere. Intangible-capital-intensive firms have been very active in accumulating further capital by way of acquisition. Some of the largest have acquired a large part of their intangible assets via acquisition. In the last 30 years just five giant tech firms (Facebook, Amazon, Microsoft, Google, and Apple) made over 800 acquisitions, and in the first half of 2020 alone Apple and Microsoft made nine acquisitions. Since 2000, these companies have completed 32 acquisitions, each valued in excess of exceeding $1 billion (CB Insight, 2021, p. 4) Indeed, so important is the buying and selling of assets (including intangible capital) as part of the business model of many intangible-capital-rich firms that they might be thought of as part industrial firm and part financial entity. Apart from financial activity in the form of M&A, intangible-capital-rich corporations also manage large sums of money capital (often held offshore). Apple, for instance, has an investment fund entity (Braeburn Capital) larger than the biggest hedge fund in the world (BlackRock). The *Wall Street Journal* has even gone so far as to describe Apple as a "hedge fund that makes phones" (Gilbert & Hrdlicka, 2018).

The emergence, and indeed now the prominence, of forms of abstract and intangible capital is clear. That rise has been quantitatively significant, but poses more than just quantitative conundrums for analysis, beginning with basic definitional issues. The International Accounting Standards Board defines intangible capital as "an identifiable non-monetary asset without physical substance. An asset is a resource that is controlled by the entity as a result of past events (e.g. purchase or self-creation) and from which future economic benefits (inflows of cash or other assets) are expected" [IAS 38.8]. The Brookings Institute defines intangible assets as "non-physical factors that contribute to, or are used in, the production of goods or the provision of services, or that are expected to generate future productive benefits to the individuals or firms that control their deployment" (Brookings Institute, 2001, p. 9). The OECD, on the other hand, defines intellectual assets (a related category to intangible capital in OECD use) as describing trends in advanced economies toward "greater dependence on knowledge, information and high skill levels, and the increasing need for ready access to these" (OECD, 2005).

In addition to definitional issues of what intangible capital is, the identification of different types of intangible capital is still the subject of ongoing research and theoretical speculation. As one OECD report noted, "various categories of intangibles are described and labels applied. Distinctions are sometimes made between trade intangibles and marketing intangibles, between 'soft' intangibles and 'hard' intangibles, between routine and non-routine intangibles, and between other classes of asset and categories of intangibles" (2015, p. 69). Corrado et al. (2006) identified 13 types of intangible assets. Of these 13 types, only five are recorded in the System of National Accounts. One category of intangible asset, economic competencies—comprised of brand, building, advertisement, market research, training of staff, management consulting, and own organizational investment—is completely absent from national accounts (Corrado, 2009; Haskell &Westlake, 2018). Both business and national income accounts have traditionally treated expenditure on intangibles as intermediate expenditure and not investment (Thum-Thysen et al., 2017, p. 5). Despite that, for many high-tech and pharmaceutical companies, intangible capital represents well over 90 percent of corporate value (Corrado, 2009). The International Accounting Standards Board stopped efforts to incorporate intangibles in measures of firm value some time ago (IASB, 2007), with the OECD noting there was only a "limited possibility to recognize intangible capital in the financial accounts" (OECD, 2006, p. 5). The recording and measurement gap has led to debates on the role of intangibles in the economy. Analyses have suggested slowdowns in growth and productivity can in part be explained by the preponderant role of (under-recorded and often "offshored") intangible assets (and their cash flows) as a source of both total factor productivity growth and national output levels (Ahmad et al., 2017; Bukht & Heeks, 2017; Thum-Thysen et al., 2017; Haskell & Westlake, 2018).

Problems with definition, identification, and measurement of intangible capital remain persistent. While there are some accepted types of intangible capital, a large proportion of the value of intangible capital and of the firms that hold it is uncategorized and unrecorded on the balance sheet. In many sectors the "undisclosed" value of intangibles exceeds both tangible and intangible capital. "Undisclosed" intangible assets include "internally generated goodwill," and accounts for the difference between the fair market value of a business and the value of its identifiable tangible and intangible assets (although this is not an intangible asset in the strictest sense—that is, a controlled "resource" expected to provide future economic benefits).

Even with emerging taxonomies that seek to disaggregate intangible capital, there remains a significant residual that is not covered. According to one measure, in 2019 the global value of firms stood at approximately $110 trillion. Of this $56.4 trillion were tangible assets and $35.4 trillion were "undisclosed value," with the residual accounted for by disclosed intangible assets and disclosed goodwill. In some cases, discrepancies between what is valued and what can be accounted for are extreme. For BAE systems (aerospace) the carrying value of its goodwill recognized because of acquisitions comprises 51 percent of firm value, whereas disclosed intangible assets comprise just 1 percent (Brand Finance, 2020, pp. 10, 19).

One problem that the rise to prominence of intangible capital poses is that there is no consensus about what sort of concept of capital is adequate to analyze the development of intangible forms of capital. A second problem is a related empirical/measurement one. Even changing the concept of intangible value from a residual one (goodwill) to a stand-alone one remains an ongoing challenge. As abstract, non-physical capital has moved beyond the vague catch-all of goodwill, the concept of intangible capital has emerged to replace it. But it too lacks specificity and clarity.

The rapid growth of intangible-rich firms and their acquisitions of rivals in their industries and related sectors has given rise to concerns that these firms are competing by virtue of their sheer size and market power (big tech, big pharma, etc), and that they earn monopolistic-type profits. Similarly, there is concern that these firms are able to use market power, acquisition or undermining of rival firms, and especially patent rights to shield themselves from market competition. Birch has termed these forms of competition and profit-making "techno-science rents" (2019).

As noted earlier, there is also an identifiable financialized logic driving the organization and reorganization of intangible capital, which extends to tax issues, whereby assets, costs, and revenues associated with intangible capital can be and are strategically located in different international jurisdictions so as to arbitrage tax codes. A notable case here is the structuring of entities and rights to intellectual capital revenues known as the double Irish Dutch sandwich. In that tax structure intangible capital takes on a triple life, with intangible capital having one home for legal protection (United States), one for the collection of revenue streams (Ireland), and one for the payment of taxes (Bermuda) (Bryan et al., 2017a, pp. 67–68). Market dominance and the low tax contributions made by these giant tech firms have begun to draw these firms into the regulatory and policy limelight.

While the determinative role of intangibles in economic life is widely recognized, it has already been noted that the concepts we deploy to understand them have not kept up with their growing significance. This inadequacy produces a concept–regulation–corporate form disjuncture where the concepts used to comprehend economic life are inadequate in informing regulation able to build traction in monitoring these innovative forms of capital (Wigan, 2021). This is apparent in the regulatory challenges posed by the digital economy to tax authorities. The traction of national tax laws on the digital economy is an ongoing and pressing policy concern. The European Union's 2018 digital tax proposal was predicated upon explicit recognition that current rules on the taxation of multinational companies (MNCs), which rest on a (national) physical nexus between the place of value creation and the taxation of profits, had become outdated (EC, 2018). Three conceptual dislocations between firms operating in the digital economy and tax rules designed for an earlier era of "atoms not bites" drive the concept–regulation–corporate form gap and point to where capital is outgrowing the institutional and policy containers previously thought to constrain or harness it.

Taxing bits not atoms

Nation-based income tax is a critical and conspicuous expression of the challenge of global intangibles to conventional value chain analysis. In intangible forms, capital has taken on a double life expressed in legal and geographical dislocation between the value chain that produces the goods and services which undergird (intangible) capitalization and the onward journey of wealth unfolding in non-linear patterns through the wealth chain. Our position is not that the implications of global intangibles can be reduced to issues of tax (or any other form of) arbitrage, but rather that tax arbitrage provides a useful "window" on the systemic transformations that are becoming apparent in the wake of the emergence of a global political economy dominated by intangible capital. The concept-regulation–corporate form disjuncture provides a means of opening up some of the analytical issues that arise in that context.

The first conceptual dislocation constraining the traction of national tax systems is about the criteria for establishing the regulatory presence of a company or activity within a given territory. Digital economy firms can supply services in a jurisdiction without (taxable) physical presence.

Software can be delivered from a cloud on a server, where the place of that server is an easily moveable feast. That place can then be strategically selected on the basis of legal affordances available, including tax rules and rates, and the interaction of those rules with rules elsewhere (Grasten et al. 2021).

The right to impose tax on an income stream or economic activity is governed by the OECD's Model Tax Convention and encoded in bilateral international treaties (Rixen, 2011). With around 3,000 in force globally, tax treaties apportion, often invidiously, the right to tax between countries on the basis of principles of "source" and "residence" (Hearson, 2018, and Chapter 3 in this volume). "Residence" refers to the home country of the investing entity.[1] "Source" is where the economic activity takes place. The distribution of the right to tax between source and residence is in part determined on the basis of the concept of permanent residence. This relies upon various temporal and substantive thresholds that determine taxable presence in a given jurisdiction, but firms, especially those with intangible revenue streams, can manage that presence to optimize tax exposure. Companies with digitalized business models frequently require neither prolonged nor substantive physical presence in a jurisdiction to maintain significant economic operations there.

Digital firms can structure sales and related activities such as warehousing in source countries as auxiliary and preparatory so these activities do not lead to the determination of permanent establishment status. Amazon, for instance, pursued a legal argument in a UK court that Amazon's UK subsidiary merely executed a trade directed elsewhere. The firm contended that the UK trade executed by the subsidiary was orchestrated by a Luxembourg resident Amazon company. In consequence, Amazon did not consider that it maintained a permanent establishment in the UK (Quentin, 2017, pp. 24–26). Tax systems rely upon stable concepts to identify a nexus between place and economic activity. This assumes a symmetry between the nation and the economic activity. That symmetry is breaking down in the face of the intangible economy.

Second, transfer pricing rules—that regulate accepted prices for exchanges between corporate entities within a firm—rest on analysis of the location of functions, risks, and assets in the value chain of a group (see Christensen, Chapter 11 in this volume). But in global wealth chains,

---

[1] Home is defined by reference to the "predominant centre of a corporation's economic interest" (OECD Glossary of Foreign Direct Investment Terms and Definitions), which is itself defined by financial calculus; not just the "site" of physical production.

the nominated location may not be readily identifiable when users provide content and data to create value and the (intangible) assets assumed to generate value are themselves not easily measured and valued. Firms with "scale without mass" often eschew the ownership of, and ties to, the physical capital that underpins the value chain analysis that informs the distribution of taxing rights. Launching its base erosion and profit-shifting initiative, the OECD pointed to "fundamental questions as to how enterprises in the digital economy add value and make their profits, and how the digital economy relates to concepts of source and residence or the characterization of income for tax purposes" (OECD, 2013, p. 10).

The allocation of tax burdens across a value chain follows analysis of points of added value and assumptions about risk bearing. Here, a linear economic process runs from financing, sourcing raw materials, through research and development, design, production, to marketing, sales, delivery, and consumption. Each point in the process is considered readily identifiable and discrete. But linearity and compartmentalization are negated by the intangible economy. Questions of "what is production?" and "what is consumption?" are increasingly ambiguous and so, thereby, are questions of the location of value creation. Intangible economy firms target advertising on grounds of information collected from user search history and patterns. Content on platforms such as Facebook, Instagram, and TikTok is "user" generated. In ongoing deliberation over how to tax the digital economy, the OECD reports that a number of member states hold that in

> some business models the collection through a digital platform of data and content contributions from users in a jurisdiction and the use of that data to attract other users to the platform and to direct advertising back at the users, are activities integral to the creation of value by the business that effectively take place in that jurisdiction, even if the platform is operated remotely.
>
> (OECD, 2018, p. 25)

Third, firms in the digital economy are disproportionately comprised of intangible assets and intangible assets are readily relocated and hard to value (OECD, 2018). In the intangible economy place is legally often quite fluid and so wealth chain assets can be strategically "placed." Attributes of intangible assets can be unbundled (into regional licensing entities located in different tax environments or other preferred states) and therefore be in several places (often at the same time), depending on financial and accounting objectives. As US Senator Carl Levin, Chairman of the Permanent Subcommittee on Investigations, remarked, launching hearings into the use of offshore financial centers by many IP-rich corporations; "High tech is probably the number-one user of offshore entities. That's because many of their assets are intangible intellectual property, which is hard to value and easy to move" (quoted in Lochhead, 2012).

The elevated mobility of intangible assets has increased along with their recognition and the ability to isolate the assets for strategic financial ends that follows. In this we see the breaking down of the corporation as capital's institutional container. The "J.Crew trapdoor" refers to what are often private equity firms incorporating into high-yield, increasingly "covenant–lite," debt contracts clauses that allow assets to be separated from the borrower and placed into a subsidiary that is not susceptible to current bond-holder claims. In 2011 TPG and Leonard Green & Partners bought the US retailer J.Crew in a $3-billion leveraged buyout. The acquired firm then borrowed a further $787 million that was largely used to fund returns to the private equity firms. In 2016, these firms used a clause in its debt covenants to strip out the IP assets that had been used as collateral for $1.5 billion of debt from the acquisition. The IP was then located in a shell company, which was later used as security for new debt that would be paid off first in the event of bankruptcy—a fate that materialized in May 2020 (Rennison, 2020).

The three conceptual dislocations highlighted here allow for heuristic delineations between firm value chains and firm wealth chains. Platform economy firm Uber relies for competitive advantage on its drivers that supply cars, fuel, labor, and rides.[2] This is the economic core of the value chain. Uber, however, does not maintain an economic presence in the vast majority of the jurisdictions in which drivers using its "matching service" operate, claiming it is an information economy firm delivering services at distance. It is on these grounds that the firm accesses the legal affordances that comprise its global wealth chain. While to date Uber has failed to post a profit and is therefore not subject to profit tax, its wealth chain does pose distinct challenges to tax authorities (Wigan, 2021). One of these challenges is the inability of tax authorities to raise value added tax (VAT) on the rides supplied by its "partner" drivers. Another is the liability of Uber to employment benefits and social insurance payments. A case at the UK Supreme Court hinged on whether Uber employs its drivers or provides an information service to them, and relatedly, whether the customer has a contract with the driver 'partner' or directly with Uber. If the court

---

[2] Uber and some other platform ride-sharing firms even have financial services to facilitate purchase of lease of vehicles.

deemed Uber an employer and the contract to be between the customer and Uber, the firm would be liable for as much as a £1.1 billion backdated VAT payment and a 20 percent VAT charge going forward. It would also be obliged to provide a minimum wage and holiday time along with paying 13.2 percent in national insurance contributions on behalf of its then drivers (Dawkins, 2020). The UK Supreme Court decided against Uber and a subsequent challenge to the decision from Uber at the High Court in London failed (Lex 2021). At stake in this on-going confrontation are the competitive advantages enjoyed by the firm on the basis of economic presence through the value chain and the legal mutability of presence (time and space) in the wealth chain.

At base, the issue of tax arbitrage in the intangible economy revolves around that concepts of value production, and the value chain analysis that is informed by them and in turn inform taxing rights, have been undermined by the intangible economy. Tax systems rely on stable concepts of the identity, location, and timing of a transaction, but intangible capital operates in fluid and mutable ways that make identity, location, and timing strategic rather than functional to the geography of firm production. Persistent definitional uncertainties and the absence of conceptual consensus around intangible capital point to a fundamental paradox. Even as the knowledge economy in advanced economies is perceived to be the key driver of growth and competitive position, concepts of capital deployed in economics and accounting (and regulation) are inadequate when faced with the task of capturing and analyzing knowledge in economic life. This is made even more challenging when we consider the way nation states have unbundled aspects of their own sovereignty in ways to get capital in different forms to "spend time" in their jurisdictions. Conceptually and empirically, we are dealing with fluid and moving targets of capital and internationalization.

Intangible capital beyond GVC

The historical question posed by these recent developments is: How generalizable are GVC and GPN across time? While these paradigms have helped researchers analyze more spatially extended and fluid forms of international commodity production and trade, as noted at the outset two developments in particular challenge GVC and GPN as general frameworks in international political economy and economic geography.

The first is the growing global role and movement of money and finance, including the exponential growth of debt in the world economy and on corporate balance sheets, as source of funds for investing in value chains and networks, and the rise of a culture of shareholder value driving corporate cost-cutting and outsourcing. But of special significance here are innovations that helped finance develop a capacity to create exposures to the performance of corporations, to various assets and liabilities of corporations, as well as to events or attributes of wider economic and financial activity, without the necessity to own the underlying bits of capital themselves (Bryan & Rafferty, 2006; Wigan, 2008). This has increased the ability to speculate and hedge increasingly uncertain futures, and in the process price attributes of assets and activities, that has helped facilitate the spatial unbundling of assets and activities that GVC and GPN approaches have attempted to describe and analyze. Financial innovation has also blurred earlier institutional boundaries between different forms of finance (equity and debt), between industry and finance (GE Capital and Apple's Braeburn Capital are notable examples), and between inside and outside of corporations (joint ventures, subcontacting, and private equity are examples here). It also means that money, capital, and finance can now live a sort of "double life," related to, but distinct from, the movement of commodities through physical value chains and production networks.

In decomposing economic activity into bits that can be thought of in terms of risk, finance has also created the capacity to trade and price these attributes. By reconceptualizing activities and assets in terms of risk, finance has provided a means of valuing and pricing (commensurating) these fluid and abstract forms of production and trade. Here, we refer especially to the roles of financial derivatives, shadow banking, offshore finance, special purpose vehicles, and so on that enable companies to decompose or respecify balance sheet items and even cash flows. This occurs in ways that both create the possibility of a different spatial and temporal "journey" for money capital and wealth, and effectively also distinguish them from the physical chains and networks of exchange (Bryan et al., 2016). While there have been a number of attempts to bring finance and money capital into GVC and GPN, these have been limited so far by conceptual limitations, as well as empirical measurement issues.

One response to that conceptual challenge has been the development of a global wealth chains (GWC) concept to supplement GVC-style analysis (Seabrooke & Wigan, 2014, 2017, and Chapters 1 and 14 in this volume). Whether GWC can or will "fill" the conceptual and empirical void, it is too early to tell. What we can say with certainty is that money and finance has from the outset been a blind spot in GVC/GPN analysis, and perhaps more speculatively, the growing scale and significance of money capital suggests that international capital may be transcending the confines of this type of analysis.

The second development, the focus of this chapter, is the rise of abstract and intangible forms of capital. The growth of intangible capital has been perhaps the most significant development in the industrial asset structure of the last quarter-century. We know that the factoryless goods producers like Apple and Nike own very little in the way of production facilities. Instead, by strategic use of design and marketing, as well as detailed control over outsourced subcontractors and supply chains, they are able to generate large profits. We also know that many companies are able to leverage their brands to earn rents that are disproportionate to the size of physical capital involved. But there are range of other developments, notably including the emergence of platform businesses like Google, Facebook, Uber, and Amazon that provide service hubs for consumers and sellers, and are being valued almost entirely on the basis of their intangible capital. These firms not only do not own factories, but their services often create or more accurately capture value being created outside of the putative factories of the Fordist era, wherever they may be and whoever owns them. This occurs variously in the labor of "affect," in prosumption and in the generation of new forms of commodification, digital objects, and big data that can then sold in various forms (Hardt, 1999; Martin, 2002; Mayer-Schönberger & Ramge, 2018; Fuchs, 2019). There is often a direct link here between intangibles and finance, where monetization is not just the direct purpose of platforms and the like, but the forms of intangible capital (like big data) are also in large part forms of financial capital (Haiven, 2014). Indeed, a decade ago the World Economic Forum suggested that data was emerging as a new asset class (WEF, 2011).

Many of the firms with large endowments of intangible assets have quite small amounts of fixed assets in buildings, plant, and equipment. For some of these intangible-asset-rich firms, actual commodity production and transfers (chains) are a small part of their turnover. Instead, their asset base is dominated by intellectual property (IP) assets, patents (especially brand names), as well as franchises and other legal affordances. This has raised the question, pace Sawhneh and Parikh (2001), not just of where value lives in a networked world, but of where it lives in abstract commodity networks. Enabled by the spatial and temporal capacities of new abstract networks, intangible capital is readily instrumentalized to relo-cate presence and strategically disaggregate the corporation in ways that are not easily captured by production-centered analytical frameworks, and the regulatory architecture that is built upon them.

In the logic of the financial derivative, value chains and production networks can be respecified so as to give lead firms exposure to the (value-generating) performance of extended production, logistical, and consumption processes, without necessarily owning much of the produc-tion assets and activities themselves (see Haslam, Leaver, and Tsitsianis, Chapter 2 in this volume, for a related depiction of the firm). Lead firms leverage their ownership or control of key attributes or stages of a value chain, such as design and marketing, via ownership of patents, trademarks, and so on. This permits the unbundling of either the production process and relocation of various activities to maximize the spread between costs and revenues from these activities, or in the case of platforms and so on, the rights to intangible capital and cash flows that accrue to that capital.

As capital becomes more liquid, mutable, financial, and intangible, GVC-type analysis is perhaps not best placed to track its development, ei-ther conceptually or empirically. The GVC approach is of course premised on the capacity to follow a commodity as it is exchanged through stages of production, which in spatio-temporal terms are more or less linear, and its imaginary inter-national. This is a value-added (adding up) discourse, familiar in standard national accounting measures of GDP. In the latter context, where data are only ever approximate, it is presumed possible to differentiate how much of the value of final output is created in each stage and each country. Applied to GVCs, it is presumed possible to decom-pose the value of final outputs to give linear precision to the exact stage of production and the location in which each element of final value is added.

Further, how can value really be "attributed" along a chain or network, any more than value creation along a mass production conveyor belt can be measured at say 10-meter intervals? Unless an "output" at any link in the chain can find a direct price, it is either misleading or trivial to attribute to it a value. Modern portfolio theory might tell us more than price theory here—that if you treat any output as an asset, its value can only be de-termined by its context—in this case its "place" and strategic importance in the portfolio flow of components and risks in the production process. What we see in the most complex wealth chains is the spatial and tem-poral linearity of exchange and nationality of capital being broken down and refigured.[3] Capital, once institutionally coherent inside of MNCs, is increasingly decentered (Desai, 2008), presenting in each nation state as a strategically optioned politico-legal space, where attributes of a partial set of assets engage regulatory conditions to optimize via unbundled state sovereignty, in tax havens, special economic zones and the like. Disaggregated components or attributes of assets engage partially to arbitrage regulatory and jurisdictional differences between and within states, and, as critical legal scholars have termed it, to optimize via "partial lift-off" and "targeted touchdown" (Wai, 2002, 2008; Biggins, 2012).

This process of decentering and spatio-temporal innovation challenges us to consider how to analyze asset forms that have the following sorts of characteristics: they are produced across a corporate calculus of space and time; can express as different forms or magnitudes of capital in different spaces; and can, in a financial and accounting sense, be in more than one place at a time, for different purposes.

Conclusion

At the outset of this chapter we noted Richard Walker's comment that the ontological primacy that the field gave to the capitalist firm elided the fact that firms are not the only way that capital as a social relation of production and trade is organized and extended on an international level. "The firm," Walker noted, "is not the only container for production . . . . It is unfortunate that the corporation was substituted for capital in the lexicon of economics and geography" (1989, p. 61). Walker concluded his review with a historical call, suggesting that recent industrial and financial innovation meant that "perhaps we have come to a time when capital is outgrowing the corporation, as presently constituted" (1989, p. 63). This was a prescient call for economic geography, but that was not the only research area that had privileged the ontological primacy of corporations as discrete units of economic analysis, so the conceptual crisis was felt across several disciplines in the early 1990s. Walker also noted that corporate geography's concept of capital had been infused with capital in use to the neglect of capital as value in motion (or perhaps as we'd put it in the derivative form, as attributes of risk and value in motion). Walker wanted a project that synthesizes the two, and for us this is the challenge that GWC analyses and

---

[3] For discussion of transformations in capital's spatiality and territoriality, see Bryan et al., 2017a, 2017b.

others that seek to respond to the rise of financial and intangible capital must meet.

This chapter has discussed how the challenge now is more than just de-institutionalizing the concept of capital. Developments since the 1990s, especially in the interaction between intangible capital and financial innovation, show that processes of unbundling capital are occurring so as both to give liquidity to capital and to valorize conceptual and locational ambiguity. Capital is not just "flowing" from one physical location to another, or existing somewhere within a network of MNCs. We need to be open to new and emerging forms of blending financial and non-financial attributes of accumulation, which organizationally are seen in firms becoming part industrial firm and part hedge fund manager, and financially can be seen in capital living an increasingly double (or triple) life. Further, we have shown that in commensurating new forms of capital such as intangible assets and giving liquidity to them, earlier spatio-temporal logics are being transcended. These are some of the challenges that this chapter poses for the GWC concept and others that wish to address intangible capital and financialization.

The impacts of these innovatory phenomena are important in their own right, not least because they support inequalities and restrict policy space. They are also important because they are pointing to where the GWC project might be heading. Intangible capital, like value chains and production networks, may exist in networks of flows, but it may not exist in the linear relations of GVC and GPN, where space and time are fixed. Thanks to its abstract nature, and especially when it is inserted into modern finance, its spatial and even temporal properties can be strategically recast. IP developed in one location and over a certain time may, for example, by granting licensing rights to a special purpose vehicle in an offshore jurisdiction, effectively become co-located. And via the ability to transform attributes of the capital via networks of financial transactions (where rights to cash flows are unbundled and reassigned), even the temporality of that capital can be reinscribed.

We have called this development (following Pryke & Allen, 2000) finance's new space–time (Bryan et al., 2017b). Financial space–time is becoming different because finance has developed the capacity not just to identify spatio-temporal mispricing, but to organize and reorganize on the basis of arbitraging difference. The basis of "difference-making" is leveraged by finance through the notion of risk and through the different exposures and strategic options made possible through finance. If this observation about new space–time relations of capital, especially intangible capital, is correct, we may need to move our conceptual and even our regulatory agendas beyond linear notions of capital toward more quantum notions of relation and movement. This challenge alone is a serious research agenda for GWC scholars.

References

Ahmad, N., Ribarsky, J., & Reinsdorf, M. (2017). Can potential mismeasurement of the digital economy explain the post-crisis slowdown in GDP and productivity growth? *OECD Statistics Working Papers 2017/09*. OECD.

Bair, J. & Werner, M. (2011). Commodity chains and the uneven geogrpahies of global capitalism: A disarticulations perspective. *Environment & Planning A*, 43, 988–997.

Baldwin, R. (2011). Trade and industrialization after globalization's 2nd unbundling. How building and joining a supply chain are different and why it matters. *NBER Working Paper 17716*. National Bureau of Economic Research.

Baldwin, R. (2016). *The Great Convergence: Information Technology and the New Globalization*. Harvard University Press.

Baldwin, R., Ito, T., & Sato, H. (2014). Portrait of factory Asia: Production network in Asia and its implication for growth—the "smile curve." *Joint Research Program Series 159*. Institute of Developing Economies-Japan External Trade Organization.

Bernstein, H. & Campling, L. (2006). Commodity studies and commodity fetishism I: *Trading Down*. *Journal of Agrarian Change*, 6(2), 239–264.

Biggins, J. (2012). "Targeted touchdown" and "partial liftoff": Post-crisis dispute resolution in the OTC derivatives markets and the challenge for ISDA. *German Law Journal*, 13(12), 1299–1328.

Birch, K. (2019) Technoscience rent: Toward a theory of *rentiership* for technoscientific capitalism. *Science, Technology & Human Values*, 45(1), 1–33.

Brand Finance. (2020). Global Intangible Finance Tracker: An annual review of the world's intangible capital. Brand Finance. https://brandfinance.com/images/upload/gift_2.pdf.

Brenner, R. (1977). The Origins of Capitalist development: A critique of neo-Smithian Marxism. *New Left review*, 104, 25–92.

Bryan, D (1995). The internationalisation of capital and Marxian value theory. *Cambridge Journal of Economics*, 19(3), 421–440.

Bryan, D. & Rafferty, M. (2006). *Capitalism with Derivatives: A Political Economy of Financial Derivatives, Capital and Class*. Palgrave Macmillan.

Bryan, D., Rafferty, M., &Wigan, D. (2016). Politics, time and space in the era of shadow banking. *Review of International Political Economy*, 23(6), 941–966.

Bryan, D., Rafferty, M., &Wigan, D. (2017a). Capital unchained: Finance, intangible assets and the double life of capital in the offshore world. *Review of International Political Economy* 24(1), 56–86.

Bryan, D., Rafferty, M., &Wigan, D. (2017b). From time–space compression to spatial spreads situating nationality in global financial liquidity. In B. Christophers, A. Leyshon, & G. Mann (Eds.), *Money and Finance After the Crisis: Critical Thinking for Uncertain Times*. Wiley-Blackwell, 43–67.

Bukht, R. &Heeks, R. (2017). Defining, conceptualising and measuring the digital economy. *Working Paper No. 68*. University of Manchester, Centre for Development Informatics, Global Development Institute.

Coe, N., Dicken, P., & Hess, M. (2008). Global production networks: realizing the potential. *Journal of Economic Geography*, 8(3), 271–295.

Coe, N. & Yeung, H. (2015). *Global Production Networks: Theorizing Economic Development in an Interconnected World*. Oxford University Press.

Corrado, C. (2009) *Intangible Assets: Measuring and Enhancing Their Contribution to Corporate Value and Economic Growth: Summary of a Workshop*. National Academies Press, National Research Council.

Corrado, C., Haskel, J., Jona-Lasinio, C. & Massimiliano, I. (2016). Intangible investment in the EU and US before and since the Great Recession and its contribution to productivity growth. *EIB Working Papers, No. 2016/08*. European Investment Bank.

Corrado, C., Hulten, C., & Sichel, D. (2006). Intangible capital and economic growth. *NBER Working Paper No. W11948*. National Bureau of Economic Research.

Dawkins, D. (2020). "Uber Vs. London: the Courtroom Battle the World is Watching." *Forbes*. July 30.

Dedrick, J. & Kraemer, K. L. (2017). Intangible assets and value capture in global value chains: the smartphone industry, *WIPO Economic Research Working Paper No. 41*. World Intellectual Property Organization.

Desai, M. (2008). The decentering of the global firm. *Working Paper 09-054*. Harvard Business School.

Dunning, J. H. (1977). Trade, location of economic activity and the multinational enterprise: A search for an eclectic approach. In B. G. Ohlin, P. O. Hesselborn, & P. M. Wijkman (eds.), *The International Allocation of Economic Activity:*

Proceedings of a Nobel Symposium Held at Stockholm. Palgrave Macmillan, 395–418.

Durand, C. & Milberg, W. (2020). Intellectual monopoly in global value chains. *Review of International Political Economy*, 27(2), 404–429.

EC (2018). Proposal for a Council Directive on the common system of a digital services tax on revenues resulting from the provision of certain digital services. COM (2018) 148. European Commission.

Fuchs, C. (2019). Karl Marx in the age of big data capitalism. In D. Chandler & C. Fuchs (eds.), *Digital Object, Digital Subjects: Interdisciplinary Perspective on Capital, Labour and Politics in ther Age of Big Data*. University of Westminster Press, 53–72.

Gereffi, G. (1994). The organization of buyer-driven global commodity chains: How US retailers shape overseas production networks. In G. Gereffi & M. Korzeniewicz, M. (eds.). *Commodity Chains and Global Capitalism*. Praeger, 95–122.

Gereffi, G., Humphrey, J., & Sturgeon, T. (2005). The governance of global value chains. *Review of International Political Economy*, 12(1), 78–104.

Gerefii, G. & Korzeniewicz, M. (eds.) (1994). *Commodity Chains and Global Capitalism*. Praeger.

Gibbon, P., Bair, J., & Ponte, S. (2008). Governing global value chains: An introduction. *Economy and Society* (37)3, 315–338.

Gilbert, T. & Hrdlicka, C. (2018). "Apple is a hedge fund that makes phones: Big companies need to disclose more about their investments." *Wall Street Journal*. August 23.

Grabs, J. & Ponte, S. (2019). The evolution of power in the global coffee value chain and production network. *Journal of Economic Geography*, 19(4), 803–828.

Grasten, M., Seabrooke, L., & Wigan, D. (2021). Legal affordances in global wealth chains: How platform firms use legal and spatial scaling. *Environment and Planning A: Economy and Space*, DOI: 10.1177/0308518X211057131.

Hagel, J. & Singer, M. (2000). Unbundling the corporation. *The McKinsey Quarterly*, 3, 148–161.

Haiven, M. (2014). *Crises of Imagination, Crises of Power: Capitalism, Creativity and the Commons*. Zed Books.

Hardt, M. (1999). Affective labour. *Boundary*, 26(2), 89–100.

Haskell, J. & Westlake, S. (2018). *Capitalism Without Capital: The Rise of the Intangible Economy*. Princeton University Press.

Hearson, M. (2018). Transnational expertise and the expansion of the international tax regime: imposing "acceptable" standards. *Review of International Political Economy*, 25(5), 647–671.

Henderson, J., Dicken, P., Hess, M., Coe, N., & Wai-Chung Yeung, H. (2002). Global production networks and the analysis of economic development. *Review of International Political Economy*, 9(3), 436–464.

Humphrey, J. & Schmitz, H. (2002). How does insertion in global value chains affect upgrading in industrial clusters? *Regional Studies*, 36(9), 1017–1027.

Hymer, S. (1970). The efficiency (contradictions) of multinational corporations. *American Economic Review*, 60(29), 411–418.

Hymer, S. (1976). *The International Operations of National Firms: A Study on Direct Foreign Investment*. MIT Press.

IASB (2007). Intangible Assets: Project Update. International Accounting Standards Board.

Jones, C. A. (1987). *International Business in the Nineteenth Century: The Rise and Fall of a Cosmopolitan Bourgoisie*. Wheatsheaf.

Kaplinsky, R. (2005). *Globalization, Inequality, and Poverty: Between a Rock and a Hard Place*. Polity.

Knickerbocker, F. T. (1973). *Oligopolistic Reaction and Multinational Enterprise*. Harvard University.

Lex (2021) "Gig economy/Uber: UK ruling adds to pressure on shakey business model." *Financial Times*. December 7.

Lochhead, C. (2012). Tech firms find havens from US taxes. https://www.sfgate.com/politics/article/Tech-firms-find-havens-from-U-S-taxes-3882486.php. *SFGATE*. September 20.

Martin, R. (2002). *Financialization of Daily Life*. Temple University Press.

Mayer-Schönberger, V. & Ramge, T. (2018). *Re-inventing Capitalism in the Age of Big Data*. Basic Books.

Nakamura, L. I. (2008). Intangible assets and national income accounting. *Working Paper No. 08-23*. Federal Reserve Board of Philadelphia.

Ocean Tomo (2020). Intangible Asset Market Value Study—Interim Update. https://www.oceantomo.com/intangible-asset-market-value-study/.

OECD (2005). The Measurement of Scientific and Technological Activities: Guidelines for Collecting and Interpreting Innovation Data: Oslo Manual, Third Edition. Working Party of National Experts on Scientific and Technology Indicators. OECD, para. 71.

OECD (2006). Intellectual Assets and Value Creation: Implications for Corporate Reporting. OECD.

OECD (2013). Action Plan on Base Erosion and Profit Shifting. OECD.

OECD (2015). Aligning Transfer Pricing Outcomes with Value Creation. OECD/G20 Base Erosion and Profit Shifting Project – Actions 8–10, Final Report. OECD.

OECD (2018). Tax Challenges Arising from Digitalisation – Interim Report 2018. OECD.

Ponemon Institute (2019). 2019 Intangible Assets Financial Statement Impact Comparison Report. Ponemon Institute LLC. https://www.aon.com/getmedia/60fbb49a-c7a5-4027-ba98-0553b29dc89f/Ponemon-Report-V24.aspx.

Price, C. (2019, June 12). The Knowledge economy, intangible assets and public wealth. On the level. OECD. https://oecdonthelevel.com/2019/06/12/the-knowledge-economy-intangible-assets-and-public-wealth/.

Pryke, M. & Allen, J. (2000). Monetized time-space: Derivatives—money's "new imaginary"? *Economy and Society*, 29(2), 264–284.

Quentin, D. (2017). Risk-mining the public exchequer. *Journal of Tax Administration* 3(2), 22–35.

Rennison, J. (2020). "Asset transfers leave creditors feeling 'J Screwed.'" *Financial Times*, June 5.

Rixen, T. (2011). From double taxation to tax competition: Explaining the institutional trajectory of international tax governance. *Review of International Political Economy*, 18(2), 197–227.

Sawhney, R. & Parikh, D. (2001). Where value lives in a networked world. *Harvard Business Review*, 79(1), 79–86.

Schwartz, H. M. (2021). Global secular stagnation and the rise of intellectual property monopoly. *Review of International Political Economy*. Advance online publication. DOI: 10.1080/09692290.2021.1918745.

Seabrooke, L. & Wigan, D. (2014). Global wealth chains in the international political economy. *Review of International Political Economy*, 21(1), 257–263.

Seabrooke, L. & Wigan, D. (2017). The governance of global wealth chains. *Review of International Political Economy*, 24(1), 1–26.

Selwyn, B. (2018). Poverty chains and global capitalism. *Competition & Change*, 23(5), 71–97.

Servan-Schrieber, J. J. (1968). *The American Challenge*. Versilio.

Thum-Thysen, A., Voigt, P., Bilbao-Osorio, B., Maier, C., & Ognyanova, D. (2017). Unlocking Investment in Intangible Assets. *Discussion Paper 047*. European Commission.

Wai, R. (2002). Transnational liftoff and juridicial touchdown: the regulatory function of private international law in the era of globalization. *Columbia Journal of Transnational Law*, 40(2), 209–274.

Wai, R. (2008). The Interlegality of International Private Law. *Law and Contemporary Problems*, 71(3), 107–127.

Walker, R. (1989). A requiem for corporate geography: New directions in industrial organization, the production of place and the uneven development. *Geografiska Annaler*, 71B(1), 43–68.

Weeks, J. & Dore, E. (1979) International exchange and the causes of backwardness. *Latin American Perspectives*, 6(2) 62–87.

Wigan, D. (2008). A global political economy of derivatives: Risk, property and the artifice of indifference. (Doctoral dissertation, University of Sussex).

Wigan, D. (2021). Uber global wealth chains. In B. Unger, L. Rossel, & J. Ferwerda (eds.), *Combatting Fiscal Fraud and Empowering Regulators*. Oxford University Press.

World Economic Forum (2011). *Personal Data: The Emergence of a New Asset Class*. World Economic Forum.

6

Private Equity

Jamie Morgan

Introduction

The global wealth chain (GWC) concept takes as its point of departure global value chain literature. It is posed as the "yin to the yang of value chains" (Seabrooke & Wigan, 2014, p. 257). The point of a GWC perspective is to orient on the many ways in which linked forms of capital capture, concentrate, and protect wealth. This underlies the conceptual nuance of the various GWC governance types set out in the editors' introductory chapter (Chapter 1; see also Seabrooke & Wigan, 2017). The GWC concept encourages investigations that explore how capital can "break loose from the location of value creation and heighten inequality" (Seabrooke & Wigan, 2014, p. 257). The contemporary organization and ownership of firms provides a prime example of GWCs (see Bryan et al., Chapter 5 in this volume). Amongst other things, financialization has introduced a new layer of ownership and management interests and concerns for the firm. A firm becomes a financial instrument (see Haslam et al., Chapter 2 in this volume on the financialization of public utilities). Private equity finance (PEF) in turn provides an illustration of how financialized practices can lead to a GWC situation and how assets as legal affordances create opportunities for the pursuance of strategies that distinguish value creation from wealth. As a point of initial clarification, in what follows the ordinary language sense of firm refers to what PEF calls an acquisition or portfolio company.

Private equity finance

Private equity typically has three distinguishable parts: the private equity firm, fund, and acquisitions. Private equity firms are organizations that

Jamie Morgan, *Private Equity*. In: *Global Wealth Chains*. Edited by Leonard Seabrooke and Duncan Wigan, Oxford University Press. © Jamie Morgan (2022). DOI: 10.1093/oso/9780198832379.003.0006 provide a general partner (GP) and a team who undertake and manage given investments (Phalippou, 2017). The firm solicits investment capital from institutional investors and high-net-worth individuals (HNWIs) and this forms a separate private equity fund. Not just anyone is eligible to invest in a fund because, as alternative investment forms, they are positioned as high risk for the investor. This is because they are illiquid since one cannot typically trade or withdraw one's investment, and they are differently regulated and subject to oversight exemptions in most jurisdictions; so one must usually establish that one can bear the potential loss and/or is aware of the nature of the investment.[1] The private equity firm sets a target solicitation for the fund, and the fund will usually have some specified focus for its activity—an industry, strategy, region, or combination (though it may also be a fund of funds whose purpose is to invest in other funds). Funds are structured as separate legal entities, typically either a limited liability partnership or limited liability company (firms are also often LLPs/LLCs).[2] Investors are contracted on the basis of a private placement memorandum (PPM), which sets out the terms and scope of the fund. Investors are referred to as limited partners (LPs) and are "passive"; the GP manages the fund on their behalf. LPs commit a given sum of capital to the fund, but may not be called upon to actually supply it until investments are made. Once the target for the fund is achieved the fund is closed and becomes operative. The year in which capital begins to be drawn down for investment purposes is usually referred to as the vintage year. Funds are typically closed-end investments, with a defined lifespan, usually 10 years.

For our purposes the main activity of private equity is the buyout. That is, the acquisition of a target business. Historically this has included divisions of conglomerates. The private equity firm typically provides some of

---

[1] For example, in the US, in order to be exempt from full registration with the SEC under Rule 506 in Regulation D of the Securities Act of 1933, a PEF firm has not been able to publicly offer its services to investors in general. It has only been able to solicit indirectly through networks of recommendations within and across the finance industry. The concept of "sophistication" is augmented by Rule 501 of Regulation D of the Securities Act, requiring that the majority of investors are "accredited"; that is, sufficiently wealthy to bear the costs of investments that fall outside the jurisdiction of the SEC. In 2011, Rule 501 stated this as a net worth for an individual exceeding $1,000,000 (excluding the value of their primary residence) and for corporations, trusts, and charitable organizations, net assets exceeding $5,000,000. The Dodd–Frank Act of 2010 has also created a number of transitional changes affecting the concept (see Morgan & Sheehan, 2015). However, the intent remains the same as it has always been, and that is to provide some degree of limit and awareness for the investor that PEF is an area of investment risk that is different than engaging in investment through publicly listed markets. The European Alternative Investment Fund Manager's Directive (AIFM) covers similar territory.

[2] Some of the larger firms may also now be partly publicly listed. Notable examples include KKR, Blackstone, and Apollo. It is also now possible to participate in private equity via listed investment vehicles. GP may also refer to more than one person.

the capital for the buyout, either directly or via an investment in one of its own funds. However, this is usually a small proportion of the total cost of the acquisition (as little as 2 percent). Some proportion of the fund capital provides the majority of the equity for the buyout, and with larger-value acquisitions firms/GPs may use capital from a combination of funds, and also engage in collaborative buyouts involving several private equity firms (consortia). Thereafter, the buyout is typically augmented by the use of debt, and this is why the term leveraged buyout (LBO) is used. The amount of debt as a proportion of the cost (usually phrased as total value) of the buyout is variable, but in large LBOs is rarely less than 50 percent, tends to increase as the scale of the buyout increases, typically ranges from 60 to 70 percent, and historically can be more than 90 percent (see Kaplan & Stein, 1993; Kaplan & Schoar, 2005; Axelson et al., 2013; Appelbaum & Batt, 2014).

The GP must consider how much credit is available and under what terms, how much debt the acquisition can service, and also the total capital within the fund in comparison to the cost of each acquisition. The fund is an investment vehicle, and the GP's role is to generate returns to the fund based on a portfolio of investments. The private equity firm and GP receive a management fee (around 2 percent of capital annually), they earn carried interest from the fund (typically 20 percent of returns) subject to a "hurdle" (a return threshold that must be exceeded), and they apply monitoring and other fees to acquisitions. The GP will look to use up the fund equity in significant blocks, since there are a limited number of acquisitions a GP can undertake and then manage within the 10-year lifespan of the fund. The typical holding of each acquisition is between three and five years. See Figure 6.1 for the main qualities of private equity firms.

Two points are significant regarding the role of leverage. First, the acquisition will be the entity that ultimately carries the debt rather than the fund or firm, both of whom have limited liability (restricted to the equity shares they have invested). For the layperson this can seem bizarre. In the case of a corporation it extends the strangeness that a corporation can effectively own itself (have legal person status) to one where it can be bought ultimately using itself as collateral for a majority of the buyout, and its own future revenues and resale price as the means to pay for it. Second, the use of debt in the buyout creates scope for financial engineering, and the concentration of equity. Concentration of equity means replacement of equity with debt, reducing the proportion of equity in the capital structure. This enables the capture of larger entities and can significantly reduce the

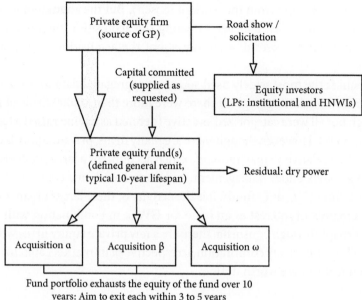

Fig. 6.1 Key aspects of private equity firms

period over which the equity is returned to the fund from the buyout. It creates further scope for additional returns through debt structures, and special dividends. It also means any pressure to restructure the acquisition and/or dispose of it for more than it was bought for, in order to realize a gain for the fund, is reduced. The GP may well be focused on these, but the point is that she need not rely on them.

One cannot emphasize enough that the basis of private equity is to generate returns to the fund and to any other participating investors. The acquisition is simply a means to this end. Specifically, a new layer of interests and concerns affects the socio-economic positioning of the acquired firm. Clearly, owners or shareholders have always had interests that affect the activity of firms. However, once a firm becomes a private equity acquisition its immediate significance for its owners is not as a source of production, but rather as a financial instrument. It is wholly owned for some period as part of an investment portfolio, and the purpose of ownership is to generate returns to the fund during the relatively short period it is part of the portfolio. The GP is managing the acquisition to manage the portfolio. In business and finance theory this is described as a competition for ownership resulting in an agency alignment of interests (classically deriving from the work of Jensen). But the alignment is on the basis of investors (as managers) owning the acquisition for some period *for investment purposes* that are not about the acquisition in any simple sense.

Preqin is the most widely used source of aggregated data for private equity. Based on data aggregated there were more than 10,000 firms in 2020, though not all were categorized as active (defined as having raised a fund in recent years). However, though there are many firms, private equity is dominated by a relatively small number, which account for a large proportion of the total assets under management, and do so based on a concentration of multi-billion ($, £, or €) funds. It is the activity of these larger organizations that is mainly of interest as an issue for GWC. In combination with debt, and perhaps through consortia, there are a few private equity firms who are able to buy almost any corporation, irrespective of its market capitalization. Several features are worth noting:

> According to Preqin, total assets under management by private equity stood at $4.11 trillion in mid-2019, with over $1.5 trillion available as 'dry powder'. Research published in 2015 reported that the top 50 firms account for over 50% of assets under management and the top 10 account for over 60% of that 50% (Jacobius, 2015). There is no reason to expect that this general situation has changed. In fact, Preqin refers to a trend of 'capital consolidation' and reports that in 2019 39% of capital raised was directed to the top 20 funds dominated by the main firms (compared to less than 30% five years previously). If one surveys the top 10 firms in 2019, each had more than $50 billion in total assets under management, and the top five more than $100 billion. Blackstone alone raised over $115 billion in fund solicitations 2005–2015. According to the 'PE 300 List', compiled by *Private Equity International* magazine, Blackstone is the largest alternative asset management firm in the world—with over $570 billion in assets under management at the beginning of 2020, if one includes its hedge funds (Carlyle Group is historically larger for private equity alone). Blackstone's Capital Partners VI fund closed at $16.2 billion in 2010, and Partners VII closed late in 2015 at $18 billion. In September 2019, Capital Partners VIII was reported at $26 billion, exceeding both its initial solicitation of $22 billion, and the previous record held by Apollo Management of $24.5 billion in 2017. The top 10 largest individual funds solicited by private equity firms are all larger than $15 billion and the majority of these have been closed since 2013. Any fund of $10 billion or more is categorized as a 'mega fund' and there are now many mega-funds. . . . According to Hammoud et al. (2017), if one aggregates the portfolio acquisitions

of the top five private equity firms, then just the top five would make private equity the second largest private sector employer in the USA (behind Walmart) and the largest in Europe.

(Morgan & Nasir, 2021, pp. 458–459)

Alliance Boots and the capture and concentration of wealth

Consider the example of the buyout of Alliance Boots in 2007 (Morgan, 2009, pp. 213–215). It remains the largest buyout of a publicly listed company in the UK. In February 2007 KKR contacted Stefano Pessina, an Alliance Boots board member with a 15 percent stake in the corporation. At the time Alliance Boots shares traded at around £8, and Pessina was reported to be unhappy with the board's strategy and with the valuation of the firm. In March 2007, KKR and Pessina put an indicative offer of £10 per share to the board as part of a buyout. However, they then become embroiled in a bidding war with the private equity firm Terra Firma. In April, KKR and Pessina finally managed to secure the primacy of an offer for £11.39 per share and a shareholder vote approved the buyout on May 31. The final offer valued Alliance Boots at just over £11 billion. However, the total value of the deal, including Alliance Boots' debt and a revolving credit facility (effectively an overdraft), was approximately £13 billion. Of this, £9.3 billion was structured as debt and £3.43 billion equity. KKR provided £1.02 billion from several funds, Pessina another £1.02 billion, and "minority investors" £1.39 billion. The latter consisted mainly of equity stakes from the consortium of banks that also provided the initial lending, which was then to be syndicated (and represents a classic case of proprietary trading activity prior to the global financial crisis).

Now, consider the power and wealth capture aspects of the deal. KKR and Pessina each provided less than 10 percent in equity of the total value of the buyout. However, each then had a claim to around 30 percent of the returns from the acquisition (subject to debt servicing). Furthermore, since minority investors have no voting rights, each had acquired 50 percent control of an £11 billion asset, based on approximately £1 billion in equity (bearing in mind that each also has limited liability and the debt is carried by the newly structured acquisition). Moreover, the eventual share price offer of £11.39 was more than £3 higher than the trading price in

February, creating a premium in excess of 35 percent. Since Pessina had a 15 percent stake in Alliance Boots, this augmented his own return from the buyout. In fact, Pessina's 15 percent stake was worth around £1.7 billion. So he was able to roll over £1.02 billion, realize an immediate return of more than half a billion, whilst actually increasing his stake from 15 to 30 percent and his controlling rights to 50 percent. The initial leverage involved in the deal can be estimated at around 70 percent. In standard ratio terms it represented around 12.5 times EBITDA.

The leverage used can be considered in simple technical terms as financial engineering. Within a positive narrative of private equity it is a disciplining force enabling agency alignment of interests. However, it is simultaneously a key component in the exercise of power that also augments power, whose consequence is the capture of a wealth asset. Concomitantly, debt vulnerability is created in the form of massive debt servicing. It seems a curious logic to argue that creating risks to the financial stability of a business is a justifiable means to ensure the further viability of that business, which is essentially what the disciplining aspect of agency alignment means. It seems also manifestly self-serving if the main articulators of this position are the private equity firms, their industry bodies, and, in some cases, research centres significantly funded by either the firms or interested banks.

Protecting wealth and issues in taxation

Private equity creates scope not only for the capture of wealth in the form of firms as acquisitions, but also for the protection of that wealth from other claims. The basic structural logics of private equity create both motives and opportunity to pursue GWC effects. The GP is highly motivated to return equity to the fund as quickly as possible in order to earn carried interest. The potentials of financing and refinancing within LBOs enable this. Though private equity firms are in many respects prominent, they are also simultaneously background entities. The financial affairs of firms and funds tend to be more obscure than those of public corporations. Though KKR, Blackstone, Bain Capital, etc are familiar within the business press, they are not prominent in quite the same way as Google, Apple, Starbucks, and other corporations. Once private equity acquires a corporation, the requirement for financial disclosure can be quite different because the acquisition is not a publicly listed company. Private equity may undertake corporate restructurings via new incorporations that different kinds of governance might resist. This creates scope for the protection of wealth and the use of chains to "break loose from the location of value creation."

For example, beginning in 2013 a variety of interest groups, activists, and tax and corporate expert-activists began to publicly criticize different alleged consequences of the Alliance Boots buyout (for broader issues of activist strategies see Seabrooke & Wigan, 2015, 2016; Baker & Wigan, 2017). In 2013 Change to Win, Unite the Union, and War on Want published a joint analysis that explored the available financial documentation of Alliance Boots since 2007, and sought to put these in the context of the various entities owned or influenced by KKR and Stefano Pessina (Change to Win et al., 2013). The report provides a map of entities, in which multiple entities in the Cayman Islands and Luxembourg, as well as singular entities in Switzerland, Monaco, and Gibraltar are prominent.

According to the report, Alliance Boots' parent company (Alliance Boots GmbH) relocated to the canton of Zug, Switzerland in 2008. Furthermore, the funds providing the initial equity and to which equity would be returned, and the holding company initially created to acquire Boots (AB Acquisitions Holdings Limited) were located in places designated by the Tax Justice Network as financial secrecy jurisdictions and tax havens (the Cayman Islands, Gibraltar, etc.). The report then notes that the initial financial engineering for the LBO has tax consequences. In 2013 Alliance Boots operated in 25 countries, but only had retail business operations in six. According to the report, retail operations (prescriptions, etc.) have higher profit margins than wholesale, and thus greater potential tax exposure. In the UK, finance costs associated with debt are deductible from taxable income. The UK is Alliance Boots' largest retail market (an estimated 33 percent of sales but 68 percent of trading profit). As such, by locating its debt in the UK Boots it would be able to significantly reduce its total tax bill, whilst at the same time any tax liabilities faced by participants in the buyout would potentially be reduced because of the location of the entities receiving benefits from Boots. Based on the available financial disclosures the report then estimated that between 2008 and 2013 Alliance Boots reduced its UK taxable income by £4.2 billion, and thereby reduced tax to be paid in the UK by an estimated £1.12 to £1.28 billion. According to a Bloomberg report this amounted to an estimated 95 percent reduction in its taxation (Thesing, 2014). To be clear, Boots had not done anything demonstrably illegal, nor is the practice of concentrating of financing costs in a firm's most profitable market a standard form of tax avoidance. However, it can in a broad sense be interpreted as a means to protect wealth from other claims.

Moreover, the practice has context. It can be interpreted as a subsidy of the buyout by the state (in terms of tax foregone). In the Alliance Boots case this raised particular issues because Boots is a healthcare provider, and is also a direct beneficiary of the state (via hospital contracts, prescriptions, etc.— an estimated 40 percent of its revenue according to MedAct). For activists there is a clear line from cuts to health services in the context of post-financial crisis austerity and the claimed failure of Boots to structure its tax affairs in line with ethical expectations. This was starkly put by translating £1.12 billion into the cost of prescriptions for the whole of England for two years.

More broadly, the practice of debt-related tax reductions frees up and/or ultimately augments income that can then be returned to investors. This is not just subsidizing debt, but creating scope for returns to the fund (see Morgan, 2009, pp. 198–207). Private equity may pay debt down more quickly, or alternatively create new debt and special dividends. Ultimately the acquisition may be disposed of in a sale where the exit involves higher net returns for any given sale price because of the way wealth has previously been protected. Significantly, the means by which income is returned to the fund, and also the GP/firm, and the locations to which it is returned can then be more readily matters of tax avoidance and profit shifting (Morgan, 2021). The degree to which this is so is open to dispute on a case-by-case basis for private equity.

In 2014 Richard Murphy and others again drew attention to matters arising from the Change to Win et al. report (Murphy, 2014a, 2014b). The report notes that Alliance Boots had not as yet disclosed its profits and income based on a country-by-country approach. It had, like many other organizations, chosen to disclose in accordance with what the law requires, rather than to exceed this based on greater transparency, which the law allows. For critics, when organizations do not meet the highest possible standards for financial disclosure, the issue is not really about proprietary information, which might put at risk some reasonably justifiable aspect of business. Nor is it typically a matter of minimizing transaction costs, since they already have more information than they disclose. It is rather that minimal information facilitates minimizing tax without giving grounds for that minimization to be challenged, either by a tax authority or by activists seeking to change practice and the law. From a critical perspective, the inference that minimal disclosure is purposive secrecy is lent further plausibility when an organization chooses to incorporate in financial secrecy jurisdictions and tax havens (see Shaxson, 2011). Defenders of the practices typically respond that matters are more legally nuanced; the location has some other purpose than tax avoidance, though "tax efficiency" may also be one of the benefits.

Core issues here are the nature of standards, the issue of disclosure, and the inference that secrecy is *chosen*, which is rather different than justifiable confidentiality. Murphy and others placed their interest in Alliance Boots in 2014 in the context of the paucity of HMRC data regarding partnerships. In drafting a new Finance Bill in 2014 it became clear that the UK HMRC held or disclosed very little information regarding LLPs. From a tax justice point of view LLPs create great scope for tax avoidance. A corporation has legal person status and so can be a member of an LLP. An LLP can then be comprised of many corporations, including foreign corporate entities. A parliamentary subcommittee raised this possibility in 2014. It noted that HMRC estimates 23,000 of 420,000 partnerships in the UK included at least one corporate member, and this enabled LLPs to create the potential for profits to be allocated to an entity incorporated in a low-tax locality, and for individuals to receive benefits in such locations. Based on this statement, Murphy and others then called for greater disclosure by HMRC of available data and for a specific investigation of Alliance Boots.

The call for greater disclosure and more data collection is indicative of context. Information has not been freely available, which at the very least creates suspicion and skepticism. The impression created by lack of transparency is that defenders of the status quo default to technical standards and marginalize the ordinary language sense of standards as justifiable ethical practice (see Christensen on transparency, Chapter 11 in this volume). Behavior is simply represented as normal practice without questioning the norms of practice: construction of LLPs with corporate legal person and individual natural person members, incorporation in financial secrecy jurisdictions and tax havens, and a flow of reporting and distribution of benefits to protect income from other claims. Prominent defenders of private equity Gilligan and Wright state:

> There are no particular arrangements available to private equity funds that are not available to others. Therefore the debate about offshore and international taxation is a manifestation of a more general debate, outside the scope of this

commentary, about the taxation of corporations and individuals generally. Our only observation is that the critics do not seem to be arguing that any laws are being broken. They appear to be arguing that the laws are wrong or wrongly interpreted. That is surely a matter for politicians and legislators. Businesses are not directly responsible for the regulatory framework and nor should they be.

(2014, p. 7)

From a critical perspective this is a curious statement. Earlier we noted that private equity does not face the same governance context as a public corporation, and so may undertake corporate restructurings via new incorporations and shifting ownership relations that different kinds of governance might resist. However, it does so in a context with overlap. Private equity shares the same set of opportunities open to public corporations. Though regulation of private equity may be different in some respects and the need to disclose in given jurisdictions may be different because an entity is not publicly listed, the legal architecture it can engage with remains to a large degree the same. Private equity is operative within financialization. An organization can create LLPs and corporations in many different jurisdictions. These can have separate legal entity status. This can then facilitate tax avoidance using multiple strategies (transfer pricing, licensing, use of bonds, etc.; see Morgan, 2016, 2017a). The ultimate point is not that opportunities are available to more than just private equity, it is that they are chosen and pursued at all.

"We do what others do," does not address whether anyone should be able to do those things, nor does it address whether the particular actor should, even as it does so. There is a difference between the law existing to facilitate an activity, and the law currently failing to effectively prevent an activity. Insofar as it does fail, it does so partly because of the way law is used. To state something is legal is a minimal statement; it does not refer to how the law has been approached, shaped by lobbying or exploited or manipulated through activity (see Picciotto, 2011; Quentin, 2017 and Chapter 13 in this volume). Not all businesses choose to minimize their tax in ways that are possible. Here one can consider two different framings of "what the law allows." First, a positive context where the law allows one to report more than is minimally required. Second, a negative context where the law allows one to exploit its specific statement or ambiguity. This is a matter of interpretation based on responsibility, ethics, and attitude. It is why defenses that begin with "we pay all legally required taxes" still generate controversy and critique.

The use of leverage also highlights issues regarding the equivalence of debt and equity, and whether tax relief should cover significant debt structures. Many countries, for example Germany, now limit the debt that can be subject to exemptions and relief to deter private equity activity.[3] Even allowing for reform, the use of leverage and thus "debt discipline" is a pressure that provides motives to undertake activity with global wealth chain effects. Private equity captures a wealth asset and then is able to protect wealth from other claims via the use of organizational structure and relations based on the negative sense of what the law will allow.

From wealth protection to power processes

When Gilligan and Wright state that private equity benefits from no specific arrangements, there are various additional points one might make. A tax policy may not exist to satisfy a special interest group, but it may be one that is specifically useful to that group, which they lobby to retain. In addition, the group may well have negotiated special arrangements, and this has been the case in the UK and US regarding the tax status of carried interest.

Carried interest is taxed as a capital gain rather than as income. This is on the basis that it is a return to an investment. However, since the GP/firm uses very little of its own equity and the basis of an LBO is fund equity plus debt then the actual return to the GP might be conceptualized as a proportional fee for a management service: the activity/work of the GP. This would make it income.[4] Taxes on income are typically higher so positioning carried interest as capital gains is clearly beneficial to private equity firms. Critics argue that a wealthy financial elite pays taxes on what is really their income that are far less as a proportion than other citizens based on their "work." Moreover, GPs can choose to be citizens of tax havens and/or be non-resident and can structure payments through LLPs and trusts. So, they can reduce capital gains liability even further. The status of carried interest is, therefore, a controversial matter. Private equity firms and industry bodies, such as the BVCA, are well aware of this, and periodically provide positional argument to defend the status of carried interest.

---

[3] The OECD BEPS process and 15-point action plan recommends adopting German practice and capping deductibility at 30 percent of operating profits.
[4] The possibility that it can be taxed as income in various jurisdictions is a matter that consultants and tax experts are perpetually concerned by (see e.g. Linklaters, 2012).

In 2003 private equity in the UK secured a "memorandum of under-standing" from HMRC that carried interest would continue to be treated as capital gains, and the BVCA in particular has thereafter lobbied government to maintain this status. Several attempts in the last decade to change the status of carried interest in the US have failed to be passed by Congress (Fleischer, 2015);[5] for example, the "Blackstone Bill," which sought to tax carried interest at 35 percent to align it with income tax. Clearly, wealth chain effects are matters of process. They include positioned argument and policy influence that affect how claims to wealth are created and protected. In the UK, the campaigning group 38 Degrees made much of this in early 2015 (Green, 2015). According to their research, 16 of 93 major Conservative Party donors who had direct access for private consultation with David Cameron and cabinet ministers in 2014 were from private equity. As part of the Party's Leader's Group they had donated more than £7 million collectively. By US standards this is a small sum, but it is significant in a UK context. As Kosman's work indicates, it is part of a broader and long-term pattern of political patronage, donations, and revolving-door employment between private equity and political office (Kosman, 2009, p. 3).[6]

It would be naïve to think that wealth chains are always a matter of how one chooses to approach the law, as though wealth chain effects were reducible only to exploitation or manipulation of law and regulation. One must also acknowledge that the law may be constructed precisely to allow— or simply not to prevent—some practices and effects. There is also a grey area where lobbying prevents the closure of loopholes, or just encourages the perpetuation of some structures of law that close loopholes whilst opening up others (rather than addressing the fundamental problem). Private equity is well resourced and its narrative fits into a mainstream business culture and discourse in a way that critique does not. This does not render critique less powerful when made, but it does make it difficult for critics to gain a sympathetic hearing. As several have argued, many nations have commercialized their sovereignty (see Palan, 2002). Though nations have an interest in protecting their tax base, they may also be captured or influenced by particular groups that reproduce specific interests in the name of general interests (Christensen et al., 2016).

---

[5] See James Maloney, director of communications, Private Equity Growth Capital Council, http://www.pegcc.org/the-hill-carried-interest-is-a-capital-gain/.

[6] For example, Margaret Thatcher served as an adviser to the hedge fund Tiger Management; John Major as chairman of Carlyle Group's European business; and Alan Milburn MP and Lord Patten have been members of the advisory board of Bridgepoint

For example, many alternative investment organizations use Eurobonds to transfer ownership and structure debt. Within a business culture discourse Eurobonds ostensibly exist to promote capital investment, and thus are part of wealth creation, employment, and growth. This underpins their tax-exempt status. In 2011, HMRC's Office of Tax Simplification reviewed the policy. The response was brief; "The original policy rationale is to encourage the growth of the UK Eurobond market, as London is one of the centres of the worldwide Eurobond market. If it were repealed, it could reduce investment in this area, and also reduce investment in the UK" (HMRC, 2011, p. 175). No evidence is given regarding the actual growth and welfare effects, and no consideration given as to whether the relief can be used to protect income from other claims. There is no mention of the potential for reduced taxation to also be a form of tax-avoidance strategy. The review simply asserts, "The policy rationale remains valid and it is a simplification for the holders" (ibid.).

In responding to an investigation by *The Independent* newspaper (Whittell & Dugan, 2013) the BVCA argued that private equity firms locate funds and other entities in particular jurisdictions and make use of opportunities such as Eurobonds because they simplify fund construction and reduce the administrative burden and cost, which would ultimately be borne by investors (BVCA, 2013). They note that institutional investors, such as pension funds, are typically tax exempt or eligible for lower taxation, so if taxes were applied then they would be simply claiming them back later. The position is predicated on several assumptions and includes several omissions. It conflates tax exemption for some investors with exemption for all. A fund is structured as essentially a pass-through entity which is tax neutral, and the implicit claim is that investors will be taxed eventually on their returns (as capital or income) in some jurisdiction based on subsequent individual reporting. This, however, puts aside the capacity to structure further entities to shift reporting to low-tax jurisdictions. It thus undercuts argument to tax the fund prior to this as an entity. It further assumes that private equity is a form of investment that should be encouraged rather than deterred. It thus undercuts the whole argument for whether private equity is a genuinely beneficial investment model and set of business practices. The BVCA position is, of course, understandable, given their remit. However, it is curious that the HMRC response seems to contradict its general statement that: "In the interest of fairness, tax reliefs should be avoided where these satisfy special interest groups or industry sectors" (HMRC, 2011, p. 18). In any case, the BVCA response does not seem to still be available from their site.

The point to carry forward here is that wealth capture leads to wealth concentration and seems to encourage wealth-protection strategies. Clearly, this is a dynamic process where power to act has consequences, power is reproduced, and power can be enhanced. This can be positional argument and influence as above and it can be the ongoing effects of pursuing core practices. Again, the case of Alliance Boots is instructive here. In 2012, KKR and Pessina agreed a trade sale (a sale of an entity to another business in the same market) of Alliance Boots to Walgreens, a US drugstore company. Walgreens agreed to buy Alliance Boots in two stages between 2012 and 2015. In the first stage Walgreens bought 45 percent of Boots, including 45 percent of each of the three equity holders' stakes, creating Walgreens Boots Alliance. Walgreens paid $6.7 billion for the equity in the first stage and exercised its option to buy the rest for a further $9.5 billion, whilst also taking on Alliance Boots' outstanding debt from the original financial engineering plus refinancing (reported at approximately £7 billion). Both Pessina and KKR received £1.4 billion each in the first stage, and so more than recouped their initial investment. KKR took 7 million shares in the new entity. Pessina also took shares, creating an 8 percent stake, and became a board member (and then CEO). Each received a further £2 billion (some as shares) in the second stage. Given the first payment exceeded the initial equity investment, the second payment alone constitutes a net return (subject to any further taxation etc.).

The original deal based on around 70 percent leverage involved committed equity from KKR and Pessina of around £1 billion each. This enabled the capture of an £11-billion asset. The initial deal also realized another half-billion for Pessina. In addition, the buyout created power through control of a firm as an asset. This in turn created further opportunity. Through the period of ownership wealth was concentrated, protected from other claims, and channeled. At the point of disposal KKR (once its share stake was sold down) realized around £3.4 billion. Pessina, meanwhile, augmented his wealth and transitioned to an ownership stake in and key management role within an even larger entity. During the period Alliance Boots did grow its sales, operating profit, and EBITDA.[7] Whether the growth is sufficient to justify a return of £2 billion and more per investment

---

[7] For example, the Annual Report for the fiscal year 2013–2014 states a 4.3 percent increase in sales revenue to £23.4 billion (in a Walgreens context). Bloomberg or Thompson Reuters provide access through their subscription trading platforms to market analyst reports on most major businesses. If one surveys recent SWOT analyses of Alliance Boots they are overwhelmingly positive (noting only a market dependency on UK sales as a vulnerability) and curiously make no mention of the LBO or debt structures.

group between 2007 and 2015 is an open question; one can consider it in terms of the relative changes in the metrics and future business potential, and one can consider it also in terms of risk, both to the acquisition and to the stability of the finance system (for context see Morgan, 2009; Christensen et al., 2016). Throughout, the acquisition has been treated as a financial instrument. Insofar as there is a counterargument, it would be that, whatever KKR's and minority investors' motives, Pessina is interested in the business as more than just a financial instrument. His participation makes the case also a management buyout (MBO). This does not preclude a financial focus, and as wealth-protection issues illustrate, does not mean his concept of good business coincides with that of other interested parties (employees, regulators, tax authorities, citizens, etc.). There are many further issues to consider here regarding entitlement, ethics, responsibility, and opportunity (see Morgan & Sheehan, 2015).

Conclusion

Private equity pre-dates financialization but clearly fits within a financialization narrative (see Froud & Williams, 2007; Erturk et al., 2010; Froud et al., 2012; Clark, 2016). There is also more to private equity than leveraged buyouts of large corporations, and there is more to the contemporary context and treatment of firms than is set out in this short chapter (Batt & Morgan, 2020; Souleles, 2019). However, one should not conflate case selection with misrepresentation. The material set out clearly illustrates that the global wealth chain concept is important. One must acknowledge that wealth capture, concentration, and protection are not new. At the same time, perennial does not entail that something is unchanging or that it receives due attention. In the contemporary world of growing inequality within states, and populist responses to the causes and consequences of that inequality, a GWC focus is both relevant and important (see Morgan, 2015, 2017b, 2021).

References

Appelbaum, E. & Batt, R. (2014). *Private Equity at Work: When Wall Street Manages Main Street*. Russell Sage Foundation.

Axelson, U., Jenkinson, T., Stromberg, P., & Weisbach, M. (2013). Borrow cheap, buy high? The determinants of leverage and pricing in buyouts. *Journal of Finance*, 68(6), 2223–2267.

Baker, A. & Wigan, D. (2017). Constructing and contesting City of London power: NGOs and the emergence of noisier financial politics. *Economy and Society*, 46(2), 185–210.

Batt, R. & Morgan, J. (2020). Private equity and public problems in a financialized world: An interview with Rosemary Batt. *Real-World Economics Review*, 94, 83–108.

BVCA (2013). *Private Equity is about Investment Not Tax Avoidance*. British Private Equity and Venture Capital Association.

Change to Win, Unite the Union, War on Want (2013). *Alliance Boots & The Tax Gap: The Case for Corporate Tax Reform*. http://www.waronwant.org/media/boots-billion-pound-tax-dodge.

Christensen, J., Shaxson, N., & Wigan D. (2016). The finance curse: Britain and the world economy. *British Journal of Politics and International Relations*, 18(1), 255–269.

Clark, I. (2016). Financialisation, ownership and employee interests under private equity at the AA (part two). *Industrial Relations Journal*, 47(3), 238–252.

Erturk, I., Froud, J., Johal, S., Leaver, A., & Williams, K. (2010). Ownership matters: Private equity and the political division of ownership. *Organisation*, 7(5), 543–561.

Fleischer, V. (2015). Two and twenty revisited: Taxing carried interest as ordinary income through executive action instead of legislation. https://papers.ssrn.com/sol3/papers.cfm?abstract_id=2661623.

Froud, J., Green, S., & Williams, K. (2012). Private equity and the concept of brittle trust. *Sociological Review*, 60(1), 1–24.

Froud, J. & Williams, K. (2007). Private equity and the culture of value extraction. *New Political Economy*, 12(3), 405–420.

Gilligan, J. & Wright, M. (2014). *Private Equity Demystified: An Explanatory Guide* (3rd edition). Institute of Chartered Accountants in England and Wales.

Green, C. (2015). Private equity bosses using £700m loophole and donating to the Tories. *The Independent*, February 19th.

HMRC (2011). *Review of Tax Reliefs Final Report*. HMRC, Office of Tax Simplification.

Jacobius, A. (2015). Big Private Equity Managers Ruling the Roost. *Pensions & Investments*, April 6th.

Kaplan, S. & Stein, J. (1993). The evolution of buyout pricing and financial structure in the 1980s. *Quarterly Journal of Economics*, 108(2), 313–357.

Kaplan, S. & Schoar, A. (2005). Private equity finance performance: returns, persistence and capital flows. *Journal of Finance*, 60(4), 1791–1823.

Kosman, J. (2009). *The Buyout of America: How Private Equity will Cause the Next Great Credit Crisis*. Portfolio.

Linklaters (2012). *Private Equity Taxation, Structuring Carried Interest in Europe and America: An Overview*. Linklaters.

Morgan, J. (2009). *Private Equity Finance: Rise and Repercussions*. Palgrave Macmillan.

Morgan, J. (2015). Piketty's calibration economics: Inequality and the dissolution of solutions. *Globalizations*, 12(5), 803–823.

Morgan, J. (2016). Corporation tax as a problem of MNC organisational circuits: The case for unitary taxation. *The British Journal of Politics and International Relations*, 18(2), 463–481.

Morgan, J. (2017a). Taxing the powerful, the rise of populism and the crisis in Europe: the case for the EU Common Consolidated Corporate Tax Base. *International Politics*, 54(5), 533–551.

Morgan, J. (2017b). Brexit: Be careful what you wish for? *Globalizations*, 14(1), 118–126.

Morgan, J. (2021). A critique of the Laffer theorem's macro-narrative consequences for corporate tax avoidance from a global wealth chain perspective. *Globalizations*, 18(2), 174–194.

Morgan, J. & Nasir, M. A. (2021). Financialised private equity finance and the debt gamble: The case of Toys R Us. *New Political Economy*, 26(3), 455–471.

Morgan, J. & Sheehan, B. (2015). Has reform of global finance been misconceived? Policy documents and the Volcker rule. *Globalizations*, 12(5), 695–709.

Murphy, R. (2014a). *Alliance Boots and the Use and Abuses of Limited Liability Partnerships*. Tax Research UK. May 30th, http://www.taxresearch.org.uk/Blog/2014/05/30/alliance-boots-and-the-use-and-abuses-of-limited-liability-partnerships/.

Murphy, R. (2014b). *Pay Up Boots*. Tax Research UK. June 11th, http://www.taxresearch.org.uk/Blog/2014/06/11/pay-up-boots/.

Palan, R. (2002). Tax havens and the commercialization of state sovereignty. *International Organization*, 56(1): 151–176.

Phalippou, L. (2017). *Private Equity Laid Bare*. CreateSpace.

Picciotto, S. (2011). *Regulating Global Corporate Capitalism*. Cambridge University Press.

Quentin, D. (2017). Risk-mining the public exchequer: Reflecting the realities of tax risk in the theory of tax avoidance. *Journal of Tax Administration*, 3(2), 22–35.

Seabrooke, L. & Wigan, D. (2014). Global wealth chains in the international political economy. *Review of International Political Economy*, 21(1), 257–263.

Seabrooke, L. & Wigan, D. (2015). How activists use benchmarks: Reformist and revolutionary benchmarks for global economic justice. *Review of International Studies*, 41(5). 887–904.

Seabrooke, L. & Wigan, D. (2016). Powering ideas through expertise: Professionals in global tax battles. *Journal of European Public Policy*, 23(3), 1–18.

Seabrooke, L. & Wigan, D. (2017). The governance of global wealth chains. *Review of International Political Economy*, 24(1), 1–29.

Shaxson, N. (2011). *Treasure Islands: Uncovering the Damage of Offshore Banking and Tax Havens*. Palgrave Macmillan.

Souleles, D. (2019). *Songs of Profit Songs of Loss: Private Equity Wealth and Inequality*. University of Nebraska Press.

Thesing, G. (2014). UK Government urged to probe Alliance Boots over tax affairs. *Bloomberg Business*, May 29th.

Whittell, R. & Dugan, E. (2013). Eurobonds scandal: The high street giants avoiding millions in tax. *The Independent*, October 23rd.

7

Beer and Pharmaceuticals

Mie Højris Dahl

Wealth management—and particularly the taxation of multinational companies (MNCs)—has become an increasingly salient issue over the last decade. Since the global financial crisis, a range of supranational initiatives have targeted banking and corporate secrecy (Engelen et al., 2010; Palan & Wigan, 2014; Sharman, 2017). More than 125 jurisdictions are at various stages of implementing the OECD base erosion and profit-shifting (BEPS) package, which provides 15 actions to combat profit shifting and gaming of tax regulation (OECD, 2018). In 2016, the European Commission presented an Anti-Tax Avoidance Package to fight aggressive tax practices by large MNCs (European Commission, 2016). Against a background of scandals following data leaks concerning significant international tax evasion and tax avoidance (such as LuxLeaks and the Panama and Paradise Papers), the taxation of MNCs has become an object of public concern and policy action.

International political economy scholarship is poorly equipped to deal with distinguishing between how firms create value and how they manage wealth. There is a tendency to focus on how firms create and capture value in global value chains (GVCs; classically Gereffi et al., 2005). Consequently, scholars have dedicated less attention to firm organization of financial and legal activities that in principle are not directly linked to the supply chain (though see Hearson, Chapter 3 in this volume, on the increasing integration of value and wealth chains). This is where global wealth chain (GWC) theory plugs an important gap. This volume broadens the range of cases and methods deployed in GWC analyses, focusing on single company cases or sectors. This chapter studies firms of national, regional, and global size in two sectors: pharmaceuticals, and beer and beverage production. It explores how sector and firm size impact the way Danish MNCs manage wealth. It does this by deploying a new methodology to study corporate wealth management. The chapter first provides

Mie Højris Dahl, *Beer and Pharmaceuticals*. In: *Global Wealth Chains*. Edited by Leonard Seabrooke and Duncan Wigan, Oxford University Press. © Mie Højris Dahl (2022). DOI: 10.1093/oso/9780198832379.003.0007 a rationale for case selection. The methodology and operationalization of GWC theory is then explained and the analysis of the six case companies presented. The chapter concludes by considering the wider significance of the study for the development of GWC scholarship.

The beer and pharmaceutical industries play an important role in the Danish economy, but the differences between them are substantial. Beer, on one hand, is a rather simple, physical product. Pharmaceutical drugs, on the other, are complex and knowledge-intensive, with intangible components far outweighing tangibles in valuations (see Bryan et al., Chapter 5 in this volume). These two very different industries provide for an interesting comparison. First, the comparison provides a means to gauge the impact of product complexity on organization in GWCs. Second, by looking at large global firms, mid-sized multiregional firms, and smaller regional firms, the role of firm size in GWCs can be identified. Case selection and rationale are illustrated in Figure 7.1.

The chapter combines a comparative approach with an embedded multiple case study design. The cases share embeddedness in the Danish institutional environment, but vary in terms of a key explanatory variable, namely industrial sector. The case units (i.e. the three case companies within each industry) share industrial sector, but vary in terms of firm size.

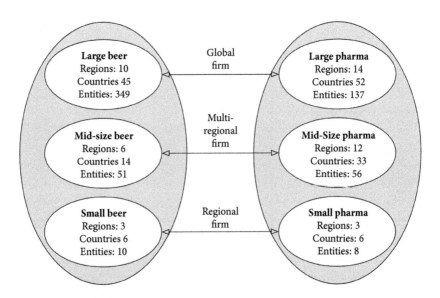

Fig. 7.1 Selection of company cases based on firm size and geographical coverage

To compare the six case companies, I deploy the five GWC types to distinguish forms of wealth chain governance. As noted by the editors of this volume, it is important to note that the GWC typology provides ideal types. We should not expect to observe such pure ideal types in reality (Seabrooke & Wigan, 2017, and Chapter 1 in this volume). Instead, it is likely that casework will reveal blends of these types and deviations from relationships and features that comprise them. The work of applying ideal types may generate new blends, which lead to the adjustment of, or additions to, original ideal types (Swedberg, 2018).

MNC multiple-case comparison

The chapter proposes a new methodology to explore MNC GWCs. It combines a mapping of corporate networks, a number of indicators on activities within corporate entities, and a number of confidential interviews to study firm organization in GWCs. Ownership links, financial information, and qualitative insights are therefore combined in the analysis of corporate wealth management. The company database Orbis is deployed to construct corporate network maps and classify corporate entities. Orbis is a comprehensive database aggregating data from more than 160 providers (Vitali et al., 2011; Heemskerk & Takes, 2016). It contains comparable data on more than 310 million companies around the world. Orbis furnishes information concerning, for example, connections between corporate entities within a firm, ownership percentages, stated purpose of business, number of employees, profit numbers, and other financial data (Garcia-Bernardo et al., 2017).

To distinguish between value and wealth, I classify corporate entities in the corporate networks of the firms studied as either value chain entities (VCEs), wealth chain entities (WCEs), or mixed entities (MEs). Additionally, some corporate entities are non-categorized entities (NEs), when there is insufficient information to evaluate the purpose and function of the entity. Classification enables an interpretation and visualization of the relationships between value and wealth. Entities are classified on the basis of an assessment of three broad indicators; the stated purpose of business, location in secrecy jurisdictions, and profit per head.

First, the stated purpose of business as reported in Orbis is recorded. This serves as an important indicator as to whether a corporate entity performs tasks that are related to the firm's supply chain activities or to the firm's legal and financial activities—or both. If the stated purpose of the corporate entity is not available, the name of the entity itself can sometimes serve as an indicator of what type of activity the entity undertakes. Further, when the purpose of the entity is not directly stated in Orbis, it is sometimes possible to find or verify the purpose through other sources such as annual reports, company registries, Bloomberg, OpenCorporates, and Crunchbase.

Second, the location of the corporate entity is recorded. If corporate entities are located in jurisdictions which have a score above 60 on the Tax Justice Network's Financial Secrecy Index (FSI), it is likely that the entities may serve wealth-maximizing objectives. The benchmark is used as an indicator that the entity may have wealth-creation or -protection purposes (Seabrooke & Wigan, 2016). "Secrecy" indicates the extent to which a jurisdiction provides facilities that enable people or entities to circumvent the laws and regulations of jurisdictions elsewhere. The FSI ranks and assesses jurisdictions based on the level of secrecy provided and the scale of offshore financial activities (see TJN, 2018). When corporate entities are located in a jurisdiction that has a high FSI score, the reason to locate corporate entities in that jurisdiction is likely to be to undertake financial and legal activities. Here, "jurisdictions with a high FSI score" are defined as jurisdictions with a FSI score of 60 or more. Such jurisdictions include Switzerland, the Cayman Islands, Hong Kong, and Singapore. Switzerland, for instance, is one of the world's largest offshore financial centers and is renowned for the protection of extensive banking secrecy. The FSI score is used when calculating the percentage of the firms' corporate entities identified as WCEs. An overview of the case companies' location in FSI jurisdictions is presented in Figures 7.2 and 7.3.

Location in FSI jurisdictions provides relevant information for assessing one of the key variables outlined in GWC theory; regulatory liability. Regulatory liability denotes the extent to which actors are informed about activities and processes that take place, and the resulting ease of regulating activities multi-jurisdictionally. GWCs are "linked forms of capital seeking to avoid accountability during processes of pecuniary wealth creation" (Seabrooke & Wigan, 2014, p. 257). Accordingly, the GWC framework emphasizes information asymmetries between supplier, regulator, and client (Seabrooke & Wigan, 2017). This also provides a rationale for deploying an indicator related to the secrecy of transactions and the ease of hiding information. This does *not* imply that WCEs in FSI jurisdictions are used for illicit activities. In the Danish beer and pharmaceutical industry, companies legally exploit the regulatory environment in FSI jurisdictions. It is important to acknowledge that while the FSI score can indicate that firms have more or less access to services that provide wealth creation and protection, it does not tell us whether the firms actually make use of the

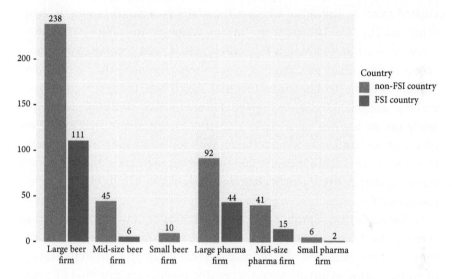

Fig. 7.2 Number of corporate entities located in FSI/non-FSI countries for all case companies

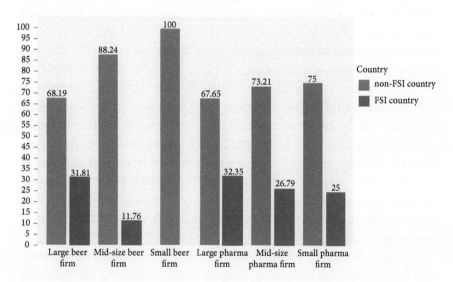

Fig. 7.3 Percentage of corporate entities located in FSI/non-FSI countries for all case companies

secrecy that these jurisdictions provide. For this reason, it is necessary to include other measures for entities located in jurisdictions with a high FSI score.

Third, for corporate entities located in jurisdictions with an FSI score above 60, the number of employees is identified and profit per head calculated as an indication of whether the entity is engaged in wealth chain activities. This is only done when financial data are available for the entity. Since jurisdictions with high FSI scores often do not provide easy, or any, access to firm financial data, this is not always the case. The rationale for looking at profit per head is that entities which have no or few employees and that are able to generate high profits are unlikely to be able to do this solely on the basis of value chain activities. Financial and legal activities, on the other hand, can be undertaken with few or no employees present. Profit per head is also a measure that is widely used by tax authorities when assessing the tax structures of companies (confidential interviews with tax professionals).

However, the use of profit per head as an indicator of wealth-maximizing activities has been questioned. On one hand, tax authorities use the indicator and researchers have also pointed out that it can provide an indication of profit shifting to jurisdictions that enable wealth maximization (Tørsløv et al., 2018). On the other hand, tax consultants as well as company tax strategists criticize the use of profit per head as a measure of wealth maximization. One tax consultant from a Big Four accounting firm highlighted that not only differences in the level of productivity of the workers, but also the placement of profit-generating intellectual property (IP), can render profit per head a misleading indicator. The abundance of Big Four accountancy firms in jurisdictions high on the FSI affirms that there is indeed a market for the management of IP and other tax-sensitive issues (Murphy et al., 2019). This may be particularly true for the pharmaceutical industry, where there exist significantly higher profits per head than in less knowledge-intensive industries (confirmed in interviews with tax experts in the pharmaceutical and beer industries). Profit per head is therefore deployed in combination with other measures, and profit is assessed in relation to firms from the same industry, to control for industry specificity.

To place a boundary on the corporate networks explored, only ownership links where the ownership share is above 10 percent are included. This threshold has been commonly used in tax literature (La Porta et al.,

1999; Sebbacon, 2013). The chapter examines not only what is owned by the firms, but also those that hold equity above 10 percent ownership, allowing ties to run between equity holders and known companies within the networks.

Mapping value and wealth

The stated purpose of business, location in FSI jurisdictions, and profit per head provide three measures to classify corporate entities as VCEs, WCEs, MEs, and NEs. These classifications allow for an interpretation of the delineation between value and wealth within the corporation. The ratio of different types of corporate entities within each of the firms is calculated. Additionally, an overview of the ratio of corporate entities located in FSI jurisdictions for each firm is generated. The classification of corporate entities into VCEs, WCEs, MEs, and NEs is summarized for all six case companies in Figures 7.4 and 7.5.

The series of confidential interviews with company representatives that inform the analysis addressed, not exhaustively, location decisions, tax management, and connections between corporate entities.

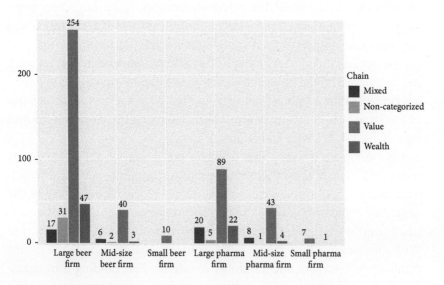

Fig. 7.4 Number of VCEs, WCEs, MEs, and NEs for all case companies

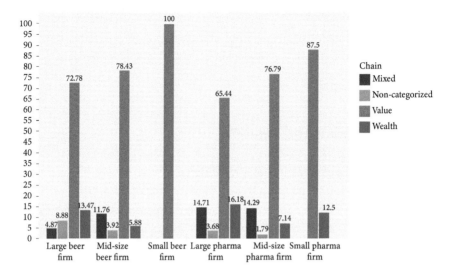

Fig. 7.5 Percentage of VCEs, WCEs, MEs, and NEs for all case companies

Beer and pharmaceutical global wealth chains

Large beer company

The largest beer company in the study includes 349 corporate entities spread over 45 countries. The corporate network of the large beer company is a very complex one; it is geographically dispersed, has many nodes (i.e. corporate entities), and it is highly interconnected with multiple ties (i.e. ownership links) connecting a large number of entities. The network has eight layers, meaning that there are up to eight intermediaries connecting entities in the corporate network. In Figure 7.6, the corporate network of the large beer company is presented, classifying the corporate entities into VCEs, WCEs, MEs, and NEs.

It is clear from the map that firms do not locate for *either* value purposes *or* wealth purposes. Corporate entities combine value and wealth objectives—which results in a high number of MEs. The majority of the large beer company's entities (73 percent) undertake value-related activities. Nevertheless, it has a significant proportion of WCEs (9 percent). The WCEs in the large beer company's corporate network include the parent company in Denmark and a number of intermediate holding companies. These often serve to channel wealth toward the parent company or protect the parent company from risks related to operations in subsidiaries.

Secrecy, risk management, local regulation, the inheritance of structures, and tax rules provide important wealth-related reasons for the structuring

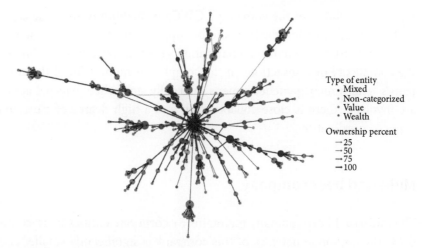

Fig. 7.6 Corporate network of a large beer company

of the large beer company's corporate network. The company has a large proportion of its corporate entities located in FSI jurisdictions (32 percent). It sometimes seeks secrecy in order to be less visible to its partners. Risk management provides a further rationale for the establishment of WCEs. The large beer company sets up intermediate companies to shield the parent company from operational risks and to avoid impairment losses for badly performing subsidiaries. Intermediate companies are also useful in shielding the parent company from political risks and regulatory change. An example of this is that the company has investment protection agreements with certain countries through some of its WCEs.

The complexity of the corporate network is to a large extent due to the company's history of growth through acquisitions, which has resulted in many inherited corporate entities. Inherited entities are often retained because of the expense and uncertain consequences associated with the dissolution of an entity. Tax rules are important for the way the large beer company structures its corporate network. The company has a dozen employees in its Danish tax department, and also local teams employed in tax management abroad. Out of all the case companies, the large beer company is the one that dedicates by far the most resources to tax management. It maintains extensive internal tax departments that are supplemented by external tax advisors. Generally, the company has moved away from aggressive tax planning, and tax activities have become increasingly focused on the complex task of compliance.

The large beer company can be characterized as a mix between a hierarchical and a relational GWC (see Chapter 1 in this volume). The regulatory liability in the company's GWCs is medium to low. The capabilities provided within the firm and by suppliers are high. There is a high degree of trust between the company and its external tax advisors. Overall, the complexity of transactions in the company is high. A lot of the company's wealth management happens internally, and when external actors are involved, there is close collaboration and a high degree of trust and explicit coordination.

Mid-sized beer company

The mid-sized beer company maintains 51 corporate entities in 14 countries. The corporate network of this company is significantly smaller and less complex than that of the large beer company. The network has four layers, which means that there are significantly fewer intermediate companies between the corporate entities than in the large beer company. The classification of the company's corporate entities into VCEs, WCEs, MEs, and NEs is presented in the corporate network map below (Figure 7.7).

As in the larger beer company, the majority of corporate entities are VCEs (78 percent). Interestingly, there is also a significant number of WCEs (6 percent) and MEs (12 percent). That the company has more MEs than WCEs may indicate that it is difficult for a small MNC to establish "pure" WCEs. It may also illustrate a shift toward MNCs aligning their GVCs and GWCs. Such a shift can potentially be observed faster in a smaller corporate network, which is easier to modify than a large one. The mid-sized beer company does not manage value and wealth separately.

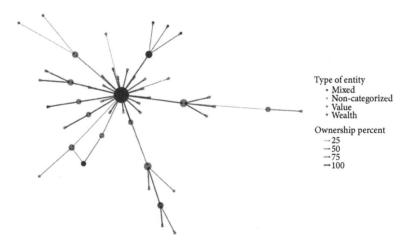

Fig. 7.7 Corporate network of a mid-sized beer company

Instead, it integrates value and wealth considerations when establishing corporate entities. When structuring its corporate network, the mid-sized beer company considers both legal and regulatory challenges, secrecy, and tax rules. The company has two tax employees in Denmark and eight to ten tax employees across the firm. Generally, tax management is far less complex than in the large beer company.

The mid-sized beer company can be characterized as a modular GWC. The regulatory liability is high; it maintains a low proportion of corporate entities located in FSI jurisdictions (12 percent) and it reports activities stringently. The complexity of transactions is low, and the company is not as financialized as the large beer company. The company's capabilities to mitigate uncertainty are medium to low, and the degree of explicit coordination is low.

Small beer company

The small beer company maintains just 10 corporate entities spread across six countries. Despite being much smaller than the other two beer companies, this company is still categorized as an MNC as it derives 77 percent of sales from foreign operations. The corporate network of the small beer company is by far the simplest of all the corporate networks examined. It only has one layer; with an intermediate company between the ultimate global parent company and one of the Danish breweries. The classification of the company's corporate entities into VCEs, WCEs, MEs, and NEs is presented in the corporate network map below (Figure 7.8).

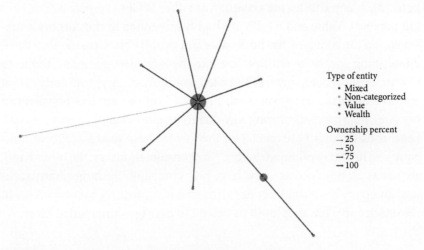

Type of entity
• Mixed
• Non-categorized
• Value
• Wealth

Ownership percent
— 25
— 50
— 75
— 100

Fig. 7.8 Corporate network of a small beer company

All of the corporate entities in the small beer company are classified as "pure" VCEs, as they are all focused on supply-chain-related activities, none of them are placed in FSI jurisdictions, and none of them have a particularly high profit per head. Hence, the company does not pursue significant wealth-creation and -protection activities. The small beer company may consider that extensive wealth management is beyond its capabilities, and therefore it relies solely on external advisors to comply with tax regulation. Unlike the large and mid-sized beer companies, the small beer company does not seem concerned about establishing an "integrated" or "tax-efficient" supply chain. With high regulatory liability, low complexity of transactions, and low capabilities to mitigate uncertainty, the small beer company can be characterized as a very simple, modular GWC.

Large pharmaceutical company

The largest pharmaceutical company in the study maintains 137 corporate entities across 52 countries and jurisdictions. Although the corporate network of the large pharmaceutical company is much smaller and less complex than that of the large beer company, the geographical coverage of the large pharmaceutical company's corporate network is more extensive. The corporate network has six layers, meaning that entities are at most owned through six other corporate entities. In Figure 7.9 below, the corporate network of the large pharmaceutical company is presented, classifying the corporate entities as VCEs, WCEs, MEs, and NEs.

The large pharmaceutical company has a relatively low ratio of VCEs (66 percent). Many entities are classified as either WCEs (16 percent) or MEs (15 percent). Value and wealth are highly integrated in the corporate network, and the company has both value and wealth objectives in mind when establishing corporate entities. Just like the large beer company, the large pharmaceutical company has inherited a number of corporate entities that are now dormant. However, such inherited entities are less prevalent in the large pharmaceutical company due to its more organic growth model. Legal considerations are crucial for the way the large pharmaceutical company sets up its corporate structure. Tax considerations, on the other hand, are not as pronounced as in the large beer company. The large pharmaceutical company has a small tax department with only three tax employees in Denmark and a few employed in Poland to manage value-added taxes.

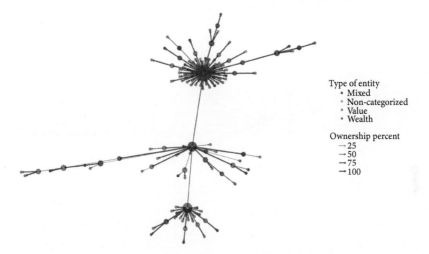

Fig. 7.9 The corporate network of a large pharmaceutical company

The large pharmaceutical company can be characterized as a captive GWC, with elements of a modular GWC. The regulatory liability is medium to high. The company works closely with the Danish tax authorities, but it has a large proportion of its corporate entities in FSI jurisdictions (32 percent). The complexity of transactions is medium to high; the company deals with highly intangible products, which are at the same time strictly regulated. The capabilities to mitigate uncertainty are medium to low; while the large pharmaceutical company is very focused on compliance, it does not—to the same extent as some of the other case companies—set up corporate structures to fend off potential threats to existing wealth.

Mid-sized pharmaceutical company

The mid-sized pharmaceutical company has 56 corporate entities across in 33 countries. The corporate network of the mid-sized company is not as complex or geographically dispersed as that of the large pharmaceutical company. Nevertheless, considering the size of the company, it has very broad coverage. The network features four layers, meaning that there are up to four intermediate companies between entities. Figure 7.10 provides a presentation of the corporate network of the mid-sized pharmaceutical

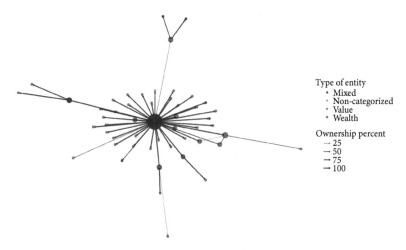

Fig. 7.10 The corporate network of a mid-sized pharmaceutical company

company, classifying the corporate entities into VCEs, WCEs, MEs, and NEs.

The majority of corporate entities are VCEs (79 percent). Yet the company still has a significant proportion of WCEs (7 percent) and MEs (13 percent). While the majority of the company's activities are determined by value considerations, value and wealth seem to be mixed and integrated. The company considers a number of wealth-related factors when managing its corporate network; compliance, risk management, and tax advantages. The company has also inherited a number of entities due to its acquisition-based growth model. Tax management in the mid-sized company is a significant task; the company has a tax department with five employees and uses external tax advisors extensively. Tax management is prioritized higher than in the large pharmaceutical company.

The mid-sized pharmaceutical company can be characterized as a captive GWC. The regulatory liability is medium to high. The company has a relatively large share of its corporate entities in FSI jurisdictions (27 percent). The complexity of transactions is medium to high; like the large pharmaceutical company, the mid-sized company also deals with highly intangible products, and a company representative stressed that it is complex for the company to manage tax and set up the apposite legal structures. The company has medium to high capabilities to mitigate uncertainty. It seems more proactive than the larger pharmaceutical company in establishing the most appropriate legal structure.

Small pharmaceutical company

The small pharmaceutical company has eight corporate entities spread across six countries. Considering the size of the company, it is notably geographically dispersed. The corporate network contains only two layers, and there is just one intermediate company between the ultimate global parent and the other corporate entities in the network. Figure 7.11 below presents the corporate network of the small pharmaceutical company, classifying the corporate entities into VCEs, WCEs, MEs, and NEs.

All of the corporate entities except one are classified as VCEs (88 percent). There is barely any distinction between value and wealth in the small pharmaceutical company. The one WCE in the corporate network is established as a holding company that collects profits. Aside from this, wealth creation and protection in the company is very simple. The company has no tax department, but relies on external tax advisors with whom it collaborates closely.

The small pharmaceutical company is characterized as a modular GWC. The regulatory liability is medium to high. The complexity of transactions is very low. Likewise, the company has low capabilities to mitigate uncertainty. The company does not focus strategically on wealth creation and protection to the same extent that the large and mid-sized case companies do.

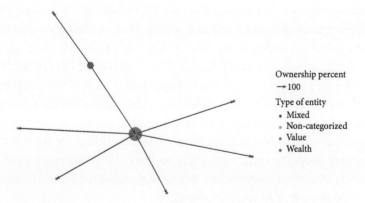

Fig. 7.11 The corporate network of a small pharmaceutical company

Industry, scale, and IP intensity

In a context where policy and analytical attention has been focused on firms that are heavily reliant on intellectual property, the findings of this chapter may, at first, seem counter-intuitive. At the industrial sector level, the simple product, beer, is associated with a complex corporate network, whereas the complex product, pharmaceuticals, is associated with a relatively simple corporate network. The differences in the way Danish beer and pharmaceutical companies structure corporate networks can be linked to product and mode of growth. Beer is a heavy product, which is expensive to transport. Beer production requires scale. Beer is not very IP-intensive, and IP in beer companies is mostly linked to advertising (Färe et al., 2004). Pharmaceuticals, on the other hand, are light and easy to transport. Due to the uniqueness of products in the pharmaceutical industry, scale is often less important than in the beer industry. Pharmaceutical drugs are very IP-intensive, and IP often exists on many different elements of the product (Wündisch & Collins, 2003).

Differences in the products and nature of the two industry sectors translate into differences in the way corporate networks are structured to create and protect wealth. That it is expensive to transport beer means that beer companies often decide to establish corporate entities to produce beer locally. That beer production requires scale means beer companies often acquire other companies and thereby develop extensive corporate networks. And that beer is not very IP-intensive contributes to value and wealth being relatively distinct in the industry. In the pharmaceutical industry, it does not make as much sense to strategically manage value and wealth separately. Pharmaceuticals are IP-based, which implies that the strategic management of value and wealth are more likely co-determined. IP is the bridge between the GVCs and GWCs. In the pharmaceutical industry, that bridge is much shorter than in the beer industry. Since pharmaceuticals are light and easy to transport, and scale is not as essential in the pharmaceutical industry, pharmaceutical companies have a tendency to establish fewer corporate entities where they are active. However, pharmaceutical companies do sometimes establish entities for legal purposes; to protect property rights or simply to have the permission to sell their products in certain markets (see Bryan et al., Chapter 5 in this volume, on the management of intangible assets).

Whereas beer companies tend to grow through acquisitions, pharmaceutical companies vary more in growth strategies. Some pharmaceutical companies have grown primarily through acquisitions (as in the example of the mid-sized pharmaceutical company) and some primarily through organic growth (as in the example of the large pharmaceutical company). Firms that follow an acquisition-based growth model often have more complex corporate network structures than firms that grow organically, because they inherit a number of existing corporate structures which may be more or less necessary in the new corporate group. Products in the pharmaceutical industry are more diverse than in the beer industry. The pharmaceutical industry produces a vast array of different pharmaceuticals, whereas the beer industry produces a limited range of the same basic product. This generates greater variation in the ways that pharmaceutical companies organize. The form of corporate planning and wealth chain is to some extent dependent on industrial sector.

In terms of firm size, larger companies have more extensive and more complex corporate networks through which they manage wealth. Larger companies are more capable of creating and protecting wealth and more purposively plan the governance of value and wealth. However, this tendency was more pronounced in the beer than in the pharmaceutical industry; in the latter the largest pharmaceutical firm maintained a fairly simple corporate network structure. The large pharmaceutical company also had a small tax department and did not govern its GWC very actively. Conversely, the large beer company had a very complex corporate network structure. This distinguished it from smaller firms in the same sector.

Perhaps surprisingly, mid-sized companies have fairly complex corporate networks and are actively trying to maximize wealth through corporate network structures. The mid-sized companies seem more agile than the larger companies in adapting the structure of corporate networks. The higher number of MNEs in the mid-sized beer company indicates that value and wealth are more closely aligned than in the larger beer firm. In the mid-sized pharmaceutical firm, wealth management seemed to carry a higher priority than in the larger pharmaceutical firm. With more people in the tax department and a significant share of GWEs and MEs, the mid-sized pharmaceutical company maintained a somewhat complex corporate network structure.

Smaller companies, however, have much simpler corporate networks. Smaller companies are not positioned to utilize complex corporate network structure. The smaller firms do not have an internal tax department. The interviewee at the small pharmaceutical company was not aware of the potential benefits of establishing corporate structures for purposes of wealth management. Small firms are largely excluded from the peer group of tax experts that larger (and sometimes mid-sized) firms are part of. Interviews reveal that large—and sometimes mid-sized—firms participate actively in tax network groups where work challenges and tax strategy are discussed. That small firms are not part of the same peer groups as larger firms contributes to the limited knowledge within these small firms in terms of wealth management. Furthermore, the limited geographical scope of small firms' GVC activities also limits their ability to build and organize GWCs. Limited resources in the smaller firms exclude them from competing on the basis of wealth management. Firms require a certain size to set up complex corporate networks and govern GWCs in an effective way. Firm size has important implications for the ways firms organize value and wealth.

Value and wealth mirror each other. They are two sides of the same coin. As this volume demonstrates, we miss important elements of the global political economy if focus is solely on value creation and capture in GVCs. In the Danish beer and pharmaceutical industries, it is not only clear that value and wealth are two sides of the same story. Value and wealth are converging (a finding shared with Hearson, Chapter 3 in this volume). Beer and pharmaceutical MNCs are moving away from corporate network structures where value and wealth are located in separate entities, marking a sharp distinction between "real and "legal/financial activities." This is a point others have made in the context of financialization and GWCs (Bryan et al., 2017, and Chapter 5 in this volume). Previously, a separation was effected by, for example, establishing shell companies in jurisdictions that provide secrecy or tax benefits, without having any business activities or employees associated with such corporate entities. Firms increasingly integrate value and wealth in what has been termed "tax-efficient supply chains" (see Hearson, this volume). The analysis in this chapter of mid-sized and large MNCs in both the beer and pharmaceutical sectors demonstrates this point.

The six case companies are shaped by their embeddedness in the Danish institutional context. Regulators, tax authorities, tax professionals, industry experts, and company representatives emphasized that the Danish tax and auditing system is both complex and comprehensive (Asen, 2019). Furthermore, the Danish system is characterized by a high level of trust and Danish tax authorities seem to have a more guiding than controlling role in relationships with companies, compared to other countries (Maskell,

1998). At the same time, there are strong expectations of compliance, and the reputational costs of managing wealth in a way that is not publicly well perceived are high (Lytken, 2018). Danish MNCs do not pursue aggressive wealth-management strategies like the US MNCs that have attracted much policy and public attention in recent years. Generally, Danish MNCs are subject to stricter regulation of wealth management, and Danish firms perceive it as necessary to govern wealth in a way that is somewhat aligned with value activities. This is in part because of recent European anti-avoidance regulation.

The future agenda on GWCs

By combining corporate network mapping with select accounting measures and confidential interviews, this chapter analyzes GWCs in a novel way. It proposes a new categorization in terms of value chain entities (VCEs), wealth chain entities (WCEs), mixed entities (MEs), and non-categorized entities (NEs)—and suggests indicators that are relevant for such classifications (i.e. stated purpose of business, location in secrecy jurisdictions, and profit per head). While the GWC framework clearly applies to MNCs (Seabrooke & Wigan, 2014), how firm size can influence wealth chain governance has not been examined. This multiple case study finds that the size of firms *is* an important factor in the governance of GVCs and GWCs. Firm size impacts on both the extent to which firms establish complex corporate structures to maximize wealth and the type of GWC, with the type of GWC often similar for firms of similar size. The chapter contributes to the GWC project by using industrial sector and firm size as explanatory variables, and exploring wealth management in a Danish context. One implication of this chapter is that GWC analyses can be usefully developed with application to different national contexts.

Conclusion

Danish beer and pharmaceutical MNCs create and protect wealth through corporate network structures in a way that depends on industry, firm size, and the national context. Industrial sector affects wealth management. Hence, a number of similarities have been demonstrated between the three beer companies and the three pharmaceutical companies. The beer industry, which generates a fairly simple, tangible product, maintains complex corporate network structures. The pharmaceutical industry, which generates rather complex, intangible-asset-rich products, maintains simple corporate network structures. Industrial sector differences in the companies' creation and protection of wealth through corporate structures can be explained by the different nature of the products and differences in modes of growth (acquisition-based or organic). The balance between value and wealth also differs between the two industries. While beer companies often handle value and wealth separately, value and wealth seem more intertwined in pharmaceutical companies due to the importance of IP. In the pharmaceutical industry, IP is related to both supply-chain activities (GVC) and the financial and legal activities of the company (GWC). IP serves as a bridge between value and wealth in the pharmaceutical industry.

Firm size has important implications for the way MNCs manage wealth. The number of corporate entities a company maintains as well as its geographical coverage matters for the way it organizes value and wealth activities. Larger firms have more complex corporate networks. While mid-sized firms have less complex corporate network structures, they still actively use these structures for wealth-creation and -protection purposes. Sometimes mid-sized firms may be even more active in organizing wealth functions. Smaller firms, on the other hand, have very simple corporate networks and do not govern wealth actively like large and mid-sized firms do. These smaller firms do not have equal opportunities for active wealth maximization, and small firm knowledge about wealth management is also often limited. Smaller firms even have difficulty complying with complex tax and auditing rules due to limited resources. Their focus is generally more on compliance than on the exploitation of regulatory gaps and opportunities.

References

Asen, E. (2019). *Corporate Income Tax Complexity in Europe | Country Tax Rankings*. Tax Foundation, March 7. https://taxfoundation.org/corporate-income-tax-complexity-europe/.

Bryan, D., Rafferty, M., & Wigan D. (2017). Capital unchained: Finance, intangible assets, and the double life of capital in the offshore world. *Review of International Political Economy*, 24(1), 56–86.

Engelen, E., Erturk, I., Froud, J., Leaver, A., & Williams. K. (2010). Reconceptualizing financial innovation: Frame, conjuncture and bricolage. *Economy and
Society*, 39(1), 33–63.

European Commission (2016). "Anti Tax Avoidance Package," September 13,
Taxation and Customs Union—European Commission, https://ec.europa.eu/
taxation_customs/business/company-tax/anti-tax-avoidance-package_en.

Färe, R., Grosskopf, S., Seldon, B. J., and Tremblay, V. J. (2004). Advertising efficiency and the choice of media mix: A case of beer. *International Journal of
Industrial Organization*, 22(4), 503–522.

Garcia-Bernardo, J., Fichtner, J., Takes, F. W., & Heemskerk, E. M. (2017). Uncovering offshore financial centers: Conduits and sinks in the global corporate
ownership network. *Scientific Reports*, 7(1), 6246.

Gereffi, G., Humphrey, J., & Sturgeon, T. (2005). The governance of global value
chains. *Review of International Political Economy*, 12(1), 78–104.

Heemskerk, E. M. & Takes, F. W. (2016). The corporate elite community structure
of global capitalism. *New Political Economy*, 21(1), 90–118.

La Porta, R., Lopez-De-Silanes, F., & Shleifer, A. (1999). Corporate ownership
around the world. *The Journal of Finance*, 54(2), 471–517.

Lytken, P. E. (2018). The anti-avoidance framework in Denmark. *Lexol-
ogy*, September 27. https://www.lexology.com/library/detail.aspx?g=b7a8c1b2-
dbe2-430d-ae61-8322a9c85bf9.

Maskell, P. (1998). Learning in the village economy of Denmark. The role of institutions and policy in sustaining competitiveness. https://doi.org/10.2139/ssrn.
54544.

Murphy, R., Seabrooke, L., & Stausholm, S. N. (2019). A tax map of global professional service firms: Where expert services are located and why. COFFERS
Working Paper D4.6. Copenhagen Business School.

OECD (2018). *OECD/G20 Inclusive Framework on BEPS: Progress Report July
2017–June 2018*. OECD. http://www.oecd.org/tax/beps/inclusive-framework-
on-beps-progress-report-june-2017-july-2018.htm.

Palan, R. & Wigan, D. (2014). Herding cats and taming tax havens: The US strategy
of "not in my backyard." *Global Policy*, 5(3), 334–343.

Seabrooke, L. & Wigan, D. (2014). Global wealth chains in the international political economy. *Review of International Political Economy*, 21(1),
257–263.

Seabrooke, L. & Wigan, D. (2016). Powering ideas through expertise: Professionals
in global tax battles. *Journal of European Public Policy*, 23(3), 357–374.

Seabrooke, L. & Wigan, D. (2017). The governance of global wealth chains. *Review
of International Political Economy*, 24(1), 1–29.

Sebbacon (2013). Understanding corporate networks. Part 1: Control via equity. OpenCorporates, October 16. https://blog.opencorporates.com/2013/10/16/understanding-corporate-networks-part-1-control-via-equity/.

Sharman, J. C. (2017). Illicit global wealth chains after the financial crisis: Microstates and an unusual suspect. *Review of International Political Economy*, 24(1), 30–55.

Swedberg, R. (2018). How to use Max Weber's ideal type in sociological analysis. *Journal of Classical Sociology*, 18(3), 181–196.

TJN (2018). Financial Secrecy Index. Tax Justice Network, January 30. https://www.financialsecrecyindex.com/introduction/introducing-the-fsi.

Tørsløv, T., Wier, L. & Zucman, G. (2018). The Missing Profits of Nations. NBER Working Paper Series, Working Paper No. 2474. National Bureau of Economic Research.

Vitali, S., Glattfelder, J. B., & Battiston, S. (2011). The network of global corporate control. *PLOS ONE*, 6(10), e25995.

Wündisch, K. & Collins, M. H. (2003). *International Transfer Pricing in the Ethical Pharmaceutical Industry*. IBFD Publications.

8

Food

Verónica Grondona and Martín Burgos

Introduction

This chapter examines the soybean sector global wealth chain (GWC) in Argentina, providing an estimation of the level of mispricing in soybean, soybean oil, and soybean meal exports by a representative sample of multinatinal companies. It draws upon transfer pricing court cases in which the sample of companies have been involved. The evidence suggests that these multinational companies are able to mitigate uncertainty in a market of high price volatility and generate wealth from transfer mispricing. While the main driver of transfer pricing manipulation is tax avoidance, transfer mispricing also has a significant role in capital flight from developing countries. Transfer mispricing enables the transfer of assets and wealth abroad as if part of normal business activity, sometimes avoiding exchange restrictions and capital controls. Capital flight through transfer mispricing can take various forms, from export underpricing, import overpricing, services, and royalties overpricing to financial transactions and business restructurings with tax-minimization objectives. These transactions are all structured with the objective of articulating GWCs, where the value created in developing countries generates profits and wealth elsewhere, often in entities strategically located in jurisdictions that provide fiscal benefits, financial secrecy, and targeted "legal affordances" (see Chapter 1 in this volume).

Transfer pricing mechanisms impact the attribution of wealth across the chain when a company produces locally—taking advantage of lower costs; production and consumer subsidies; and proximity to natural resources, local human resources, and infrastructure—but the company also uses transfer pricing mechanisms to erode the tax base and shift value out of the country. Several methodologies have been used to estimate the volume of illicit financial flows occurring through transfer pricing. These can

Verónica Grondona and Martín Burgos, *Food*. In: *Global Wealth Chains*. Edited by Leonard Seabrooke and Duncan Wigan, Oxford University Press. © Verónica Grondona and Martín Burgos (2022). DOI: 10.1093/oso/9780198832379.003.0008 be divided in two broad groups: those using trade data to estimate what is usually referred to as trade mispricing or misinvoicing and its impact; and those using foreign direct investment (FDI) data to estimate the amount of profit shifted.

Methodologies based on FDI data, though useful for capturing a global picture, are difficult to apply at a local level due to a lack of information in developing countries on multinational entity investments (and the bureaucratic difficulties in obtaining such information). Moreover, such analyses (UNCTAD, 2015) address illicit financial flows ocurring through debt and interest payments, not those occurring through under- and over-pricing of goods, or those relating to intragroup services and/or royalties. Using trade data, methodologies deployed to generate a global number from macro-data, for example comparing the export data of a country with imports registered in another (country-partner methodologies), ultimately run up against the impossibility of isolating that which they are measuring. Moreover, they generally rely on the comparison of the exports of one country with the imports of another, assuming that the difference represents under-invoicing of exports, when the difference could represent over-invoicing of imports. Methodologies using micro-data require sufficiently comparable prices, or must resort to price-filter analysis and risk underestimating the value of mispricing (Pak, 2012). They also do not address illicit financial flows occurring through payments for intragroup services, royalties, or financial transactions.

In this chapter we use micro-data in analysing Argentinian soybean exports. Here perfect comparables are available: international market quotes. It should be noted that this methodology does not allow for an estimation of illicit financial flows ocurring through payments for intragroup services, royalties, or financial transactions, as there is very limited information for an analysis of this sector based on FDI data. The extensive second section of the chapter summarizes the main characteristics of the soybean sector and classifies it in the GWC framework. The third section presents the data analysis. The final section provides an interpretation of the data.

Argentinian soybean exports and global value chains

The soybean sector

The main producers of soybean are the United States, Brazil, Argentina, China, and India. China is also the largest importer, followed by the

European Union, Mexico, and Japan. The United States is the largest exporter, followed by Brazil, Argentina, Paraguay, and Canada. Argentina is by far the largest exporter of soybean oil, followed by Brazil, the United States, the Netherlands, and Paraguay (Murphy, Burch, & Clapp, 2012). Archer Daniels Midland (ADM), Bunge, Cargill, and Louis Dreyfus (known as the ABCD companies) are the largest four grain traders in the world. The global soybean market is dominated by the ABCD companies (Murphy, Burch, & Clapp, 2012).

The soybean sector in Argentina grew since the 1990s due to changes in the means of production (increases in scale, direct sowing, new machinery, implementation of new chemicals) and in the actors involved (sowing pools, contractors, oil industries), and due to a new institutional framework driven by the approval of the use of transgenics in 1996 in response to increased international prices as a result of demand from China and the rest of Asia. This institutional framework emerged in the context of political shifts in Latin American government policies in which privatization was used as a way of financing fiscal and financial deficits. In this context, the privatization of railways, national highways, and public warehouses, and the elimination of the National Grain Boards and changes in the fideicomisos legislation[1] were central to the move to a new agricultural "model" (Burgos, Mattos, & Medina, 2014). In this shift, local economic groups and multinational enterprises gained leverage, concentrating power in the core nodes of the agricultural value chain. Increased vertical integration of the big grain exporters resulted, facilitating the creation of private ports, plants for the soybean industrialization, private warehouses and, in some cases, the private administration of the railways.

This new configuration of the logic of production and decisions taken by the actors in the sector led to enterprises integrating and diversifying activities. Soybean oil manufacturers sell products to exporters in the same economic group which export goods through private ports which they own, through related intermediaries, to affiliated companies located in India or China. Integration and diversification of activities make the regulators' task acutely difficult, as it very difficult for local regulators in Argentina to access to the full picture of the related companies and diverse activities in which these companies engage, particularly abroad. Integration allows for transfer pricing within related companies in the country, something that is not yet regulated in Argentina (nor in most countries).

---

[1] The fideicomisos legislation (Law 24.441 from 1994) enabled the creation of "cultivation financial pools" for investment in the agricultural sector.

Table 8.1 Soybean exports as a percentage of total Argentinian exports

Year	2010	2011	2012	2013
Soybean meal	12%	12%	13%	14%
Soybean oil	6%	6%	5%	5%
Soybean	7%	6%	4%	5%
Subtotal	25%	24%	22%	24%

Source: Trademap

Table 8.2 Companies' share of Argentinian soybean exports

Year	2010	2011	2012	2013
Soybean meal	73%	68%	67%	69%
Soybean oil	81%	71%	71%	67%
Soybean	61%	51%	46%	48%

Source: Trademap and Penta Transaction

Agricultural products in general, and soybean in particular, are key for Argentina due to their importance in generating foreign exchange and tax revenue.[2]

As shown in Table 8.1, soybean-related exports represented 24 per cent of total Argentinian exports in 2013. Soybean is the main export to China, Argentina's second-largest commercial partner after Brazil. It is notable that these exports are concentrated in a very few enterprises, including Cargill, Bunge, Nidera, Dreyfus, Toepfer, Deheza, Vicentin, and Oleaginosa Moreno, which are the companies analyzed here.

Table 8.2 shows that the eight exporters analyzed in this chapter accounted for 48 percent of the soybean exports and 67 percent of soybean oil and meal exports in 2013.

As noted by Pierri and Cosenza (2014), the soybean market is particularly concentrated at the level of the exporters in Argentina—even more, for example, than the wheat market—mainly because Argentina sells an important part of its production with the added value provided by the milling process (soybean meal) and the sector is highly integrated. While

---

[2] Argentina had export tariffs of 35 percent for soybean, and 32 percent for both soybean oil and soybean meal between 2008 and 2015. The revenue from all export tariffs (which also included those applied to other sectors, such as mining) represented 4 percent of total government revenues in 2015. Also, soybean export companies were subject to a nominal corporate income tax of 35 percent.

the two other main exporters of soybean (Brazil and the United States) concentrate their exports in soybean (70 percent for Brazil and 80 percent for the United States), Argentina only exports 25 percent of its total soybean production in the form of soybeans; 50 percent is exported as meal and 25 percent as oil.[3]

In the Chinese context, the "soybean crisis" of 2004 provided the opportunity for the ABCD traders to enter the crushing industry by buying Chinese companies. By 2016, the share of the soybean market held by international traders (principally the ABCD companies) was 70 percent, and nearly 35 percent in the crushing industry (Jamet & Chaumet, 2016).

The main soybean buying and selling offices of the ABCD firms are located in Singapore and Geneva. The Geneva Bunge office provides origination for the Singapore office and trades all freight for international operations, also buying soybeans and soy products from North and South America for the office in Singapore. Bunge's Singapore office sends its daily sales to Geneva who in turn will buy soybeans and meal CIF ("cost, insurance, and freight" up to the import port) to match these sales from Bunge's major origination offices (USSEC, 2011, p. 58). Cargill's Asian headquarters in Singapore is responsible for selling soybeans and soybeans products to Asian customers. Their products are purchased from Cargill's major grain origination offices by the Geneva office, which is also responsible for the freight. In the same way, Louis Dreyfus also has an office in Singapore responsible for all trading operations and logistical support activities in Asia. The company buys its products CIF from major origination offices and sells them in Asia (USSEC, 2011, pp. 55–57).

The vertical integration of the soybean exporters and the localization of their main commercial offices in financial secrecy jurisdictions or tax heavens like Singapore and Switzerland[4] provides a lot of margin for the manipulation of the valuation of internal transactions (transfer mispricing) within the multinational companies for the purpose of allocating profits in the most convenient way, for example where corporate income tax is lower. Moreover, as the justification of such valuations of transactions is so complex in the context of the separate entity criteria and the arm's-length

---

[3] Source: COMTRADE.
[4] Switzerland is the number-one jurisdiction in the Tax Justice Network's 2018 Financial Secrecy Index (FSI), while Singapore is number five (see https://www.financialsecrecyindex.com/introduction/fsi-2018-results). Oxfam (2017) developed a blacklist of 35 tax havens using the criteria of the Council of Europe, and both Switzerland and Singapore were on that list.

principle[5] (incorporated to the Argentinian legislation in 1976), transfer mispricing can also serve the purpose of eluding financial controls for capital flight.

Transfer pricing mechanisms

In the context of the global validation provided to the arm's-length principle—which attempts to generate intragroup prices by comparing transactions within multinational groups with often hypothetical transactions between independent entities—and the separate entity principle—which treats entities belonging to integrated multinational enterprises as distinct for tax purposes—transactions can be used to virtually locate assets and wealth anywhere without any necessary connection to the economic reality of which group entity produces the value that is transferred (Grondona, 2014). Bryan et al. (2017, also Chapter 5 in this volume) note that regulatory frameworks have been transcended by the development of forms of capital which are increasingly abstract. In this context, the anti-tax-avoidance regulations seem unable to keep pace with the organization of multinational enterprises.

Enterprises in the soybean sector not only export goods to related parties but carry out financial and service transactions with related parties, and make commission and logistics payments with related and unrelated parties that are used for base erosion and profit shifting (Argibay Molina, 2013). Notably, of the 50 enterprises or multinational groups making the highest capital transfers (corresponding to debt payments, interest payments, tourism, services, etc.) abroad in the year 2001 (the year in which the Argentinian crisis that had begun in 1998 finally erupted), those by soybean exporters analyzed in this chapter stand out. In descending order by volume Nidera, Bunge Ceval SA, SA L. Dreyfus y Cía, Cargill SA, Vicentin SA and Aceitera General Deheza made combined transfers of $1.9 billion. Our calculation is based on information gathered by the Central Bank of Argentina in the context of the research commission created by Argentina's Chamber of Deputies to analyze capital flight during the economic crisis of 2001, in which foreign exchange restrictions had been the final detonator (Comisión Especial de la Cámara de Diputados 2001, 2005).

---

[5] Transfer prices are the prices used by related parties for valuing the transactions taking place between them. When two parties are not related, prices are settled through negotiation. However, the acknowledgement of the existence of a price, which is in itself a contract, between one party and another subject to it (as it is normally the case between two related parties) is already contradictory, as the lack of independence between the two parties results means no independent contract is possible, and thus the valuation of the internal transaction is unilaterally decided (Corti, 2012).

Global value chains and global wealth chains

The literature on global value chains and how they are governed began on the premise that production across the globe is increasingly fragmented. As trade became more integrated, production became more disintegrated with the rise of component manufacturing and modularity. Global value chain literature argues that information asymmetries between different levels of the chain—characterized as market, modular, relational, captive, and hierarchy—are important in determining the potential for genuine economic development, fostering human capital, and reducing trade barriers (Gereffi et al., 2005; Seabrooke & Wigan, 2017). Various international organizations (the WTO, OECD, and World Bank, among others) have deployed global value chain analyses to identify production processes, trade opportunities, and ways to reduce information asymmetries as a means to encourage growth and development.

The segmentation of multinational groups into components holding distinct functions, risks, and assets (the separate entity combined with the arm's-length criteria tends to the same segmentation also occurring within the same entity)[6] ends in limited profits in high tax jurisdictions and increased base erosion and profit shifting. Several factors have compounded this tendency. Amongst these are: the weight given to the intellectual property rights in global value chains (see Bryan et al., Chapter 5 in this volume); the possibility of contractually locating such property rights in entities optimally located for tax and regulatory purposes; the system of tax treaties (see Hearson, Chapter 3 in this volume); and the facilities provided for corporate tax inversions[7] and earnings stripping.[8] In this context, wealth chains serve the purpose of hiding, obscuring, and relocating wealth by breaking loose from the location of value creation.

The GWC typology is delineated on the basis of the complexity of information and knowledge related to the product or service provided by the supplier, the ease of multi-jurisdictional regulatory intervention, and the capability of suppliers to mitigate challenges. Due to the fact that soybean and its by-products are commodities and that the main players in

---

[6] For example, the contract manufacturing activities for related companies are segmented from the manufacturing activities that are performed for the local market; the contract distribution and sales commissioning activities are segmented from the sales to third parties performed locally. Such financial segmentation is used to set differentiated prices and profit margins for each intragroup transaction.

[7] Corporate tax inversion is a practice by which multinational corporations are acquired by smaller companies located in a zero- or low-tax jurisdiction so as to reduce the combined firm's overall tax burden.

[8] Earnings stripping can be achieved through tax-deductible payments (e.g. in the form of loans, royalties, and services) to a zero or low-tax jurisdiction.

the sector are multinational entities that have the possibility of acting as highly integrated suppliers acquiring the raw materials from smaller players, soybean exporters described in this chapter could fit a transition from a market toward captive forms in the national trade segment (producer to crusher/trader). This form is appropriate since the soybean market in Argentina is not integrated by small and medium enterprises as observed in other cases (Montalbano, Nenci, & Salvatici, 2015)). Market wealth chains are present when there are multiple suppliers competing on price and quality in accordance with clear market mechanisms. Captive chains occur when lead suppliers dominate smaller suppliers by dominating the legal apparatus and financial technology. As our case shows, there has been a clear move toward lead supplier coordination. The power of soybean exporters is reflected in the fact that the Minister of Agriculture since December 2015, Ricardo Buryaile, used to be the Vice President of the Argentine Rural Confederation between 2007 and 2009.

Due to the participation of large cooperative producers working at the same level as multinational corporations in the soybean production sector, we could also classify the soybean sector in the national trade segment as a "market model" in GVC terms; sector linkages could be taking place at arm's length, established legal regimes are of low complexity, and there are multiple suppliers who compete on price and capacity. In the soybean international segment (crusher/trader to customer) where clients and suppliers are highly integrated, the governance of the soybean GWC reflects the hierarchy type. Even when the ABCD firms are not dealing, in the case of soybean, with highly complex products, the tax planning transactions are increasingly complex, deploying several entities dealing with marketing, insurance, and freight activities located in tax havens.

Since 2000, the Argentinian tax authority (Administración Federal de Ingresos Públicos—AFIP) has examined transfer pricing (i) during the course of general tax audits; (ii) during specific transfer pricing audits in industries previously identified based on the documentation and declarations presented by the companies (e.g. automotive, pharmaceutical, iron and steel, fishing, cereals, oil); (iii) of companies with operations in tax havens; and (iv) of companies that have registered technology transfers or brand licensing agreements with the National Institute of Industrial Property. 28 percent of taxpayers audited in 2009 operated in the "cereals" sector.

Grondona and Knobel (2017) provide a comprehensive review of transfer pricing cases that have reached different court levels in Argentina over

Table 8.3 Price differences in commodity exports by typical intermediaries and end clients found by the AFIP since 2009

Residence	Intermediary	End client	Price difference
Dutch capital	Related company, Asia	China, Europe,Brazil	5%
US capital	America branch	China, Spain, Malaysia India	5%
German capital	Parent company Europe	China, Spain, Brazil, Chile	5–10%
Argentinian capital	America branch	China, Spain	5–10%
US capital	US parent company	China, Saudi Arabia, Syria	5%

Source: Echegaray, Michel, & Barzola (2013, p. 86).

time. Among those cases involving the companies analyzed in this chapter, Cargill claimed in defence that prices established verbally differed from those on the date of shipping. Charges of tax evasion were overturned on appeal. From the review of cases it can be gleaned that: (i) cereal exporters tend to use intermediary companies; (ii) in some cases, the AFIP found that there was no contract in place for related party transactions; and (iii) the AFIP has noted that prices of exports conducted through intermediaries tend to be lower than for other exports from the same exporter, and at a price lower to that of a recognized international quote at the shipping date. Such intermediaries tend to be located in tax havens or secrecy jurisdictions. The AFIP has also analyzed price differences between the origin and destination of Argentinian commodity exports by large concentrated export groups (mainly linked to the oil and oilseeds sector), noting that in some cases there is a 5–10 percent price difference between origin and destination (see Table 8.3).

Under- and over-pricing of soybean exports in Argentina

Export set under analysis

This section analyzes the exports of soybean, soybean oil, and soybean meal from Argentina. The exports of these three products represented 24 percent of all of Argentinian exports in 2013, 22 percent in 2012, 24 percent in

Table 8.4 Exporters, group membership, and headquarters location

Exporter	Group to which it belongs	Headquarters	Jurisdiction of HQ location
Aceitera General Deheza	Urquía Group	Aceitera General Deheza S.A.	Argentina
Bunge	Bunge	Bunge Limited	Bermuda
Cargill	Cargill	Cargill, Inc.	United States
Dreyfus	Louis Dreyfus	Louis Dreyfus Holding B.V.	Netherlands
Nidera	Nidera	Nidera B.V.	Netherlands
Oleaginosa Moreno	Glencore	Glencore plc	Switzerland
Toepfer	ADM	Archer-Daniels-Midland Company	United States
Vicentin	Vicentin	Vicentin S.A.I.C.	Argentina

Source: Based on company websites, annual reports, and Gaggero et al., (2013, p. 107)

2011, and 25 percent in 2010. Eight companies dedicated to the export of soybean and related products have been selected for analysis. The selection is based on a list of companies fined by the Argentinian tax authorities for paying export duties below the level required for soybean exports. These firms referenced an outdated export duty lower than that in place at the moment of the purchase of the grains to be exported. A total of $787 million in fines had been levied on the cereal companies by May 2013, with Cargill subject to the largest fine of $228 million, LDC (Dreyfus) next with $141 million, and Nidera $132 million (Gaggero, Rua, & Gaggero, 2013).

As can be observed in Table 8.4, the companies selected for the analysis are part of transnational groups with headquarters in Argentina, Bermuda, the United States of America, the Netherlands,[9] and Switzerland.

It is quite remarkable that most of these companies have their headquarters in known tax havens. Bermuda, the United States, and Switzerland were among the 92 countries recently screened by the European Union for the building of the EU list of non-cooperative jurisdictions for tax purposes, and both Bermuda and Switzerland are still on the EU's grey

---

[9] LDC Argentina S.A. has been controlled since 2007 by Galba SA (75 percent), a company resident in Switzerland, and related to LDC. The headquarters of the LDC group are in the Netherlands. Ultimate control is in a trust named Akira, whose beneficial owner is the Luis Dreyfus family.

list.[10] The Netherlands was also recently identified by the European Commission as a jurisdiction providing opportunities for "aggressive tax planning,"[11] a euphemism for tax avoidance. This suggests that these companies may be using such jurisdictions for tax avoidance, or for the financial secrecy they grant.

The exports of these companies represented 69 percent of soybean meal exports in 2013, 67 percent of soybean oil exports, and 48 percent of soybean exports. Soybean exports by the selected exporters are less significant because soybean oil and meal are processed by the multinational companies and subsequently exported. This processing implies higher entrepreneurial content in soybean meal and oil exports, and lower in soybean, where there is some participation of national exporters and cooperatives.

Methodology

This section compares the average price of daily customs registrations at the shipping date of the set of eight companies listed in Table 8.5 between 2010 and 2013 with the daily price of an international quote.

The application of this methodology is possible only when customs registrations are publicly available and if there are public quotes available that match the goods under analysis. This methodology is the closest to what is known as the "sixth method" in transfer pricing, applicable according to Argentinian law to "exports made to related parties, that relate to cereals, oil products, and other products of the earth, hydrocarbons and its by-products, and, in general, goods that have a known quote in international markets, in which an international intermediary is involved that is not the effective recipient of the merchandise." In such cases, the price should be calculated based on "the trading value of the goods in a transparent market on the date on which the goods are shipped." According to Argentinian legislation, the sixth method is not applicable when the taxpayer can demonstrate that the foreign intermediary has economic substance.[12] In such cases the best of the five remaining methods prescribed

---

[10] See Council of the EU. 2018, June 8. Code of Conduct Group (Business Taxation): Report to the Council/ Endorsement. 9637/18.

[11] See https://ec.europa.eu/info/publications/2018-european-semester-country-reports_en.

[12] An international intermediary is understood to have economic substance if the main activity of the intermediary does not consist in receiving passive rents, that the intermediary has a "real" presence in the residence jurisdiction, and that the intermediary performs activities with other entities outside the multinational group.

Table 8.5 Summary with transfer-pricing-related court decisions

Company	Ruling from	Fiscal year in question	Date of last ruling	Result in favour of	Details
Cargill S.A.C.E.I.	Camara Nacional de Apelaciones en lo Penal Tributario (CNAPT—National Appeal Court for Tax Crimes)	2000, 2001, 2002, 2003	February 22, 2011	Taxpayer	The case related to exports from Argentina through a branch located in Uruguay. The company argued that the prices from Montevideo were settled with different importers throughout the world and that these prices were agreed verbally by telephone or through different types of mail, in relation to the demand and supply at the date of these communications, and that this was the reason why the prices differed from those at the shipping date taken by the tax authority. Cargill's directors were charged for the crime of tax evasion, and the Court on Economic Crimes ruled against them on the grounds that there was no definitive date of agreement; but on appeal to the CNAPT that court ruled in their favour, considering that the pricing methodology involved had not always resulted in a lower export price.
Nidera S.A.	Ruling by TFN ratified by the CCAF	1999	June 6, 2013	Tax authority	Nidera S.A. exported commodities (cereals and oils) through intermediaries resident in tax havens, and argued that its export prices were based on the export prices at the date of the agreement. The case discussed whether the "sixth method," Article 8 of the Income Tax Law (Ley de Impuesto a las Ganancias (LIG) in Spanish), or the Comparable Uncontrolled Price (CUP) Method (Article 15 of the LIG) should have been applied. Article 8 of the LIG required that the value of exported goods, for the purpose of the determination of income, should be established "subtracting from the wholesale price at destination the cost of such goods,

Continued

			Taxpayer/tax authority

transport and insurance expenses, sales commissions and expenses, and other expenses incurred in Argentina" while the CUP Method is one of the OECD recommended transfer pricing methods, based on the arm's-length principle, which recommends the comparison of the price of the intercompany transaction with a price of a comparable transaction between non-related entities. The tax authority finally stipulated the use of the CUP Method based on prices published by the Secretary of Agriculture in Argentina at the shipping date and corresponding to an analysis of the behavior of other comparable companies (Alfred C. Toepfer and La Plata Cereal S.A.). The TFN ruled in favour of the tax authority and the CCAF upheld the decision of the TFN.

Oleaginosa Moreno exported commodities to Atlantic Oils & Meals (a related party resident in Switzerland), priced free on board (FOB), at international prices on the contract date. The invoice date was relatively close to the shipping date, but the price reflected in the invoice was based on a prior contract, which did not have a specific date. In the transfer pricing documentation presented by the taxpayer, Deloitte used the CUP method to validate Oleaginosa Moreno's prices, comparing the company's averaged prices with the ones published by the Secretary of Agriculture for the invoice date. The tax authority made the tax adjustments based on the highest price (referring to Article 8 of the LIG, although it did not use the prices at destination and nor did the taxpayer) published by the Secretary of Agriculture between the invoice and the shipping date for the commodities exported to Atlantic Oils & Meals, in a transaction by transaction analysis. The tax authority also observed that the exports made to an independent party in Chile had been priced using the quotes

Oleaginosa Moreno S.A.C.I.F.I.A   TFN   1999   September 9, 2014

Table 8.5 *Continued*

Company	Ruling from	Fiscal year in question	Date of last ruling	Result in favour of	Details
					published by the Secretary of Agriculture for the invoice date. The adjustments made by the tax authority reduced the tax loss carry forward of the taxpayer. The taxpayer questioned the use of the shipping date, alleging that the sixth method had been applied retroactively (as the sixth method was introduced into the legislation in 2003); and it objected to the internal comparables (the transactions with the independent party in Chile) used, alleging that the transactions had significant differences for which no adjustments had been made. The TFN found that there had not been a retroactive application of the sixth method. However, it ruled in favour of the taxpayer since the legislation in place in the fiscal year under analysis did not indicate that the price to be used should be that of the international exchange quoted price at the shipping date, so a valid quoted price at the date for the contract could be used. The TFN also observed that the transactions with the independent party in Chile could not be used as a reference for the date to be used due to the significant differences they had with the transactions with related parties. Nevertheless, the TFN ruled in favour of the tax authority in relation to the use of a transaction by transaction analysis, instead of the average global analysis employed by the taxpayer.
Oleaginosa Moreno S.A.C.I.F.I.A.	CSJN	2000	September 2, 2014	Taxpayer	The AFIP objected to the export price of commodities sold to Atlantic Oils & Meals, a related party located in Switzerland, because for 36 transactions the price had been documented as an average

instead of individually. The AFIP proposed that such prices shouloud be calculated individually and in relation to the price at the shipping date. The TFN partially confirmed the AFIP's position, observing that the legislation in place was consistent with the methodology chosen by the AFIP, although the use of the contract date could also be permitted—as suggested by the company—since the legislation in place at the time of the operations did not indicate the use of any specific date. The AFIP had also observed a difference between the price paid for the export of commodities to related parties and to independent parties located in Chile. However, the TFN accepted the complaint of the company observing that there were differences in the conditions of these transactions that precluded such transactions from being used as internal comparables. Both the AFIP and Oleaginosa Moreno appealed to the CCAF, which ruled in favour of Oleaginosa Moreno, and the AFIP's further appeal to the CSJN was also rejected.

| Alfred C. Toepfer Internacional | CSJN | 1999 | March 25, 2015 | Taxpayer | Toepfer had been selling commodities to two non-resident associated traders: one based in Liechtenstein acting as an intermediary for independent clients based in Europe, Africa, and Asia, and the other in Brazil dealing with the South American market. The exchange-quoted price of the commodity at the shipping date was consistently higher than the intragroup price. The tax authority argued that the sixth method was applicable, but the tax court ruled that it could only be applied prospectively, from the date on which the law introducing this rule had become effective, October 22, 2003. On appeal, the CCAF accepted the adjustments proposed by the tax authority, but only for those transactions for which the taxpayer could not prove the transaction date. It also observed that the tax authority had been able to prove that when the taxpayer exported to independent clients its prices when the |

Continued

Table 8.5 *Continued*

Company	Ruling from	Fiscal year in question	Date of last ruling	Result in favour of	Details
					taxpayer exported to independent clients its prices were in general higher than the exchange-quoted prices at the shipping date, and that for such sales the transaction dates were much closer to the shipping date than for the transactions with related parties). Toepfer appealed, observing that the previous ruling had only considered the underpriced cases and not the overpriced ones, when comparing with the prices published by the Secretary of Agriculture at the shipping date. The CSJN ruled in favour of the taxpayer based on administrative grounds, as well as the interpretation that the regulations in place before 2003 did not provide for taking only the cases of underpricing when comparing with the commodity price at the shipping date.

Source: Based on Grondona (2019)

by law should be applied; which are based on the arm's-length principle that requires that transactions between related parties should mirror
a similar (often theoretically construed) transaction between unrelated
parties.

Here, the comparison was drawn with price quotes on the Gulf of Mexico
(one of the two international markets for trading soybean products; the
other is Chicago). In Argentina, the Ministry of Agriculture also publishes
soybean product prices used by the tax authority for the application of the
sixth method, but even when such prices follow those of the Gulf of Mexico,
they are not market quotes. Therefore, for the purpose of our analysis we
use Gulf of Mexico prices. The local trading markets of Rosario and Buenos
Aires in Argentina were not used because prices here do not reflect export
prices but local prices (transactions between producers and exporters).

The stipulation to use prices available on the shipping date is often
disputed due to the fact that the sector usually uses future quotes when
negotiating prices with third parties. Even though this argument may be legitimate in relation to current practices in the sector, it is difficult to verify
when the agreement has been made between related parties, since in practice there are joint interests. Further, when dealing between related parties,
a futures contract does not necessarily make sense, since any uncertainty
that a futures contract is meant to mitigate by definition remains within the
same group—shifting such real economic risks within a group will only in-
frequently be strategically coherent. Futures contracts are more likely to be
appropriate therefore in transactions with third parties. When transacting
with a related intermediary sitting between the local exporter and the unrelated party local income will be affected by the margin retained by such
an intermediary after negotiating the price with the unrelated third party
based on future prices, and having settled the price with the local producer.
Our analysis of customs data suggests that export underpricing is everyday
practice.

Data

Applying the methodology outlined above, the average mispricing of exports in the soybean sector was 10 percent in 2010, 7 percent in 2011, 13
percent in 2012, and 9 percent in 2013, amounting to as much as $1,500
million in 2012 (see Table 8.6).

Table 8.6 Soybean export underpricing ($ and %)

Year	Soybean meal	Soybean oil	Soybean	Total
2010	– 672,689,866	– 327,886,389	– 242,665,029	– 1,243,241,284
2011	– 553,279,766	– 257,674,139	– 117,655,984	– 928,609,890
2012	– 1,134,870,549	– 163,414,113	– 212,319,241	– 1,510,603,903
2013	– 717,142,518	– 251,908,091	– 168,319,051	– 1,137,369,659
2010	–11%	–10%	–8%	–10%
2011	–8%	–7%	–4%	–7%
2012	–16%	–5%	–15%	–13%
2013	–10%	–10%	–9%	–9%

Source: Reuters and Penta-Transaction

Table 8.7 Soybean export overpricing ($ and %)

Year	Soybean meal	Soybean oil	Soybean	Total
2010	21,182,572	2,336,356	43,365	23,562,293
2011	32,390,020	12,470,257	44,528,967	89,389,244
2012	42,196,592	24,541,622	8,603,375	75,341,589
2013	66,439,464	2,041,905	5,372,137	73,853,506
2010	0%	0%	0%	0%
2011	0%	0%	2%	1%
2012	1%	1%	1%	1%
2013	1%	0%	0%	1%

Source: Reuters and Penta-Transaction

Export overpricing did not exceed 2 percent over the same period, being on average in the soybean sector 0 percent in 2010, 1 percent in 2011, 1 percent in 2012, and 1 percent in 2013, and amounting to $89 million in 2011 (Table 8.7).

These findings stand for soybean, soybean oil, and soybean meal, even after accounting for the tendency of commodity prices to rise and fall and display considerable volatility.

As can be seen in Figure 8.1, the underpricing in the soybean meal is constant through the whole period, and particularly relevant in 2012. There are also a few moments of clear overpricing; in the first months of 2010,

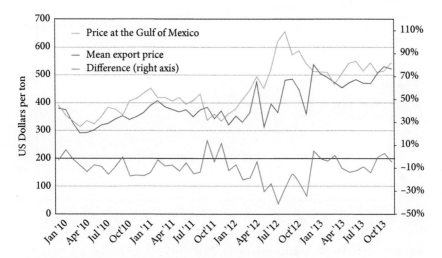

Fig. 8.1 Soybean meal—daily price difference, 2010/2013
Source: Reuters and Penta-Transaction

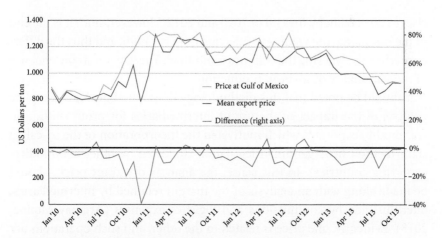

Fig. 8.2 Soybean oil—daily price difference, 2010/2013
Source: Reuters and Penta-Transaction

between October 2011 and January 2012, in January 2013, and in October 2013.

A similar situation is observed in the case of soybean oil, presented in Figure 8.2, where underpricing is seen throughout the period (with few exceptions).

In the case of the exports of soybean, underpricing can also be observed throughout the period (Figure 8.3). The average daily difference in prices

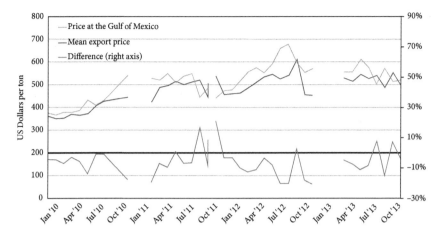

Fig. 8.3 Soybean—daily price difference, 2010/2013
Source: Reuters and Penta-Transaction

rises to 20 percent by the end of 2010 and 2012. However, since it is the end of the campaign, the volumes traded are not very high, and thus the difference when considering the volumes is minimal. The gaps are a consequence of the seasonality of soybean production.

It should be noted that this methodology does not allow for a complete analysis of the impact of the use of intermediaries for profit shifting in commodity exports,[13] which motivated the incorporation of the so-called sixth method in Argentinian legislation (followed by other commodity-exporting countries). In this sense, the analysis of export prices should be made along with an analysis of the margin retained by intermediaries, often justified by commissions and logistics expenses (Argibay Molina, 2013). Evidently, one price is related to the other, and such operations are interrelated (Grondona & Picciotto, 2015).

Similarly, the analysis here does not shed light on illicit financial flows channeled through alternative transfer pricing mechanisms, such as financial transactions, payments for intangibles or services, and the import of overpriced goods. Estimates of the money value attached to the manipulation of intragroup prices are likely to be higher where these alternative transfer pricing mechanisms can be identified and incorporated into analysis. Finally, it is not possible to provide a comprehensive analysis of the

---

[13] This has been attempted in Cobham, Jansky, & Prats (2014).

taxes paid by these multinational entities in Argentina,[14] as only firms listed on the Buenos Aires stock exchange are required to provide this information publicly. However, evaluating export underpricing in developing countries provides additional information on the role assigned to developing countries in significant global value chains and how global wealth chains circumscribe the resources accruing to developing countries on the basis of their contribution to global economic processes.

Differences in prices and values by country of destination and probable exporters

We analyzed the accumulated differences in prices and value per country of destination and "probable exporter"[15] for the month of March in 2010, 2011, 2012, and 2013. Regarding the accumulated difference in values for the month of March over 2010–2013 by country of destination of Argentinian soybean meal exports, it can be noted that the Netherlands appears in the top position for most "probable exporters" (it is in first place for Aceitera General Deheza and Oleaginosa Moreno, and in second place for Luis Dreyfus and Vicentin). Other destinations are remarkable also for the differences in values observed in the exports conducted through them. This is the case for Poland as a destination for Cargill as "probable exporter" (where an accumulated difference in value of $13 million is seen in March of 2010–2013).

When we analyze the accumulated difference in price for the month of March over 2010–2013, the largest differences are observed for destinations such as the United Kingdom and the Netherlands (for "probable exporters" Cargill in the first case, and Aceitera General Deheza, Louis Dreyfus, Vicentin, and Oleaginosa Moreno in the second case). However, other destinations are remarkable for the differences in prices that are observed in the soybean meal exports going through them. These are the cases of Colombia and Italy (Grondona & Burgos (2015).

---

[14] While companies resident in Argentina are required to make annual accounts publicly available, there are bureaucratic impediments to accessing this information. Access is by application for each individual company. Although searches can be made online, applications are required to be made in person and on paper, the accounts are provided on paper, and a legitimate interest in the use of the data needs to be proved by means of a letter from the institution requesting the data.

[15] Exporters identified in the database Penta-Transactions are 'probable exporters' since the information is not made public by the Argentinian customs, but is obtained by Penta-Transactions through their own investigations.

Interpretation

A possible explanation

International prices for soybean-related products displayed significant volatility between September 2008 and 2009 and between 2011 and 2013 due to the deepening international economic crisis. In each of these episodes, a bubble-type rise in prices was followed by a substantial fall. Comparing the monthly average price with a monthly average international quote (Chicago International prices in this case), in the soybean oil case, we can see that differences between these two are smaller in 2014 and 2015 were prices seem to have stabilized again. Therefore, it seems that transfer mispricing has been used to hedge against international price instability. Most importantly, as can be seen in Figure 8.4, differences are higher when international prices rise and lower when international prices go down, indicating that when international prices are high there is more margin for profit shifting.

Argentina had export tariffs of 35 percent for soybean, and 32 percent for soybean oil and soybean meal between 2008 and 2015. Underpricing allows exporters to avoid not only corporate income tax, but also export tariffs. Changes in exchange rates do not seem to have a clear impact on export underpricing: while the devaluation of January 2014 seems to have had no

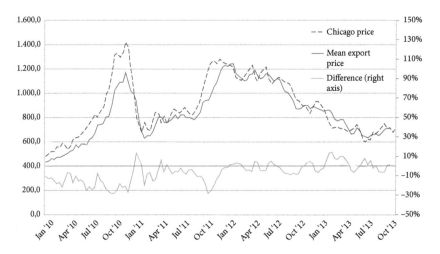

Fig. 8.4 Soybean oil—monthly price difference 2006/2016
Source: Trademap and Argentina's Ministry of Economy

impact on the differences between the monthly average of the export price of soybean meal and the international quote, that of December 2015 seems to correspond with a moment in which significant export underpricing is observed.[16] Moreover, exchange market controls do not seem to be an underlying reason for export underpricing: from 2012 to the end of 2015, the government intervened in the exchange market restricting the acquisition of foreign exchange; however, there does not seem to be a particular change in the pattern of underpricing at that time.

Intragroup prices can be used to mitigate the effects of international price volatility. Even though the analysis in this chapter does not differentiate between exports to related and unrelated parties, based on the characteristics of the sector it can be assumed that there is either an economic linkage between parties or the possibility of applying trade mispricing mechanisms as if such a linkage existed (Argibay Molina, 2013). As demonstrated by Bernard, Jensen, and Schott (2006), intragroup transactions are often used to mitigate negative impacts on corporate income that arise for a variety of reasons.[17]

Analysis of the margin obtained by intermediate jurisdictions

The analysis of customs data shows that there is not one tax haven that is significantly more relevant as country of destination for Argentinian soybean exports. It is however in the export of soybean meal and soybean oil where more countries are used as intermediaries.

In the case of soybean meal, while Argentina, Brazil, and the United States account for more than 70 percent of global exports, the Netherlands appears to have an important role in the global circulation of this product, accounting for between 7 and 9 percent between 2010 and 2014. This may be explained by the importance of the port of Rotterdam in the redistribution of products to the main destinations of France, Germany, the United Kingdom, Belgium, and Denmark.[18]

---

[16] In January 2014, the government devaluated the peso by 12 percent. In December 2015, the new Argentinian government devalued the peso by more than 30 percent in one day.

[17] Bernard et al. (2006) analyzed intragroup prices against unrelated ones, for different product characteristics, firm size, export share, oligopoly markets, taxation, exchange rate, and import duties. They did not analyze the use of intragroup prices for price stabilization, but we have extended their conclusions to such cases.

[18] *Source*: Trademap.

Table 8.8 Difference of prices of soybean meal exports. Argentina and the Netherlands. $ FOB per ton

Year	2010	2011	2012	2013
Average FOB price Argentina	328	367	444	488
Average FOB price the Netherlands	393	436	499	568
Difference	1.2	1.19	1.12	1.16

Source: Penta-Transaction and UN Comtrade

Based on this, the annual median FOB[19] prices of Argentinian soybean meal exports between 2010 and 2013 are compared with the annual median FOB prices of the Netherlands' exports of soybean meal (Table 8.8). The difference is estimated to range between 20 percent in 2010 and 12 percent in 2012. It cannot be unequivocally concluded from this difference in prices that abusive practice is at play. However, it should be noted that even when costs of insurance and freight may vary, these tend to represent 5 or 8 percent of the differences and cannot in themselves explain the observed difference in prices.[20]

Conclusion

Many developing countries are particularly concerned with problems of transfer pricing in the commodity sector, which often account for a significant proportion of developing country economies. Similar to other sectors, profit attribution may be highly dependent on the valuation assigned to commodity exports. For this reason, a number of developing countries have adopted the so-called sixth method, following the Argentinian experience. This method aims to establish a clear and easily administered benchmark and avoid the need for subjective judgment and discretion (Grondona & Picciotto, 2015).

The analysis provided in this chapter of the Argentinian soybean related exports by a set of companies represents between a minimum of 46 percent

---

[19] The term free on board (FOB) indicates that the price is the price of the good up to the export port, and includes neither the cost of transport, nor the insurance, nor any other cost incurred from the export port to its destination. The balance of payments indicates exports at FOB prices and imports at CIF prices.

[20] See Burgos (2012) and Basualdo and Kulfas (2002).

(of soybean exports in 2012) and a maximum of 81 percent (of soybean oil exports in 2010) of the soybean, soybean oil, and soybean meal exports between 2010 and 2013. The underpricing of exports, when compared to the export price recorded in customs registrations and price quotes on the Gulf of Mexico, per day is, on average, 10 percent in 2010, 7 percent in 2011, 13 percent in 2012, and 9 percent in 2013. For the same period, export overpricing did not amount to more than 2 percent of the value of the exports. While this analysis does not differentiate between exports to related and unrelated parties, based on the levels of concentration and integration in this sector, it should be assumed that there is either an economic linkage between parties or the possibility of applying trade mispricing mechanisms as if such a linkage existed (Argibay Molina, 2013). Intragroup pricing may be used to dampen the effect of international price volatility. In the context of GWCs, the captive form of GWC could be used to understand the behavior of the soybean, soybean oil, and soybean meal exporters in Argentina. These are highly integrated companies that acquire raw materials from smaller players, and can use the pricing of their intragroup transactions for risk mitigation and wealth creation.

References

Argibay Molina, J. A. (2013). *The Phenomenon of Trade Mispricing: Untying the Knot for a Legal Analysis*. McGill University, Faculty of Law.

Basualdo, E. & Kulfas, M. (2002). La fuga de capitales en la Argentina. In J. Gambina, *La Globalización Económico-Financiera. Su Impacto en América Latina*. Buenos Aires. http://biblioteca.clacso.edu.ar/clacso/gt/20101004085849/5.pdf.

Bernard, A., Jensen, J., & Schott, P. (2006). *Transfer Pricing by US-Based Multinational Firms*. National Bureau of Economic Research. http://www.nber.org/papers/w12493.

Bryan, D., Rafferty, M., & Wigan, D. (2017). Capital unchained: Finance, intangible assets and the double life of capital in the offshore world. *Review of International Political Economy*, 24(1), 56–86.

Burgos, M. (2012). La ruta de la soja: Aportes para el entendimiento de la relación Argentina–China. *La revista del CCC* (online), 16.

Burgos, M., Mattos, E., & Medina, A. (2014). *La soja en Argentina (1990–2013): Cambios en la cadena de valor y nueva articulación de los actores sociales*. Centro de Economía y Finanzas para el Desarrollo de la Argentina (CEFID-AR). CEFID-AR.

Cobham, A., Jansky, P., & Prats, A. (2014). Estimating illicit flows of capital via trade mispricing: A Forensic analysis of data on Switzerland. Center for Global Development.

Comisión Especial de la Cámara de Diputados 2001 (2005). *Fuga de Divisas en la Argentina. Informe Final.* Siglo XXI Editores.

Corti, A. (2012). *Algunas Reflexiones Sobre los Mecanismos de Exacción de la Renta Impositiva Nacional: A Propósito de las Ficciones de Contratos al Interior de los Conjuntos Económicos. Derecho Público,* 2.

Echegaray, R., Michel, G., & Barzola, J. P. (2013). *La Administración Tributaria Frente al Contribuyente Global: Aspectos Técnicos y Prácticos Relevantes.* La Ley.

Gaggero, J., Rua, M., & Gaggero, A. (2013). *Fuga de Capitales III. Argentina (2002– 2012). Magnitudes, Evolución, Políticas Públicas y Cuestiones Fiscales Relevantes.* Centro de Economía y Finanzas para el Desarrollo de la Argentina (CEFID-AR). CEFID-AR.

Gereffi, G., Humphrey, J., & Sturgeon, T. (2005). The governance of global value chains. *Review of International Political Economy,* 12(1), 78–104.

Grondona, V. (2014). *Fuga de Capitales IV. Argentina. 2014. La Manipulación de los Precios de Transferencia.* Centro de Economía y Finanzas para el Desarrollo de la Argentina (CEFID-AR). CEFID-AR.

Grondona, V., & Knobel, A. (2017). *Transfer Pricing in Argentina 1932-2015.* International Centre for Tax and Development (ICTD).

Grondona, V. (2019). Transfer pricing: Concepts and practices of the "sixth method" in transfer pricing. In M. F. Montes, A. Bernardo, & D. Bernardo (eds.), *International Tax Cooperation: Perspectives from the Global South.* South Centre.

Grondona, V. & Burgos, M. (2015). *Fuga de Capitales VI. Argentina 2015. Estimación de los Precios de Transferencia. El Caso del Complejo Sojero.* Centro de Economía y Finanzas para el Desarrollo de la Argentina (CEFID-AR). CEFID-AR.

Grondona, V. & Picciotto, S. (2015). Response to Action 10 discussion draft on the transfer pricing aspects of cross border commodity transactions. BEPS monitoring group. https://bepsmonitoringgroup.files.wordpress.com/2015/02/ ap-10-commodities.pdf.

Jamet, J. P. & Chaumet, J. M. (2016). Soybean in China: adapting to the liberalization. *Oilseed and Fats Crops and Lipids Journal,* 23(6). D604.

Montalbano, P., Nenci, S., & Salvatici, L. (2015). *Trade, Value Chains and Food Security.* FAO-UN.

Murphy, S., Burch, D., & Clapp, J. (2012). Cereal Secrets. *The World's Largest Grain Traders and Global Agriculture.* Oxfam.

Oxfam. (2017). *Blacklist or Whitewash? What a Real EU Blacklist of Tax Havens should Look Like*. Oxfam. https://www.oxfam.org/en/research/blacklist-or-whitewash-what-real-eu-blacklist-tax-havens-should-look.

Pak, S. (2012). *Lost Billions. Transfer Pricing in the Extractive Industries*. Trade Research Institute Inc. https://www.publishwhatyoupay.no/sites/default/files/import/1008a-PWYP_TransferPricing_ENG_DOWNLOAD.pdf.

Pierri, J. & Cosenza, L. (2014). *El Diferencial de Precios en el Comercio Exterior de Granos, 1980–2010*. Biblos.

Seabrooke, L. & Wigan, D. (2017). The governance of global wealth chains. *Review of International Political Economy*, 24(1), 1–29.

UNCTAD. (2015). FDI, Tax and Development. The Fiscal Role of Multinational Enterprises: Towards Guidelines for Coherent International Tax and Investment Policies. United Nations.

USSEC. (2011). How the Global Oilseed and Grain Trade Works. US Soybean Export Council (USSEC).

9

Art

Oddný Helgadóttir

Introduction

Times have changed in the art world. Paul Gauguin spent a decade as a stockbroker in the Paris Bourse before he set sail for Tahiti in search of "a more natural," if also a more impoverished, existence as an artist (Mendelsohn, 2017). A hundred years later, Jeff Koons transitioned seamlessly from his career as a commodities trader to that of an artist, putting the skills of this previous trade to efficient use as the producer of highly lucrative and unabashedly commercial works (Landi, 2007). He and other leading lights of his generation embraced Andy Warhol's tenet that "good business is the best art," and have largely treated the artistic endeavor as the trade of selling luxury goods to the highest bidder (Schroeder, 2013; Adam, 2017). While this embrace between art and finance is by no means a novelty, it is now tighter and more intimate than ever before (Adam, 2014, 2017).[1]

Koons' generation of artist has been central to an art market that has been in an almost relentless boom since the 1980s (Adam, 2014, 2017). While much of the economy has been in the doldrums since the Lehman crisis of 2008, it only registered as a brief blip in the art world. In fact, an auction of Damien Hirst's work fetched a record-breaking £111 million at a Sotheby's auction on the very day that Lehman Brothers went under, portending the surprising resilience of the market.[2] Since then, the estimated annual turnover of the art market has reached record heights time and again, and unprecedented prices for individual works of art continue to feature in the news.[3] As the price gains on art continue to outperform those of other investments, it is increasingly treated as a serious transnational asset

---

[1] For a historical perspective informed by information economics see Nelson, Zeckhauser, & Spence, 2014.

[2] However, Hirst's personal brand, seen as overinflated in the aftermath of this exhibition, took a hit, though it has since recovered (Salmon, 2017).

[3] The $450 million auction of Leonardo da Vinci's *Salvator Mundi* is the most recent record-breaking sale (Freeman, 2017).

Oddný Helgadóttir, *Art*. In: *Global Wealth Chains*. Edited by Leonard Seabrooke and Duncan Wigan, Oxford University Press.
© Oddný Helgadóttir (2022). DOI: 10.1093/oso/9780198832379.003.0009

class in its own right, with the attendant institutional infrastructure, including price indices, dedicated investment funds, and a host of specialized consultancies (Adam, 2017).

Yet matters are hardly as simple as such portrayals suggest. The "art world" is very much shaped by forces and institutions that can hardly be understood as either predominantly economic or rational.[4] The combination of unique investment characteristics on one hand and specific institutional norms and social conventions on the other constrain the potential of art to act as a stable store of value or reliable investment instrument. The motivation to buy art is therefore not analogous to that of other assets in global wealth chains (GWCs). Thus, while art is certainly an important link in such chains, it is rather a special one.

This chapter attempts to identify some of the distinctive functions that art plays in the governance of GWCs. The editors of this volume have described five types of wealth chains. The first is composed of market linkages, or transparent, simple, open, and legal arm's-length relationships. This form of global wealth chain accounts for a large proportion of transactions in the art world, primarily those where buyers are inexpert newcomers. Most of the value, however, comes from modular and relational wealth chains carried out through classic auction house, gallery, or private dealer activities (Halperin & Kinsella, 2017; McAndrew, 2017).

Modular wealth chains offer both parties the opportunity to buy and sell using tailor-made financial and art consulting services. This restricts both supplier and client flexibility. Bespoke suppliers such as global auction houses (Christie's, Sotheby's) and independent fine art funds reconstruct the art market into complex information that can nevertheless be exchanged with little explicit coordination between the participants. While they are equally complex, relational wealth chains involving art are less explicit. Instead, they are more sociological, thriving on transacting tacit information, requiring high levels of explicit coordination and depending on trust relationships anchored in claims to prestige and status. Private dealers—the suppliers in such chains–generate highly complex, albeit deeply social, tacit, and malleable, "knowledge" about the market, which they transfer to buyers at a steep price.[5] Given that the art market is

---

[4] The art critic Arthur Coleman Danto coined the term "art world" in the mid 1960s. He argued that in its contemporary form, distinct from earlier art production dominated by the Church and aristocracy, the artistic universe is best understood through reference to a combination of economic, sociopolitical, academic, and philosophical contexts.

[5] The ongoing legal feud between art world magnate Yves Bouvier and billionaire collector Dmitry Rybolovlev centers on disagreement over whether, when facilitating Rybolovlev's billions of dollars'

"the least transparent and least regulated major commercial activity in the world," sociological forms of power are most likely to be mobilized here (Thompson, 2008, p. 31).

To advance our understanding of how modular and relational wealth chains centered on art operate, this chapter focuses on how these relationships are articulated in three main commercial uses of art: (1) art as prestige acquisition, (2) art as a financial instrument, and (3) art as a tax-avoidance mechanism. In addition to the framework provided by the editors, this choice of cases departs from Veblen's insight that the prestige and economic functions of the assets of the leisure class are closely intertwined and should be treated as such (Veblen, 1994).

In recent years, global inequalities and the capacity of the wealthy to obscure their wealth have become highly salient items on the agenda of states and international financial institutions (Palan, 2003; Palan et al., 2013; Seabrooke & Wigan, 2016). In light of this, these three functions of art should be of particular scholarly and policy interest. But while the prestige, financial and tax avoidance functions of premium real estate and other assets classes have come to the attention of policymakers as reservoirs of taxable revenue (Helgadóttir, 2020), art still remains below the radar. This chapter is a scholarly first cut at filling this knowledge gap.

The first part of this empirical analysis of the role of art in GWCs explores its function as a supplier of aesthetic pleasure and social prestige. Then, it delves into its uses as a form of investment, as a financial collateral and as a selling pitch for luxury real estate. The third section deals with art as a mechanism of tax avoidance. A final section concludes and relates these findings more concretely to the literature on global wealth chains.

Pleasure and prestige

The oldest function of art is the delivery of pleasure and/or prestige. In 1986, economist William Baumol argued that art is a worthwhile investment for those "who derive a high rate of return in the form of aesthetic pleasure"—but, due to unstable valuation, not for others. Pushing this insight to rather improbable levels of precision Atukeren and Seckin estimate that the "psychic returns" of art are about 28% (2007), up considerably from the 1.6% reported in 1977 (Stein, 1977).

worth of art purchases, Bouvier was acting as Rybolovlev's agent or as a seller in his own right. This disagreement exemplifies how ambiguous and social transactions of this kind can be (Kinsella, 2018).

Whether it can be quantified so precisely or not, art certainly has a classic Veblenian conspicuous consumption function that buys social prestige in a given social context. It is an archetypal "positional good" (Mandel, 2009). It is thus not surprising that a recent Deloitte survey revealed that 61% of collectors think that the social perks of collecting—being thought of as a person of taste and receiving invitations to the right dinners and openings—was part of the allure of collecting (Gapper, 2015). The conjecture that growing demand for art is at least in part driven by such dynamics is supported by the rapid proliferation of private collections that are open to the public, though these have no doubt also been spurred on legislation in both the USA and UK that confers tax benefits to collectors that open their collections to the public (Brown & Gill, 2013; Wallop, 2015; Oralkan, 2016). Bank of America Merrill Lynch's research division has taken heed and now actively researches what it calls "the vanity capital market," in which art plays a significant role (Bain, 2015).

Art buys prestige not only for wealthy individuals but for corporates as well. Thus, Japanese real estate companies triggered the impressionist art boom of the 1980s. Similarly, Deutsche Bank invested systematically in the so-called "young British artists" and turned its headquarters into a gallery featuring their art. Until its collapse, Lehman Bothers did the same in its London headquarters. In both cases, multimillion dollar Damien Hirst and Jeff Koons pieces were a compulsory presence (Harris, 2013. p. 29).

Alongside these developments, a rapidly expanding industry of art purchasing services has sprung up. This includes, for example, investment advisories like New York City based Artvest, and the online service Art-Wise, which promises to connect buyers and sellers while preserving their anonymity. Jumping on this bandwagon, the normally conservative big auction houses have begun offering a new range of services, including on-line auctions geared towards a younger generation of collectors (Dizard, 2014; Adam, 2017). Artnet.com, in turn, provides information about the auction prices of individual artists. New art sales fairs, catering to every taste, are also established with increasing frequency (Pickford, 2013). In addition to the established Mei Moses All Art index financial media like the *Financial Times* and *The Economist* now offer their own art indices and analyses for interested investors (Brewster, 2007).[6]

---

[6] The Moses Mei index was developed by New York University Stern School of Business professors Jianping Mai and David Moses in 2001 and was purchased by Sotheby's in 2016.

Another recent innovation in using art for prestige signaling is the intertwining of art and high-end real estate markets in global cities. Thus, the *Financial Times* has reported that just as Europe turned to harsh austerity in 2010, a new practice emerged, centered on marketing prestige real estate as particularly suitable for housing and displaying art collections. Another trend, referred to as "dressing" properties, takes several forms. One is to time open houses for real estate to coincide with art fairs and turn the property for sale into a temporary gallery. Thus, art exhibitions containing work of artists such as Poussin and Picasso have been used by developers to promote luxury London flats during high-profile art fairs (Frieze, Walpole Mayfair). Another tactic is to redefine the boundaries of the professions of interior design and art critique, with new professional networks developing between the designers of high-end property interiors and gallerists from high-prestige sites such as London, New York, and Berlin (Adam, 2017; Knight Frank, 2018).

The rise of new fortunes in emerging markets has also opened up new opportunities and incentives for prestige dealers in art. For example, the newly wealthy in Asia and Russia have sought to boost their prestige at home by buying back the artistic heritage of their cultures. Experts at Christie's connect the fact that Asian art is now the auction house's second-strongest category to this particular reconfiguration of wealth chains (Adam & Burns, 2011).

Just another asset class

Investment, collateral, and marketing tool for luxury properties

Art has been used as a reservoir of value since the Medicis, and scholars have long noted the close relationship between art and finance (Parks, 2005). Yet, over the past two decades, financialization has brought this dynamic to a new level. This transformation does not only concern the marketing of contemporary art and corporations acting as patrons of art museums. More importantly, in spite of economists' longstanding consensus that art is a poor investment, it is increasingly treated as a commodity and art buyers and intermediaries act much like commodity brokers.[7] As another *Financial Times* report notes:

> Today's new collectors may be trendsetters but few are tastemakers—that role is now played by the dealers and gallerists. Unlike many of the great patrons of the past, from the Medicis to the Mellons, who were interested in curating art of earlier periods or in discovering and nurturing new talent, a growing number of those buying art at the highest level now see themselves primarily as investors. They might already own a portfolio of properties around the world, each with an immaculate, if rather soulless interior, and they want to buy into blue chip artists whose works offer them financial security rather than a reflection of their own personality.
>
> (Battle, 2012)

Thus, over the course of the last few years, art has defied its reputation as a poor investment in and of itself. This conventional wisdom seems to be giving way as the economic trends dictating rising demand for art, most notably a growing pool of very wealthy collectors, remain on course (Goetzmann, Renneboog, & Spaenjers, 2011). While the global financial crisis has decimated or made other kinds of investment less certain, the art market has benefitted. Specifically, two years into the recession, the proportion of the wealthy interested in art investments rose significantly, likely due to the dual mechanisms of traditional investment uncertainty and greater concentration of wealth (Knight Frank, 2018).

In spite of a slowdown in 2015 and 2016, there is no doubt that the value of the global art market has been rising rapidly (McAndrew, 2017; Knight Frank, 2018). According to Art Market Research, a leading analyst of art market trends, 2014 prices were up by 121 percent since 2010 and 634 percent since 2000 (Barker, 2014). This is true of emerging markets as well, with recent reports noting striking booms in China (780 percent) and India (830 percent).[8] These, however, can only be rough estimates since precise values for art sales are hard to come by, as the bulk of transactions are not reported (Schrager, 2013; Gapper, 2014; Adam, 2017).

Public auctions, which are only one way of trading art, provide some indication of price levels and volume of sales. In 2014 both of the big auction houses, Christie's and Sotheby's, witnessed record sales of £5 billion and $6

---

[7] For a sociological perspective on art prices see Velthuis, 2007.

[8] Art Market Insight, http://www.artprice.com.

billion, respectively. This, however, only gives us part of the picture. McAndrew, an economist for the European Fine Art Fair, has surveyed both dealers and collectors and estimates that private unreported sales account for 70 percent of all transactions. By that logic the total level of transactions should be close to $50 billion. Economist Nouriel Roubini believes that the number is higher yet, and has stated that capitalization of $1 trillion is a reasonable guess (2015).

In this market, art investment funds have been proliferating, with their structure, strategies, calculative devices, or credit ratings resembling those of modern finance:

> New innovative art funds, such as the London-based Fine Art Fund, which launched in 2004, have been set up with prices of artworks carefully tracked on databases such as Artnet "like stock market indices". At least ten launched between 2005 and 2007, including Artistic Investment Advisers (AIA)'s London-based Art Trading Fund and the Swiss-based Art Collectors Fund. In a manner analogous to a mutual fund or a private equity fund, these have focused on short-term art trades, buying directly from living artists and "distressed sellers", while often hedging themselves by shorting derivatives correlated to art market performance, such as the shares of Sotheby's stock.
>
> (Harris, 2013, p. 31)

While such efforts to turn art into a fungible and continuously tradable asset have yet to prove substantively successful, new efforts in this direction are continuously being launched (Adam, 2017). Winners of globalization in the global south have entered the fray as well. In China, local auction companies (Beijing Poly, Beijing Marina Time, Beijing Hanhai) and the Hong Kong subsidiaries of Western houses (Sotheby's Hong Kong, Christie's Hong Kong) perform a variety of financial investment services. Spring and autumn auctions in Shanghai run art trades worth an estimated $1.5 billion for each season.

Critically, the Chinese art market is shaped to a much greater extent by art investment funds than is the case in Europe and North America. Chinese Minsheng Banking Corporation launched its first art fund in June 2007 and a second in July 2009. Beijing-based Zhong Bo Auctions Company and Shanghai-based Terry Art Fund Management also have two funds each, with more on the way. These are no small operations. One of the latest entrants on the market (Noah Management) is the first wealth-management fund from China that was listed on the New York

Table 9.1 Global art investment funds and assets under management (billions of $)

	Assets under management, $billion total	Number of funds, Europe & US	Number of funds, China	≈ % Europe & US/China
2011	1.55	23	60	43/57
2012	2.13	25	90	41/59
2013	1.46	17	87	28/72
2014	1.27	17	53	36/64
2015	1.20	20	34	46/54

Source: Deloitte Luxembourg and ArtTactic Art and Finance Report 2016

Stock Exchange. Noah distributed more than $3.9 billion of wealth management products in the third quarter of 2016 and had $17.2 billion in assets. Some funds report returns as high as 25 percent a year, and while the holding period for art is around seven years in the United States, it is on average two years in China. As Table 9.1 below shows, in China both the number of global art investment funds and their assets under management far exceed those of Europe and the US combined. However, the art funds of the old capitalist core manage a relatively stable level of art assets, while the Chinese ones fluctuate more.

In addition to acting as an investment in its own right, art can be used for collateral. An international environment in which demand for traditional forms of collateral (mortgage-backed securities, government bonds) increasingly outstrips supply, has catalyzed such uses for art. Indeed, a new vehicle has recently emerged to manage the flows of art acquisitions through wealth chains: loans operations collateralized with art by bespoke financial firms. These art loan firms are typically run by wealth-management firms that have developed bespoke services in the art market, such as art advisory, alongside more conventional wealth management (Adam, 2017). Consider the case of the Fine Art Group, one of the newcomers in the business. Its founder, Philip Hoffman, who manages seven investment funds, has been running an art advisory service for the past few years and its new art lending business is headed by a former finance lawyer and senior legal counsel at Christie's. The firm is expected to lend against works valued between $250,000 and $20 million and has been involved in transactions worth $325 million at Christie's and Sotheby's over a two-year period (Gerlis, 2016).

In addition to these legible forms of imbrication of art into GWCs, there are subtler trends that lend even greater agency to finance. Increasingly, the boundaries between art production and the art market have begun to blur, with financial firms becoming involved in art production itself. The convention-defying and market-centric art production of Damien Hirst, an art market insider with close links to financial firms whose process is often used as a case study in business school classes, and the fact that "the supply of identical art works has often been ramped up to meet demand—in contrast to the inelastic supply of work by deceased artists," are cases in point (Harris, 2013, pp. 30–31; Adam, 2017).

Tax-avoidance device

Conspicuous consumption, wealth storage, and the need for collateral are, however, not the only reasons to invest in art. Importantly, art can also be appealing for tax reasons. The US art market is largely unregulated and the EU only began requiring that galleries report sales in cash over €7,500 and file notices about suspicious transactions in 2013. In this regulatory environment, the opaque practices of the art market make it ideal for reducing one's tax footprint. Economist Nouriel Roubini is quoted in the following:

> Whether we like it or not, art is used for tax avoidance and evasion. . . . It can be used for money laundering. You can buy something for half a million, not show a passport, and ship it. Plenty of people are using it for laundering. . . . While art looks as if it is all about beauty, as a business it is full of shady stuff. We should correct it or it will be undermined over time
>
> (Kaminska, 2015)

This volume departs from the observation that the mobility of transacted capital and the ease with which it takes new forms in ever-shifting jurisdictions "has raised the specter of a permanent schism between the location of value creation and the geographical allocation of profits and wealth" (Seabrooke & Wigan, 2017, p. 2). Art gives new valence to this insight. While prestige investments in art often result in private collections being made open to the public, growing investment in art for tax purposes has the opposite effect.

Increasingly, invaluable works of art are tucked away in high-security storage spaces close to global financial centers, where they are not subject to taxation. In that sense trade in art fits more and more the definition of GWCs as "transacted forms of capital operating multi-jurisdictionally for the purposes of pecuniary wealth creation and protection." On the spectrum posited by the editors of the volume, when it is used in this way art sits closer to "'off-the-shelf' products shielded from regulators by advantageous international tax laws" than to "highly complex and flexible innovative financial products offered by large financial institutions and firms" (Seabrooke & Wigan, 2017, p.1).

Indeed, one can easily set up shell companies to sell art in ways that minimize tax obligations. Incorporating these companies in tax havens is key to this process. Thus, the Panama Papers scandal revealed that "freeport king" Yves Bouvier, one of the largest players in the global art market, was also expert at "setting up offshore companies—Diva, Blancaflor, Eagle Overseas—to enable galleries to buy specific works and mask the identity of other investors in a transaction" (Salmon, 2016). Such expertise was key to making sure that the chain of buyers and sellers was complex enough to preclude difficult questions about the dealer's markups. This effectively blindfolded tax authorities and made it nearly impossible to tell whether taxes were duly paid.

Critically, a great deal of valuable art disappears from view once it is bought in this way, and is never displayed, even in private homes. Rather, it is kept in specialized storage facilities called "freeports," which offer "*temporary* exemption of taxes and duties for an *unlimited period of time*"[9] (sic). No transaction, capital gains, value added, or inheritance taxes are due on goods traded in freeports (Segal, 2012; Adam, 2017; Zarobell, 2017). The original art freeport, which measures over 50,000 square meters and stores a variety of undisclosed assets besides art, is in Geneva. Since reporting and inventory standards are both lax and lightly enforced it is very difficult to estimate the value of artworks stored there. There is, however, no doubt that the sums in question are very high. A *New York Times* article on the freeport in Geneva reports that art dealers and insurers believe that the art housed in that facility alone would suffice "to create one of the world's great museums." In a similar vein, a London-based insurer stated that there isn't "a piece of paper wide enough to write down all the zeros" (Segal, 2012).

Importantly, the Geneva freeport is not a global aberration, but rather a corporate form that is proliferating worldwide in lockstep with growing wealth inequality. Recently, in a physical testimony to the nearby

[9] https://www.nlc.ch/en/about/, retrieved April 2016, emphasis added.

concentration of wealth, similar facilities have spread to other important financial and economic hubs such as Luxembourg, Monaco, Dubai, Singapore, Beijing, and Shanghai.[10]

The West Bund Fine Art Warehouses (WBFAW), located in Shanghai, was opened in 2014 with much fanfare and with the support of local officials keen to project the city's cultural as well as economic clout. It stores art for about 30 art organizations such as Long Museum West Bund, Yuz Art Museum, and Sotheby's. Importantly for the Chinese case, art can be used not just for tax avoidance, but also to circumvent constraints on capital mobility. Where capital controls and high import duties exist and are enforced, art can be a useful vehicle to get around restrictions. In China individuals are legally prohibited from taking more than $50,000 out of the country per year. A Hong Kong art consultancy firm reported that this makes art smuggling a tempting option while also opening up a market for importing art at prices lowered on import forms by art shipping companies (Adam, 2017; see also Grondona & Burgos, Chapter 8 in this volume).

Notably, the global spread of freeports has largely been spearheaded by Swiss managers. This has led to speculation that the export of the freeport model constitutes a Swiss strategy to continue to capture the gains of undeclared money and anonymous investments, even as such operations are squeezed through new regulation in Switzerland. For years, Swiss banks and foreign banks with Swiss subsidiaries have raked in considerable profits due to their proximity to the Geneva freeport.[11] For example, leaks revealed allegations that HSBC's Swiss subsidiary offered bespoke services to big-name artists and buyers through complex techniques that made it difficult to tell who owns what. There has been some regulatory response to this, led by the US, which has made bilateral agreements with Switzerland to report large withdrawals and transfers (*The Economist*, 2013; O'Murchu, 2015; Adam, 2015, 2017).

Most of the assets kept in freeports are likely acquired legally. Yet, as the editors argue, the activities constituting GWCs "range from the legitimate, to the illicit, where wealth chains are used as channels for aggressive avoidance, corruption, appropriation, and evasion." Thus, illicit art has been discovered in freeports. For example, in 2003 a huge scandal erupted as hundreds of antiques, including mummies, sarcophagi, and statues, all of which had been stolen from excavation sites in Egypt, were traced back

[10] Recently, the Tax Justice Network has incorporated the presence of freeports into its Financial Secrecy Index (https://financialsecrecyindex.com/introduction/fsi-2018-results).
[11] http://www.artlyst.com/articles/hsbc-leak-reveals-key-art-world-connections.

to the Geneva Freeport. Some items had been painted in shrill colors so that they could be smuggled as inexpensive trinkets. Following this discovery, new surveillance and reporting were ramped up. Nevertheless, similar scandals erupted in 2016 and 2017 as priceless antique artworks were found stored in the Geneva Freeport (Muñoz-Alonso, 2016; Bradley, 2017).

Such salacious scandals are, however, the exception rather than the rule. The bigger story is the legal use of art for tax planning purposes in an environment that is not legible to the tax authorities. As a recent report put it:

> The purpose behind such corporate maneuvers nearly always involves opacity: to ensure that no one knows who the sellers might be, or what other art they might own. "The tax laws in art make it basically legal to not pay taxes on art. If you're a serious art buyer, you just get a good tax accountant," former New York-based art consultant Beth Fiore tells Hopes & Fears. "If you show newly purchased works in certain museums then you never have to pay taxes on it." Edward Winkleman of Winkleman Gallery maintains that his gallery keeps fastidious records of all transactions and pays taxes even on cash sales. But he admits that "the state generally wouldn't question what is reported." He also tells us that individual sales don't need to be reported, only the totals for each quarter. Hypothetically, someone could buy millions of dollars' worth of art without the IRS knowing, and then later sell those works for a "legitimate" profit that looks clean on taxes.
>
> (Salmon, 2016)

Equally common are reports and rumors that in addition to offering tax benefits, freeports also take advantage of the gray zone outside regulation in which they operate to offer a place to store undeclared goods and funds. Thus, both the *Economist* and the *Financial Times* have reported on speculation that Swiss banks, feeling the heat from international anti-money-laundering efforts, have been advising clients to invest in assets such as art or wine and store them in freeports (Helgadóttir, 2020).

The use of art for tax avoidance came to the fore in public debates in the wake of the Panama Papers scandal, with the law firm Mossack Fonseca supplying critical expertise. Journalist Jake Bernstein reported that the tax benefits of the Geneva Freeport come with costs (Swiss court jurisdiction) that could be avoided with the help of such expertise. Take the example of the Rybolovlev case. Dmitri Rybolovlev is a Russian billionaire who incorporated a company (Xitrans Finance) in the British Virgin Islands to purchase a raft of A-list works of art by the likes of Picasso, Rodin, Monet, and Rothko. The art was stored in Switzerland but, when faced with divorce and the likelihood that the Swiss courts would have jurisdiction over the paintings, he used Xitrans to whisk the paintings out of Switzerland. In this, Mossack Fonseca's task was to keep the art and its owner secret and grease the cogs of a largely relational market "where dynastic fortunes can be made on the basis of nothing more than knowing who owns what." Indeed, as the editors have hypothesized, complex tacit information, high levels of explicit coordination, and strong trust relationships managed by prestige and status interactions are the bread and butter of these relational global wealth chains.

Conclusion

The market value of art is difficult to gauge due to the often byzantine and restrictive social norms of the art world. But the opaque and complex social conventions of the art world are now changing rapidly. There used to be a strong division between primary and secondary markets in art. The primary market was composed of galleries that groomed and recruited artists and sold their works to various clients and collectors. The galleries set the prices for art pieces, and did not lower them at any cost, preferring instead to keep or gift them (Velthuis, 2003).

Yet prices were not the same for all clients. Various fees were often waived for prestigious buyers, especially prominent museums or trend-setting collectors, whose opinions shaped the market (Gapper, 2014). If these clients then decided to sell the works they could do so through either public auctions or private dealers. This was not without social risk. Galleries would disfavor collectors that were perceived to engage in speculative behavior or too frequent "flipping," endangering the reputation and value of the galleries' artists or flooding fragile markets (Schrager, 2013; Adam, 2017). Such sanctions could include restricted access to artists, less favorable terms of sale, higher fees, and less access to auctions and special auction financing.

Recently, however, these rules of the game have been changing and even the established players increasingly treat art as an asset class, granting clients better access to price information and offering more client-oriented services. Moreover, while the auction houses used to focus exclusively on very expensive pieces, they have begun expanding to cheaper works sold through online auctions. The most notable example of this trend is Sotheby's cooperation with online commerce giant eBay (Dalley, 2014; Gapper, 2014). At a first glance one might conclude that as art is increasingly treated as an asset in its own right, the governance of GWCs in art would become more *market* oriented, characterized by transparent, simple, open, and legal arm's-length relationships. Yet, such a conclusion would not be warranted.

Rather, in the relational universe of the art world, market actors have begun raiding the turf of the traditional counterpart of the artist, the art critic. For example, influential dealers and collectors like Charles Saatchi have used their strategic positioning in the market to generate trends irrespective of what art magazines say. Some artists, particularly high-profile ones, now bypass galleries altogether and put their works straight to auction. In order to garner more business, the auction houses are also increasingly offering minimum guarantees for the works they put up for sale (Adam, 2017; Harris, 2013). In other words, if there are no bids above a certain agreed-upon price, the auction house buys the work, acting much like an underwriter in an initial public offering of stock. Conversely, private collectors and dealers can also underwrite auctions, in return for a cut in deals that exceed the guaranteed bid (Adam, 2014).[12]

Thus, while there is a trend towards more prices being disclosed—a change that dealers and galleries have long tried to avoid—still various actors take cuts along the way, often in opaque and undisclosed ways. The case of the 14-foot tiger shark put in formaldehyde by Damien Hirst and called "The Physical Impossibility of Death in the Mind of Someone Living" is a relevant example. This work was put up for sale in 2005 for an asking price of $12 million by an agent acting on behalf of its then owner, the British advertising magnate Charles Saatchi. The actual price that was eventually paid was not revealed; the parties involved agreed not to discuss the amount publicly. Yet, the $12-million figure circulated will have helped increase the value of the other Hirst works in Saatchi's collection. Another feat of ingenuity was that the buyer was purchasing the artistic intention rather than the original piece. The shark—which Damien Hirst had had shipped over from Australia for £,6000 in 1991—"had deteriorated greatly and was replaced as part of the deal by one of Hirst's production staff."(Harris, 2013, p. 31).

---

[12] Sotheby's disclosed last year that it had made $279 million of guarantees, of which $65 million had been laid off to third parties, and the latter figure has since risen.

In light of the general lack of oversight and regulation and the strong emphasis on preserving prestige and status as key markers of relational wealth chains, price manipulation is likely very common. Even at auctions, then, price signals are not necessarily market price signals. Indeed, Schrager argues that "high-end art is one of the most manipulated markets in the world" (2013) and key actors go to great lengths to hide price fluctuations. Still, it seems that the balance of information and power may be shifting away from sellers and towards increasingly cash-rich buyers.

The relational nature of wealth chains comprising art is reinforced by the density, opacity, and heterogeneity of the professional expertise involved, not unlike the case of finance:

> Financial innovations, such as credit-default swaps, yield curve arbitrage and synthetic collaterised debt obligations have reached a point where not only the language is increasingly opaque and impenetrable but the statistical models underlying them are harder to compute and analyse effectively. Similarly, much recent contemporary art generally requires knowledge of accumulated layers of art history, insights into different games of irony, and familiarity with new conceptual ideas such as relational aesthetics and the distribution of the sensible.
>
> (Harris, 2013, p. 32)

As suggested, art is not just an investment asset. It also triggers what could be called a "dual depletion" of public spaces: not only are states' tax revenues lowered, but prized works of art are also removed from circulation. Such practices are beginning to raise serious questions about whether the lightly regulated art market needs to be re-examined. Indeed, at the Davos conference in 2015 Nouriel Roubini warned that the art market is the last big unregulated market and that the lack of oversight masks shady dealings of all kinds, including tax evasion, money laundering, and what in other sectors would be considered insider trading (Egan, 2015).

More oversight and regulation, as suggested by Roubini, would likely lead the market to bifurcate—into more resolutely modular and relational wealth chains for wealthy buyers, and into market wealth chains for everyone else. The latter are increasingly buying art through relatively transparent and arms-length online platforms where competition is open. The former are, by contrast, seeking out bespoke services and legal advice from a small pool of suppliers.

References

Adam, G. & Burns, C. (2011). Qatar revealed as the world's biggest contemporary art buyer. *Art Newspaper*, 226 (July–August).

Adam, G. (2014). How long can the art market boom last? *Financial Times*, June 6. https://beaumontnathan.com/2014/06/10/long-can-art-market-boom-last.

Adam, G. (2015). The art market: Freeport magnate unstuck. *Financial Times*, March 6. http://www.ft.com/intl/cms/s/0/ee459744-c1d4-11e4-bd24-00144feab7de.html#axzz3btKx8bSi.

Adam, G. (2014). *Big Bucks: The Explosion of the Art Market in the 21st Century*. Lund Humphries.

Adam, G.(2017). *Dark Side of the Boom: The Excesses Of The Art Market In The 21st Century*. Lund Humphries.

Atukeren, E. & Seçkin, A. (2007). On the valuation of psychic returns to art market investments. *Economics Bulletin*, 26(5), 1–12.

Bain, M. (2015). "'Vanity capital' is the new metric for narcissism, and its value is greater than Germany's GDP. *Quartz*, May 11. http://qz.com/393171/vanity-capital-is-the-new-metric-for-narcissism-and-analysts-say-its-value-worldwide-is-greater-than-germanys-gdp/.

Barker, G. (2014). "The shark is dead but the price has a bite." *Financial Times*, July 1. http://www.ft.com/intl/cms/s/0/ddfb22e6-0109-11e4-a938-00144feab7de.html#axzz3btB0XXxI.

Battle, L. (2012). "The estate of the art." *Financial Times*, April 15. https://www.ft.com/content/440ea16e-7e41-11e1-b009-00144feab49a.

Bradley, S. (2017). "Priceless Roman sarcophagus heads home after legal saga." *SWI swissinfo.ch*. https://www.swissinfo.ch/eng/geneva-to-turkey_priceless-roman-sarcophagus-heads-home-after-legal-saga/43495484.

Brewster, D. (2007). "Market jitters to hit high art costs." *Financial Times*, November 4. http://www.ft.com/intl/cms/s/0/35d28c32-8b02-11dc-95f7-0000779fd2ac.html#axzz3btKx8bSi.

Brown, M. & Gil, N. (2013). "Tax exemption for public access to treasured artworks is a 'racket.'" *The Guardian*, December 27. https://www.theguardian.com/artanddesign/2013/dec/27/tax-exemption-public-access-treasured-artworks-racket.

Dalley, J. (2014). "Winners and losers from the art market's new rules." *Financial Times*, June 27. http://www.ft.com/intl/cms/s/0/55ba02ec-fc51-11e3-98b8-00144feab7de.html.

Dizard, J. (2014). "Auction Houses embracing digital technology to sell to the new global rich." *Financial Times*, September 19. http://www.ft.com/intl/cms/s/0/83b85b78-382c-11e4-a687-00144feabdc0.html#axzz3btKx8bSi.

The Economist (2013). "Über-warehouses for the ultra-rich." November 23. http://www.economist.com/news/briefing/21590353-ever-more-wealth-being-parked-fancy-storage-facilities-some-customers-they-are.

Egan, M. (2015). "Dr. Doom's latest warning: the art market is 'shady'" *CNN Business*, May 11. https://money.cnn.com/2015/05/11/investing/art-market-shady-nouriel-roubini/index.html.

Freeman, N. (2017). "Leonardo da Vinci's 'Salvator Mundi' sells for $450.3 M. at Christie's in New York, shattering market records." *ArtNet*, November 15. http://www.artnews.com/2017/11/15/leonardo-da-vincis-salvator-mundi-sells-450-3-m-christies-new-york.

Gapper, J. (2014). "Modern art auctions are as baffling as the paintings." *Financial Times*, May 7. http://www.ft.com/intl/cms/s/2/1d20e4b6-d47c-11e3-bf4e-00144feabdc0.html#axzz3btKx8bSi.

Gapper, J. (2015). "Picasso is not just a valuable abstract." *Financial Times*, May 13. http://www.ft.com/intl/cms/s/0/b4ea7a1a-f955-11e4-ae65-00144feab7de.html#axzz3btKx8bSi.

Goetzmann, W. N., Renneboog, L., & Spaenjers, C. (2011). Art and money. *American Economic Review*, 101(3), 222–26.

Harris, A. (2013). Financial artscapes: Damien Hirst, crisis and the City of London. *Cities* (33), 29–35.

Halperin, J. & Kinsella, E. (2017). "The 'winner takes all' art market: 25 artists account for nearly 50% of all contemporary auction sales." *Artnet News*, September 20 https://news.artnet.com/market/25-artists-account-nearly-50-percent-postwar-contemporary-auction-sales-1077026.

Helgadóttir, O. (2020). The new luxury freeports: Offshore storage, tax avoidance, and 'invisible' art. *Environment and Planning A: Economy and Space*, 0308518X20972712.

Kaminska, I. (2015). Roubini Vs. the so-called "art" industry. *FT Alphaville*, https://www.ft.com/content/7b8ad458-7efe-361a-89bf-0e2f85301d1a

Kinsella, E. (2018). "Russian billionaire Dmitry Rybolovlev continues his epic legal crusade over the 'largest art fraud in history.'" *Artnet News*, February 13 https://news.artnet.com/art-world/rybolovlev-bouvier-lawsuit-art-fraud-1221968.

Knight Frank (2018). The Wealth Report. http://www.knightfrank.com/resources/wealthreport2018/the-wealth-report-2018.pdf.

Landi, A. (2007). "Top ten ARTnews stories: How Jeff Koons became a super-star." *Art News*, November 1. https://www.artnews.com/art-news/news/top-ten-artnews-stories-how-jeff-koons-became-a-superstar-188/.

Mandel, B. R. (2009). Art as an investment and conspicuous consumption good. *American Economic Review*, 99(4), 1653–63.

McAndrew, C. (2017). "The Art Market 2017." *Art Basel and UBS*.

Mendelsohn, M. (2017). "Why is the art world divided over Gauguin's legacy?" *Artsy* https://www.artsy.net/article/artsy-editorial-art-divided-gauguins-legacy.

Melnik, A. L. & Plaut, S. E. (2008). "Art as a component in investment portfolios." Unpublished paper. https://www.researchgate.net/publication/255593223_Art_as_a_Component_in_Investment_Portfolios.

Muñoz-Alonso, L. (2016). "Trove of looted antiquities belonging to disgraced dealer Robin Symes found in Geneva Freeport." *Artnet News* https://news.artnet.com/art-world/trove-looted-antiquities-belonging-disgraced-dealer-robin-symes-found-geneva-freeport-418157.

Nelson, J., Zeckhauser, R., & Spence, M. (2014). *The Patron's Payoff: Conspicuous Commissions in Italian Renaissance Art*. Princeton University Press.

O'Murchu, C. (2015). "Art: A market laid bare." *Financial Times*, April 7. http://www.ft.com/intl/cms/s/2/a91a1608-d887-11e4-8a23-00144feab7de.html#axzz3btKx8bSi.

Oralkan, E. (2016). "Private art becomes public." *Observer*, March 3. http://observer.com/2016/03/private-art-becomes-public/.

Pickford, J. (2013). "Frieze finds its limits in battle against 'fair fatigue.'" *Financial Times*, October 21. http://www.ft.com/intl/cms/s/2/6231dbf6-3a75-11e3-9243-00144feab7de.html.

Palan, R., Murphy, R., & Chavagneux, C. (2013). *Tax Havens: How Globalization Really Works*. Cornell University Press.

Palan, R. (2003). *The Offshore World: Sovereign Markets, Virtual Places, And Nomad Millionaires*. Cornell University Press.

Salmon, F. (2016). "Panama Papers show how the very rich use art to get richer." *Fusion*, April 7. https://fusion.tv/story/288515/panama-papers-leak-art-market.

Salmon, F. (2017). "The false narrative of Damien Hirst's rise and fall." *The New Yorker*, December 6. https://www.newyorker.com/culture/culture-desk/the-false-narrative-of-damien-hirsts-rise-and-fall.

Schrager, A. (2013). "High-end art is one of the most manipulated markets in the world." *Quartz*, July 11. http://qz.com/103091/high-end-art-is-one-of-the-most-manipulated-markets-in-the-world/.

Schroeder, J. (2013). The artist and the brand. *European Journal of Marketing,* 39(11/12), 1291–1305.

Seabrooke, L. & Wigan, D. (2016). Powering ideas through expertise: Professionals in global tax battles. *Journal of European Public Policy,* 23(3), 357–374.

Seabrooke, L. & Wigan, D. (2017). The governance of global wealth chains. *Review of International Political Economy,* 24(1), 1–29.

Segal, D. (2012). "Swiss freeports are home for a growing treasury of art." *The New York Times,* July 21. http://www.nytimes.com/2012/07/22/business/swiss-freeports-are-home-for-a-growing-treasury-of-art.html.

Stein, J. P. (1977). The monetary appreciation of paintings. *Journal of Political Economy,* 85 (5), 1021–1035.

Thompson, D. (2008). *The $12 Million Stuffed Shark: The Curious Economics of Contemporary Art and Auction Houses.* Aurum.

Veblen, T. (1994). *The Theory of the Leisure Class.* Penguin Books.

Velthuis, O. (2003). Symbolic meanings of prices: Constructing the value of contemporary art in Amsterdam and New York galleries. *Theory and Society,* 32 (2), 181–215.

Velthuis, O. (2007). *Talking Prices—Symbolic Meanings of Prices on the Market for Contemporary Art.* Princeton University Press.

Wallop, H. (2015). "What are the new status symbols for the ultra rich?" *The Telegraph,* April 21. http://www.telegraph.co.uk/culture/art/artsales/11551843/What-are-the-new-status-symbols-for-the-ultra-rich.html.

Zarobell, J. (2017). *Art and the Global Economy.* University of California Press.

10

Family Generations

Mariana Santos

In 2016, UBS estimated that, over the following 20 years, fewer than 500 individuals would pass on $2.1 trillion to their heirs (UBS/PwC, 2016). Keen on taking part in what has been described as the largest ever intergenerational transfer of billionaire wealth, the private banking and wealth-management (PBWM) industry pledges its tools and expertise to assure clients that their wealth will endure through succession. This chapter focuses on one dimension of transgenerational wealth-protection strategies which wealth managers address with clients: children's preparation for inheritance.

Recent work has taken interest in dynastic fortunes and their constitutive entanglements with multiple financial and legal services providers (Beaverstock et al., 2013; Hay & Beaverstock, 2016; Harrington, 2016). As work in this volume documents, the different structures and products deployed in wealth protection entail distinct modes of coordination. In the PBWM sector, the task of devising a fit between clients' needs and products and services supplied might, for instance, go from standard, arms-length outsourcing of asset management to third-party suppliers (in so-called open-architecture approaches) to confidential face-to-face conversations between client and manager inside the private bank's hermetic meeting room. This chapter zooms in on the latter, relational (Seabrooke & Wigan, 2017) forms of coordination between the high-net-worth (HNW) client and their PBWM suppliers, by taking the (often sensitive) topic of inheritance as entry point.

As ethnographic research with 30 managers in Lisbon, London, Geneva, and Zurich suggested, the issue of children's preparation for wealth is rendered a matter of service delivery—that is, an issue of wealth protection to be addressed through specific services and resources—as well as a way of engendering the kind of trust and intimacy that solidify client–supplier ties. Managers cultivate this emotional investment of the commercial

Mariana Santos, *Family Generations*. In: *Global Wealth Chains*. Edited by Leonard Seabrooke and Duncan Wigan, Oxford University Press. © Mariana Santos (2022). DOI: 10.1093/oso/9780198832379.003.0010 relation not only to secure clients' preferences vis-à-vis competitors, but also to access and establish timely rapport with those comprising the following generations of family wealth—the so-called next-gens.

The chapter thus brings into the GWC framework the concern with how everyday life and affectivity come to bear on market participation which has motivated research in economic sociology and cultural economy (Çaliskan & Callon, 2009, 2010; McFall, 2014; Deville, 2015; Cochoy et al., 2017). Particularly paying attention to what Cochoy et al. (2017) have called "arts of market attachments" promises thick, grounded, accounts of how suppliers seek to attach clients' preferences/detach them from competitors; such understanding of how market ties are practically constructed and sustained meets GWCs' concern with how structures and products are selected in wealth chains (Seabrooke & Wigan, 2017), and how these solidify or dissolve particular constellations of suppliers.

Drawing on interviews and informational material provided, the chapter looks at concrete practices, tools, and techniques through which the topic of children's preparation for wealth is explored in the ongoing practical accomplishment of client–manager relationships. Specifically, the first section considers how clients' descendants are brought into the routines of account management through mundane—"quaint" (McFall, 2014)—devices such as credit cards, account-opening forms, or smaller investment accounts. The second section analyzes two booklets on children-related topics that firms supply to clients; objects like these equip managers in their task of enrolling clients at a more intimate, private level, while also creating opportunities for enquiries on services and products. The third section considers events that firms organize to ensure the financial education of clients' inheritors, unpacking them as curated environments where the latter are prompted to develop distinctive kinds of financial subjectivities (Langley, 2008; Kear, 2016; Santos, 2021), and where the continuity of "market attachments" (Cochoy et al., 2017) to firms can be afforded.

The concluding section discusses the chapter's contribution to the GWC heuristic. Notably, taking succession planning and inheritors' preparation within private wealth management as entry point offers significant insights into how the techno-financial interpretative work developed in relation to the legal affordances of transgenerational asset transfer is carefully interwoven with culturally charged understandings of dynastic wealth in relational coordination modes within GWCs. Analytically, the grounded approach proposed here does not just promise a thicker grasp of how GWC coordination modes take place in practice than that offered by network representations. It also unlocks understandings of wealth chains as topological spaces (Allen, 2011), enacted through manifold material, sociotechnical, affective binds and folds that dissolve distances and conjure proximities; topological representations of wealth can be fruitfully considered as alongside, and constantly entangled with topographic, transjurisdictional spacings, contributing to an understanding of GWCs as "more-than-economic" spaces (Gibson-Graham, 2014; Harker, 2017).

Bringing the "next-gens" in

Antonio[1] could not pin down exactly the moment when he became a private banking client. His history of relations with private bankers went back to when he was young and he and his siblings had signatory powers on his father's account. "He trusted his children," he said; "he'd let us sign in the account and use a credit card when we were travelling. But it wasn't our account, we didn't have the money to be clients.". The father had a close relationship with his US bank manager who, while living in New York, always dedicated at least three annual visits to his clients in Portugal. But Antonio's first contact with private banking consisted in little more than a signature, a credit card, and having his father's manager sorting it out whenever he could not use his card abroad or needed extra funds to buy unexpected flights back home from New York where he studied.

Four decades later, encouraging clients to appoint coholders is still a pervasive strategy through which wealth managers access clients' inheritors. In Lisbon, Elsa, head of private banking at a German bank, stressed the importance of account coholder(s) for the permanence of the assets in family hands, as well as in the bank's.

> Because of the banking legislation, the account should always have another co-holder should something happen to the investor and they become unable to access the account. And this coholder is generally the spouse, or a son, and this in itself opens a door into the family's inner circle. By appointing their children in the account, they [clients] facilitate us a proximity to them. This grasp of the second generation is crucial, because once the parents are no longer fit or die, and the wealth is transmitted to the children, the account is already open so it's just a matter of keeping on managing that wealth.

[1] For confidentiality reasons, all interviewees are here referred to under false names; where interviews were conducted in Portuguese, translation to English is by the author.

Where children are appointed coholders or granted signatory powers, the account-opening meeting becomes the first opportunity to meet the client's descendants who must also be present to fill in and sign the forms. Banks try as much as possible to preserve this as a ritual enacted within their premises—"it's a bit like going to the notary to sign the deed to a property," Rui, a Geneva-based manager said the importance of this foundational act should not be underestimated. It inscribes the wealth-management firm into the scripts and spaces of family life as a site of intergenerational communication about patrimonial wealth. In this context, Rui also noted, the manager, "the gentleman from the bank," assumed a key mediating, neutral role for many clients—especially in southern European countries "where parents do not talk about money with their children."

Once open, the new field rapidly fits with the flow of the family's everyday life, habits and regular events. This was particularly noticeable for Geneva and London-based managers dealing with offshore clients (i.e. those resident in other countries). They noted how many of these clients combined their visits to the bank (namely, the account-opening one) with other affairs they had in the city or habits they cultivated a doctor's appointment, a business meeting, a shopping weekend, or the family skiing holidays. "I'll come by the bank with my son the next time I'm there," Rui said his Portuguese clients often told him.

Economic sociologist Viviana Zelizer (2005) has consistently argued that, as friends, co-workers, employers, parents, intimate partners, etc. one constantly engages in multiple forms of what she terms the "relational work" of combining personal ties and monetary forms in "differentiated ties that distinguish the relations at hand from others with which they might become confused" (p. 35). As private wealth increasingly takes on legal and financial forms, legal and financial tools and procedures such as beneficial ownership, nominee coholder, authorized signatures, and credit cards become the language and resources through which families earmark intimate and intergenerational relations and rites. Mediated by the figure of "the gentleman from the bank," the bank and the meeting room afford a sort of liminal space where elite (gendered) adulthood becomes enacted through multiple forms of financial authorization and autonomy, like using a credit card, or gaining access to assets in trust when reaching a stipulated age.

For Antonio, four decades ago, an authorized signature and a credit card were markers conveying the trust his father had in his children. But wealth managers constantly work to bring families' forms of relational work in line with their business interests. In devising this fit, a critical role is played by cultural discourses and representations of financial literacy and, in particular, the preparation of children for dealing with increasingly complex financial investments and markets. This notion that heirs should be prepared for the financial form of wealth has performative effects. Notably, some managers observed how many families had the tradition of marking certain life events of their children—reaching legal majority, starting or finishing a university degree, getting married, etc.—by gifting them money.

> In order to bring more money in, but also to motivate them, I sometimes suggest that when children reach majority—especially those studying business or economics—I ask whether they would like to open an account for their children, even if just with a small amount, so that they start to have notions of what it is like to manage financial wealth.
>
> (Private banking manager, Lisbon)

Beyond their role as markers of private meanings and ties, donations have long been a main form of intergenerational wealth transfer; under the manager's advice, money gifts often assume forms that cultivate particular financial subjects (Santos, 2021). Judith, a London-based manager, told me about one couple who wanted to make a donation to their children; after discussing with them how to do this, the parents concluded that rather than simply appointing them as beneficiaries of a savings account or trust, this could be a good time to begin activating their daughters as investors.

> For instance, the family I was just thinking about there, the mother and father were the first to take up the relationship with us. Then they brought on their two daughters who are at university and they gifted them some money. So it's all about the education. What they want is for their children to have a portfolio of their own, to learn about investments.

While firms would hardly take a new client seeking to open an account of only €100 thousand or €200 thousand, these sorts of training portfolios, set parallell to clients' main accounts in order to motivate and educate their children, have a strategic value. One manager at the Lisbon offices of a Swiss private bank priding itself on requiring a minimum wealth threshold of €1 million noted how these portfolios of around €200 thousand, €300 thousand would never be taken by the bank in isolation, but "are part of the service the bank offers to its clients." More than fee-yielding devices, these portfolios are meant to work as affective thermostats, nurturing the right sort of emotional orientations toward investing—namely, long-term investing, investment of total returns, etc.—and keeping a foothold in descendants' life events:

> And then if the son wants to buy a house, for instance, we are already there to offer him credit. So we try to slowly involve him more and more because if we keep having him as a client and he progresses in his career over time, he can eventually become an interesting client.
>
> (Private banking manager, Lisbon)

Thus, while making sure that an account remaining under their management after a client's incapacitation or death is a core drive behind wealth managers' efforts to engage their descendants, the latter's own life events also hold business promise—maybe a well-paid job after finishing the said business or economics degree, or a mortgage to buy property; maybe their succession in the family's business (with some business potential for the investment banking department), or the eventual cash injections of a bonus, inheritances, or from the sale of some property or shares; maybe a few referrals to the friend from the university alumni network, or to the colleague at the firm who has been unhappy with their own bank. Wealth managers nurture their clients' descendants not merely as the passive future recipients of their fortunes, but as ongoing active amplifiers of their net worth.

When it comes to accommodating next-gens within the fabric of PBWM firms, it is a rather ambivalent relational task that managers must perform. On one hand, these next-gens must be disentangled just about enough to allow for the new ties to be created. At the same time, this disentanglement must be perceived by clients not as a predatory commercial act, but as bespoke performances of care for them and their family. Judith recalls how, to motivate the daughters to get involved with the portfolios, she suggested that the daughters would be "looked after" by one of the younger members in the bank's team.

> I look after the mum, and the daughters are looked after by a younger colleague of my team who's about the same age as they are. And that was done in discussion with the mum. I said "well, I can look after their portfolios; but you met my colleague, and he can look after them." And she thought "actually, that would be a really good thing to do!" But as we work as a team, I know their portfolios, and he also knows the mum's portfolio.

Carefully woven into the conversation, the suggestion surfaces as a thoughtful solution from the empathic manager who also has children of the same age. Knowing that the two managers work as a team reassures the parents that service delivery is tailored to their personal circumstances. At the same time, a younger manager embodies not only better chances at conjuring empathy, but also the possibility of a longer-lasting relationship.

The inclusion of young(er) managers (of different genders, languages, and cultural/religious backgrounds) in PBWM teams is thus a common organizational strategy that firms deploy to facilitate the connection with younger generations and smooth the disentanglement of new commercial relationships from already-existing ones. Occasions for contact are fabricated with the aid of the kind of mundane, "quaint" (McFall, 2014) objects and practices reviewed above, through which managers lure clients' descendants into the spaces and routines of wealth management (e.g. the credit card they can use, the form they must sign, the "training" portfolio, etc.). But firms also develop tools and resources exclusively geared at devising and supporting acquaintance and bonding between managers and younger members of clients' families, such as financial education events or programmes organized exclusively for them.

"I get the younger people involved with the younger people on the team," Judith continues, "and then they can invite them along to meetings so they get to meet other young clients of the bank, which is quite a nice thing for them." I ask her to tell me more about these meetings but, in her sixties, she seems to have only a general knowledge of them: "Yes, they have these young persons' events where they get speakers in, run quizzes," she says, before adding with a laugh, "I don't get invited, funnily enough. Too old for them!"

Problematizing the preparation of children

Before looking at these events, it is worth considering how the trigger of the financial education of children works in relation to broader problematizations of children's preparation for wealth. While limiting advice to financial matters was often referred to as a mark of professionalism, managers were conscious that conversations about family and children played a key role in solidifying ties with clients. Occasions inevitably emerge "as a result of us being involved in the conversations about money," one London-based manager noted, but managers also rely on a variety of tools, objects, and environments. In this section, I consider two booklets that managers offered me during interviews at two firms in London.

The first was provided by the London-based manager referred to above. He had just been telling me how succession was a difficult topic because "money changes relationships between people," when he rose from the black leather chair to fetch a small booklet on the topic of preparing children for inheritance. It had just come out, he explained, and was designed to share with clients insights collected by the firm from its network, including families of clients, wealth managers, heads of schools, and other experts.

A few months later, Eve, manager of international clients at a London-based private bank, would also momentarily leave the room where we were chatting to get me a copy of a guide on British private schools. Commissioned by the bank, the guide reviewed different schools according to several criteria: percentage of pupils achieving A*–B grades at A-level, percentage entering Oxbridge universities every year, sports and arts programmes, day school or full boarding, Single sex or co-ed, the organization of pastoral care, and things to look for on open days. Each topic gathered viewpoints of heads of schools, parents, pupils, and alumni sharing experiences of managing, attending, or sending kids to British private schools. These were complemented by glossaries of relevant terminology and textboxes with "insider's tips" on "how to make sure you get them in" (including registration at birth), or with the dates of schools' fairs in London, Geneva, Dubai, Singapore, and Istanbul.

On both occasions, as I held the booklets and conversations resumed, I wondered what role those objects played in the client–manager relationship; what were they meant to *do*, through what they promised? Undoubtedly, both objects embodied the firms' distinctive capacities to mine knowledge from their networks and congeal this into resources available to their clients. As Eve remarked referring to the guide: "we like to share intellectual capital with clients."

But the way in which objects like these work to capture clients' preferences for suppliers goes beyond knowledge-sourcing as part of service delivery. As I revisited the booklets away from the managers and their alluring meeting rooms and lobbies, I sensed an effect similar to what Deville (2015) noted about the credit cards and letters through which consumer credit and debt-collection firms seek to activate borrowers' attachment to their debts by enfolding spaces of everyday life. The effectiveness of the booklets' encroachment into clients' realms of private experience had not just to do with a capacity, afforded by their materiality and mundanity, to follow them into their offices, cars, homes, etc., but also with a particular mode of address. In fact, where a brochure on the firm's wealth-planning products and services might easily be resisted or dismissed as market-ing material, addressing clients as caring, concerned parents rather than buyers promised a greater effect. Unpacking how this mode of address is devised in the booklets through a combination of discursive and visual ele-ments is instructive of how the problematization of children's preparation is accomplished as an art of market attachment.

A key role seems to be ascribed to a certain ambivalent discourse about money, in which money is at once always present and also that which must be surpassed, rendered secondary, or placed in particular forms of arms-length subjective relations. In the schools guide, for instance, despite its aim to help parents select a school, costs, fees, or monetary issues are never referred to. Rather, the institutional message which the bank inscribes in the guide—that "the most important investment you'll ever make is in your children"—expresses the attempt to address and engage clients at the deeper, more intimate level of that which is cared for beyond money.

This trope is particularly developed in the inheritance booklet, where this kind of intimate interpellation of the client is procured through the imagined forum of others with resonating experiences, concerns, and tales, such as talking to children about the family wealth—a conversation that "might be harder than talking about sex, but [which] is just as important"— or teaching them the value of money, and the importance of budgeting and thrift. The youngest of three children in Switzerland recalls how his father instilled in him and his siblings the habit of saving by asking each of them to choose between receiving 100 francs immediately or having 300 francs in a savings account. A couple voiced their expectations about introducing a system of allowances to the three children, replacing the previous habit of buying them whatever they asked for. They were keen on children learning to make choices and saving toward something they really wanted. Another father recalled discussing with his wife the right amount they should give their children as an allowance; the sum should be large enough so they be-came familiarized with having a large volume of wealth to budget, allocate, and invest, but not so much that they became "spoiled or got into trouble."

Learning to avoid the "troubles" arising from failing to teach chil-dren how to have money—afflictions jeopardizing their physical bodies as much as their wealth (e.g. spendthrift and drinking, gambling, and drugs, etc.)[2]—is also deployed as a compelling topic. Accordingly, parents share experiences of using monetary incentives to get children to make healthy choices, providing a repertoire of modes of tying monetary forms (pocket money, allowances, rewards) to valued, meaningful behaviors and habits: one mother spoke of introducing an allowance which the son could either spend on fast food or keep for other things should he opt for a healthier packed lunch from home; a father mentioned the arrangement he and his wife made with the kids that if they did not smoke until they were eighteen they would get £1,000.

But the best way to avoid the "threats of wealth," the booklet's key point seemed to be, was by instilling in children a sense of purpose—encouraging them to find a "motivation," a "passion," a "career." Indeed, parents were adamant: children should explore their talents and capacities to find what motivates them. It is in the context of this compelling interpellation that the issue of the right school and imaginaries of the well-prepared child can be explored as tools for engaging the client-reader at the level of core values and ideals. More than "intellectual capital" supplied to customers, the guide functions as a device through which the bank can simultaneously affirm and appeal to a specific ethos, which Eve describes as "conservative."

Accordingly, the schools' offer of international placement schemes such as UN programs, the International Baccalaureate Diploma, or charity programs is viewed as a way of children acquiring leadership and teamwork skills "through empathy and service," learning how to deal with disaster and solve "real-life problems," and becoming "the truly global citizen" that top universities and "companies like Goldman Sachs" look for in graduate trainees. The "global citizen" envisaged in the booklet, however, is a pervasively anglophile, not to say colonial subject. Throughout the pages, (mostly white) boys and girls in uniforms can be spotted playing sports "created in 19th-century Britain and embodying Victorian ideals": hockey, lacrosse, rugby, cricket, polo. Green playing grounds, where a visitor may expect to be "welcomed by eager spaniels" or "girls returning from a ride

---

[2] It is interesting to note how this association between the health of bodies and wealth preservation is captured by the now widespread industry term *affluenza*, the rich kids' "disease"; see, for example, https://www.theguardian.com/society/2016/jan/04/affluenza-history-disease-wealth-privilege-ethan-couch (accessed on July 25, 2017).

up the hill," and Elizabethan buildings complete the affective atmosphere of an "almost Enid Blythonesque ethos."

This anglophile dream of British education is amplified through international voices meant to appeal to British and non-British clients alike. A Singapore-resident couple recall sending their children 7,000 miles away to an Oxford boarding prep school. Having attended a British university, the wife had agreed that a UK boarding school would be the best choice for the childrens' "extra-curricular education" and "the experience of living with others." A few pages ahead, three girls from Hong Kong, Russia, and Mumbai reveal their experience at a Westminster boarding school, marked by different sports and morning jogs at the Royal Parks.

Moreover, military education programs are also viewed as appealing to parents keen on children finishing school with plenty of "military values" such as leadership, self-discipline, and responsibility: from the Combined Cadet Force units available in several UK schools to the Britannia Royal Naval College and the Royal Military Academy Sandhurst "where the gentlemen cadets were prepared for the infantry, cavalry and the Indian army."

It is hard to miss how gender is deployed in the booklet as a lure for attachments. For boys, life at boarding school is portrayed as filled with fishing, woodland adventures, and bonfires, whereas girls live in "dreamy" 16th-century manor houses where they "can bring their pony or share someone else's," and "galloping matrons pull them out of bed for pre-breakfast rides." An Olympic 110-meter hurdler explains how his time at Eton shaped his confidence, competitiveness, and self-discipline alongside his physical capacity, while the deputy head girl of a Catholic girls' school tells of how boarding with other girls with "shared faith and experience" made up for being a single child. As for parents, the schools' "premium on good manners" is praised for easing the task of raising young children, "especially if dad's not around to remind boys to 'respect' their mother."

To conclude, objects like these booklets assist managers in the task of channelling affective affordances conjured into the firm's machinery. Like the leaflets, merchandising, and other materials used by doorstep finance companies in the early 20th-century US analyzed by McFall (2014), the booklets integrate a "promotional mix ... deployed to enhance the impact of different platforms ... in order to generate enquiries" (p. 104). The schools guide, for instance, closes with a directory of companies supporting different aspects of (private international and/or boarding) school life. These include educational consultancy companies advising on requirements and procedures for entering schools, including companies dedicated to assisting overseas children academically and socially with the language skills and social habits necessary for entering the UK boarding school system. There are also companies for ensuring children's safety and healthcare arrangements outside school, including security providers, guardians to look after overseas pupils during exeats, and agents to accompany travelling minors. Finally, there is a comprehensive range of complementary concierge services: airlines providing services for travelling minors, agents sourcing chauffeurs and household staff (butlers, chef, nannies), child therapists and consultants, English language coaching, gap year planners, lifestyle/travel consultants, etc.

Facilitating these networks of specialized suppliers is the wealth manager. The booklet on inheritance bears reference not only to the firm's trust and estate planning services, but also to the family governance consultants it can connect clients with. Likewise, should parents want to invest in a property near children's schools, or take advantage of parents' visa/residency rights that come attached to children's student visas, the guide informs the reader of the bank's real estate advisors and wealth-management services.

The Mandarin Oriental

The scene: Geneva, late July. A few dozen future heirs in their 20s gather from all over the world for an intensive program led by senior managers of their parents' or grandparents' private bank. The day starts early. Breakfast is served at 8.30 a.m. in a special room of the Mandarin Oriental, the five-star hotel which the cohort leaves only to go for meals. From 9 a.m., the next generation of private wealth sits around tables of six or seven to hear the bank's finest talk expertly about different facets of wealth and business succession. Occasionally, participants take notes, or use the bank's app on their tablets to answer poll questionnaires or simulate investment exercises. Morning coffee break, and networking ensues, followed by a strategy expert speaking on the challenges of owning a business. Lunch is at one of Geneva's top restaurants, with a terrace overlooking Lac Léman, with its rims of banks and watchmakers, and the Alps behind. Back at the Mandarin, the afternoon is filled with more seminars on market and business hot topics—alternative investments, entrepreneurship, emerging markets—duly punctuated with another networking break. Before heading off for dinner, there is some free time for leisure and socializing.

Captured in a three-minute-long summary video,[3] the Geneva program addressing the financial preparation of heirs is part of the wealth-management services that HSBC Private Banking—like many PBWM firms—offers clients. The video recasts the bank's machinery of technical expertise as a training device for clients' inheritors. On a tablet's screen, the event app introduces a lineup of speakers composed mainly of HSBC senior staff: wealth planners, heads of different regional units, corporate advisors, and alternative investment and emerging markets specialists. Dressed in suits, they nonetheless appear smiling and approachable, as they go back and forth through slideshow presentations with their pointers. Glimpses of tablets, slideshows, and scribbled whiteboards show portfolio-management simulations, wealth succession case studies, business plans for fictitious entrepreneurial ideas, and a variety of polling questionnaires on topics such as "do you know how wealthy your family is?" This visual narrative of technologically enabled hands-on financial education is punctuated with thoughts shared by speakers on the challenges ahead for their young participants. For the "future business leaders" and "young investors," the future is problematized as immanently financial: they will face higher market volatility; increasingly complex investment products; and globally dispersed structures of wealth, business, and family relations, etc. The sooner they understand "how the laws of compound interest" can work in their favor, and the sooner they appreciate the benefits of conservative, long-term investing, the better equipped they will be to protect and grow their wealth.

The event reassembles the bank's financial services machinery as a field of knowledge where managers gain a renewed epistemic status and authority over the problematization of children's future and preparation. Contributing to this epistemic makeover of the wealth-management machine is not just the enactment of classroom imaginary through the sequence of talks, presentations, practical exercises, and devices like the slideshow, the presentation pointer, and the whiteboard. Often, wealth managers seek the partnership of academic and/or research institutions that can lend to these events the hallmark of scientific respectability. Thus, the Zurich-based manager mentioned earlier told me how the Swiss private bank he worked

[3] https://www.hsbcprivatebank.com/en/discover/news-room/2015/looking-ahead; accessed on January 21, 2017.

for has its own annual "young investors" programme where the clients' children "spend a week in Switzerland talking with senior managers and university professors and networking." Eve, the London-based manager mentioned above, referred to the "future leaders programme" the bank would be running "in the summer for some of the children of [its] top clients, where [they would be doing] education in business with [an Ivy League] Business School." Through their new roles as knowledge providers rather than product sellers, managers gain enhanced forms of access to the next-gens. Undoubtedly this is the ultimate goal of these kinds of programs, as Elsa, the head of private banking unit referred to in the first section, made clear:

> We might say that they have an educational goal; it sounds much nicer. We sometimes do seminars and stuff like that and we say they have an educational goal. But the ultimate goal is captivation, is to secure the loyalty of those children who are now twenty years old. I pretend to give them loads of fantastic seminars on macroeconomics, and many highlights so that they think they are very important. I don't care about that one bit. What I want is to get them as clients when their parents kick the bucket.

But Eve also sees in these programs the opportunity to cut across the layer of professional intermediation imposed by the family offices that, as manager of UHNW (Ultra High Net Worth) clients, she usually deals with.

> We've just taken one of the UK's billionaires in here a couple of weeks ago and said "yes, we'll deal with your family office, but we really want to be able to talk to you occasionally as well, and get to know what drives you, what your key concerns are." Not to try to do the same job as the family office, but to make sure that we're supporting the family office in the right way. . . . So this individual, he's got a daughter who is 23. We're doing a future leaders programme in the Summer . . . and basically that would be perfect for her. So we need to know what he thinks about that so that we can invite her and bring her into that opportunity.

As noted before, private banking relations—at least at the higher end of the wealth spectrum—are becoming increasingly mediated by entities such as family offices or multi-family offices which coordinate multiple asset managers and private banks selected and assessed on the basis of financial performance. To the 350-year-old London-based private bank—traditionally focused on banking and cashflow management services—devising such forms of (value-added) direct engagement is critical for maintaining the relevance of the relationship, in a context of increasing intermediation by family offices and competition from investment banks. "If we disinterme- diate," Eve says, "there's no value in being part of Y [the bank]. They might as well just do it with Credit Suisse for product." But competing with big- ger banks for relevance also means that Y's future leaders program must be grounded in something more than elaborate and resourceful in-house machineries of financial expertise. By associating it with an Ivy League in- stitution, the relevance of the market attachment to Y is renewed for father and daughter by a version of children's preparation marked not only by the expert financial and business knowledge the bank can source, but by the elite circuits of cultural and social capital it can unlock.

Another example of events organized for clients' descendants was given by Jorge, founder of a multi-family office in Lisbon. In his view, outsourcing family-office services to firms that specialize in providing these services to multiple families was the best way of professionalizing family wealth man- agement. One of the benefits, he noted, was the opportunity for clients' children to meet each other and share experiences with peers as well as with the older generations of other wealthy, business-owning families like theirs. Each year, "four or five young members of clients' families gather over a week around the cherrywood table" of one of the firm's meeting rooms, to have seminars with experts on investment-related topics but also to hear older family members sharing family stories of business and wealth transition.

"A grandson already listens to his own grandfather at home; teaching the children of others is something that clients don't mind at all," Jorge continues, before noting how hearing the stories, problems, and solutions of other families engenders a sense of collective identity that strengthens their engagement as heirs.

That the financial education of future generations is better accomplished alongside peers is thus a logic complementary to the notion that a timely financial education is necessary to adequately prepare children for inheri- tance. And despite the variegated forms they take—from HSBC's luxurious emulation of a business forum, to the "young persons' meetings" referred to by Judith earlier—they all attempt to contract the heir as a collec- tive, class subject enmeshed in and marked by the ties with their PBWM supplier.

When Judith mentions the young persons events that, "funnily enough," she is not invited to, she is emphasizing not only the advantages of aligning descendants with young managers on the basis of enhanced commonality, but also the role that enabling a social community of younger people plays in achieving stronger, more durable attachments to the bank.

At the Mandarin Oriental, socialization is a side effect not just of spending three days sleeping, eating, and engaging in learning activities with the same people under the same roof, but also of a thorough planning of how bodies move and affects circulate in the different spaces and temporalities of the event. From the outset and throughout, participants contemplate a common landscape of future risks and uncertainties: market volatility, taxation, divorces, fallings-out with business partners, lawsuits related to the latter two, difficulties of keeping several members and branches of the family together when the founder of the business and fortune is no longer around.

Learning techniques and technologies are applied to elicit common experiences of wealth. For instance, at one point in the video, the tablet of a participant displays the case of a patriarch who sets up a trust to transfer the shares of his company, a holiday property at the Hamptons worth $10 million, and two bank accounts to his sons. Beside the use of case studies familiar to the cohort of future heirs, activities occasionally include polling exercises, whereby each participant can confront their own views and experiences regarding the question given with the majority sentiment in the room.

The case study and the poll integrate a discursive–affective apparatus designed to establish a common ground of knowledge and the contracting of subjects, with the former inviting family stories, cases of wealth, and succession, and the latter compiling them into norms, means, and other forms of "weak generalities" (Deleuze, 2014). The parameterized environment of the event thus forms a particular response to the Deleuzian question of "under what conditions experimentation ensures repetition" (ibid., p. 3). The event works as a laboratorial device whereby wealth managers attempt to secure the conditions of repetition of market attachments. The Mandarin Oriental and other similar venues constitute "closed environments" where heirs and managers, financial expertise and social class, whichever "chosen factors" have been selected, retained, and disposed relative to each other according to two types of relations: hierarchical relations of knowledge, recasting a commercial relational field into an epistemic and pedagogic one; and heterarchical relations of social normalization among peers.

Conclusion

As high-net-worth families plan for succession, their wealth managers seek to engage and secure the financial preparation as well as the commercial preference of their heirs. As they do so, "quaint" objects and practices like credit cards, account-opening forms, money gifts in the form of "training" portfolios, or booklets sharing "intellectual capital" suggest that wealth-management firms figure as privileged sites of problematization and management of family wealth transfer. Traversing these strategies, the trope of children's preparation for wealth—and as holders of financial portfolios more narrowly—is a compelling mode of address, enabling forms, or "arts" (Cochoy et al., 2017) of market attachment whereby wealth managers distinguish themselves from other suppliers, both within and without clients' constellations of wealth organization and management.

By taking the PBWM sector—and its entwinements with succession more narrowly—as analytical and empirical entry point, this chapter sheds light on how relational forms of coordination take place and work to materialize a specific type of wealth chain—private/ family wealth. The chapter has highlighted key factors intervening in the organization of wealth chains beside the liability criteria advanced in the original GWC formulation (see Seabrooke & Wigan, 2017)—namely, the reservoirs of trust and intimate knowledge accumulated by managers, which render suppliers harder to replace (cf. also Harrington, 2016). It also nuances the notion of liability itself, to account for threats arising from wealth's embeddedness in interpersonal and sociocultural dynamics—divorces, unprepared heirs, family quarrels, etc.—which coalesce with tax and regulatory liability in the wealth-management solutions designed by suppliers.[4]

At the analytical and methodological levels, if the types of wealth chain governance outlined in the GWC framework—market, modular, relational, hierarchical, and captive (Seabrooke & Wigan, 2017)—are not to be taken as silos but as a heuristic sensitized to the empirical variegation of wealth chains, then an analytical toolkit is necessary to account for how governance types are accomplished, sustained, and combined in *practice*, amidst the messiness and contingency of everyday life. Borrowing from economic sociology and cultural economy, the orientation here toward

---

[4] A good example is the variety of offshore asset-holding structures (trusts, companies, foundations, etc.) that enable avoiding, or minimizing, not only tax liability, but also forced-heirship legislation and divorce-settlement rulings in clients' home countries.

market attachments and methodological attunement to the "arts" and the devices enabling them, provides analytical traction in that endeavor. By focusing on the subtleties of client–manager exchanges around the issue of children's preparation for inheriting wealth, the chapter has offered insights into how interpretative work entailed with the legal affordances of transgenerational asset transfer is carefully woven with culturally charged understandings of dynastic wealth in relational coordination modes within GWCs.

This privileging of a grounded approach over institutional or network representation has consequences for how space and the role of spatiality in wealth chains should be conceptualized. Notably, what the cases analyzed here show is a relational work geared at enacting binds and folds, distances and proximities that are not reduceable to the (multi)jurisdictional organization of wealth. Through tools and techniques such as the ones reviewed here, trust in the "gentleman from the bank," empathy with the manager of the same age, or the allure of a British private bank's "conservative" ethos incentivize clients to bring children to meetings or send them abroad on financial education programmes. Understanding suppliers' capacities for attaining these fluid, contingent, and more or less temporary forms of dissolving distances and enfolding spaces of private and family life is key to understanding how private and family wealth solidify, or rather dissolve particular constellations of financial and legal services suppliers. The chapter thus makes the case for attuning the GWC framework to the co-constitutive entanglements between topographical and topological spatiality (Allen, 2011) that materialize wealth chains as always already "more-than-economic spaces" (Gibson-Graham, 2014; Harker, 2017).

Finally, the chapter's signposting of family wealth as a key type of wealth chain must be read as opening scope for, and calling for further work on, the overlaps and modes of articulation between corporate and private wealth chains (namely, while not exclusively, of family-owned company formations).

References

Allen, J. (2011). Making space for topology. *Dialogues in Human Geography*, 1(3), 316–318.

Beaverstock, J. V., Hall, S. J., & Wainwright, T. (2013). Overseeing the fortunes of the global super-rich: The nature of private wealth management in London's financial district. In I. Hay (ed.), *Geographies of the Super-rich*. Edward Elgar Publishing, 43–60.

Çalışkan, K. & Callon, M. (2009). Economization, part 1: Shifting attention from the economy towards processes of economization. *Economy and society*, 38(3), 369–398.

Çalışkan, K. & Callon, M. (2010). Economization, part 2: A research programme for the study of markets. *Economy and Society*, 39(1), 1–32.

Cochoy, F., Deville, J. & McFall, L. (eds.). (2017). *Markets and the Arts of Attachment*. Routledge.

Deleuze, G. (2014). *Difference and Repetition*. Bloomsbury Revelations.

Deville, J. (2015). *Lived Economies of Default: Consumer Credit, Debt Collection and the Capture of Affect*. Routledge.

Gibson-Graham, J. K. (2014). Rethinking the economy with thick description and weak theory. *Current Anthropology*, 55(S9), S147–S153.

Harker, C. (2017). Debt space: Topologies, ecologies and Ramallah, Palestine. *Environment and Planning D: Society and Space*, 35(4), 600–619.

Harrington, B. (2016). *Capital Without Borders*. Harvard University Press.

Hay, I., & Beaverstock, J. V. (eds.), (2016). *Handbook on Wealth and the Super-Rich*. Edward Elgar Publishing.

Kear, M. (2016). Peer lending and the subsumption of the informal. *Journal of Cultural Economy*, 9(3), 261–276.

Langley, P. (2008). *The Everyday Life of Global Finance: Saving and Borrowing in Anglo-America*. Oxford University Press.

McFall, L. (2014). *Devising Consumption: Cultural Economies of Insurance, Credit and Spending*. Routledge.

Santos, M. (2021). High net-worth attachments: Emotional labour, relational work, and financial subjectivities in private wealth management. *Journal of Cultural Economy*, 14(6), 750–764.

Seabrooke, L. & Wigan, D. (2017). The governance of global wealth chains. *Review of International Political Economy*, 24(1), 1–29.

UBS/PwC (2016). Billionaires Insights: Are Billionaires Feeling the Pressure?, available at https://uhnw-greatwealth.ubs.com/media/8616/billionaires-report-2016.pdf.

Zelizer, V. (2005). *The Purchase of Intimacy*. Princeton University Press.

11

Transparency

Rasmus Corlin Christensen

Introduction

Following the global financial crisis, the transparency of corporate tax practices gained substantial momentum as a key global policy goal. Rapid economic integration had created increasing opportunities for corporate capital to exploit national tax systems through international regulatory arbitrage. The international corporate tax system rested on century-old principles, originally designed in the 1920s, unable to deal with contemporary economic realities. World leaders agreed that there was an urgent need to shore up national fiscal systems, address rising debt burdens, and alleviate social injustices, and corporate taxation emerged as a central reform target (Christensen & Hearson, 2019). In 2013, the Organisation for Economic Cooperation and Development (OECD) and the G20 launched the Base Erosion and Profit Shifting (BEPS) project. BEPS introduced 15 concrete action points aimed at comprehensive and coordinated global policy change, with a particular emphasis upon corporate tax transparency (OECD, 2013). The aim was to make more information available to stakeholders on companies' tax affairs, including a controversial demand for an unprecedented level of publicity and geographical segmentation through so-called *country-by-country reporting* (CBCR). Combining strong political backing from the G20 with the OECD's technical expertise on tax policy, the project was able to produce new globally accepted standards on corporate tax transparency by 2014.

New tax transparency rules have wide-ranging economic, normative, and political consequences for the regulatory context of global wealth chains (GWCs). Tax transparency is a critical wealth chain asset, a legal affordance that shapes the information asymmetries between wealth chain "insiders" and "outsiders," and a key component of corporate financial and reputational management (Christensen et al., 2021). More transparency

Rasmus Corlin Christensen, *Transparency*. In: *Global Wealth Chains*. Edited by Leonard Seabrooke and Duncan Wigan, Oxford University Press. © Rasmus Corlin Christensen (2022). DOI: 10.1093/oso/9780198832379.003.0011 means more information available for outsiders to mount regulatory and reputational challenges to corporate tax practices—a risk to the differential returns earned by firms able to obscure information around their tax practices. In particular, the global introduction of CBCR would place significant pressure on corporate wealth chains by mandating unprecedented (public) disclosure by multinational companies (MNCs) of taxes paid in each jurisdiction of operation, alongside a number of real economic activity indicators, allowing for simple quantitative comparisons by outside stakeholders. Consequently, the BEPS process brought stakeholders with various levels of investment in GWCs to the table, vigorously contesting the proposed regulatory changes (Büttner & Thiemann, 2017).

How did the new rules for corporate tax transparency develop, and to whose benefit? As the introductory Chapter 1 of this volume contends, there is an urgent need to understand how wealth chains are regulated, how they are affected by regulatory innovation, and the role of interpretive communities of professionals—lawyers, economists, and accountants—in enabling or constraining wealth creation and protection. This chapter addresses these issues by analyzing the BEPS policy process and the ostensibly technical but fundamentally political battles between professional actors over the right to define new global standards on corporate tax transparency. It draws on literature on professional micropolitics in global governance, which has highlighted the influence of such competition in technical settings reshaping global corporate tax politics (Seabrooke & Wigan, 2016; Büttner & Thiemann, 2017; Hearson, 2018; Christensen, 2020). This chapter adds to this literature by exploring competitive dynamics amongst professionals in a particularly crucial area of the regulatory context of corporate wealth chains, namely corporate tax transparency, and specifically CBCR.

The argument proposed here is that technicization of the BEPS policy process constrained the post-crisis political momentum for expanded transparency of corporate wealth chains. Technicization is the process of embedding highly political discussions in a specialized, knowledge-intensive policy context. Such settings mask fundamental politics as "technical" or "neutral," favouring expertise and technical efficiency, as opposed to public politicized policy settings where explicit political interests dominate. I argue that this technicization effectively constrained the broadly established post-crisis political momentum for expansive corporate tax transparency through three key processes: policy insulation, reframing, and appropriateness judgments. These processes of technicization

influenced the views of technical experts and policymakers on key policy issues and solutions, effectively shaping policy outcomes. Evidence is
drawn from qualitative content analysis of the policy debates surrounding
BEPS, in particular its "Action 13" on corporate tax transparency, as well
as interviews with select informants involved in the policy process. Based
on these data, the chapter emphasizes professional and technical–political
dynamics in defining the changing regulatory context of GWCs.

The chapter is structured as follows. The next section outlines the key
battle lines and implications for global wealth chains of corporate tax transparency. I emphasize how expanded transparency reduces information
asymmetries, challenges financial and reputational capital, and presents
opportunities for increased regulatory traction in captive and hierarchy
wealth chains. The third section introduces the policy context and policy
process of BEPS Action 13, detailing the eventual "transparency compromise" that emerged. The fourth section discusses the technical–political
battles over the right to define new corporate tax transparency standards,
and details the professional arguments used for and against. I highlight the
process of technicization—how it creates knowledge barriers to mobilization, how it masks political viewpoints, and its implications for the policy
environment, which was characterized by a strong presence of practitioners with private sector tax expertise cautioning against expansive transparency. I argue that technicization influenced the final policy outcomes
by constraining the political momentum for expanded transparency, limiting regulatory traction in GWCs. The concluding section reflects on the
analysis and its implications, suggesting that the chapter highlights the potential of further research on the technical–political processes shaping the
changing regulatory context of GWCs.

Global wealth chains and corporate tax transparency

The global wealth chains framework allows us to systematically link global
regulatory innovations with the practices and micropolitics of wealth chain
actors. It directs our attention toward the micro-level underpinnings of
wealth-creation and -protection regimes, requiring analyses of the professional and social networks that maintain global wealth chains. Furthermore, by analyzing the impact of global regulatory reform on global wealth
chains, GWC research can contribute insights on the impact of regulatory
innovations on financial accumulation practices. Such investigating allows

us to expand knowledge of policy influence and adaptation by wealth chain actors, including the role of professionals in enabling or constraining socio-economic change.

In the case of corporate tax transparency, regulatory innovations touch directly upon captive and hierarchy wealth chains. Captive wealth chains involve major global advisory firms (lead suppliers) providing complex tax advice to corporate tax officers (small suppliers) and MNCs (clients). Here, existing transparency schemes provide authorities with limited regulatory traction.[1] In hierarchy wealth chains, suppliers and clients are more closely integrated, with in-house tax advisers largely performing the tax structuring. This integration provides regulators less transparency about tax practice, and thus clouds oversight. Within these two types of chains, corporate tax planning is central to wealth strategies, and transparency crucial to potential regulatory intervention. Aggressive tax behavior has allowed some companies to shift profits artificially to low-tax jurisdictions, minimizing tax burdens significantly (Dharmapala, 2014). In response, regulators have identified increased transparency as a central lever for combating these strategies, enabling governments to identify and act on key risk areas (OECD, 2013).

Expanded transparency, if adopted across the world, would enable unprecedented challenges to corporate financial and reputational capital by reducing information asymmetries in corporate wealth chains (Seabrooke & Wigan, 2017). Transparency and its absence are key strategic assets in the governance of global wealth chains, providing benefits and costs for wealth chain actors. For clients and suppliers, lack of transparency can contribute to holding outsiders at bay, protecting wealth-accumulation strategies and reputational capital. If authorities and the public are unable to decipher financial structures and tax-related transactions, they are unlikely to mount effective regulatory and reputational interventions. For regulators, lack of transparency obscures oversight. Importantly, "regulators" here is understood broadly, including the media and civil society activists alongside government authorities. While the later perform a *legislative* regulatory function, the former perform a *normative* regulatory function. More information provides regulators with more power, easing normative, administrative, and legislative intervention and critique by strengthening regulatory capacity. In turn, more information would impose financial

---

[1] Most developed countries, and increasingly developing countries as well, have legislated and expanded tax transparency documentation requirements over the past two decades.

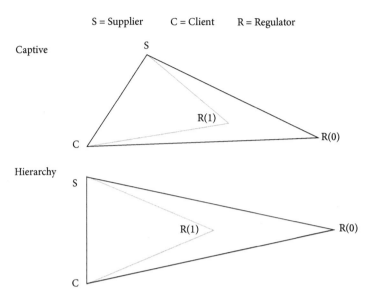

Fig. 11.1 Potential effects of transparency on wealth chain information asymmetries

and reputational costs upon MNCs (whether or not any legal misconduct had taken place). For instance, previous advances in corporate tax transparency have allowed civil society activists to advance impactful criticisms of banks' tax practices as expressions of misalignment of taxable profits toward low-tax jurisdictions (Murphy, 2014; Dyreng, Hoopes & Wilde, 2016; CCFD-Terre Solidaire et al., 2016; Oxfam, 2017). Thus, if expansive CBCR were to be required of companies through BEPS 13, it would bring regulators closer to clients/suppliers, increasing the likelihood of regulatory and normative liability for captive and hierarchy wealth chains. Figure 11.1 illustrates this, contrasting the status quo (position 0) with potential effects of BEPS 13 (position 1) on tax transparency.

If information asymmetries were reduced through transparency, beneficiaries of captive and hierarchy chains might well need to rethink wealth strategies entirely. Given the imposition of extra costs of fiscal arbitrage (in the form of administrative compliance burdens or reputational risk, etc.), wealth chain suppliers might need to mobilize increasingly high-level capabilities to help clients restructure tax affairs to conform to a new regulatory environment. This could take the form of either reorganization to avoid reputational exposure through "creative compliance" or reorganization to meet new norms and minimize reputational challenges altogether. In the former scenario, MNCs might restructure to maintain tax advantages whilst formally meeting regulatory demands, bolstering information asymmetries and existing wealth chain strategies. For instance, captive wealth chain suppliers are increasingly marketing "tax-effective supply chain management" services, enabling clients to establish integrated operational structures that are "tax sustainable" in the face of regulatory action (Hearson, Chapter 3 in in this volume). In the latter scenario, MNCs might de-risk and simplify financial structures, moving toward more market-based wealth chain structures of lower complexity and lower regulatory liability. In this vein, surges toward increased transparency of corporate tax affairs since the financial crisis have led businesses to rethink tax practices due to potential reputational pressures, with tax reputation management becoming a key issue for high-level corporate executives (EY, 2016; PwC, 2016). A 2016 industry survey of American CEOs summarizes the point:

> Many companies are restructuring their global operations and looking at their supply chains, with a view to minimizing any potential brand or reputational risk. . . . They don't want to deal with the potential fallout of negative publicity should a tax arrangement attract attention from media or shareholders.
>
> (KPMG, 2016, p. 26)

BEPS Action 13: A transparency compromise

In the wake of the 2007–2008 financial crisis, the BEPS project emerged as the key initiative to enhance corporate tax transparency. However, corporate tax transparency was not initially on the post-crisis agenda for global leaders, although they had begun to criticize tax havens and opaque corporate practices as sources of financial instability (Lesage & Kaçar, 2013; Rixen, 2013). As international tax reform moved into the global spotlight, OECD bureaucrats and activists mobilized powerfully, leveraging years of work "in the shadows" on proposals to strengthen the international tax system. Alongside civil society activists, they lobbied G8 and G20 officials successfully, bringing key policy asks—including transparency—onto the agenda (Eccleston & Woodward, 2014, p. 223). Thus, formally prompted by the G20 leaders at the June 2012 Summit in Los Cabos, Mexico (G20, 2012), the work began. The OECD issued a scoping report in February 2013, followed by the project launch and the BEPS Action Plan in July.

The envisioned regulatory changes were far-reaching, targeting a broad range of issues; abuse of bilateral tax treaties, international tax mismatches, corporate debt gaming, multilateral tax cooperation, and, importantly, corporate tax transparency (OECD, 2013).

Action 13 on transfer pricing documentation and country-by-country reporting (CBCR) was the most controversial project item. CBCR had been a hotly contested issue for years, with civil society activists seeking to mandate extensive *public* disclosure by MNCs. For them, it was about "putting MNC activity 'on the record'" (Murphy, 2012). However, CBCR had faced substantial opposition from policymakers, businesses, and tax professionals due to its perceived threat to entrenched legal principles, to corporate privacy, and to competitiveness (Lesage & Kaçar, 2013; Baden & Wigan, 2017). Activists had found some momentum with the adoption of Dodd–Frank in the US and the Accounting and Transparency Directives in the EU, both of which required publication of "lite" versions of CBCR in targeted industries. Emboldened, civil society activists worked to push CBCR onto the BEPS agenda after it had been entirely absent from the initial OECD scoping report. This was successful, and the G8 leaders in June 2013 formally called on the OECD to develop a global standard for CBCR (G8, 2013).

As the BEPS project commenced, the technicization of policy discussions took hold. Formally, the political direction had been set by global leaders in the G8, the G20, and the OECD Council, and key points of decision-making continued to formally rest with ministers and high-level diplomats. Within that setting, the practical policy-formulation process now lay largely at the technical level, specifically with OECD bureaucrats and the broader interest ecology of tax experts in public administrations, business, academia, and (to a lesser extent) civil society. The Action 13 work was managed by Working Party 6 (WP6) of the OECD's Committee of Fiscal Affairs (CFA). WP6 and the CFA both consist of national delegates, who meet every 3–4 months in addition to informal bilateral talks. WP6 and the CFA had support from a dedicated BEPS secretariat in the OECD's tax directorate, responsible for preparing most documentation and advancing discussions, drafting policy recommendations, and engaging proactively with stakeholders throughout the process. From July 2013 to May 2014, WP6 and the OECD secretariat planned six official consultations on CBCR, receiving a range of inputs from stakeholders. They held four "regional" consultations (in Korea, Colombia, South Africa, and France (in Paris)) and also two events for the wider public in Paris. Then, in June 2014, the WP6 presented the policy recommendations following the technical discussions to the CFA, which were approved and later ratified by the G20 Finance Ministers in September.

The outcome of the BEPS Action 13 policy process can be labelled a "transparency compromise." Issued in September 2014, the final Action 13 report contained recommendations for countries to adopt national documentation requirements on corporate tax transparency, asking for more information than ever before, including the controversial addition of CBCR (OECD, 2014c). However, the recommendations had also re-formulated the purpose of CBCR from prior political discussions. Far removed from "putting MNCs on the record," the stated purpose of CBCR was now to enhance risk assessment by tax administrations, subject to considerations of business compliance costs. The CBCR template itself included seven data points for economic comparison, down from fif-teen in the initial draft, and less than had initially been advocated by CBCR inventors (Murphy, 2003), notably excluding cross-border pay-ments and labor costs. Furthermore, the report stipulated that CBCRs should be disclosed to tax administrations in the MNC groups' parent headquarter country (i.e. largely the global North), and be obtained by other countries through bilateral tax agreements. This was another depar-ture from prior political discourse, which had emphasized broad-based access for the non-North (who generally have few tax agreements in place for such exchanges). Finally, the disclosure requirements were limited to companies with more than €750 million in annual revenue, represent-ing around 10 percent of global MNCs, again a narrowing compared to the original activist intentions and previous regulation in the EU and the US.

In wealth chain terms, the final recommendations will undoubtedly reduce wealth chain asymmetries by providing authorities with more information—but less so than initial post-crisis political momentum had envisioned. With more than 100 countries committing to implementing the Action 13 recommendations, the transparency compromise is certain to have global effect. While the CBCR recommendations have been suc-cessfully diffused, their scope and nature have become critically limited compared to the intentions of those who pushed them onto the global agenda. Consequently, the potential for new regulatory traction on global wealth chains remains constrained. Figure 11.2 illustrates this, contrasting the status quo (position 0), the original activist intentions (position 1), and the actual recommendations (position 2) in terms of effect on wealth chain information asymmetries.

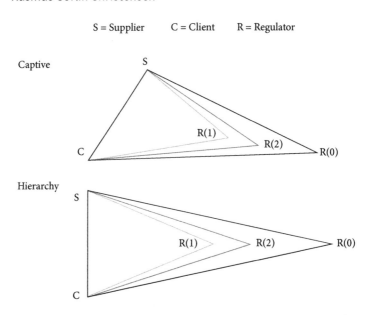

Fig. 11.2 Actual effects of transparency on wealth chain information asymmetries

Technical–political battles

How did this transparency compromise come about? With the main stakes and the policy process outlined, I now turn to the technical–political battles around new global standards for tax transparency. I argue that techniciza-tion of the policy process subdued the surge for expanded transparency of corporate wealth chains through three key dynamics: policy insulation, re-framing, and appropriateness judgments. I consider each of these in turn. These processes influenced the view of technical experts and policymak-ers on key policy issues and solutions, effectively shaping policy outcomes. Evidence is drawn from qualitative content analysis (QCA) of the two pub-lic consultations in BEPS 13, as well as interviews with select informants involved in the policy process. Alongside 24 hours of video footage, 183 comment letters were mapped, detailing the respondent, its type, and pol-icy positions on key issues of debate. For each comment letter, the stated policy position on these issues was coded on a scale of 1 to 3, with 1 demarking a general preference for expansive wealth chain transparency and 3 demarking a general opposition thereto. The policy positions pro-vide an overview of the structure of the debate but they also reflect the main wealth chain politics: more transparency means less information asymmetry and thus more scope for reputational challenges and regulatory traction, and vice versa.

The first key dynamic of technicization was *policy insulation*. Policy insulation prevents outside influence on established institutions by infusing them with structural ideational inertia, making such settings more likely to resist change (Drezner, 2000; Figueiredo, 2002). This is a well-established dynamic in the case of the OECD's international tax policymaking, where insulation from popular politics had "facilitated normative settlement and the emergence of a transnational 'epistemic community' embodying it" (Genschel & Rixen, 2015, p. 36). At its core, the technical policy setting insulated professionals involved in policymaking from politicization and public conflict. In the political sphere, the conditions for uptake of CBCR had been favorable. Extensive media coverage, crisis momentum, and rising popular salience of issues related to corporate tax avoidance and inequality had provided an ideal platform on which to push tax transparency. However, the technical policy space was entirely different. As opposed to politicians, media, and the wider public, the technical environment featured primarily expert stakeholders, such as national delegates, OECD bureaucrats, and the wider community of tax professionals, all of which had considerable interaction throughout the discussions. Such professionals can be more closely connected amongst each other within the technical community, sharing policy ideas and epistemic frames, than they are through affiliations with a particular organization or nation (see Seabrooke & Sending, 2020). As one interviewee noted, "the group of people involved in the process is relatively small; we see each other regularly" (interview with tax advisor #1), while another said "they all know each other very well, by first name; they are extremely chummy" (interview with OECD official #1). By embedding key policy discussions in such an "epistemic community" (Haas, 1992), policymaking professionals were effectively insulated from messy popular politics, enabling a strong technical unity, upon which other formal authorities involved in the policy process—such as ministers and high-level diplomats—relied.

An overwhelming majority of private sector tax specialists in the policy discussions, cautioning against transparency, furthered policy insulation. There was dominant mobilization of private sector tax expertise in the public policy consultation as well as in informal discussions (Christensen, 2020). And the majority were strongly against expansive new transparency demands. Figure 11.3 below shows a density plot (smoothed

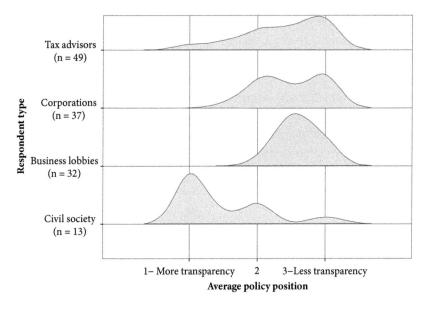

Fig. 11.3 Distribution of policy positions on tax transparency

histograms)[2] of the distribution of average policy positions in comment letters sent to the OECD, broken down by respondent type.[3] The significant
right skew—except for civil society activists—indicates a broad consensus
amongst contributors warning *against CBCR*. Across the comment letters,
the average policy position scored 2.4 (median 2.5). This aligns with the
composition of respondents, largely dominated by tax advisors, corporations, and business lobbies, that is, groups with a high degree of technical
expertise on tax matters as well as political investment in existing global
wealth chains. In opposition, marginal voices from civil society, including
researchers and developing-country actors, remained in a small minority.
As one interviewee said of these groups' influence in the policy deliberations, "we can have a voice but not a vote" (interview with civil society
activist #1).

A central reason for the structure of mobilization was knowledge barriers. Technicization creates obstacles to political inclusion and engagement,
requiring detailed practical expertise and thus limiting the range of actors
able to credibly contest policy debates. Policy discussions were conducted
in a highly technical, specialized language, thick with specific legal and

[2] Density kernel joint bandwidth of 0.221.
[3] Comment letters that did not express any particular policy opinions on the key issues were
excluded (21 in total).

economic terminology. While many tax practitioners found this natural, activists and other non-specialists were absent by choice or necessity. A number of national representations and critical NGOs thus participated very little or not at all in the technical policy discussions. This excluded a number of voices, critical of global wealth chains and favoring more transparency, from the deliberations, thus contributing to relative consensus amongst participants against expansive transparency.

It should be noted that a small minority of activists took on the challenge, banding together relevant expertise to participate meaningfully in technical discussions. In particular, the BEPS Monitoring Group, a coalition of civil society tax experts, sought to aggregate activist knowledge on tax matters in order to mobilize counter-expertise (Quack, 2016). The Group's engagement with technical discussions was led by Richard Murphy, an accountant-turned-activist and creator of the activist-backed CBCR standard (Murphy, 2003); Sol Picciotto, emeritus professor of law; and Jeffery Kadet, a tax accountant and former tax partner at Arthur Andersen. Alongside attempts to make explicit the broader political implications of the corporate tax transparency discussions, the Group argued their case using specific technical comments. Their comment letter, for instance, leveraged economic expertise in arguing that CBCR should be made public, as it "would make the system more effective by promoting consistency" (OECD, 2014b). It also argued in extensive detail for a "top-down" approach to CBCR, noting that such an approach would minimize double taxation by aligning with recognized accounting standards (OECD, 2014b). Such structured organization of counter-expertise and detailed expertise-based arguments was largely unprecedented from activists in technical tax processes.

The second key dynamic of technicization was *reframing*. Framing is the process by which events or ideas are made sense of, which in turn "organize experiences and guide action" (Snow et al., 1986). The way corporate tax transparency and CBCR was made sense of and talked about shaped reactions to the proposals. In particular, the technicized policy process *re*framed CBCR, re-engineered conventional understandings of the purpose of CBCR by institutionalizing and diffusing an alternative framing of corporate tax transparency measures. Already, in the June G8 declaration, and shortly thereafter in the July OECD Action Plan, the signs of expert reframing had been evident. Whereas activists had advanced *public* CBCR as a financial reporting standard to expose corporate tax avoidance, the adoption onto the global agenda framed CBCR as "for tax authorities."

Suddenly, CBCR had shifted from a public concern and an accounting issue to a private administrative matter under the rubric of "transfer pricing documentation," over which OECD had exclusive authority as the global standard-setter. Furthermore, the idea of CBCR as a lever for systemic change was abandoned. Activists had promoted CBCR as a tool for fundamentally reshaping the international corporate tax system, which they saw as easily manipulated and unjustly favorable to MNCs (Murphy, 2013; Tax Justice Network, 2013). They hoped that creating transparency for MNCs' (mis)allocation of profit in relation to economic activity (sales, labor, assets) would help usher in a new era. However, the G8 declaration and the OECD Plan defined CBCR as exclusively a risk-assessment tool for governments, in line with existing OECD framing of transfer pricing documentation, and thus activist framings and aspirations suffered a significant blow.

This reframing of CBCR was furthered in the technical policy discussions, with significant political implications. While it may not be surprising that expert professionals, under political pressure to adopt CBCR into policy discussions on their "home turf," framed CBCR in (for them) conventional terms, such as transfer pricing risk assessment, this co-optation is by no means a "neutral" process. What is technical is political. Technicization and reframing steered discussion toward a limited range of topics, effectively eliminating certain political viewpoints and avenues. As one interviewee noted, "By breaking it down into technical, detailed topics, people focus on those minor technical issues rather than the larger ones" (interview with tax advisor #2). The discussion of CBCR as a technical issue of risk assessment for tax administrations and part of the standard transfer pricing documentation package, rather than a revolutionary tool (as in the activist framing), precluded debate on the fundamentals of international corporate taxation. Instead, the experts discussed such issues as the costs of language translations. Still, even such "minor technical issues" have significant political and distributional implications. For instance, the exclusion of data points on national economic activity from the CBCR, such as local labor costs, was largely justified in terms of its (lack of) necessity for risk assessment. However, as labor costs are amongst the most popular benchmarks for cross-border comparison of corporate profit (mis)alignment, its exclusion was a blow to "outsiders" looking to mount reputational and financial challenges to MNC tax strategies.

Interestingly, reframing also contributed in some ways to further professional *support* for (a specific idea of) CBCR, rather than exclusively *opposition.* Because CBCR was accepted into the "home turf" framing of the technical tax community as a risk-assessment tool under the rubric of transfer pricing documentation, debate focused on the *scope* and *content* of the CBCR requirements more than its introduction altogether. Very few comment letters by tax experts argued that CBCR should be abandoned altogether; rather, the technical community recognized the idea for the purposes of risk assessment, focusing on tailoring the CBCR to suit such requirements. Largely, this meant limiting its scope and content, but not rejecting the very idea of country-by-country reporting. One particularly critical comment letter, from the International Alliance for Principled Taxation (IAPT), noted:

> [T]he extraordinarily detailed template demands far more information than is needed for the high-level risk-assessment tool the OECD was mandated to develop. The IAPT therefore recommends limiting the CbC template data elements to those identified by the G8 and G20 as needed to provide a high-level risk-assessment tool.
>
> (OECD, 2014b)

The third key dynamic of technicization is *appropriateness judgments.* In a policy discussion, different actors put forth different arguments to establish control over the discussions, with each argument evaluated according to its "appropriateness" (Lazega, 1992). Such appropriateness is defined socially in the organizational setting. In the case of BEPS Action 13, where an overwhelming majority of participants in a technical–political setting were insulated from diverse and conflicting political views, and using consistent and narrow framing, the "appropriateness" of different arguments was clearly visible and consequential. Specifically, the "benchmark" for accepted arguments was largely based on technical legal and economic expertise, particularly from private sector experience, and this favored certain policy arguments over others, fostering a consensus around what constituted feasible policy solutions. Here, practitioners' expertise-based arguments against expansive transparency clashed most notably with moral arguments of activists and emerging countries. Tax professionals emphasized legal uncertainties and economic inefficiencies in technical discussions. Concerned with the trade-offs of expansive new transparency requirements, opponents of wide-ranging CBCR framed new demands as raising the risk of double taxation and posing a threat to competitiveness. On the former, practitioners argued that such tax transparency would challenge tax administrations' processes, inclining them toward irrelevant analyses, thus obscuring overall tax compliance, creating double taxation and unnecessary administrative burdens. The comment letter from A3F, a French tax practitioner collective, warned of "a significant risk that the DD [discussion draft] opens the door to formula-based allocation of income or systematic application of profit-split upon audit by some countries, ignoring the taxpayer's business and value-creation model, functional analysis and related transfer pricing methodology" (OECD, 2014b). On the latter, commenters opined that corporate competitiveness would suffer from added transparency demands, exposing commercial secrets and putting companies at a competitive disadvantage. The comment letter from BIAC, an institutionalized business advisory group to the OECD, found that the proposed documentation "largely relates to highly confidential or commercially sensitive information, and, if inadvertently shared beyond the intended recipient, could present a significant risk to the group in question (OECD, 2014b).

In opposition, activists and others largely argued for expanded disclosure based on moral persuasion. The few activists and delegates from non-core OECD countries attending the technical debates often made normative claims, transposed into the technical setting from a politicized starting point. For instance, at the public consultation in Paris, the Chinese WP6 delegate argued for *local* filing of the CBCR report (rather than home-country filing with sharing through tax treaties) in moral terms, noting it was needed to "ensure proper tax is paid in China." This contrasted with, for example, the Japanese delegate, who defended treaty sharing in legal and economic terms, noting the advantage of sharing through tax treaties because they "contain dispute-resolution mechanisms" that could "properly resolve double taxation." Civil society professionals from Eurodad, Christian Aid, Oxfam, and the Jubilee USA Network also largely refrained from technical comments in the BEPS 13 consultation, instead problematizing the policy forum (OECD) itself and the lack of developing-country involvement. For instance, the Eurodad comment letter noted, "[W]e also find it problematic that the decision by the OECD to suggest a confidential country-by-country reporting system seems to have been taken before the regional BEPS consultations of developing countries have even started" (OECD, 2014b). This was in tune with the arguments of ActionAid, an activist organization that did not participate in the technical discussions, whose public call to the UK government was headlined "The BEPS process: failing to deliver for developing countries" (ActionAid, 2014). Similarly, there was hardly any difference between the framing in Oxfam's consultation letter to the OECD (OECD, 2014b) and their public BEPS briefing paper (Oxfam, 2014), both of which stressed the structural inequality faced by developing countries in international tax cooperation.

While moral appeals fell largely on deaf ears as they were not deemed "appropriate" in the technical–political setting, arguments based on tax-specific expertise were far more likely to be perceived as acceptable. The reactions to "justice" claims was, in large part, disinterest. Instead, the technical community took account of expertise-based arguments, providing authority to claims about corporate competitiveness, confidentiality, and compliance costs. Such technical comments held primacy with the OECD pen-holders. As one WP6 member noted in the second consultation meeting, "We always benefit from consulting with business, but in this area it has been particularly helpful, and I think it is going to allow us to come out with a more balanced product and hopefully, eventually, allow us to reach consensus, a broad consensus." One informant noted that civil society was "pretty much excluded from everything," while practitioners had a "strong relationship and involvement with OECD staff" (interview with OECD official #2). Another WP6 delegate noted in the consultation meeting that it was "a good chance to hear from business." This notion was reflected on the practitioner side. One interviewee found that practitioners had been "successful in convincing the OECD that you don't need all that information [in the CBCR]" (interview with tax professional #2), and another noted that discussions amongst professionals had "reduced the number of CBCR data points" (interview with tax professional #3). Simply put, in an environment of tax practitioners and specialists with a technical frame of reference, discussants with only general knowledge of tax issues were unlikely to find support for claims based on non-specific expertise. Knowledgeable practitioners, on the other hand, found the ground more fertile for arguments based on technical expertise. For activists, who had been successful in pushing tax transparency onto the global agenda through broad-based campaigning and targeted lobbying, as well as for developing countries and other marginalized actors, the technicized process of BEPS 13 provided a frustrating experience. Tax professionals, bureaucrats, and officials involved clearly expressed a particular shared openness to well-established technical expertise.

Having discussed the key dynamics of technicization, I now turn to its sources and impact. Technicization is a well-known phenomenon in complex global fiscal policy processes (Picciotto, 2015; Pagliari & Young, 2015), but it is not a given. In the context of BEPS Action 13, three interrelated reasons for technicization can be identified. First, the policy forum: The *modus operandi* of OECD tax policy processes is consensus-based, technical deliberations, which aim to find common ground among experts and practitioners, specifically avoiding the muddy distributional discussions of high politics. Second, the design of the policy process: The purpose set out for tax transparency in the Action 13 draft was to strengthen tax administrations' risk assessment, considering compliance costs. As such, the official narrative limited, *a priori*, the pool of relevant stakeholders to tax practitioners, and technical experts from governments and the OECD thus specifically sought inspiration preferably from like-minded private sector experts as opposed to other stakeholders. Moreover, comment requests were specifically centered on largely practical details, such as whether the CBCR should be compiled "bottom up" (from local statutory accounts) or "top down" (from MNC groups' consolidated income statements), or regarding the most appropriate approach to translation requirements (OECD, 2014a). Third, the consultation participants themselves: Practitioners from tax law, economics, or transfer pricing backgrounds were simply more concerned with technical issues, with incremental adjustments to the existing tax transparency regime, rather than radical overhauls. In an established professional territory such as tax, it can be particularly difficult to introduce radical new policy ideas because of the high levels of professional consensus on policy issues and solutions (Suddaby, Cooper, & Greenwood, 2007).

The impact of technicization was clear: It contributed to a taming of the surge for expanded transparency that had been established in a broader political sphere, thus limiting new pressures on corporate wealth chains. Rather than a broad-based public debate, the BEPS 13 discussions were characterized by a specialized, knowledge-intensive policy context. Technical knowledge barriers and professional dynamics enabled an overwhelming consensus amongst the policy-engaged community of professionals that cautioned against expansive new transparency requirements. In particular, this consensus featured arguments based on economic and legal expertise against "unnecessarily burdensome" CBCR, which was consistently framed as a tool for risk assessment only, as a threat to corporate commercial sensitivity and competitiveness, and as risking double taxation and legal uncertainty. This provided an effective counter, within the technical setting, to wider calls for transparency from popular politics, which had initially been pushed by activist groups. The effect was an outcome that restrained the potential for reputational challenges to captive and hierarchy wealth chains, limiting the ability of regulators to launch challenges to corporate wealth chains.

Conclusion

This chapter has argued that the technicization of policy discussions around corporate tax transparency helped subdue political momentum for new transparency demands. Through policy insulation, reframing, and appropriateness judgments, technicization contributed to blunting new financial and reputational challenges to corporate wealth chains. Policy insulation fostered technical unity, established knowledge barriers to participation, and contributed to the diffusion of policy consensus against expansive transparency amongst technical experts and policymakers. Reframing moved CBCR from a revolutionary public lever to a confidential risk-assessment tool, thus institutionalizing a new understanding of CBCR, subject primarily to concerns of economic efficiency and legal uncertainty. The dynamics of appropriateness judgments promoted a favoring of tax-specific expertise-based arguments over moral claims. By embedding discussions where participants' expertise and frame of reference were predominantly defined by corporate competitiveness, confidentiality, and compliance costs, those concerns came to determine the feasibility of policy proposals. The result was a "transparency compromise," a limited expansion of transparency, less than that intended by those who originally pushed CBCR onto the global policy agenda. The new global rules for corporate tax transparency will provide less firepower for political and public critique of corporate tax affairs than originally intended by activists, thus reducing the potential for reputational and financial challenges to captive and hierarchy wealth chains.

The case of BEPS Action 13 suggests a need to pay attention to technicization in the making of international tax rules and in the changing regulatory context of wealth chains. Professional interactions and technicization play a central yet often-overlooked role in highly technical, complex policy processes, influencing the definition of new rules for global wealth chains. These rules have profoundly political consequences, affecting information asymmetries, regulatory liability, and the overall relationship and governance among actors within global wealth chains. The case here demonstrates the power of professional dynamics in reworking such information asymmetries and regulatory traction for captive and hierarchy wealth chains, where transparency of tax and transfer pricing strategies are central. However, as the case is limited to one particular policy process around corporate tax transparency under the auspices of the OECD, there is significant scope for further research on the mobilization and interplay of knowledge-based actors in policy processes shaping wealth chain regulation at the national, regional, and international levels.

References

ActionAid (2014). The BEPS Process: Failing to Deliver for Developing Countries. https://actionaid.org/publications/2014/beps-process-failing-deliver-poor-countries.

Baden, A. & Wigan, D. (2017). Professional activists on tax transparency. In L. Seabrooke & L. Folke Henriksen (eds.), *Professional Networks in Transnational Governance*. Cambridge University Press, 130–146.

Büttner, T. & Matthias, T. (2017). Breaking regime stability? The politicization of expertise in the OECD/G20 Process on BEPS and the potential transformation of international taxation. *Accounting, Economics, and Law: A Convivium*, 7(1), 20160069.

CCFD-Terre Solidaire, Oxfam France, Secours Catholique, & la Plateforme Paradis Fiscaux et Judiciaires (2016). En quête de transparence: Sur la piste des banques francaises dans les paradis fiscaux. https://www.asso-sherpa.org/nouveau-rapport-en-quete-de-transparence-sur-la-piste-des-banques-francaises-dans-les-paradis-fiscaux.

Christensen, R. C. (2020). Elite professionals in transnational tax governance. *Global Networks*, 21(2), 265–293.

Christensen, R. C. & Hearson, M. (2019). The new politics of global tax governance: Taking stock a decade after the financial crisis. *Review of International Political Economy* 26 (5), 1068–1088.

Christensen, R. C., Seabrooke, L., & Wigan, D. (2021). Professional action in global wealth chains. *Regulation & Governance*. https://doi.org/10.1111/rego.12370.

Dharmapala, D. (2014). What do we know about base erosion and profit shifting? A review of the empirical literature. http://papers.ssrn.com/sol3/papers.cfm?abstract_id=2398285.

Drezner, D. W. (2000). Ideas, bureaucratic politics, and the crafting of foreign policy. *American Journal of Political Science*, 44(4), 733–749.

Dyreng, S. D., Hoopes, J. L., & Wilde, J. H. (2016). Public pressure and corporate tax behavior. *Journal of Accounting Research* 54 (1), 147–186.

Eccleston, R. & Woodward, R. (2014). Pathologies in international policy transfer: The Case of the OECD tax transparency initiative. *Journal of Comparative Policy Analysis: Research and Practice*, 16 (3), 216–229.

EY (2016). *A New Mountain to Climb: Tax Reputation Risk, Growing Transparency Demands and the Importance of Data Readiness*. Tax risk and controversy survey series. EY. https://cupdf.com/document/tax-reputation-risk-growing-transparency-demands-and-new-mountain-to-climb.html.

Figueiredo, Rui J. P. de (2002). Electoral competition, political uncertainty, and policy insulation. *American Political Science Review*, 96(2), 321–333.

G8 (2013). 2013 Lough Erne G8 Leaders' Communiqué. https://www.gov.uk/government/publications/2013-lough-erne-g8-leaders-communique.

G20 (2012). G20 Leaders Declaration. Los Cabos, Mexico, 18–19 June 2012. http://www.g20.utoronto.ca/2012/2012-0619-loscabos.html.

Genschel, P. & Rixen, T. (2015). Settling and unsettling the transnational legal order of international taxation. In T. C. Halliday & G. Shaffer (eds.), *Transnational Legal Orders*. Cambridge University Press, 154–184.

Haas, P. M. (1992). Introduction: Epistemic communities and international policy coordination. *International Organization*, 46 (1), 1–35.

Hearson, M. (2018). Transnational expertise and the expansion of the international tax regime: Imposing "acceptable" standards. *Review of International Political Economy*, 25(5), 647–671.

KPMG (2016). *2016 US CEO Survey*. https://home.kpmg/us/en/home/insights/2016/06/us-ceo-outlook-2016-its-now-or-never.html.

Lazega, E. (1992). *Micropolitics of Knowledge: Communication and Indirect Control in Workgroups*. Aldine de Gruyter.

Lesage, D. and Kaçar, Y. (2013). Tax justice through country-by-country reporting: An analysis of the idea's political journey. In J. Leaman and A. Waris (eds.), *Tax Justice and the Political Economy of Global Capitalism, 1945 to the Present*. Berghahn Books, 262–282.

Murphy, R. (2003). A Proposed International Accounting Standard: Reporting Turnover and Tax by Location. Association for Accountancy and Business Affairs. https://www.taxjustice.net/cms/upload/pdf/new_int._Account_Standard.pdf.

Murphy, R. (2012). Why Country-by-Country Reporting by Multinational Corporations Matters. *Tax Research UK* (blog). http://www.taxresearch.org.uk/Blog/2012/02/20/why-country-by-country-reporting-by-multinational-corporations-matters/.

Murphy, R. (2013). Lough Erne and country-by-country reporting. *Tax Notes International*, 71 (3), 249–253.

Murphy, R. (2014). Barclays: The Bank That Just Loves Luxembourg and Jersey, but Not the UK. *Tax Research UK* (blog). http://www.taxresearch. org.uk/Blog/2014/06/30/barclays-the-bank-that-just-loves-luxembourg-and-jersey/.

OECD (2013). *Action Plan on Base Erosion and Profit Shifting*. OECD Publishing.

OECD (2014a). *Discussion Draft on Transfer Pricing Documentation and CbC Reporting*. OECD Publishing.

OECD (2014b). *Public Comments Received: Discussion Draft on Transfer Pricing Documentation and CbC Reporting*. OECD Publishing.

OECD (2014c). *Guidance on Transfer Pricing Documentation and Country-by-Country Reporting*. OECD/G20 Base Erosion and Profit Shifting Project. OECD Publishing.

Oxfam (2014). *Business among Friends: Why Corporate Tax Dodgers Are Not yet Losing Sleep over Global Tax Reform*. https://policy-practice.oxfam.org/resources/business-among-friends-why-corporate-tax-dodgers-are-not-yet-losing-sleep-over-316405/.

Oxfam (2017). *Opening the Vaults: The Use of Tax Havens by Europe's Biggest Banks*. https://policy-practice.oxfam.org/resources/opening-the-vaults-the-use -of-tax-havens-by-europes-biggest-banks-620234/.

Pagliari, S. & Young, K. (2015). The interest ecology of financial regulation: Interest group plurality in the design of financial regulatory policies. *Socio-Economic Review*, 14(2), 309–337.

Picciotto, S. (2015). Indeterminacy, Complexity, technocracy and the reform of international corporate taxation. *Social & Legal Studies* 24 (2), 165–184.

PwC (2016). *Tax Strategy and Corporate Reputation: a tax issue, a Business Issue*. 16th Annual Global CEO Survey. https://docplayer.net/2476577-Tax-strategy-and-corporate-reputation-a-tax-issue-a-business-issue.html.

Quack, S. (2016). Organizing counter-expertise: Critical professional communities in transnational governance. In A. Werr & S. Furusten (eds.), *The Organization of the Expert Society*. Taylor & Francis, 113–128.

Rixen, T. (2013). Why reregulation after the crisis is feeble: Shadow banking, offshore financial centers, and jurisdictional competition. *Regulation & Governance*, 7(4), 435–459.

Seabrooke, L. & Sending, O. J. (2020). Contracting development: Managerialism and consultants in intergovernmental organizations. *Review of International Political Economy*, 27(4), 802–827.

Seabrooke, L. & Wigan, D. (2016). Powering ideas through expertise: Professionals in global tax battles. *Journal of European Public Policy*, 23(3), 357–374.

Seabrooke, L. & Wigan, D. (2017). The governance of global wealth chains. *Review of International Political Economy*, 24 (1), 1–29.

Snow, D. A., Burke Rochford, E., Worden, S. K., & Benford, R. D. (1986). Frame alignment processes, micromobilization, and movement participation. *American Sociological Review* 51(4), 464–481.

Suddaby, R., Cooper, D. J., & Greenwood, R. (2007). Transnational regulation of professional services: Governance dynamics of field level organizational change. *Accounting, Organizations and Society* 32(4–5), 333–362.

Tax Justice Network (2013). Confronting Transfer Mispricing by the Use of Country by Country Reporting. https://www.taxjustice.net/cms/upload/pdf/CbC_100319_reporting_-_TJN_summary.pdf.

12

Mining

Saila Stausholm

What form does wealth protection take in an industry where value creation is geographically fixed, and assets fall under government control? The location of natural resources cannot be manipulated in the ways intangible goods and assets are moved across jurisdictions. Permission to extract these resources must also be granted by national authorities. This chapter analyzes how claims to wealth are made by mining companies operating in resource-rich developing countries. These companies accrue wealth by obtaining tax advantages arising within mining countries as well as from the strategic placement of ownership rights in low-tax jurisdictions. On the basis of a close reading of 113 mining contracts across 21 developing countries, this chapter finds strong evidence that firms in the mining sector are able to piece together tax advantages via government deals and multi-jurisdictional structures. Three types of global wealth chain are combined in ways that provide opportunities for wealth accrual and protection by mining firms.

The distribution of wealth arising from natural resources is a contentious issue, as historically wealth arising from these resources has not been distributed in ways that benefited source country's economy or population. Many resource-rich economies remain poor, a paradox captured in the concepts of a "resource curse" and "Dutch disease" (Auty & Warhurst, 1993; Sachs & Warner, 2001; Davis & Tilton, 2005). These outcomes have been linked to corruption (Marshall, 2001; Caripis 2017), lack of administrative capacity (Arezki et al., 2012), and inadequate tax payments from multinationals (Le Billon, 2011). Unequal distribution and unstable institutions have also been linked to social unrest and civil war (Klosek, 2018). Claims to wealth arising from the mining industry are particularly important in developing countries, where the loss of rights to mineral wealth negatively impacts poverty levels and sustainable development.

Saila Stausholm, *Mining*. In: *Global Wealth Chains*. Edited by Leonard Seabrooke and Duncan Wigan, Oxford University Press. © Saila Stausholm (2022). DOI: 10.1093/oso/9780198832379.003.0012

More than half of the value added in the mining sector is internal to mining firms. There are few job-creating linkages with other firms and industries, making upgrading in the mining industry challenging for resource-rich countries (Korinek, 2020). While locally owned mining companies source some input and services domestically, most foreign-owned mining firms do not vertically integrate within the mining country (Katz & Pietrobelli, 2018). Across most mineral and metal types, the mining global value chain consists of a long exploration and feasibility stage and a mine construction stage, before value is generated. Construction is followed by the extraction phase. All of these activities are fixed geographically. The potential global scope of the value chain arises mostly at the processing stage, with, for example, India the main location for cutting and polishing raw diamonds (Linde et al., 2021). The final phase is the retail of finished products or sale of inputs to other industries. The value added within the value chain is mostly in the geographically fixed extraction phase.

The mining value chain consists of the extraction of raw material, and processing into valuable forms of minerals and metals. The mining wealth chain consists of the legal affordances which control the distribution and transfer of the wealth arising from mining after the export of raw materials, after the sale of processed materials, and after the sale of final products. Profits arising from these operations are claimed by corporate entities operating in different or several parts of the value chain and are protected from taxation by governments in both the mining country and elsewhere. Strategies for the protection of wealth include tax advantages obtained *within* mining countries in the form of contracts containing favorable fiscal regimes and the strategic use of ownership over mining rights in tax havens to obtain tax advantages by transacting wealth *between* jurisdictions.

As multinational corporations have organized their operations in global value chains, the globalization of capital has put states in a position of competing for investment, and tax policy has become one tool utilized to lure investors (Devereux, Griffith, & Klemm, 2002; Genschel, 2002; Rixen, 2011; Abbas & Klemm, 2013; Egger & Raff, 2015). The pitting of states against each other has driven a downward trend in corporate tax rates (Devereux, Griffith, & Klemm, 2002; Keen & Konrad, 2013) as well as discretionary tax advantages provided to firms to incentivize investment. Thomson Reuters (2015) recorded 10,000 instances globally since 2005 where states awarded discretionary incentives to investors, with an average incentive value of almost one fifth of the investment, or $8.19 million.

Such incentives include opportunities for firms to decrease their tax bill within the jurisdiction where value-generating activities take place. Even in mining, where geology rather than business climate is the key location determinant, tax advantages are granted *within* countries through statutory and discretionary tax policy.

Given the differences between legal and taxation systems across countries, multinational firms have increasingly been able to take advantage of differences in the legal treatment of assets to obtain lower global tax rates (Jansky & Prats, 2013; Seabrooke & Wigan, 2014; Zucman & Piketty, 2015; Janský & Kokeš, 2016). The OECD's Base Erosion and Profit Shifting initiative was motivated by the prevalence of the under- or over-pricing of transactions between corporate entities within the firm, treaty shopping, and the strategic shifting of debt internationally (Beer et al., 2018; UN & ECA, 2018).

Tax incentives and multi-jurisdictional tax advantages afforded by offshore jurisdictions comprise firm tax strategy in combination. The goal of tax-minimizing firms is that profits fall *between* jurisdictions and legal categories so as to exist beyond the reach of tax authorities—to be placed "elsewhere, ideally nowhere" (Murphy, 2009, p.16; cf. Bryan et al., 2017). While the strategic deployment of intangible assets for purposes of wealth creation and protection has extenuated an imbalance between governments seeking revenue and firms active within their jurisdictions (Bryan et al., Chapter 5 in this volume), the fact of geographically fixed assets does not necessarily constrain the use of global wealth chains. The geographical fixity of assets, however, may well change the *type* of global wealth chain governance that is engaged, as tax treatments within the mining country are more important in this context. For mining companies, the global value chain is geographically fixed as is the most of the value arising from the mining itself (Korinek, 2020). This is why obtaining tax advantages *within* countries becomes as important as obtaining tax advantages *between* countries for this industry. This chapter demonstrates the prevalence of wealth creation and protection schemes in the mining industry, and discusses what forms of global wealth chain governance are implicated.

Exploration, mining machinery and extraction, the refinement and processing of metals, and final manufacture into consumer goods are the value-adding productive activities which constitute the value chain. The wealth chain consists of the legal affordances around the value chain, which distribute rights to the wealth that arises from these activities. Claims to wealth arising from mining arise and are bolstered by a diverse and overlapping set of sources, including national law, international law, and corporate legal documents (Dezalay, 2019; Mann, 2015). National legislation in the mining code and tax code stipulate the tax rates, royalty rates, and other payments which should be made from the firm to the government. However, the fiscal regime is often negotiated in further detail in the contracts granting mining rights to firms. The legal framework, and in particular the contract, therefore is an asset in the sense that it provides entitlements to wealth. Contracts typically grant significant tax advantages, enabling the mining firm to accrue disproportionate amounts of wealth arising from the value-creating activity. Most contracts between mining firms and governments are confidential, but recent transparency initiatives have made a push toward higher levels of disclosure (EITI, 2021; Resourcecontracts.org, 2021). Analyzing 113 contracts from 21 countries, this chapter provides an overview of how mining contracts comprise legal affordances that create and protect wealth.

Data description

The fiscal regime for mining companies derives from several overlapping sources of law. Between countries, international investment treaties and tax treaties govern how income from cross-border economic activity is treated (Hearson, Chapter 3 in this volume). Within mining countries, the tax code and mining code detail the fiscal rules for mining investors, including incentives which are provided industry wide. Additionally, for each mining project contracts detail special fiscal rules governing the project (Mann, 2015). Contracts which grant mining licenses provide the legal basis for the rights to extract minerals and metals. This practice has arisen since the privatization of the mining industry from the 1980s (Dezalay, 2019; Mann, 2015). These contracts provide the legal and economic basis for global value chains and global wealth chains in mining, and are negotiated between governments of resource-rich countries, mining firms, and in some cases third-party legal professionals (Dezalay, 2019). Contracts constitute an important data source for research in global wealth chain analysis, as they specify the relationship between buyers and suppliers, or in this case, between investors and governments (Cutler & Dietz, 2017).

This chapter analyzes a large number and range of publicly available legal documents from 21 developing, resource-rich countries (see Table 12.1).

Table 12.1 Number of contracts by country

Country	Number of contracts
Afghanistan	6
Burkina Faso	7
Burundi	1
Cameroon	3
Colombia	5
DRC	9
Ecuador	1
Guinea	10
Liberia	17
Madagascar	1
Malawi	2
Mali	12
Mongolia	3
Mozambique	4
Niger	1
Peru	5
Philippines	7
Senegal	5
Sierra Leone	6
Tunisia	2
Zambia	6

These documents include the mining, tax, and in some cases investment codes (54 documents in total). Additionally, 113 contracts provided by the Resouce Contracts public repository[1] are analyzed.[2] The contracts span the years from 1978 to 2016, but most are from 1990 onwards. The legislation used is the most recent available at the time of research (2018). The contracts analyzed span a wide range of mineral types. Most of the contracts regard refined base and precious metals such as gold, copper, and silver. The second-largest group of contracts are for bulk commodities, especially iron ore. A few contracts pertain to the mining of metallurgical products such as alumina, gemstones (usually diamonds), and heavy mineral sands. The contracts sometimes combine different categories of minerals, such as gold and diamonds.

[1] http://www.resourcecontracts.org.
[2] Data collection was conducted by the author with three legal consultants with expertise in the mining sector and French and Spanish language skills. The data and analysis can be found in Readhead (2018) and IGF (2019).

After identifying 11 relevant areas of tax, the documents were sorted through and coded according to these 11 areas.[3] Each mention of something pertaining to tax within a document related to either regulation or a contract would be copied into the corresponding field in a spreadsheet. Tax incentives that were coded from legislation and contracts range from lower taxes such as a lower corporate income tax rate, tax holidays, property, VAT or sales tax exemptions, and lower withholding tax rates to provisions which allow for deductions on expenditure, such as accelerated depreciation or capital expenditure deductions. Others include extended loss carry-forward periods and royalty rates set on a discretionary basis. Stability clauses in which the tax regime cannot be changed are also counted as a tax incentive.

After translating and summarizing these tax provisions, each field was analyzed to determine whether it constituted an incentive. The assessment of the legislation as an incentive was based upon whether it afforded greater benefits than those offered in other sectors. In a second step, the corresponding text in the contract (if there was anything specified) was assessed to see if it afforded greater benefits than those already available in the law. If so, it was marked as an incentive. It is therefore possible for a country to have an incentive in the law and in the contract, if the contract provides something more extensive than the legislation.

Statutory and discretionary tax incentives in mining

The analysis of mining codes, tax codes, and mining contracts reveals that mining companies are commonly granted statutory tax advantages within mining countries. Contracts across 21 mining countries show that mining companies furthermore obtain discretionary tax incentives. Figure 12.1 illustrates the widespread nature of these tax exemptions across mining countries. Seventeen of the countries included fiscal concessions in both legislation and contracts. Looking at the subfields these are in, there are overlaps. This implies that mining firms in some instances receive concessions beyond the incentives already granted in the legislation of that country.

---

[3] For most countries, all contracts were analyzed provided they were available in English, Spanish, or French. However, for the Philippines, Guinea, the DRC, and Peru only a limited selection of contracts was analyzed due to the large number of available contracts. The sample analyzed was selected so it reflected the different types of minerals mined in the country.

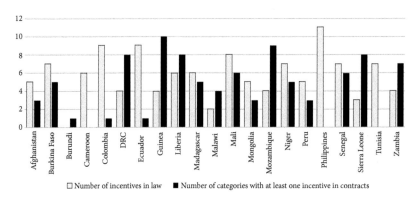

Fig. 12.1 Tax incentives by country

The three types of tax incentives that pose the highest risks of base erosion and profit shifting are lower (or exemptions from) corporate income tax rates, and concessions on withholding tax and royalty rates. Corporate income tax concessions are provided by 15 out of the 21 countries through either contract or legislation, in many cases in both. Over half the countries provide either lower royalty rates or withholding tax rates, the latter in some cases being completely exempt. The most extreme form of tax incentive is a tax holiday, which suspends corporate income tax for a period of time. These are often the most generous tax incentives, and pose the risk that they are used for tax minimization beyond that intended if the firm is able to register income such that it falls under the umbrella of the holiday (Fletcher, 2002; Zee, Stotsky, & Ley, 2002). Over half the countries provide tax incentives in either contracts or legislation. Nine out of the 21 countries have offered tax holidays with total exemptions of 3–15 years to mining firms, and a further three countries offered a semi-tax holiday where they exempt some taxes or apply a lower rate (Figure 12.2).

Protections are built into contracts that mitigate against risks of future regulation. Almost all firms analyzed have a stability clause in the contract or are subject to a statutory stability clause, and there are many cases where the stability period granted in the legislation is exceeded in the contract. These clauses limit the ability of the government—including future governments—to change fiscal rules, or, in some cases, even implement human rights legislation effectively (Shemberg, 2009). The period of stability ranges from very few years to 99 years or the entirety of contract duration. The mining company can therefore be effectively protected against new regulation. At the same time, there are also clauses that ensure that the

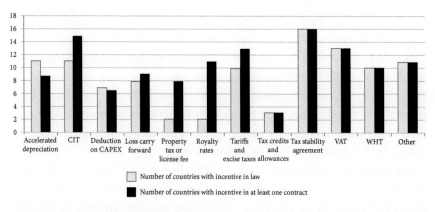

Fig. 12.2 Tax incentives by category

fiscal regime becomes more beneficial over time. Some contracts include a provision that the firm will enjoy the same affordances that any competitor receives. In consequence if other contractors can be argued to be competitors then a concession given to one firm might be applied more broadly even when that concession is not specified in the contract. For example, one contract "shall entitle [company] to take advantage of any more favorable regime applicable specifically to and agreed individually with any company whether in a development agreement or otherwise." (retrieved from resourcecontracts.org, 2018). This can be understood in terms of the creation of fair competition and a level playing field. It also means that a contract affording the most extensive benefits might create ripple effects that extend across the entire industry, effectively ensuring a built-in race to the bottom.

The advantageousness of contracts depends on the institutional setting. Comparing contracts shows that there is variation, but that variation is limited within countries. It is therefore not the case that firms mining a specific type of mineral receive the same treatment from different governments. One type of mining is not treated more favorably than another across the board. Variation is driven more by what a country has granted than the type of mineral or metal that is mined.

Market-relational global wealth chains through government tax deals

Global wealth chains consist of legal, economic, and social relationships between clients, suppliers, and regulators (Seabrooke & Wigan, 2017). In the mining industry, the value creation for mining firms—the client—is tightly linked to government control, and so is wealth protection. While the government in this instance acts in the capacity of both supplier and regulator, it is important that these are different agencies with different and sometimes conflicting interests, information, and capacities (Readhead, 2016). The government acts as the supplier when providing tax advantages in legal codes and contracts through the ministries of mining or other politically appointed officials (Kienzler et al., 2015), and as the regulator when acting in the capacity of the tax administration.

Wealth protection through statutory and discretionary tax incentives can be seen as a combination of market and relational global wealth chains. In the case of statutory tax incentives, all mining investors are equally entitled to them, and there is no need to engage in complex negotiations, knowledge sharing, or planning. This is akin to a market type of global wealth chain, in which the product—the tax exemption—is readily available for qualifying investors. While the structural power of mining companies can influence the existence of statutory tax incentives (Bell & Hindmoor, 2014, Marsh et al., 2014; Elbra, 2014), the firm does not negotiate directly and no complex information sharing is involved in obtaining this type of wealth protection.

In the case of discretionary incentives granted in contracts, this is more akin to a relational type of global wealth chain. The process of negotiating these contracts is long, often spanning several years, during which coordination and exchange of information is required between a small number of officials, officers of the firm, and professionals. On the government side, the negotiation is often led by political appointees or experienced civil servants, with input from a range of technical and legal experts (Kienzler et al., 2015). The use of external expertise is however limited on the government side as they often don't trust foreign experts or simply can't afford their fees (Radon, 2006).The firm team will be tailored depending on the relationship with the government. The team will usually include technical experts, such as engineers or geologists, in-house and outside legal counsel, financial modelers and economists, and, in some cases, firm managers (Radon, 2006; Kienzler et al., 2015). Mining companies have an advantage in their ability to deploy in negotiations greater levels of expertise and numbers of experts, and more experienced negotiators (Radon, 2006). In some cases, mining companies even hire members of the government team after negotiations have begun, gaining insight into government strategy and leading to turnover and instability in the government team (Kienzler et al., 2015). While perhaps not a strong trust relationship, it is a relational interaction between two teams of professionals and appointees. Over the period of negotiation, these teams will share and come to agreement on an understanding of complex geological data, infrastructure plans, timelines for construction, and job-creation prospects, explicitly coordinating on a wide-ranging list of issues, including fiscal terms.

Relational does not imply an equal relationship between the two parties. While there is a lot of knowledge sharing and trust generation in the negotiations, there remains strong information asymmetry between the government and the mining firm. Sharing financial and geological data in itself, and in the absence of requisite scientific and economic expertise, does not produce equality between negotiating parties. The firm is most likely to hold such requisite expertise (Radon, 2006; Kienzler et al., 2015). Valuing a mining reserve is inherently difficult, as it is impossible to know either the exact amount of resource in the ground or the costs of extraction, and because prices may fluctuate considerably (Otto, 2017). The mining firm does, however, hold more expertise, and might be better able to translate geological data into a value assessment (ICMM, 2009; Readhead, 2016). Contracts may be especially skewed in favor of the firm when the firm rather than the government has conducted feasibility studies and asset evaluations (Kienzler et al., 2015).

The government's involvement as supplier is distinct from its role as regulator and tax collector. These roles and the processes in which they play out are temporally and functionally separated. Negotiation occurs prior to tax collection, and is sometimes conducted under the authority of ministers who are no longer in power when the mine is operational and tax is to be collected. While mining ministries aim to promote development and investment, they may be less concerned with the fiscal implications down the line—both because they might no longer be in office and because they have been convinced they need to compete for scarce investment (Mann, 2015; Dezalay, 2019). The tax authorities aim to secure tax collection, but face the challenges of insufficient information, lack of sector-specific expertise, and the lack of an incentive to audit firms when they are beneficiaries of concessions and exemptions (Readhead, 2016).

Hierarchical global wealth chains through international ownership structures

Though the source of the wealth is fixed, multijurisdictional ownership structures employed by mining firms enable them to engage in global wealth chains similar to other multinational companies. Intrafirm transactions through strategically placed corporate entities are a means of profit shifting and effective tax minimization. Prices for services and intermediate products or byproducts from mining (e.g. minerals that are not the main product of the project), as well as interest rates on loans, should be reported at market prices according to the "arms-length principle." However, these prices may be subject to manipulation in transactions between related parties (Redhead, 2016; Beer & Devlin, 2021). In addition to debt financing between entities and mispricing internal sales of products and services, capital gains may be realized within offshore jurisdictions that offer a combination of low taxes and tax treaties protecting against other governments claims (see Hearson, Chapter 3 in this volume).

Even where a fiscal regime does not provide tax advantages, transfer pricing poses risk to tax collection (Otto, 2017). In a multi-country statistical analysis, Beer and Devlin (2021) find that reported profits in the mining sector are sensitive to country tax rates, estimating revenue losses from profit shifting amount to be 0.06 percent of the GDP of selected countries, or around $44 billion. Finér and Ylönen (2017) show how firms in the Finnish mining sector employ a wide range of tax-minimization strategies based on strategic choices around intragroup relationships and transactions. Global Financial Integrity (2014) found widespread instances of trade mis-invoicing in the mining sector in Africa (see also Grondona and Burgos on the soybean sector, Chapter 8 in this volume). Legal disputes between governments and firms may shed light on the tax avoidance of multinational mining firms. In the case of Acacia Mining in Tanzania, the firm paid large dividends to shareholders in years when they did not pay any taxes. This is likely due to a combination of the generosity of tax incentives and profit shifting through inter-company loans (Forstater & Readhead, 2017; Haines, 2017).

The ownership structure within multinational mining firms is not usually described in contracts, but in one case the appendix provided an overview. The firm in question operates a refinery project in Guinea. Figure 12.3 outlines the ownership structure, in which the local firm responsible for the mine is owned by a firm in Canada through two tiers of entities in the British Virgin Islands. The appendix states "by retaining this two-tiered [tax haven] corporate structure, [company] is preserving for its investors the most tax-efficient means for off-shore investment strategies." The British Virgin Islands is described as "a widely accepted jurisdiction which imposes no income tax on companies incorporated within its jurisdiction" (contract retrieved from resourcecontracts.org, 2018). This arrangement allows dividends from the refinery project to be reinvested

Fig. 12.3 Ownership structure of mining company

without first incurring a tax liability from investors' home jurisdictions. It also allows for the deferral of capital gains tax and tax on production profit, and prolongs the benefits of the tax holiday because taxes paid in the mining country after the tax holiday can be used to claim tax credits when remitting earlier profits from the haven. All these benefits are detailed in a letter from PwC, a professional service firm known for providing multinational corporations with advice on tax-minimization strategies. This highlights the significance of legal and tax experts in supplying these types of complicated tax haven structures (Jones et al., 2017; Murphy et al., 2019; Ajdacic et al., 2020).

Dynamic effects of combining of global wealth chain types in mining

Combining different types of wealth chains increases the level of wealth protection beyond the use of one standalone strategy. Table 12.2 outlines the different wealth-protection strategies employed in the mining industry, which can be combined. Statutory tax incentives as granted in legislation

Table 12.2 Wealth-protection strategies in mining

Wealth protection strategy	Complexity of products and services	Regulatory liability	Capabilities to mitigate uncertainty	Degree of explicit co-ordination	GWC form
Statutory tax incentives	Low	Low	High	Low	Market
Contractual tax incentives	↕	Low	High	↕	Relational
International structures	High	Low	High	High	Hierarchy

require low levels of coordination, are not complex, are widely accessible, and generate low levels of regulatory liability. Statutory tax incentives can be easily accessed by any investor, and this type of wealth protection is closest to a "market" form in the global wealth chain typology. The low uncertainty and risk of regulatory liability also applies to contractual terms, particularly if backed up by stability clauses, which a majority of the contracts examined here were. As the contract is a consequence of the relational interaction in the negotiation, in which the status/authority of negotiators impacts the outcome, and in which the notion of a mutual exchange (e.g. jobs for incentives) is important, this is best reflected in the relational global wealth chain type. The use of international ownership structures to take advantage of tax differences and obtain tax advantages *between* jurisdictions is more complex and requires a high degree of explicit coordination with tax planning expertise to the fore. This strategy might be devised and executed in-house such that the supplier–client relationship is internal to the corporation, or sourced through a professional service firm. Such a configuration conforms to a hierarchy type of global wealth chain.

Mining firms can combine market, relational and hierarchy wealth chain strategies to create and protect wealth. In the case of the firm examined above, the two-tiered tax haven structure is only the cherry on top of what is already a nice sundae. The government in question already offers mining companies a lower tax rate (30 rather than 35 percent), a 3-year tax holiday and a 15-year stabilization clause. The contract also provides the firm a 15-year tax holiday, a 15-year amortization of startup-costs and 5-year loss carry-forwards after the period of the tax holiday, a 5 percent investment credit, a cap on customs expenses, and (not least) a stabilization clause which will stay in place throughout the duration of the contract. The firm thereby combines statutory and contractual tax advantages with the opportunities afforded by placing ownership in a tax haven. This is a hybrid market–relational–hierarchy global wealth chain.

Global wealth chain governance turns on managing the degrees to which on one hand explicit coordination is necessary, and on the other information asymmetries characterize relationships. The mining firm's objective is to maintain a large information asymmetry with tax authorities (Kienzler et al., 2015). Downplaying or misrepresenting production volumes, sales relationships, and by-product exports through missing documents or unreliable record-keeping is prevalent in the sector (Readhead, 2016). This is a challenge for tax authorities because of a lack of resources and expertise, but is exacerbated by the contractual and statutory exemptions which limit the incentive to audit, and by the complex ownership structures which make it unclear whether parties to a transaction are related parties. In this way, the already existing information asymmetry between the firm and the regulator is increased through the use of market, relational, and hierarchical wealth chains. Even if authorities can overcome the information asymmetry, firms may use the concessions and exemptions that they have been afforded to repel efforts to tax them. In one case in Ghana a stability clause was initially (though ultimately unsuccessfully) used to argue for immunity from transfer-pricing legislation (Readhead, 2016).

Conclusion

Mining firms extract value from the ground in developing countries, and extract wealth from the same countries by using legal structures to claim disproportionate ownership of the profits from the sale of mining products. Multinational mining corporations are able to protect wealth by combining different strategies and affordances arising both *within* and *between* countries. Interest in mining investment incentivizes governments and government officials, in the form of mining ministries and officials, to provide statutory and discretionary tax incentives. These are articulated in market and relational global wealth chain governance modes, providing very large tax savings with very low liability and uncertainty for investors. Policies to encourage investment and intended to ensure upgrading in global value chains ultimately serve as the key building blocks in global wealth chains. Mining firms can also enjoy the dynamic upgrading of the output of their global wealth chains when in many cases they are protected against future regulatory intervention and promised equal treatment in case any more favorable policy is ever extended to another firm. At the same time, these firms are able to draw upon hierarchical global wealth chains by deploying tax and legal expertise to produce tax-efficient ownership structures and organize internal transactions and finance in ways that ensure profits are transferred outside of the mining country.

The power governments hold over natural resources raises the question of why these incentives are provided at all. These are valuable resources that no one can mine without a license. The puzzle is especially acute given that tax incentives in general are not at the top of investors' lists of reasons to invest (Unido, 2011). In some cases, the motive might be political or corrupt (Marshall, 2001; Readhead, 2016; Carpis, 2017). While corruption might explain single cases, it cannot explain the widespread nature of the practices. Notably, these practices are also prevalent in other industries (Klemm & van Parys, 2011). The incentives might be provided under conditions of imperfect information and bounded rationality (Poulsen, 2015). Information asymmetries between governments and investors mean that governments don't know to what extent tax incentives are necessary. Accepted ideas that incentives could potentially be important for investors might lead governments to use them excessively (Bell & Hindmoor, 2014). The puzzle might also be explained by the structural power of mining companies, exercised in negotiations and lobbying efforts (Marsh et al., 2014; Elbra, 2014).

While tax incentives are generally discouraged now (UNCTAD, 2012), multilateral organizations such as the World Bank and the OECD previously advised governments to provide incentives and legal protections in order to attract investment. Given a perceived scarcity of investment, governments were encouraged to compete to attract it (Mann, 2015). Tax incentives in mining and particularly stability clauses were historically motivated by the privatization and deregulation wave of the 1980s and the concomitant need to provide investors confidence that new regulations or nationalization would not occur (Mann, 2015). Such affordances contributed to investor-friendly environments and were particularly prevalent in sub-Saharan Africa, where the perceived need to "roll out the red carpet" was strong (Mann, 2015). A naïve take could be that these are phenomena

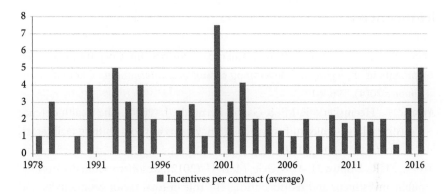

Fig. 12.4 Number of incentives over time

of the past, and improvements in institutions will mean tax incentives become less prevalent. However, the failure of institutions to ensure a fair distribution of natural resource wealth cannot be understood as a failure that can be improved simply by imposing the right legal framework. The willingness of governments to engage in tax competition enables most corporate tax minimization, and it is not being addressed by current attempts to reform the international tax system. Figure 12.4 shows that the provision of incentives has not decreased over time. These institutionalized practices should be understood as part of the colonial history of the countries that provide them, as well as a manifestation of new imperialist practices (Dezalay, 2019).

Further research might test how far the geographical fixity of the underlying value chain asset increases the importance of tax incentives and other tax advantages granted within countries. It is evidently an important element of mining wealth chains, but firms in other sectors also seek, and attain, tax exemptions. While it is likely the negotiated nature of firm tax liabilities increases the likelihood of at least some kind of fiscal incentive, discretionary deals are by no means unique to the mining sector. What is clear from this investigation of mining global wealth chains is the widespread use of wealth-creation and-protection strategies. Most of these are possible because countries to varying degrees enable them. The question remains as to the extent governments are able to transcend a perceived compulsion to compete via tax system design and discretionary tax affordances.

References

Abbas, S. & Klemm, A. (2013). A partial race to the bottom: Corporate tax developments in emerging and developing economies. *International Tax and Public Finance* 20(4), 596–617.

Ajdacic, L., Heemskerk, E. M., & Garcia-Bernardo, J. (2020). The wealth defence industry: a large-scale study on accountancy firms as profit shifting facilitators. *New Political Economy*, 1–17.

Arezki, M. R., Dupuy, M. A., & Gelb, M. A. H. (2012). Resource windfalls, optimal public investment and redistribution: The role of total factor productivity and administrative capacity. International Monetary Fund.

Auty, R. & Warhurst, A. (1993). Sustainable development in mineral exporting economies. *Resource Policy*, 19(1), 14-29.

Beer, S. & Devlin, D. (2021). Is there money on the table? Evidence on the magnitude of profit shifting in the extractive industries. International Monetary Fund.

Beer, S., De Mooij, R. A., & Liu, M. L. (2018). International corporate tax avoidance: A review of the channels, magnitudes, and blind spots. Working Paper No. 18/168. Internatioanl Monetary Fund.

Bell, S. & Hindmoor, A. (2014). The structural power of business and the power of ideas: The strange case of the Australian mining tax. *New Political Economy* 19(3), 470–486..

Bryan, D., Rafferty, M., & Wigan, D. (2017). Capital unchained: Finance, intangible assets and the double life of capital in the offshore world. *Review of International Political Economy* 24(1), 56–86.

Caripis, L. (2017). Combatting corruption in mining approvals: Assessing the risks in 18 resource-rich countries. Transparency International.

Commonwealth Secretariat & International Council on Mining and Metals (ICMM) (2009). *Minerals Taxation Regimes*.

Cutler, A. C. & Dietz, T. (eds.). (2017). *The Politics of Private Transnational Governance by Contract*. Taylor & Francis.

Davis, G. A. & Tilton, J. E. (2005). The resource curse. *Natural Resources Forum* 29(3): 233–242). Blackwell Publishing.

Devereux, M. P., Griffith, R., & Klemm, A. (2002). Corporate Income tax reforms and international tax competition. *Economic Policy* 17(35), 449–495.

Dezalay, S. (2019). Lawyers and the "new extraction" in Africa. *International Journal of Social Economics*, 46(11), 1305–1318.

Egger, P. & Raff, H. (2015). Tax rate and tax base competition for foreign direct investment. *International Tax and Public Finance* 22(5), 777–810.

EITI (2021). Contract transparency. https://eiti.org/contract-transparency.

Elbra, A. D. (2014). Interests need not be pursued if they can be created: private governance in African gold mining. *Business and Politics*, 16(2), 247–266.

Finér, L. & Ylönen, M. (2017). Tax-driven wealth chains: A multiple case study of tax avoidance in the Finnish mining sector. *Critical Perspectives on Accounting* 48 (supplement C), 53–81.

Fletcher, K. (2002). Tax incentives in Cambodia, Lao PDR and Vietnam. Hanoi, Vietnam. https://www.imf.org/external/pubs/ft/seminar/2002/fdi/eng/pdf/fletcher.pdf.

Forstater, M. & Readhead, A. (2017). Inflated expectations about mineral export misinvoicing are having real consequences in Tanzania. Center for Global Development. https://www.cgdev.org/blog/inflated-expectations-about-mineral-export-misinvoicing-are-having-real-consequences-tanzania.

Genschel, P. (2002). Globalization, Tax competition, and the welfare state. *Politics & Society* 30(2), 245–275.

Global Financial Integrity GFI (2014). Hiding in plain sight. https://gfintegrity.org/report/report-trade-misinvoicing-in-ghana-kenya-mozambique-tanzania-and-uganda/hiding_in_plain_sight_report-final/.

Haines, A. (2017). Acacia's $190 billion Tanzania tax bill sends shockwaves through mining sector. *International Tax Review*. https://www.internationaltaxreview.com/article/b1f7n87v940m2l/acacias-$190-billion-tanzania-tax-bill-sends-shockwaves-through-mining-sector.

IGF. (2019). Insights on Incentives: Tax competition in mining. Intergovernmental Forum on Mining, Minerals and Sustainable Development. The International Institute for Sustainable Development.

Janský, P. & Prats, A. (2013). Multinational corporations and the profit-shifting lure of tax havens. Christian Aid occasional paper, no. 9. https://pdfs.semanticscholar.org/8013/a32109d8abf68a67a9d125e6699c139d4ee6.pdf.

Janský, P. & Kokeš, O. (2016). Profit-shifting from Czech multinational companies to European tax havens. *Applied Economics Letters* 23(16), 1130–1133.

Jones, C., Temouri, Y., & Cobham, A. (2017). Tax haven networks and the role of the Big 4 accountancy firms. *Journal of World Business*. 53(2), 177–193.

Katz, J. & Pietrobelli, C. (2018). Natural resource based growth, global value chains and domestic capabilities in the mining industry. *Resources Policy*, 58, 11–20.

Keen, M. & Konrad, K. (2013). Chapter 5: The theory of international tax competition and coordination. In A. J. Auerbach, R. Chetty, M. Feldstein, & E. Saez (eds.), *Handbook of Public Economics*, Elsevier, vol. 5, 257–328.

Kienzler, D., Toledano, P., Thomashausen, S., & Szoke-Burke, S. (2015). Natural Resource Contracts as a Tool for Managing the Mining Sector. Columbia Center on Sustainable Investment staff publications. https://scholarship.law.columbia.edu/sustainable_investment_staffpubs/21/.

Klemm, A. & Parys, S. V. (2011). Empirical evidence on the effects of tax incentives. *International Tax and Public Finance* 19(3), 393–423.

Klosek, K. C. (2018). Catalysts of violence: How do natural resource extractive technologies influence civil war outbreak and incidence in sub-Saharan Africa? *The Extractive Industries and Society*, 5(2), 344–353.

Korinek, J. (2020), The mining global value chain. *OECD Trade Policy Papers*, No. 235, OECD Publishing. http://dx.doi.org/10.1787/2827283e-en.

Le Billon, P. (2011). Extractive sectors and illicit financial flows: What role for revenue governance initiatives?. U4 Issue.

Linde, O., Kravchenko, S., Ari Epstein, A., & Rentmeesters K. (2021). The global diamond industry 2021: Brilliant under pressure. https://www.awdc.be/sites/awdc2016/files/documents/210208_AWDC_Bain_Diamond_report_2020-21.pdf.

Mann, H. (2015). IISD handbook on mining contract negotiations for developing countries. International Institute for Sustainable Development.

Marsh, D., Lewis, C., & Chesters, J. (2014). The Australian mining tax and the political power of business. *Australian Journal of Political Science*, 49(4), 711–725.

Marshall, I. E. (2001). A survey of corruption issues in the mining and mineral sector. *International Institute for Environment and Development*, 15, 3–52.

Murphy, R. (2009). Defining the secrecy world. Rethinking the language of "offshore." Tax Justice Network. https://fsi.taxjustice.net/Archive2011/Notes%20and%20Reports/SecrecyWorld.pdf.

Murphy, R., Seabrooke, L., & Stausholm, S. N. (2019). A Tax map of global professional service firms: Where expert services are located and why. COFFERS Working Paper D4.6. https://openaccess.city.ac.uk/id/eprint/21868/.

Otto, J. M. (2017). The taxation of extractive industries. In T. Addison and A. Roe (eds.) *Extractive Industries: The Management of Resources as a Driver of Sustainable Development*, 275–297.

Poulsen, L. (2015). Bounded rationality and economic diplomacy: The politics of investment treaties in developing countries. Cambridge University Press.

Radon, J. (2006). How to negotiate your oil agreement. *Initiative for policy dialogue working paper series*.

Readhead, A. (2016). Preventing tax base erosion in Africa: A regional study of transfer pricing challenges in the mining sector. Natural Resource Governance Institute.

Readhead, A. (2018). Tax incentives in mining: Minimising risks to revenue. The International Institute for Sustainable Development and the Organisation for Economic Co-operation and Development.

ResourceContracts.org. (2021). ResourceContracts.org—About the site. Natural Resource Governance Institute, the World Bank, and the Columbia Center on Sustainable Investment https://resourcecontracts.org/about.

Rixen, T. (2011). From double tax avoidance to tax competition: Explaining the institutional trajectory of international tax governance. *Review of International Political Economy* 18(2), 197–227.

Sachs, J. D. & Warner, A. M. (2001). The curse of natural resources. *European Economic Review*, 45(4–6), 827–838.

Seabrooke, L. & Wigan, D. (2014). Global wealth chains in the international political economy. *Review of International Political Economy*, 21(1), 257–63.

Seabrooke, L. & Wigan, D. (2017). The governance of global wealth chains. *Review of International Political Economy*, 24(1), 1–29.

Shemberg, A. (2009). Stabilization clauses and human rights: A research project conducted for IFC and the United Nations Special Representative of the Secretary-General on Business and Human Rights. International Finance Corporation.

Thomson Reuters (2015). Let's make a deal: Understanding the opportunities in discretionary incentives. Thomson Reuters Tax & Accounting. https://tax.thomsonreuters.com/CreditsIncentives/ThankYou-Download/.

UN & ECA (2018). Economic Commission for Africa annual report 2018. https://digitallibrary.un.org/record/3830983?ln=en#record-files-collapse-header.

UNCTAD (2012). Tax incentives and foreign direct investment: A global survey. ASIT Advisory Studies No. 16. United Nations Conference on Trade and Development. https://unctad.org/system/files/official-document/iteipcmisc3_en.pdf.

UNIDO (United Nations Industrial Development Organization) (2011). Africa Investor Report 2011. Towards Evidence-Based Investment Promotion Strategies.

Zee, H., Janet, H., Stotsky, G., & Ley, E. (2002). Tax incentives for business investment: A primer for policy makers in developing countries. *World Development* 30(9), 1497–1516.

Zucman, G. & Piketty, T. (2015). *The Hidden Wealth of Nations: The Scourge of Tax Havens*. University of Chicago Press.

13

Legal Opinion

Clair Quentin

This chapter discusses legal opinion as an asset class within global wealth chains. It opens with a discussion of a phenomenon whereby some of the highest-status tax advisers in the UK have been in the habit of (apparently deliberately) giving incorrect advice. The second section proceeds to examine this phenomenon as an emanation of certain institutional characteristics of the profession in question. The discussion in the third section is then widened into a one of tax risk, so as to yield a general theory of the legal opinion on a tax matter as a species of "offshore." Then, in Section 4, in order to locate that theory within the global wealth chain analytic, information asymmetries that arise where legal opinions form part of global wealth chains are discussed. The chapter's final section offers a summary of conclusions which in addition suggests routes which might be pursued by policy development in this area.

Good money for bad advice

The market for legal services in England and Wales has until very recently been divided into two strictly regulated professional monopolies. There are solicitors, who until recently had a monopoly over giving advice to the public, and barristers who until recently had a monopoly over addressing the courts. Broadly, if you want legal advice you go to a solicitor, and if you have to go to court, your solicitor instructs a barrister to do the advocacy. You are the "lay client," and the solicitor is the barrister's "professional client."

These historic monopolies have led to deeply embedded cultures within the two professions. Solicitors, as they specialize, will tend on the whole to focus on specific spheres of client activity and therefore the transactional needs of their business sectors, whereas barristers tend to specialize in categories of litigation, and therefore acquire deep familiarity with specific

Clair Quentin, *Legal Opinion*. In: *Global Wealth Chains*. Edited by Leonard Seabrooke and Duncan Wigan, Oxford University Press. © Clair Quentin (2022). DOI: 10.1093/oso/9780198832379.003.0013 realms of legal doctrine. This has meant that barristers have developed an additional function as lawyer's lawyers, giving authoritative advice on the law to professional clients whose focus is more on the lay clients' commercial needs.

This institutionally embedded association with particular legal expertise on the part of barristers is accentuated by the cultural associations of the courtroom advocate, with their perceived forensic intellect and oratorical flair. It is also amplified by the scarcity value and arcane traditions of this small, old-fashioned profession; there is roughly one barrister for every ten solicitors, and in contrast to the efforts of firms of solicitors to seem as corporate as their clients in spanking new glass-and-steel offices, the business practices and jargon (and, until very recent times, courtroom apparel) of barristers seem more contemporaneous with the elegant Georgian town houses from which so many of them still practice. All in all, in view of these and related phenomena, it is fair to say that barristers have a cultural and professional cachet that solicitors do not share.

But the cachet commanded by an ordinary barrister is as nothing compared to that of a "Queen's Counsel" or "QC." QCs are barristers who have achieved sufficient reputation and standing to be endorsed by the state as pre-eminent within their profession, but that endorsement (as the name suggests) is bestowed not by some chartered regulator but (on the recommendation of an appointments panel) by the Crown itself. The status is very "establishment," very high-status, and quite exceptionally advantageous from the point of view of the pricing of the QC's services. QCs are rich, powerful, privileged people with (to adapt the words of David Bowie in "Ziggy Stardust") god-given gravitas. A QC's opinion, which will inevitably cost many thousands or tens of thousands of pounds, is the acme of authoritative legal advice in England and Wales.

That being the case, there has been something going on among the few dozen QCs specializing in tax law which is very odd indeed. The first public acknowledgment that there was an anti-social behavior problem emanating from the senior members of, as the case may be, 11 New Square, or 15 Old Square (barristers traditionally style their place of business simply by reference to their addresses, often if they are London-based within the estates of medieval professional institutions known as "Inns of Court") was a suggestion made by Member of Parliament Margaret Hodge in her capacity as the chairman of the UK Parliament's Public Accounts Committee, while taking evidence in a public session on marketed tax-avoidance schemes on December 6, 2012. She put it to a witness that Jonathan Peacock, Rex Bretten, Andrew Thornhill, and Giles Goodfellow (all tax QCs) "seem to be the guys who prostitute themselves" to the providers of tax-avoidance schemes (House of Commons, 2012). Giving tax advice is what these men do for a living—why then is what they are doing in relation to tax-avoidance schemes attracting this language, which is no doubt (engaging as it does the social stigma attaching to sex work) intended to be strongly derogatory?

A few months later, on March 14, 2013, one of those very same tax QCs, Rex Bretten, whose advice on tax law should be of the utmost authority, had his own personal tax planning publicly defeated by Her Majesty's Revenue and Customs (HMRC) before the UK's humble First Tier Tax Tribunal, both on the basis of HMRC's primary argument and also on the basis of their secondary, back-up argument.[1] Why did this tax QC give *himself* such bad tax advice? Is the giving of bad tax advice in any way connected to the "prostitution" among these men that Margaret Hodge identified?

At least a component of the answer was provided in a blog post by tax barrister Jolyon Maugham (now himself a QC) posted on August 7, 2014, the first paragraph of which read as follows:

> I have on my desk an Opinion—a piece of formal tax advice—from a prominent QC at the Tax Bar. In it, he expresses a view on the law that is so far removed from legal reality that I do not believe he can genuinely hold the view he says he has. At best he is incompetent. But at worst, he is criminally fraudulent: he is obtaining his fee by deception. And this is not the first such Opinion I have seen. Such pass my desk All The Time.
>
> (Maugham, 2014)

The piece goes on to explain the dynamic thus:

> Assume you are a seller of tax planning ideas—a "House". You have developed a planning idea that you wish to sell to taxpayers. But your customers will typically want independent corroboration—from a member of the Bar—that your idea "works", that is to say that it delivers a beneficial tax treatment. Or, to use the preferred euphemism, that it "mitigates" your tax liability.
>
> The fees that can be generated from bringing a planning idea to market are substantial: I am aware of instances where a single planning idea has generated fees of about £100 million pounds for the House. But without barrister sign-off, you have nothing to sell.

---

[1] *George Rex Bretten QC v Revenue & Customs* [2013] UKFTT 189 (TC), available at http://www.bailii.org/uk/cases/UKFTT/TC/2013/TC02604.html.

This fact creates predictable temptations for the Bar. If you are prepared to sign off a planning idea, the House will pay you handsomely. In some instances hundreds of thousands of pounds for a few days' work.

But this dynamic alone—that (a) people are prepared to pay good money for bad advice, and (b) anyone can be tempted to breach their obligations if the reward is sufficient—does not explain why the bad advice is so desirable in the first place; so desirable, in fact, that Mr Bretten would actually give it to himself. The explanation for that lies in an earlier post on Jolyon Maugham's blog, dated June 13, 2013. In that post he explains that

> when you file your tax return and pay your tax you're paying the tax you think—or your advisers have told you—you are liable to pay. Not what tax you are *actually* liable to pay. And if you've participated in the Big Idea [i.e. the tax-avoidance scheme] you're going to be telling HMRC that you have less income than you would otherwise have and you're therefore going to be paying less tax. Now, not everyone's return gets checked. And if your return doesn't get checked, it doesn't matter whether the Big Idea works or not, because, either way, you've paid less tax
>
> (Maugham, 2013)

The point here—sometimes referred to as the "risk-mining" theory of tax avoidance (Quentin, 2017)—is that a tax-avoidance scheme that does not work as a matter of law can nonetheless result in reducing the amount of tax the taxpayer pays, since the taxpayer's wrong tax return may never be challenged by HMRC. And so in circumstances where tax cannot "legally" be avoided, a tax-avoidance scheme that does not work nonetheless produces an *opportunity* to avoid the tax.

But in order to file on the basis of a tax-avoidance scheme that does not work, the taxpayer needs to have been advised that the scheme works. This is because it is only with the benefit of professional advice backing up the filing position that the taxpayer is able to say that reasonable care was taken in arriving at it, so that a penalty in respect of negligence is not applicable. And so professional advice backing up a legally ineffective tax-avoidance scheme serves the purpose of creating an opportunity to not pay tax which is legally payable, with reduced downside risk and certainly without the criminal downside risk of tax evasion. Which is why it is worth paying good money for bad advice.

Adviser/advocate role-substitution bifurcating the sovereign space of the state

No doubt there is an extent to which participation by eminent establishment men in the dynamic described above can simply be characterized as typical of the venality and corruption of their class. Indeed one of the tax QCs named by Margaret Hodge, Andrew Thornhill QC, was given a formal reprimand and a £10,000 fine for professional misconduct in connection with some disreputable financial transactions on April 27, 2018 by the barristers' regulatory body the Bar Standards Board (Bar Standards Board, 2018). There may also be an element of ideology; certainly some promotional material emanating from their places of business suggests that there is. Promotional material for a tax planning seminar held on October 2, 2013 by 15 Old Square, the chambers from which Rex Bretten QC formerly practiced, contained the following paragraph:

> The productive members of society are constantly being lectured that taxpayers must pay their fair share of tax. Yet, unless they are astutely advised, they will pay far more than their fair share. The aim of this seminar is to help ensure they pay no more than that
>
> (Key Haven Publications, 2013)

This ideological positioning—the suggestion that the ultra-wealthy are society's "productive" members as opposed to, say, rentiers accruing wealth out of all proportion to their putative marginal productivity—could be taken to be mere puff for the seminar. The chairman at this seminar Robert Venables QC (Rex Bretten QC's successor as head of chambers at 15 Old Square) is, however, notable for his angry outburst at UK Uncut tax-avoidance protesters captured on one of their videos: "you are trespassing scum; go!"[2] This outburst suggests that the positioning is held more strongly (by him at least) than is required for the purposes of drafting a promotional flyer. (As if to emphasize how tiny this world is, the person restraining Venables in that video is another of the so-called prostitutes, Giles Goodfellow QC.)

Venality and ideology are, however, not the story here. What is going on is structural, and it is more than merely the fact that QCs are better positioned than anyone else to profit from the dynamic described above

---

[2] https://youtu.be/uWbpyDLZMLM?t=187.

because their advice is more authoritative than anyone else's. The contention in this chapter is that the key feature of the matrix from which this phenomenon emanates is the fact of these men's practices being at one and the same time as expert advisers and as specialist advocates.

To illustrate, let us examine the behavior of the tax QC in what might be described (bearing in mind the historic monopolies noted above) as its natural habitat: a courtroom. When tax cases come to court it is generally in connection with a dispute between a taxpayer and HMRC over how much tax is payable. That dispute may arise because the taxpayer has deliberately courted controversy by implementing a tax-avoidance scheme, or it might be because there is uncertainty over the application of the relevant tax law to the taxpayer's purely commercial (i.e. non-fiscally motivated) arrangements; it matters not for the purposes of understanding the role of the advocate. The advocate's job is simply to present the taxpayer's case as best they can.

Often in tax cases the facts are not substantially in dispute, or there is one overall factual question which hinges on a broad factual picture the details of which are not in dispute, and the principal question before the court is how the law is to be interpreted so as to determine whether it applies on the facts. If, in such a case, the taxpayer loses, then his or her advocate has been advancing an interpretation of the law that turns out to be wrong. But prior to such determination, the interpretation may or may not be wrong, and a key skill of an advocate in tax matters is to (a) develop interpretations of the law which favor their client and are arguably correct, and to (b) present them as persuasively as possible. There is no moral, legal, or regulatory impediment standing in the way of an advocate's inventiveness in this regard; no upper limit to the scope for a skilled advocate to press upon a court speculative interpretations of the law which turn out to be wrong, in the hope that they are right. An example of this process in action, nicely flagged up for us by some pointed judicial sarcasm, may be found in the case of *Interfish v HMRC* [2014] EWCA Civ 876.[3] The advocate in question is Jonathan Peacock QC, another of the QCs named as a "prostitute" by Margaret Hodge. (To be clear, this is not an avoidance case—it is just an illustration of the basic mechanism of advocacy regarding legal interpretation in the context of a tax dispute.)

On its face the case raised no new issues of law; it was a classic matter of the court determining whether or not a certain item of expenditure

[3] http://www.bailii.org/ew/cases/EWCA/Civ/2014/876.html.

was deductible against trading profits on the basis of having been incurred solely for the purposes of that trade. In this case the payments were donations to a rugby club which were partly to benefit the taxpayer (being in the nature of corporate sponsorship for the purposes self-promotion) and partly to prop up the ailing rugby club financially. The paragraphs of the Court of Appeal's judgment in which Jonathan Peacock's arguments are described are worth quoting at some length, in order to get a feel for the audacity of those arguments through the court's unjudicial departure of tone into raw tongue-in-cheek:

> Courts have never wavered from the proposition that the business purpose must be the sole purpose. You might have thought, therefore, that once it had been found as a fact by the First-Tier Tribunal that the payments by Interfish had two purposes, that was the end of its appeal. If you had thought that, you had not reckoned with the advocacy of Mr Peacock QC. In beguiling submissions, he accepted that essential proposition but argued that Interfish did, in fact, have only one purpose in making its payments and that was a business purpose. The purpose of improving the financial position of the rugby club was merely a necessary and intermediate purpose on the way to the sole and ultimate purpose of improving the financial position of Interfish [and the FTT had so found—FTT paragraphs 47, 48].

As I have already indicated, Mr Peacock QC was not foolhardy enough to seek to gainsay the proposition of law that the statutory restriction on deductibility requires the business purpose to be the sole purpose. If authority is needed for so elementary a proposition, it can be found in the judgment of Romer LJ in *Bentley Stokes and Lowless v Beeson* [1952] 33 TC 491 at 504. The proposition was repeated by Lord Brightman in *Mallalieu v Drummond* [1989] 2 AC 861 at 870:

> "If it appears that the object of the taxpayer at the time of the expenditure was to serve two purposes, the purposes of his business and other purposes, it is immaterial . . . that the business purposes are the predominant purposes intended to be served."
>
> Nothing daunted by so clear a statement of principle, Mr Peacock QC seeks to find in *Bentley* authority for the proposition that an intermediate purpose on the way to achieving an ultimate purpose may be disregarded. The authority for his proposition, he says, is to be found in *Bentley* itself.

Mr Peacock QC, on behalf of the taxpayer, relied upon a passage which I must set out in full:

> "Was the entertaining [i.e. the expenditure claimed as a deduction in the *Bentley* case] undertaken *solely* for the purposes of business, that is, solely with the object of promoting the business or its profit earning capacity? It is, as we have said, a question of fact. And it is quite clear that the purpose must be the sole purpose. The paragraph says so in clear terms. If the activity be undertaken with the object both of promoting business and also with some other purpose, for example, with the object of indulging an independent wish of entertaining a friend or stranger or of supporting a charitable or benevolent object, then the paragraph is not satisfied, though in the mind of the actor, the business motive may predominate. For the statute so prescribes. [. . .]
>
> Mr Peacock QC sought to underline the word "independent". Interfish's purpose in benefiting the rugby club's financial position was not independent of its purpose of furthering Interfish's trade. The promotion of Interfish's business by payments to the rugby club necessarily involved the attainment or furtherance of financial support for the rugby club. Financial support of the rugby club was "necessarily inherent in the promotion of Interfish's business".
>
> This ingenious deployment of particular words and phrases in a paragraph of Romer LJ's judgment is, in my view, contrary to the principles expressed and the decisions themselves in a number of unquestioned revenue cases dealing with the requirement of exclusivity (paras 4–9).

What Jonathan Peacock QC is doing here is advancing a proposition of law (i.e. that an additional purpose not independent from the business purpose does not rule out deductibility) that is in the nature of an orthogonal departure from the true position (i.e. that the business purpose must be the sole purpose in order for the expenditure to be deductible), in the hope that the court accepts it as a refinement on the established interpretation, so as to save his client some money that would otherwise be payable in tax. In other words it is a fundamentally speculative proposition, having an at-best-indeterminate relation to normative propositions of law, potentially aligned with the normative position but probably antithetical to it. And it is his job as an advocate to advance such propositions.

This kind of proposition of law is, however, fundamentally different to the kind of proposition of law that one might expect an expert acting in an advisory capacity to offer. In such a context one might expect an adviser to deploy a proposition of law that most closely approximates to the law that a court might be expected to impose. But there is, in the UK at least, no strict formal obstacle preventing someone who is both an expert adviser and a specialist advocate from advancing in an *advisory* context the speculative propositions of law that are more suited to an *advocacy* context.[4] And where there is a tacit understanding that what the client actually wants is just such speculative propositions of law, in the expectation that they will yield an opportunity to not pay tax that is legally payable (and where the adviser is also adequately cushioned from liability in the event the propositions turn out to be wrong), that might well be what the adviser in fact does.

To imagine Jonathan Peacock acting in this (alleged) "prostitute" capacity, one might suppose a vendor of tax schemes coming to him for a favorable legal opinion on a tax scheme which is legally ineffective because it relies on a deduction where the business purpose is not the sole purpose of the expenditure. Mr Peacock could of course advise that it fails for that reason, and might perhaps even be paid a small amount for this trite and disappointing advice, but prior to the decision in *Interfish* he might alternatively have advised (for a fee more commensurate with his eminent standing) that it succeeds on the basis of the plausible but incorrect speculative proposition of law which he advanced *qua* advocate in that case. The argument in this chapter is that this adviser/advocate role-substitution, rather than mere venality or bourgeois economics, is behind the behavior of these QCs who take good money for bad advice.[5]

In effect this role-substitution creates a parallel tax regime—a tax regime where the rules are as wealthy taxpayers and/or their advisers would want them to be in order to minimize tax liabilities, standing alongside the actual tax regime applied by responsible advisers and the courts in accordance with normative propositions of law. In other words it is a species of "offshore." The classic conception of "offshore" is a "set of juridical realms marked by more or less withdrawal of regulation and taxation" effecting a "bifurcation of the sovereign space of the state" (Palan, 2003, p.19). The parallel legal universe created by Her Majesty's tax counsel, insofar as they act in the way that attracted Margaret Hodge's opprobrium, appears to come within this definition.

---

[4] This is not the case in, for example, the US: see IRS Circular 230, §10.37.

[5] It should be noted that since the phenomenon of tax QCs who "prostitute themselves" was publicly identified, a regime has been enacted which penalizes tax advisers for having enabled failed avoidance (to be found in Schedule 16 Finance (No. 2) Act 2017). Sadly the penalty is limited to the amount of the adviser's fee and so while the adviser's upside is at greater risk than previously, there continues to be no downside for them. The deterrent effect of this regime is therefore likely to be limited.

All legal opinions in respect of tax planning not guaranteed to succeed introduce an "offshore" element

A legal opinion taking a position antithetical to the actual law and sold by a tax QC in support of an aggressive tax-avoidance scheme that should fail upon challenge is, however, an extreme example of a more general phenomenon. In order to analyze this general phenomenon it is necessary to recognize that the idea of tax advice that is right or wrong, and the concomitant idea of a tax scheme that will or won't fail upon challenge, is a false binary where we should in fact be seeing a spectrum. Any filing position will inhabit a position between the theoretical extremes of inevitable success or inevitable failure upon putative challenge, and so the use of legal opinions to enable filing positions should be theorized in terms of *risk*.

It will be recalled that, in the case of a maximally unlikely to succeed filing position, the advantage is that the tax saving can still be achieved if the filing position is not challenged. As the likelihood of success of the filing position increases, this advantage is augmented by the possibility that the filing position *will* succeed upon challenge, the tax saving thereby being realized in accordance with the relevant law rather than in spite of it. It follows that, where a tax saving is enabled by a legal opinion, the legal opinion should be understood as providing two routes to a tax saving; the "onshore" route where the filing position is correct, and the "offshore" route where the filing position is wrong but goes unchallenged. As in the case of a quantum wave function, these two alternative routes exist simultaneously. The wave function is collapsed either by tax authority challenge, or by the time limit for tax authority challenge expiring.

In the case of tax planning relying on a QC's opinion which, as Jolyon Maugham put it, is so far removed from legal reality that he does not believe the QC can genuinely hold the view he says he has, the "offshore" element is unalloyed by any realistic possibility of success upon challenge, disclosing its fundamental nature. In the case of a responsible and conscientious legal opinion supplying a qualified endorsement of less aggressive arrangements (perhaps provided by a less expensive barrister, or a solicitor, or the tax department of a firm of accountants), that element is nonetheless present to the extent that the planning introduces a risk factor on the basis of which the planning *might* fail upon challenge, even if the planning is more likely than not to succeed. In such a case there still exists a possibility that the planning might be legally ineffective but go unchallenged.

And if that possibility eventuates, tax which is legally payable will go unpaid. This private appropriation of money belonging to the public purse will have been enabled by a favorable but false opinion as to the legal effectiveness of the arrangements, hence the value of the legal opinion generally as an asset in global wealth chains.

This is not to say that any specific instance of legal-opinion-endorsed tax planning introducing a risk factor results in private appropriation of money belonging to the public purse. In any specific instance it may be the case that the legal opinion is correct. And in the case of planning which is more likely than not to succeed upon challenge that is, by definition, more likely to be the case. The aggregate effect of any arbitrarily large number of such positions being taken, however, will as a matter of statistical inevitability yield such appropriation. This effect is augmented by the fact that planning which is more likely than not to succeed is unlikely to be challenged by a tax authority even where the tax authority finds out about it. Paradoxically, the less aggressive the tax avoidance, the more likely it is that this "offshore" element of the upside will accrue (this dynamic is explored in full in Quentin, 2017).

Once appropriated (e.g. in the form of untaxed income or gains) the wealth can be moved into more conventional offshore spaces; for instance a bank account (perhaps in the name of a company or a trustee), in a secrecy jurisdiction. Typically, tax-avoidance arrangements used by multinational enterprises, by offshore finance capital, and by internationally mobile wealthy individuals will deploy a combination of legal-opinion-endorsed tax-free accumulation in a jurisdiction with non-negligible rates of tax (for example the UK) and conventional offshore facilities. In many instances the legal opinion may therefore be the first offshore link in a global wealth chain.

Legal opinions and information asymmetries in global wealth chains

A key focus of global wealth chain analysis is information asymmetries as between "supplier," "client," and "regulator," and these schematic abstractions can be treated as corresponding to participants in the dynamic whereby legal opinions become assets within global wealth chains. The "supplier" is the person giving the legal opinion. As discussed above, in the case of a legal opinion wrongly endorsing an aggressive scheme that supplier is likely (in the UK at least) to be a tax QC, whereas in the case of a responsible and conscientious legal opinion supplying a qualified endorsement of less aggressive arrangements which are likely to succeed upon challenge, the supplier may be a lower-status barrister, solicitor, or accountant. Wherever on that spectrum the advice sits, standing behind the supplier are regulatory bodies which sanction the professional activities of the adviser (for example the Bar Standards Board or the Solicitors Regulation Authority), and behind those bodies stands the statutory and institutional apparatus governing the provision of legal services. This institutional framework constitutes the state as indirect supplier, and as we have seen in the case of the legal opinions of tax QCs, that framework implicates as indirect supplier the UK's head of state herself.

The "regulator" is the tax authority of the onshore jurisdiction in relation to which the legal opinion is given; in the UK that would be HMRC. The "client" is the lay client whose tax liability is potentially being side-stepped. A complicating factor in the case of legal opinions given by barristers is that the intermediary instructing the barrister (i.e. the professional client or tax-avoidance vendor) is both a "client" of the supplier and a "supplier" to the client. Broadly, insofar as concerns legal opinions as assets within global wealth chains, there are three key information asymmetries potentially at play; (a) potential unawareness of the tax authority as to the fact that the tax position has been taken at all, (b) potential unawareness of the lay client as to the fact that the scheme may be predicated on bad advice, and (c) potential unawareness of the person giving the legal opinion, as at implementation, regarding the effectiveness of subsequent tax risk mitigation.

As regards the first of these (i.e. tax authority unawareness), this is only really relevant in cases where the planning is likely to fail upon challenge (as we have seen, where it is likely to succeed upon challenge the tax authority will probably not challenge even where it is aware of the planning). Tax authorities have increasingly sophisticated tools for uncovering tax-avoidance schemes that rely on speculative propositions of law; for example the UK's "DOTAS" (i.e. disclosure of tax avoidance schemes) regime. In broad principle the regime requires taxpayers to make a disclosure when they have implemented a scheme.

The effectiveness of DOTAS is constrained, however, by its strategic targeting of widely marketed tax-avoidance schemes. In the case of a widely marketed and therefore standardized scheme a single assessment upheld in the courts can generally be treated as applicable to all instances of it. In addition, the UK has implemented mechanisms whereby in such cases the tax can be collected in advance from huge numbers of scheme customers pending the outcome of such litigation. In order to pursue these efficiencies, and in order to avoid the notorious indeterminacy of the concept of tax avoidance, the DOTAS rules focus on the commercial "hallmarks" of standardized schemes rather than the putative juridical hallmarks of tax avoidance per se. It is therefore in relation to tailor-made tax avoidance relying on speculative propositions of law that the legal opinion retains its value from the point of view of this particular information asymmetry. This speaks to a mix of what Seabrooke and Wigan (Chapter 1 in this volume) refer to as captive and relational global wealth chains.

As regards unsophisticated clients yielding the second of the aforementioned information asymmetries—that is, unawareness of the lay client as to the fact that the scheme carries risk—there has in the UK been a rash of instances of celebrities being taken to task in the press over their failed tax-avoidance arrangements, and claiming by way of response that they were advised that the "investments" were legitimate. Singer Katie Melua, for example, issued the following statement upon the revelation that (notwithstanding her public stance against tax avoidance) she had participated in a scheme:

> From what I can remember in 2008 when the Liberty scheme was presented to me it was not presented as "an aggressive tax avoidance scheme". It was presented as an "investment scheme" that had the potential to legally reduce yearly income tax. [. . .] Totally legal and legit and my accountants and advisers would take care to complete the formalities which included dealing with HMRC. Seemed pretty straight-forward and simple, so I signed up
>
> (Hickey, 2014)

In these instances, where the ultimate client lacks commercial understanding of the risk profile of the tax position they are being persuaded to take, the take-up of the scheme is being driven by the intermediaries (who stand to earn significant fees from the transaction), and those intermediaries are perhaps the true "client" of the supplier's services, insofar as they are the party turning those services to commercial account (the ultimate client being effectively the victim of a kind of confidence trick). Given the low success rate of the standardized schemes marketed to unsophisticated clients, and the vulnerability of such schemes to tax authority tools such as DOTAS, it is questionable whether this category of information asymmetry is of particular interest for the purposes of global wealth chain analysis, except to flag up that any number of governance types might be in play.

The third category of information asymmetry—that is, unawareness of the person giving the legal opinion, as at implementation, regarding the effectiveness of subsequent tax risk mitigation—is perhaps the most interesting. As we shall see, this asymmetry further undermines the distinction that might conventionally be observed between a legal opinion wrongly endorsing an aggressive scheme and a responsible and conscientious legal opinion endorsing less aggressive arrangements (a distinction which is, as we have seen, already undermined by the fact that the former only contains in unalloyed form the "offshore" element of the latter).

It will be recalled that tax litigation often hinges on disputed interpretations of the law, but it remains the case that, in order for tax-avoidance schemes to succeed upon tax authority challenge the facts on which it relies also have to be established. An example might be the "Working Wheels" scheme of which UK celebrity radio DJ Chris Moyles was a famous user. This scheme relied on the court finding as a fact that, alongside being a radio DJ, he was also a used car dealer, and this was a factual finding that the court was not able to make.[6]

When a legal adviser opines favorably on the viability of a tax-avoidance scheme, the factual propositions are not their responsibility. In the UK at least, factual assertions can in principle simply be assumed to be true for the purposes of a legal opinion.[7] A conscientious legal opinion regarding tax planning will generally include risk-management recommendations assisting the client in implementing the proposed arrangement in such a way that the factual assertions are more likely to be found to be true, but of course in practice those recommendations may be ignored. A client's tax risk management failings can therefore have the consequence that a responsible and conscientious legal opinion endorsing less aggressive arrangements may nonetheless endorse a scheme which, *as implemented*, is likely to fail upon challenge.

An example is Amazon's former UK corporation tax structuring. In very broad summary the structuring relied on a separation of the functions of Amazon's UK business into the actual contractual selling, which was done by a Luxembourg entity, and auxiliary functions performed by a UK entity,

---

[6] *Eoghan Flanagan & Christopher David Moyles & Allan Stennett v Revenue & Customs* [2014] UKFTT 175 (TC), available at http://www.bailii.org/uk/cases/UKFTT/TC/2014/TC03314.html.

[7] Again, the position is somewhat more constrained in the US.

which were (applying the relevant UK and international tax law) not sufficient to give rise to a taxable presence—in the UK—of the Luxembourg entity in which the profits were being booked. This arrangement could in principle have been legally effective to avoid UK corporation tax, and was no doubt endorsed prior to implementation by advice to that effect.

Such advice or opinion would have proceeded on the basis that the functions would be formally separated by means of a contract for services between the UK and Luxembourg entities, whereby the UK entity would contract to perform its auxiliary functions, but the opinion should also have included a recommendation that the actual conduct of the two sets of functions be kept substantively separate, and in particular that the substantive processes of selling to UK customers be clearly and discretely effected by the Luxembourg entity.

In the event the activities were not kept separate at all: in non-tax-related litigation it has been found that the purported separation of functions was "wholly unreal and divorced from the commercial reality of the situation," and the two entities were consequently found to have acted jointly in relation to the operation of the UK business.[8] It is quite reasonable to speculate that, had this finding been made in tax litigation, the profits of the Luxembourg entity would have been held to be taxable in the UK after all (the case study of Amazon's UK tax structuring is addressed in greater detail in Quentin, 2017). The correct analysis may therefore be that Amazon should have been assessing itself as liable to UK tax on the profits arising from its UK sales all along. It would appear, therefore, that the opinion on the basis of which Amazon did *not* so assess itself, however conscientious and reasonable that opinion may have been, and however plausible its factual assumptions at the time it was given, may have been as effective to divert public money into private hands as the most eye-poppingly speculative opinion that any of Margaret Hodge's "prostitute" QCs may have issued.

Conclusion

In summary, the role of legal opinions as an asset class within global wealth chains is to bifurcate an onshore tax system so as to create a parallel "offshore" system where the laws are as wealthy individuals and multinational

---

[8] *Cosmetic Warriors Ltd & Anor v amazon.co.uk Ltd & Anor* [2014] EWHC 181 (Ch), available at http://www.bailii.org/ew/cases/EWHC/Ch/2014/1316.html.

corporate groups want them to be rather than as they would be interpreted by the courts. This phenomenon takes effect in unalloyed form in a case where a high-status advocate sells a speculative proposition of law, suitable only for the adversarial context of tax litigation, as if it were legal advice. The phenomenon nonetheless pervades almost the entire spectrum of tax planning, since it is only in the case of tax planning which is guaranteed to succeed upon tax authority challenge that the potential upside of entering into planning which may succeed by default notwithstanding that it would fail upon challenge is absent.

From an enforcement (and therefore policy) perspective, the most significant categories of information asymmetry are (a) tax authority unawareness of instances of bespoke tax planning relying on speculative propositions of law, and (b) potentially false assumptions on the part of tax advisers as to the effectiveness of subsequent implementation, enabling them to give opinions which do *not* rely on speculative propositions of law, but which nonetheless endorse planning which would fail upon challenge, giving rise to a dynamic analogous to the more obviously abusive one of tax QCs lying about the law. As a final observation regarding policy implications, the debate around enforcement presupposes that the dynamic discussed here is one to be addressed on a civil basis, but the tax QC conduct considered in this chapter is manifestly dishonest, and in principle could form the basis of prosecutions for the offence of cheating the public revenue (Ormerod, 1998; All Party Parliamentary Group on Anti-Corruption and Responsible Tax, 2020).

References

All Party Parliamentary Group on Anti-Corruption and Responsible Tax (2020). *Ineffective tax avoidance: Targeting the enablers.* https://www.kcl.ac.uk/policy-institute/assets/targeting-the-enablers-of-tax-avoidance-appg-on-acrt.pdf.

Bar Standards Board (2018). *Disciplinary finding 183496.* https://web.archive.org/web/20180704083943/https://www.barstandardsboard.org.uk/complaints-and-professional-conduct/disciplinary-tribunals-and-findings/past-findings-and-future-hearings/?DisciplineID=183496.

Hickey, S. (2014). Katie Melua admits being 'clueless' about tax avoidance scheme. *The Guardian*, June 12. https://www.theguardian.com/music/2014/jul/12/katie-melua-clueless-liberty-tax-avoidance-scheme.

House of Commons (2012). *Uncorrected transcript of oral evidence to be published as HC 788-i.* https://web.archive.org/web/20180704071601/https://publications. parliament.uk/pa/cm201213/cmselect/cmpubacc/uc788-i/uc78801.htm.

Maugham, J. (2013, June 13). How do you solve a problem like tax avoidance: But I digress. http://waitingfortax.com/2013/06/13/how-do-you-solve-a-problem-like-tax-avoidance-but-i-digress/.

Maugham, J. (2014, August 7). Weak transmission mechanisms—and the boys who won't say no. https://waitingfortax.com/2014/08/07/weak-transmission-mechanisms-and-boys-who-wont-say-no/.

Key Haven Publications (2013). Practical Tax Planning: An Afternoon Seminar at the Law Society. https://web.archive.org/web/20131224201848/ http://www. khpplc.co.uk/products/58/PRACTICAL-TAX-PLANNING.

Ormerod, D. (1998). Cheating the Public Revenue. *Crim. L. R.,* 627–645.

Palan, R. (2003). *The Offshore World.* Cornell University Press.

Quentin, D. (2017). Risk-Mining the Public Exchequer. *Journal of Tax Administration,* 3(2), 22–35.

14

Articulating Global Wealth Chains

Leonard Seabrooke and Duncan Wigan

This volume has been concerned with identifying and delineating asset strategies in the world economy through the management of global wealth chains (hereafter GWCs). By "asset strategies" we mean the overarching plans used by firms, elites, and professionals to create and protect wealth. Such plans engage a range of tactics and often rely on power structures in the world economy, including the replication of social and economic networks that can realize asset strategies. We suggested in the introductory chapter to this volume (Chapter 1) that an asset can be considered a *legal affordance that provides differential claims on wealth*. This affordance is typically held in the form of a legal document (paper or digital) that entitles the account holder or bearer to discrete rights. The financial and legal worth of the asset, and the rights surrounding who can access it, know about it, monetize it, or destroy it, are protected by an interpretative community of professionals. They commonly include lawyers, accountants, entrepreneurs, regulators, and other professionals. Asset strategies in the world economy typically concentrate on activities to harness legal affordances across multiple jurisdictions. It is the sustained articulation of legal affordances across jurisdictions that gives stability to GWCs, allowing firms, elites, and professionals to plan their use and maintenance.

In Chapter 1 we made the case for using ideal types of abstracted forms of behavior to locate asset strategies in GWCs. The logic here is that by comparing empirical findings from cases of GWCs with the typology of market, modular, relational, captive, and hierarchy types, one can reflect on how asset strategies are articulated. We have mirrored the types first put forward by Gereffi, Humphrey, & Sturgeon (2005) to analyze global value chains (hereafter GVCs). This is to highlight how the treatment of value and wealth differ, and how asset strategies used by firms and professionals choose different paths when the aim is not to produce value but to create, protect, or store wealth. The purpose of ideal types and typology

Leonard Seabrooke and Duncan Wigan, *Articulating Global Wealth Chains*. In: *Global Wealth Chains*.
Edited by Leonard Seabrooke and Duncan Wigan, Oxford University Press.
© Leonard Seabrooke and Duncan Wigan (2022). DOI: 10.1093/oso/9780198832379.003.0014

is to provide abstract benchmarks against which empirical realities can be compared to reveal information. A further purpose is to permit a conversation between researchers over what is happening in their cases compared to others, and what collective lessons can be fostered through comparison. Our hope is that the original contributions in this volume provoke such conversations among readers, as they did among the authors. Discerning whether a case best fits with a modular or captive type, for example, is not about getting it right, but about how comparison reveals information that increases our knowledge about how asset strategies are developed through GWCs.

In this concluding chapter we suggest that the sum of contributions to this volume forces us to think through: (i) how firms and corporations act and differ; (ii) how professional strategies find stability in an interpretative community to select GWCs; and (iii) the future research agenda. We take each of these conceptual considerations in turn. First, we need to distinguish the firm from the corporation (Robé, 2011). This allows us to see how GWCs are articulated through the development of corporate structures rather than conflating the firm and the corporation as a single entity, or having an outdated vision of multijurisdictional activity as typified by multinational enterprises' (MNEs) foreign direct investment portfolio. Second, we need improved theoretical tools to locate how suppliers, clients, and regulators forge relationships that underpin the selection and maintenance of GWCs. Such a conceptual step can help us make micro-to-macro connections to improve case comparability and try to explain the sources of GWC strategies. Third, if we can think through the first two steps then we can also mark out what kinds of issues may be included in a future research agenda on GWCs. This includes some considerations about what factors replicate power asymmetries in both value chains and wealth chains.

Firm and corporate strategies

As stated in Chapter 1, it is important to distinguish between the firm and the corporation to delineate how asset strategies are articulated in GWCs (see, especially, Robé, 2011). Conceptually, the distinction between the "going concern" of the firm—those who preside over decision-making—and the legal structures used as part of strategy has long been identified. Veblen (1921, 1923) was concerned that managers were separating from the industrial purpose of production and scientific advance, with managers in search of pecuniary gain. The contributions to this volume attest to the continuing relevance of this insight with the logic of action in firms not easily delineated through a binary of circulation and production. The firm and the corporation are not one and the same. The latter is the servant of the former, and this relationship is the key source of wealth chain articulation.

Following this logic in a multijurisdictional context recasts some well-worn stereotypes of how firms and corporations behave internationally. As has been pointed out, theoretical advances are stymied by attributing canon-like status to old theories of the firm and the corporation (Suddaby et al., 2011; Mathieu, 2016; Bryan et al., Chapter 5 in this volume), and there is a view that more can be done to study the fields and mechanisms that provide variation in corporate forms (Davis & Marquis, 2005). Thinking about how GWCs are articulated can assist this aim. With this in mind, Figure 14.1 illustrates three stylized conceptions of the firm. In image (i) we have the conflation of the firm and the corporation within a single legal jurisdiction. As suggested above, this conflation is common, with the chief executive officer (CEO) seen as running both the firm and the corporation and with a view that shareholders own this structure (the key bugbear for Robé, 2011). An example can be seen in the significant literature in economic and organizational sociology on shareholder activism (Jung, 2016; Hirsh & Cha, 2018). Here the key question is how the corporation can be held to account and reflect shareholders' priorities; a question that is most easily answered when the firm and the corporation are seen as synonymous (Campbell, 2007).

In image (ii) we have a standard view of how firms/corporations directly control their subsidiaries in multinational jurisdictions. Again the firm and the corporation are seen as one and the same, with an understanding of the corporate entity that is the "parent" company and HQ of the operation. The important aspect here is that the firm controls the parent corporate entity and the multinational entities are then tied to these interests. From there the CEO, chief financial officer (CFO), and chief operating officer (COO) coordinate to ensure they have control over foreign subsidiaries for strategic planning over financial interests and production (see e.g. Kristensen & Zeitlin, 2005). However, at the same time that this view of the firm came to prominence, some scholars noted the increasing prevalence of financialization within the firm. The rise of the finance-minded CEO using multi-divisional forms (Fligstein, 1985), as well as CFOs and COOs focused on financial returns (Zorn, 2004), has been important to the

(i)

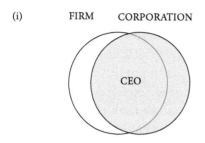

(ii)

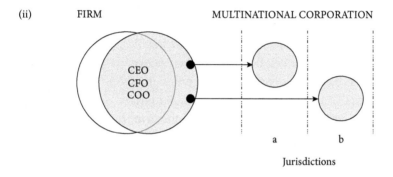

(iii)

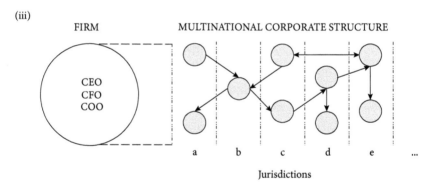

Fig. 14.1 Stylized representations of firm to corporate structure dynamics

articulation of such corporate structures since the 1980s. Scholars have also noted that even when the focus is on foreign direct investment (the kind of relationship in image (ii)), firms have significantly invested in regional networks that draw on imperial legacies that provide legal affordances, rather than hub-and-spoke strategies based on efficiencies in production and market access (Haberly & Wójcik, 2015).

In image (iii) the firm and the corporate structure are separated. The CEO, CFO, and COO are all present within the firm with coordination duties. As officers they are charged with the duty of controlling assets owned by entities within the multinational corporate structure. They do not work for shareholders (Ireland, 1999; Robé, 2011). They oversee the structure. From a hub they direct activity within an ecosystem of corporate entities. The dashed lines represent such oversight. The corporate entities are present in many jurisdictions that may offer tax advantages but also risk- and liability-management services. It is a combination of affordances available in the ecosystem that determines the articulation of GWCs. Entities that manage value creation and those that protect wealth are delineated according to opportunities offered by different jurisdictions (Seabrooke & Wigan, 2017). This includes the location of wealth and functional differentiation in its placement, with some jurisdictions acting as "conduits" while others are "sinks" (Garcia-Bernardo et al., 2017). Levels of ownership are often ten layers deep and in multiple jurisdictions, reflecting the "decentering" and "great fragmentation of the firm" (Desai, 2008; Reurink & Garcia-Bernardo, 2020). This enables risk-management strategies and the avoidance of detection through corporate reporting that focuses on aggregations more beneficial in a world where image (ii) is dominant. This third image is the most accurate depiction of corporate reality for leading multinational enterprises.

The contributions concerned with firms in this volume confirm the relevance of this third image. As Haslam, Leaver, and Tsitsianis argue, noting the "Jekyll and Hyde" relationship between information transparency in value chains and non-disclosure and obfuscation in wealth chains, complex financial relationships are not well understood in the scholarship on GVCs and supply chain management. They show how a firm can strategize to combine the use of regulations, such as pricing floors on a public utility, with multijurisdictional corporate entity management, and accounting practices that essentially transfer booked profits from the UK subsidiaries to the French parent company. The outcome is that "the firm has become a conduit between debt markets and investor returns and a site that backs extended chains of financial engineering" (Haslam et al. in Chapter 2, p. 30). Similarly, Morgan (Chapter 6) describes how for private equity firms the practice of debt-related tax reductions is not about subsidizing debt but providing more room for maneuver in paying or creating new debts and dividends. The use of the multinational corporate structure is to maximize the return to investors from the sale of acquisitions where the "exit involves higher net returns for any given sale price because of the way wealth has previously been protected" (Morgan in Chapter 6, p. 122). Bryan et al.

(Chapter 5) suggest that one consequence of the corporate logic depicted in image (iii) is that the view of the firm should focus more on movement and flows within the corporate ecosystem than linear relationships emerging from the parent company.

While many of the asset strategies that arise from the merger of financial and productive logics are marked in their complexity, others are audacious in their simplicity, yet are nonetheless effective. For example, Grondona and Burgos (Chapter 8) show the significant distributional impact of misreporting export prices to authority and the manipulation of profits through internal transactions (see also Vet et al., 2021). Similarly, as Stausholm (Chapter 12) demonstrates in the case of mining, even where the value chain assets are geographically fixed, wealth chain articulation is not necessarily constrained. Legal affordances can be provided in statutory law or negotiated contracts with little coordination or management needed for them to be realized.

Not all GWCs are, in the first instance, motivated by pecuniary reward. The establishment of layers of corporate entities can also service contiguous ends, such as regulatory and reputational risk mitigation. This is especially important in maintaining information asymmetries between the parties involved in GWC transactions. For example, Dahl (Chapter 7) notes with a large beer firm that the parent "sets up intermediate companies to shield the parent company from operational risks and to avoid impairment losses for badly performing subsidiaries. Intermediate companies are also useful in shielding the parent company from political risks and regulatory change" (Dahl in Chapter 7, p. 141). In a different context, Hearson (Chapter 3) walked us through the stages of international tax treaty negotiation, which had reflected the second image of the firm in Figure 14.1, but are now better represented by the third image. "Treaty shopping" is now incorporated into the multinational corporate structure rather than reflecting a simple relationship between a headquarters, a strategically placed "base" company, and operational jurisdictions. In the wake of regulatory upgrading by the OECD, firms are harnessing tax treaties by placing high value business functions and risks in "hub" companies in low tax jurisdictions. "In contrast to "base" company tax avoidance, which has little connection to the firm's tangible activities, "hub" company structures . . . are the leveraging of the value chain in order to create a wealth chain" (Hearson in Chapter 3, p. 63).

We note that variation in firms' strategies operating multinationally, or across national jurisdictions, has expanded beyond the conventional image of a firm engaged in foreign direct investment. These trends have been noted in the literature but are not currently integrated into GWC research. Examples here include the rise of firms in the passive index fund industry—such as BlackRock, Vanguard, and State Street—especially notable in affirming the kinds of concerns between pecuniary and industrial goals noted by Veblen above (Fichtner et al., 2017; Fichtner & Heemskerk, 2020; Petry et al., 2021). The power of such entities is affirmed by their introduction into digital platforms that accentuate reliance on passive indices (Haberly et al., 2019), including forms of everyday finance, such as automated app-based trading (Hayes, 2021).

Delineating professional strategies

Given that firms and corporations are separate in how they are articulated in asset strategies, we need theoretical tools to establish the kinds of micro-level relationships that underpin the articulation of GWCs. Legal affordances emerge from negotiations between clients, suppliers, and regulators. In the cases provided in this volume, the suppliers are commonly professionals that belong to established interpretative communities, and are enmeshed in professional and social networks, as well as working on behalf of private geopolitical actors, such as GPSFs (Boussebaa & Faulconbridge, 2019). It is professionals in these interpretative communities that secure legal affordances, in that what is legitimate and acceptable is shaped by relationships of dominance and deference that emerge from professional standing and social hierarchy. Veblen (1899, 1919) had a great deal to say on this, linking social status dynamics to the production of "suitable legal decisions bearing on the inviolability of vested interests and intangible assets," which underpins a great deal of wealth protection (Veblen, 1919, p. 60). In the same spirit, we suggest that linking micro-level forms of interaction to macro outcomes is important in the articulation of GWCs. The focus on firms above reveals much about the circuits of capital in GWCs, but social circuits that produce, bolster, and maintain GWCs are less known. As Collins has noted, we have "yet to measure, and to conceptualize, the mechanisms by which 'profit' moves across circuits" (Collins 2004, p. 267).

One way to develop this is to focus on the relationships and relations among the triad of clients, professionals (suppliers), and regulators. We follow the view from Martin (2009, 2011) that agents develop "action profiles" that give regularity to their conduct and how it is seen by others. Shortcuts on likely forms of action are provided internally through identity maintenance and shared "habitus" (Spence & Carter, 2014), and signaled externally through styles of professional engagement and qualification, including how knowledge is codified in corporate and professional organizations (Morris, 2001; Suddaby & Greenwood, 2001). Relationships within the triad of clients, professionals, and regulators define what information is available to act upon, and the boundaries that define which behavior is permitted or sanctioned (Thiemann & Lepoutre, 2017). For GWCs, the professionals commonly involved are lawyers, accountants, financiers, etc. who have a foothold in national regulatory systems but are also used to working in a transnational social space that provides them with some freedom of movement (Seabrooke, 2014).

Figure 14.2 provides a conceptualization of the links between micro-level relationships between clients, professionals, and regulators and the selection of asset strategies via GWC types. These selections are then embedded in the transnational economic and legal order, and affirmed through recursive cycles of conflict and consensus (Halliday & Carruthers, 2007; Halliday, 2009; Broome & Seabrooke, 2020).

At the bottom of Figure 14.2 we can see the triadic relationship between clients, professionals (again, suppliers in the broader GWC framework), and regulators. These parties engage in the transfer or withholding of information, have the potential to sanction (through law, professional censure, or financially), and are all involved in exchanging status and identity affirmations. They can agree on common goals and understandings, seek to exploit each other, or fail to generate any meaningful engagement. In

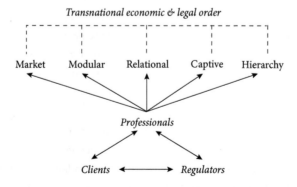

Fig. 14.2 Linking micro-level actions to global wealth chain articulation

principle the relationships are dyadic (client ↔ professional, professional ↔ regulator, regulator ↔ client), where the action profiles are intensely developed. From these relationships builds a cumulative profile where consensus in this interpretative community develops on what is legitimate and permittable behavior. Relationships become relations that are more regular and permit GWC articulations.

Variations in the kinds of relations within the triad support different asset strategies. Variation is strongly informed by information asymmetries between the parties, on who is willing to share knowledge, who is guarding information, and how expertise about information is conveyed to other parties. Given this, understanding more about the micro-level relationships tells us what undergirds asset strategies and GWC selection. Critical here is the management of uncertainties. These uncertainties include social relations and role performance, the interpretation of signals from other parties, and the potential for shocks from the external environment (White, Godart, & Thiemann, 2013). Information asymmetries and perceptions of uncertainty among the parties inform interactions in the selection of GWCs, including clients' appetite for risk, fear of regulatory incursions, and compliance with the spirit and letter of the text in legal affordances.

Many of the contributions in this volume shed light on these interactions and processes that link the micro level to macro outcomes. This includes the role of status and social hierarchy in relations, as well as the presentation of knowledge to induce deference in others. Such dynamics are also critical to the operations of organizations heavily involved in the articulation of GWCs, such as GPSFs and especially the Big Four global accounting firms.

The most obvious assertions of power through social hierarchy can be seen from elite professionals. As Clair Quentin (Chapter 13) writes in their view on Queen's Counsel barristers, some professionals have "god-given gravitas." As Quentin describes, where status and prestige is extenuated what is possible expands considerably. Queen's Counsel barristers operate in an interpretative community that is extremely permissive. They write that there

is no moral, legal or regulatory impediment standing in the way of an advocate's inventiveness in this regard; no upper limit to the scope for a skilled advocate to press upon a court speculative interpretations of the law which turn out to be wrong, in the hope that they are right.

(Quentin, in Chapter 13, p. 267)

This creates an "offshore" system for wealthy elites and professionals that is at the heart of English jurisprudence.

In a different case, but in reference to elite networks and their replication, Santos (Chapter 10) shows how professionals cultivate relationships with "next-gens" to maintain intergenerational wealth management through GWCs. Here the role of professional–client relations is not only to maintain a financial connection but to foster an emotional one. As Santos writes, "portfolios are meant to work as affective thermostats, nurturing the right sort of emotional orientations toward investing—namely, long-term investing, investment of total returns, etc.—and keeping a foothold in descendants' life events" (Santos, in Chapter 10, pp. 205–6). These relationships are maintained among peers and in closed environments with physical co-presence—such as Santos's Mandarin Oriental example—to ensure that there is emotional intensity and collective agreement on shared goals.

What Santos describes has been called by others a "Zelizer circuit," after Viviana Zelizer's (1994, 2005) foundational work, where what is being exchanged is shared interpretations of worth that enable GWC articulation, including a preference for asset strategies that signal social standing to peers. Emotional and financial energies flow together and affirm each other (Collins 2004; Gammon & Wigan, 2015). Such relationships are important in elite replication, establishing what is socially acceptable (Friedman & Reeves, 2020; Adamson & Johansson, 2020), as has been noted in scholarship on transnational elites and advanced business services (Beaverstock et al., 2004, 2013; Wójcik, 2013). As noted by Santos, micro-level preference formation occurs at the educational level in repeated staged interactions, and is especially noteworthy among Anglophone elites who are transnationally mobile (see Santos in Chapter 10; Harrington & Seabrooke, 2020). At a macro level this also helps maintain the educational and racial composition of global elite networks (Young et al., 2021).

Many of the contributions to this volume note that deference and hierarchy are fortified through interactions between professionals and clients, or professionals and regulators. The rituals of esteem and rarefication in the high-value art market are an essential part of controlling wealth. Helgadóttir (Chapter 9) notes how GWC articulation in the context of high-value art is largely a function of sending and affirming the right signals between professionals and clients, construing access to a sacred arena. Global art investment funds have boomed in Europe and the US, and especially in China, to facilitate this global market. The reformulation of professional networks has followed the success of GWC asset strategies, such as changing relationships between designers of high-end property interiors and gallerists for the promotion of art, and between freeport managers and investors for its storage.

Christensen shows (in Chapter 11) how professionals can use technical language to overwhelm those opposing their views. He details how professionals involved in policy processes aimed at making GWCs more transparent—the OECD and G20's Base Erosion and Profit Shifting project—used "technicization" to constrain who was able to speak to policy and to guide policy content. As Christensen notes: "Policy discussions were conducted in a highly technical, specialized language, thick with specific legal and economic terminology" (Chapter 11, pp. 231–2). These types of constructed information asymmetries are omnipotent in GWCs. They can be found in the stretching of accounting regulations (Haslam et al. in Chapter 2), or in the filigree of structured finance (Bryan et al. in Chapter 5). Stausholm illustrates (Chapter 12) how in the negotiation of mining contracts government officials are disempowered in the face of overwhelming expertise deployed by firms. While they have clear options in what they can offer mining firms, the professionals and clients have much greater knowledge on what can be exploited from beneath the ground and the costs of its extraction. The elevated profits provided by the legal affordances written into contracts then travel beyond the reach of government through strategically placed multinational corporate entities to maximize wealth creation and protection.

The coordination of GWC asset strategies is a task often dominated by GPSFs. The role of these actors is especially prominent in tax treaties and advance pricing agreements, as discussed by Hearson (Chapter 3) and Ylönen (Chapter 4). Hearson argues that, due to the widespread use of "tax-efficient supply chain management," GPSFs are now inverting the relationship between the value chain and the wealth chain, so now the "tail now wags the dog" (Chapter 3, p. 50). This occurs in parallel to the shift from image (ii) to image (iii) in Figure 14.1. Ylönen (Chapter 4) also points to the power of GPSFs, in particular the Big Four global accounting firms, in facilitating advance pricing agreements and advanced tax rulings, with the intervention of professionals from these firms who determine the character of wealth chains. The sovereign capacity to provide such legal affordances is also now commercialized. Ylönen describes how some sovereign entities that authorize advance tax rulings and advance price agreements have effectively outsourced the allocation of these affordances to GPSFs and consultancies, further affirming their power (Boussebaa & Faulconbridge, 2019; Elemes et al., 2021).

The future research agenda

Our first step in this concluding chapter has been to set out how firms and corporations are not one and the same and how we can see firm management of GWCs through multinational corporate structures. The second step is to suggest ways of thinking about how micro-level interactions are stabilized through social relations that enable the selection of asset strategies in GWCs. The third step is then to think through how connections between the first two steps can inform a future research agenda.

Figure 14.3 complicates the third image presented in Figure 14.1. These are useful complications that can provoke a discussion. On the left side of the image is the firm, including the CEO, CFO, and COO. On the right-hand side are suppliers of services to the maintenance of multinational corporate structures, including GPSFs and professionals. Both are involved in the management of GVCs and GWCs. In the middle of the illustration we can see not only wealth chain entities but also value chain entities. Knowing how to distinguish between the two is critical for the future research agenda. Scholars working in this area suggest a great degree of caution is necessary in this pursuit, especially with "big data" (Heemskerk et al., 2018). Jerry Davis warns that while the data to answer many questions may be available, "We are drowning in a sea of data, much of it conveniently formatted, which eliminates a traditional constraint on building knowledge

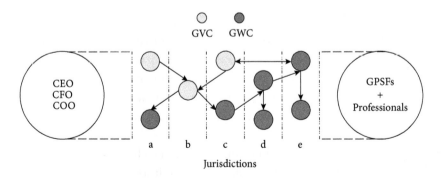

Fig. 14.3 Distinguishing global value chains from global wealth chains

about organizations" (Davis, 2010, p. 705). A solution to this problem is to build cases that follow multiple lines of data verification. Building a series of comparative cases follows the logic of ideal types presented in Chapter 1, and permits a common conversation on how GWCs are articulated, and how we can distinguish wealth and value in practice.

Dahl (Chapter 7) takes a big step here in proposing a concrete method in her investigation of beer and pharmaceutical firms and the link between firm size, their regional or global ambitions, and value/wealth chain mix. Her method is to find the entities associated with a known firm in the Orbis database and then note the stated purpose of business for each entity. This provides a rough indicator as to whether the entity is related to production and supply chain activity, or to legal and financial management. The second step is to note the jurisdictional location of corporate entities, linking these to the presence of known sectors in the same geographic location (cf. Garcia-Bernardo et al., 2017; Reurink & Garcia-Bernardo, 2020), as well as known information on levels of financial secrecy in the jurisdiction (Cobham, Janský, & Meinzer, 2015). Third, based on estimates from the first two steps, it is possible to then assess the number of employees in each entity and profit per head. Low numbers and high profit per head are likely indicators of wealth chain activity (Murphy et al., 2019). In combination such methods can be used to distinguish value and wealth corporate entities. Furthermore, "equity mapping" can also be conducted, in which Orbis data is cleaned to distinguish direct and indirect forms of ownership, and to eliminate double counting. Visualizing such data can distinguish between "stand-alone" and "in-betweener" corporate entities (Phillips et al., 2021). From there it would be possible to harness insight from teams of professionals (lawyers, financiers, accountants, etc.) to identify the purpose of each entity and its role in the overall corporate structure.

In developing the GWCs framework our opening gambit was to state that "wealth chains are the yin to the yang of value chains" (Seabrooke & Wigan, 2014, p. 257). This pithy remark has attracted some attention to promote the idea that multinational enterprises can be viewed as "organisational circuits" (Morgan, 2016) and that we should recognize the hidden costs of legal practices that underpin value chain activity (Cutler & Lark, 2021). These are early signs that there is a clear intellectual and policy desire to understand and explain how value chains and wealth chains are entangled. There are also clear policy implications from such research. For instance, it would allow us to locate the link between multinational financial management and labor and wage suppression, which is a function not of power asymmetries in production but of access to the numerous legal affordances that allow wealth extraction to dominate corporate strategy (LeBaron, 2021; Selwyn & Leyden, 2021). More information on how firms use multinational corporate structures would also permit pressure on international organizations to not promote development in a manner that ignores the effects of GWCs on development (Bair et al., 2021).

The development of a broader conversation on how to build cases that can distinguish or capture the integration of value and wealth is fundamental to the future research agenda. As it stands we have scholars working on GVCs, global production networks (e.g. Yeung & Coe, 2015), financialized global value chains (e.g. Durand & Milberg, 2020), global financial networks (Haberly & Wójcik 2021), and GWCs. This scholarly interpretative community has noted transformations in internationalization and capital accumulation. The GWC project raises the question of how to conceptualize and trace these transformations in a world where capital in commodity form and capital in money form are not easily parsed (see Bryan et al. in Chapter 5). It may be that the GVC project, despite its numerous achievements, has limitations in its understanding of how value and wealth differ, and how they are integrated. A new community of scholars has begun to interrogate how wealth is created and protected across jurisdictions, and how wealth and value are related in the asset strategies used by elites and firms. This community of scholars, as shown in this volume, has begun the process of developing conceptual, theoretical, and methodological tools. Such development will benefit from a broader interdisciplinary input and dialogue. Ultimately, the concern of the approaches noted above is the same. What is sought to be explained are the distributional outcomes from global economic activity. The common enterprise is to locate the macro-, meso-, and micro-level relationships and processes that underpin distributional outcomes, and then determine how to correct them.

References

Adamson, M. & Johansson, M. (2020). Writing class in and out: Constructions of class in elite businesswomen's autobiographies. *Sociology*, 0038038520962393.

Bair, J., Mahutga, M., Werner, M., & Campling, L. (2021). Capitalist crisis in the "age of global value chains." *Environment and Planning A: Economy and Space*, 0308518X211006718.

Beaverstock, J. V., Hall, S., & Wainwright, T. (2013). Servicing the super-rich: New financial elites and the rise of the private wealth management retail ecology. *Regional Studies*, 47(6), 834–849.

Beaverstock, J. V., Hubbard, P., & Short, J. R. (2004). Getting away with it? Exposing the geographies of the super-rich. *Geoforum*, 35(4), 401–407.

Boussebaa, M. & Faulconbridge, J. R. (2019). Professional service firms as agents of economic globalization: A political perspective. *Journal of Professions and Organization*, 6(1), 72–90.

Broome, A. & Seabrooke, L. (2020). Recursive recognition in the international political economy. *Review of International Political Economy*, 28(2), 369–381.

Campbell, J. L. 2007. Why would corporations behave in socially responsible ways? An institutional theory of corporate social responsibility. *Academy of Management Review*, 32, 946–967.

Christensen, R. C., Seabrooke, L., & Wigan, D. (2021). Professional action in global wealth chains. *Regulation & Governance*, forthcoming. https://doi.org/10.1111/rego.12370

Cobham, A., Janský, P., & Meinzer, M. (2015). The financial secrecy index: Shedding new light on the geography of secrecy. *Economic Geography*, 91(3), 281–303.

Collins, R. (2004) *Interaction Ritual Chains*. Princeton University Press.

Cutler, A. C. & Lark, D. (2021). The hidden costs of law in the governance of global supply chains: The turn to arbitration. *Review of International Political Economy*, forthcoming. DOI: 10.1080/09692290.2020.1821748

Davis, G. F. (2010). Do theories of organizations progress? *Organizational Research Methods*, 13(4), 690–709.

Davis, G. F. & Marquis, C. (2005). Prospects for organization theory in the early 21st century: Institutional fields and mechanisms. *Organization Science*, 16, 332–343.

Desai, M. (2008). The Decentering of the Global Firm, *Working Paper 09-054*. Harvard Business School.

Durand, C. & Milberg, W. (2020). Intellectual monopoly in global value chains. *Review of International Political Economy*, 27(2), 404–429.

Elemes, A., Blaylock, B., & Spence, C. (2021). Tax-motivated profit shifting in big 4 networks: Evidence from Europe. *Accounting, Organizations and Society*, 95, 101267, https://doi.org/10.1016/j.aos.2021.101267.

Faulconbridge, J. R., Henriksen, L. F., & Seabrooke, L. (2021). How professional actions connect and protect. *Journal of Professions and Organization*, 8(2), 214–227.

Fichtner, J. & Heemskerk, E. M. (2020). The New permanent universal owners: Index funds, patient capital, and the distinction between feeble and forceful stewardship. *Economy and Society*, 49(4), 493–515.

Fichtner, J., Heemskerk, E. M., & Garcia-Bernardo, J. (2017). Hidden power of the Big Three? Passive index funds, re-concentration of corporate ownership, and new financial risk. *Business and Politics*, 19(2), 298–326.

Fligstein, N. (1985). The spread of the multidivisional form among large firms, 1919–1979. *American Sociological Review* 50, 377–391.

Friedman, S. & Reeves, A. (2020). From aristocratic to ordinary: Shifting modes of elite distinction. *American Sociological Review*, 85(2), 323–350.

Gammon, E. & Wigan, D. (2015). Veblen, Bataille and financial innovation. *Theory, Culture & Society*, 32(4), 105–131.

Garcia-Bernardo, J., Fichtner, J., Takes, F. W., & Heemskerk, E. M. (2017). Uncovering offshore financial centers: Conduits and sinks in the global corporate ownership network. *Scientific Reports*, 7(1), 1–10.

Gereffi, G., Humphrey, J., & Sturgeon, T. (2005). The governance of global value chains. *Review of International Political Economy*, 12(1), 78–104.

Haberly, D., MacDonald-Korth, D., Urban, M., & Wójcik, D. (2019). Asset management as a digital platform industry: A global financial network perspective. *Geoforum*, 106, 167–181.

Haberly, D. & Wójcik, D. (2015). Regional blocks and imperial legacies: Mapping the global offshore FDI network. *Economic Geography*, 91(3), 251–280.

Haberly, D. & Wójcik, D. (eds.). (2021). *Global Financial Networks: What They Are and Where They Come From*. Oxford University Press.

Halliday, T. C. (2009). Recursivity of global normmaking: A sociolegal agenda. *Annual Review of Law and Social Science*, 5, 263–289.

Halliday, T. C. & Carruthers, B. G. (2007). The recursivity of law: Global norm making and national lawmaking in the globalization of corporate insolvency regimes. *American Journal of Sociology*, 112(4), 1135–1202.

Harrington, B. & Seabrooke, L. (2020). Transnational professionals. *Annual Review of Sociology*, 46: 399–417.

Hayes, A. S. (2021). The active construction of passive investors: Roboadvisors and algorithmic "low-finance." *Socio-Economic Review*, 19(1), 83–110.

Heemskerk, E., Young, K., Takes, F. W., Cronin, B., Garcia-Bernando, J., Henriksen, L. F., Winecoff, W. K., Popov, V., & Laurin-Lamothe, A. Y. (2018). The promise and perils of using big data in the study of corporate networks: Problems, diagnostics and fixes. *Global Networks*, 18(1), 3–32.

Hirsh, E. & Cha, Y. (2018). For law and markets: Employment discrimination lawsuits, market performance, and managerial diversity. *American Journal of Sociology*, 123(4), 1117–1160.

Ireland, P. (1999). Law and the myth of shareholder ownership. *The Modern Law Review*, 62(1), 32–57.

Jung, J. (2016). Through the contested terrain: Implementation of downsizing announcements by large US firms, 1984 to 2005. *American Sociological Review*, 81(2), 347–373.

Kristensen, P. H. & Zeitlin, J. (2005). *Local Players in Global Games: The Strategic Constitution of a Multinational Corporation*. Oxford University Press.

Laage-Thomsen, J. & Seabrooke, L. (2021). Actors and authority in the international tax ecosystem. In B. Unger, L. Rossel, & J. Ferwerda (eds.), *Combating Fiscal Fraud and Empowering Regulators*. Oxford University Press, 9–34.

LeBaron, G. (2021). The role of supply chains in the global business of forced labour. *Journal of Supply Chain Management*, 57(2), 29–42.

Martin, J. L. (2009). *Social Structures*. Princeton University Press.

Martin, J. L. (2011). *The Explanation of Social Action*. Oxford University Press.

Mathieu, J. (2016). The problem with [in] management theory. *Journal of Organizational Behavior*, 37(8), 1132–1141.

Morgan, J. (2016). Corporation tax as a problem of MNC organisational circuits: The case for unitary taxation. *The British Journal of Politics and International Relations*, 18(2), 463–481.

Morris, T. (2001) Asserting property rights: Knowledge codification in the professional service firm. *Human Relations* 54(7), 819–838.

Murphy, R., Seabrooke, L., & Stausholm, S. N. (2019). A tax map of global professional service firms: Where expert services are located and why. *COFFERS Working Paper 4.6*. Copenhagen Business School.

Petry, J., Fichtner, J., & Heemskerk, E. (2021). Steering capital: The growing private authority of index providers in the age of passive asset management. *Review of International Political Economy*, 28(1), 152–176.

Phillips, R., Petersen, H., & Palan, R. (2021). Group subsidiaries, tax minimization and offshore financial centres: Mapping organizational structures to establish the "in-betweener" advantage. *Journal of International Business Policy*, 4(2), 286–307.

Reurink, A. & Garcia-Bernardo, J. (2020). Competing for capitals: The great fragmentation of the firm and varieties of FDI attraction profiles in the European Union. *Review of International Political Economy*, 1–34.

Robé, J. P. (2011). The legal structure of the firm. *Accounting, Economics, and Law* 1(1): 2152–2820.

Santos, M. (2021). High net-worth attachments: Emotional labour, relational work, and financial subjectivities in private wealth management. *Journal of Cultural Economy*, https://doi.org/10.1080/17530350.2021.1952097.

Seabrooke, L. (2014). Epistemic arbitrage: Transnational professional knowledge in action. *Journal of Professions and Organization*, 1(1), 49–64.

Seabrooke, L. & Wigan, D. (2014). Global wealth chains in the international political economy. *Review of International Political Economy*, 21(1), 257–263.

Seabrooke, L. & Wigan, D. (2017). The governance of global wealth chains. *Review of International Political Economy*, 24(1), 1–29.

Selmier, W. T. (2017). An institutional perspective on governance, power, and politics of financial risk. *Business and Politics*, 19(2), 215–240.

Selwyn, B. & Leyden, D. (2021). Oligopoly-driven development: The Word Bank's trading for development in the age of global value chains in perspective. *Competition & Change*, 1024529421995351.

Spence, C. & Carter, C. (2014). An exploration of the professional habitus in the Big 4 accounting firms. *Work, Employment and Society*, 28(6), 946–962.

Suddaby, R. & Greenwood, R. (2001) Colonizing knowledge: Commodification as a dynamic of jurisdictional expansion in professional service firms. *Human Relations*, 54(7), 933–953.

Suddaby, R., Hardy, C., & Huy, Q. N. (2011). Where are the new theories of organization? *Academy of Management Review*, 36, 236–246.

Thiemann, M. & Lepoutre, J. (2017). Stitched on the edge: Rule evasion, embedded regulators, and the evolution of markets. *American Journal of Sociology*, 122(6), 1775–1821.

Veblen, T. (1899). *The Theory of the Leisure Class*. MacMillan.

Veblen, T. (1919). *The Vested Interests and the Common Man*. McMaster University Archive for the History of Economic Thought.

Veblen, T. (1921). *The Engineers and the Price System*. B. W. Huebsch.

Veblen, T. (1923). *Absentee Ownership and Business Enterprise in Recent Times: The Case of America*. B. W. Huebsch.

Vet, C., Cassimon, D., & Van De Vijver, A. (2021). Getting the short end of the stick: Power relations and their distributive outcomes for lower-income countries in transfer pricing governance. In *Taxation, International Cooperation and the 2030 Sustainable Development Agenda*, 19, 1. United Nations University Series. https://doi.org/10.1007/978-3-030-64857-2_1.

White, H. C., Godart, F. C., & Thiemann, M. (2013) Turning points and the space of possibles: A relational perspective on the different forms of uncertainty. In F. Dépelteau & C. Powell (eds.), *Applying Relational Sociology*. Palgrave Macmillan, 137–154.

Wójcik, D. (2013). Where governance fails: Advanced business services and the offshore world. *Progress in Human Geography*, 37(3), 330–347.

Yeung, H. W. C. & Coe, N. (2015). Toward a dynamic theory of global production networks. *Economic Geography*, 91(1), 29–58.

Young, K. L., Goldman, S. K., O'Connor, B., & Chuluun, T. (2021). How white is the global elite? An analysis of race, gender and network structure. *Global Networks*, 21(2), 365–392.

Zelizer, V. (1994). *The Social Meaning of Money*. Basic Books.

Zelizer, V. (2005). *The Purchase of Intimacy*. Princeton University Press.

Zorn, D. (2004). Here a Chief, There a Chief: The Rise of the CFO in the American Firm. *American Sociological Review*, 69(3), 345–364.

Index

Activists, 121–22, 224–27, 230–35, 236–37
Accountants, 2, 21, 193, 221, 231, 271, 274, 279, 286
Accounting, 2, 10, 19, 279, 281, 286–87, 289
  in advance pricing agreements, 75, 77
  in art markets, 193
  in intangible capital, 89, 95–96, 100–2, 105–6
  in beer and pharmaceuticals, 151
  in family wealth management, (201–219)
  in legal opinion, (271, 273–74)
  in tax transparency, 226, 231–32
  in tax treaties, 60
  in utilities markets, 30, 34, 38, 41–42, 44
Administración Federal de Ingresos Públicos (Argentina), 162–63, 168–69
Advance Pricing Agreements,
  as private governance, 69, 80–81
  Big Four global accounting firms, 74, 77–79, 81
  commercialization of sovereignty, 69, 78–81
Advance Tax Rulings, 17, 68–72, 74, 77–83, 289
Alliance Boots, 22, 120–23, 128–32
Amazon, 62, 94–95, 99, 104, 275–76
Anglophone identity, 210–11, 288
Apple, 11, 22, 62, 73, 88, 94, 103–4, 110, 120
Arbitrage, v, 19, 38–39, 49, 63–64, 97–98, 102, 196, 220, 224
Argentina, 155–60, 163–67, 175–79
Arm's length principle, 12, 15, 70–72, 84–85, 159–62, 165–67, 183, 195
Art,
  'dual depletion' of public space, 196
  expertise on, 186, 191–93, 196
  freeports, 16–17, 191–93, 289
  tax avoidance, 191

Asset,
  'socio-legal' definition, 2
  strategies, 2, 4–5, 8–9, 11, 15, 22–23, 279–83, 283–84, 287–89
  in art markets, 192
  in family wealth management, 203
  in mining, 244
  in private equity, 115, 119
  in tax transparency, 223
  in tax treaties, 62, 65
  in utilities markets, 30, 36, 38, 41
Authority claims, 5, 7–8, 14, 63, 122, 235, 274

Base erosion and profit shifting, 8, 19–20, 60–61, 63, 82, 84, 133, 221–28, 231, 233–34, 235–37, 238
Big Four global accounting firms, 19–20, 50, 65, 68, 74, 77–79, 81, 138, 287, 289
Beer,
  embedded multiple case study design, 134–39
  tax departments in, 140–44
  tax expertise, 138, 150
Beijing, 188, 192
Belgium, 68, 177
Beneficial ownership, 8, 11, 59, 100, 164fn9, 204, 243, 251–52, 255
BlackRock, 95, 285
Brazil, 59, 156–59, 163, 169, 177
British Private Equity & Venture Capital Association, 125–27
British Virgin Islands, 19, 193–94, 252–53
Bryan, Dick, 90

Cameron, David, 126
Capitalism, 1, 3, 90
Captive wealth chain, 13, 16, 18–21, 280
  in utilities markets, 33
  in tax treaties, 65
  in food, 162, 179

in tax transparency, 222–25, 237–38
in legal opinion, 274
Canada, 35, 52, 157, 252–53
Cargill, 157–60; 163–64, 175
Carnegie, Andrew, 3
Cayman Islands, 22, 44, 121, 136
Chief Financial Officer, 13, 281–82, 290
China, 187–88, 156–59, 163, 187–89, 192,
   234, 288–89
Christie's, 183, 186–89, 198
Coase, Ronald, 31
Colonial subjects, 210, 257
Commons, John, 3, 18
   futurity, 3
   goodwill, 3
Corporation,
   as agent and structure, 4–5
   firm vs. corporation, 5–7, 280–83
Country-by-country reporting, 220–21,
   229–37

Davis, Jerry, 290–91
Debt structuring, 3, 22, 283
   in art markets, 196
   in food, 156, 160
   in family wealth management, 208–9
   in intangible capital, 101–3
   in mining, 244, 252
   in private equity, 116–28
   in tax transparency, 220, 226
   in utilities markets, 30–31, 34, 39–42, 45
Deloitte, 17, 74, 167, 185
Denmark, 140, 143–44, 153, 177, see also
   Beer, Pharmaceuticals
Deville, Joe, 208
Digital economy, 21–22, 82, 98–100, 104,
   285
Dividend payments, 38, 40, 51–53, 59, 122,
   252, 283
Double taxation, 20, 50, 54–61, 64–67,
   74fn2, 231, 234–36
Dunning, John, 53–54

Education,
   elite, 18, 208–12, 214, 288
   financial, 190, 205–7, 213–18, 288
Ernst & Young, 17, 60, 74
Eurobond market, 127
European Commission, 68, 82–83, 133

European Parliament, 68, 83
European Union, 37, 157
   Accounting and Transparency
      Directive, 226
   black and greylists, 164–65
   digital tax proposal, 98
   Directive on Administrative Cooperation
      in the Field of Taxation, 83
Expertise, 7–8, 19–20, 287–89
   in art markets, 186, 191–93, 196
   in beer and pharmaceuticals, 138, 150
   in family wealth management, 201,
      212–13, 215, 218
   in legal opinion, 263, 267–70
   in mining, 250–51, 253–255
   in private equity, 121
   in tax transparency, 222, 226, 229–33,
      235–37
   in tax treaties, 56, 59, 62–63
   in utilities markets, 41

Facebook, 94–95, 100, 104
Family wealth management
   education in, 18, 205–12, 214, 213–18,
      288
   'next gen' management, 203–7
Financial secrecy index, 16, 136–39, 141,
   143, 145, 159fn4, 192fn10
Financialization, v, 33–34, 45, 107, 114,
   129, 150, 186, 281
Firms,
   actorness of, 6–8, 280–81
   as 'going concern', 280
   as 'legal fiction', 6, 60
   as organizational unit, 282–84
Fligstein, Neil, 5, 34fn1, 281
Food,
   capital flight and, 15, 155, 160
   legal affordances in, 155
   transfer pricing and, 155–58, 159–60,
      162, 165–67, 174–79
Foreign Direct Investment, 91, 156
Futurity, see Commons
Freeports, see Art

Geneva, 17–18, 159, 191, 192–93, 199, 201,
   204, 208, 212–13
Gereffi, Gary, 10, 33
Global Financial Networks, 8, 282

Global Production Networks, 2, 89, 89–93, 102–4, 292
Global Value Chains, 1, 10–11, 290–92
  Gereffi, Humphrey and Sturgeon typology , *vii*, 10–11
  international organizations and, *v*, 1, 10
  in beer and pharmaceuticals, 16, 135, 138, 151
  in food, 15, 157, 161
  in intangible capital, 98–102, 105
  in mining, 243–44, 257, 284
  in tax treaties, 49, 51, 53–54, 62–65, 289
  in public utilities, 36
  typology, 10–11
Global Wealth Chains,
  client-supplier-regulator triad, 4
  definition, 136, 191
  information asymmetries, see also *Information asymmetries* for cases
  legal affordances in, 3–4, 7, 10, 23, 38, 283, 279, 282, 292, see *Legal affordances* for cases
  regulatory liability, 1, 7, 11–12, see also *Regulatory liability* for cases
  transaction complexity, 10–13, 284, see also *Transaction complexity* for cases
  typology, 11–14, 76–77, 135, 279–80
Google, 62, 95, 104, 120
Group of Twenty, 220, 225–27, 233, 289

Hedge funds, 25, 107, 110, 118, 126fn6, 176
Her Majesty's Revenue and Customs (U.K.), 123, 126–27, 264–65, 267, 273–74
Hierarchy wealth chain, 13, 17, 20–23
  in utilities markets, 44
  in advance pricing agreements, 77
  in tax transparency, 222–24, 237–38
  in mining, 255
Hirst, Damien, 182, 185, 190, 195
Hodge, Margaret, 263–64, 266–67, 270
Hong Kong, 35, 136, 168, 192, 211
HSBC, 192, 213, 215
Hybrid wealth chains, 12, 30, 38, 44, 255

Ideal Types, 4, 9, 23
Illicit financial flows, 155–56, 192–93
Inequalities, 1, 17, 27, 29, 33, 88, 107, 111, 114, 129, 131–32, 184, 191, 229, 235
Information asymmetries, 4, 11, 15, 280, 284, 287, 289, 292
  in advance pricing agreements, 78
  in beer and pharmaceuticals, 136
  in food, 161
  in legal opinion, 277
  in mining, 251, 256
  in tax transparency, 220, 222–24, 227–29, 237
Intangible capital, 3
  defining, 95–97
  goodwill and, 89, 96–97
  legal affordances in, 99, 104
Intellectual property, 22, 33, 60, 101, 104, 138, 148, 161
International Accounting Standards Board, 95
Interpretive community, 2–4

Japan, 35, 157, 165, 234

KKR, 22, 35, 115, 119–21, 128–29
Koons, Jeff, 182, 185
KPMG, 17, 64, 74–75, 225

Lawyers, 2, 56, 189, 221, 263, 279, 286, 291
  barristers vs. solicitors, 262–63
  see also *Legal opinion, Queen's Counsel*
League of Nations, 55–57, 70
Legal affordance, 3–4, 7, 10, 23, 38, 283, 279, 282, 292
  in advanced pricing agreements, 289
  in food sector, 155
  in intangible capital, 99, 104
  in mining, 19, 243–45, 249, 256–57, 284
  in private equity, 114
  in professional strategies, 285
  in public utilities, 30, 38
  in tax transparency, 220
  in wealth management, 202, 218
  supported by interpretive communities, 2, 283
Legal opinion,
  expertise in, 263, 267–70

use of legal status, 14, 72, 81, 99, 116, 123–27
Lehman Brothers, 182, 185
Lisbon, 18, 201, 203, 206, 215
Lobbying, 51–52, 55, 59, 73, 124–26, 225, 230, 235, 256
London, *vi*, 18, 102, 127, 186–86, 188, 191, 201, 204–5, 207–8, 214, 263
Luxembourg, 22, 68, 77–78, 81, 89, 121, 192, 275–76

Mandarin Oriental, 212–16
Maugham, Jolyon, 264–65
Market wealth chain, 12, 15, 18, 225, 250, 254, 255
Martin, John Levi, 285–86
Mauritius, 52–53, 58, 61
Mining,
  expertise on, 250–51, 253–255
  legal affordances in, 19, 243–45, 249, 256–57, 284
  resource curse, 242
  tax holidays, 247–48, 252–54
  value chain dynamics, 243–44, 257, 284
Modular wealth chain, 11–12, 16–17, 280
  in advance pricing agreements, 76–78, 81
  in art markets, 183–84
  in beer and pharmaceuticals, 143–47
  in food, 162
Money laundering, 13, 16–17, 190, 193, 196
Multilateral policy coordination, 21, 31, 57, 73, 226, 256
Multinational corporations, see
  Multinational corporate enterprise
Multinational corporate enterprise, 280, 291–83
  in advance pricing agreements, 68, 70–71
  in intangible capital, 90–93, 98, 106–7, 109
  in beer and pharmaceuticals, 133, 135, 142–43, 150–52
  in food, 160
  in tax transparency, 221, 223–27, 232, 236
  see also *Corporation*
Murphy, Richard, *vii*, 122–23, 231

Netherlands, 15, 52–53, 68, 71, 79, 81, 157, 164–65, 175–77
Networks, 16
  commodity and production, 69, 90–93, 103–5, 107, 292
  corporate, 21–22, 31–32, 36, 135–39, 143, 148–50, 152
  expert and professional, 2, 7–8, 14, 19, 186, 212, 222, 285, 289
  regional, 282
  regulatory, 19
  social, 115fn1, 208, 222, 288
  tax treaty, 60–61

Offshore finance, *v*, 7–8, 14, 19, 23, 286,
  in art markets, 191
  in beer and pharmaceuticals, 136
  in family wealth management, 204, 217
  in intangible capital, 95–96, 101–03, 107
  in legal opinion, 262, 270–72, 275
  in mining, 244, 252
  in private equity, 123–24
  in tax treaties, 52–53
  in utilities markets, 40
'Onshore' finance, 53, 271, 273, 276
Orbis database, 16, 136–36, 291
Organisation for Economic Co-operation and Development, 8, 10, 19–20, 284, 289,
  advance pricing agreements and, 69–71, 74, 79, 82–84
  beer and pharmaceuticals and, 135
  food and, 161, 167
  intangible capital and, 95–96, 99–100
  mining and, 244, 256
  private equity and, 125
  tax transparency and, 224–26, 229–38
  tax treaties and, 55, 57–59, 62, 64–65
  see also *Base erosion and profit shifting*
Oxfam, 159fn4, 234–35

Palan, Ronen, *vi*, 64
Peacock, Jonathan, 267–70
Pharmaceuticals,
  embedded multiple case study design, 134–39
  tax departments in, 144–47
  tax expertise, 138, 150
Picciotto, Sol, 7, 56

Poland, 144, 175
PriceWaterhouseCoopers, 17, 59, 63, 68, 74, 77–78, 253
Private banking, 12, 18, 188, 201–3, 206, 213–17
Private equity,
    expertise on, 121
    legal affordances in, 114
    leveraged buyouts and, 116, 120–21, 125, 128
    solicitation in, 115, 117–19
Privatization, 37–38, 157, 245, 256
Production, 33, 91–92
Professionals,
    legal affordances and, 2–3, 285
    strategies of, 285–87

Queen's Counsel, 14, 263, 266–71, 273, 276–77, 287

Real estate, 13, 184–86, 206, 212, 216
Regulators, 4, 10–11, 13, 17–18, 279–80, 285–88
    in art markets, 191
    in beer and pharmaceuticals, 150
    in food, 157
    in mining, 249–50
    in private equity, 129
    in tax transparency, 223–24, 236–37
    in tax treaties, 49
    in utilities markets, 38
    legislative vs. normative functions, 223–24
Regulatory capital value, 38–39
Regulatory liability, 1, 7, 11–12
    in beer and pharmaceuticals, 136–37, 142–47
    in family wealth management, 217
    in mining, 254
    in tax transparency, 225, 237
    In utilities markets, 36–37
Relational wealth chain, 12, 17–19, 44, 196, 255, 274
Residency status, 51, 99, 125, 162, 166–67, 169, 175, 204, 211
Robé, Jean-Philippe, 5–7, 281, 283
Roubini, Nouriel, 188, 190, 196

Secrecy jurisdictions, 16–17, 78–79, 121, 123, 136–38, 140–41, 151, 155, 163
Shanghai, 188, 192
Shareholders, 5–6, 34, 36, 38–39, 41, 44–46, 103, 117, 119, 225, 252, 281, 283
Sovereignty, commercialization of, 289–90
    in advance pricing agreements, 69, 78–81
    in intangible capital, 102, 106
    in legal opinion, 266, 270
    in private equity, 126
    in tax treaties, 52–53, 61, 65
Status dynamics, 12, 15, 17–18, 282, 285–87
    in advance pricing agreements, 81
    in art markets, 183–86, 190, 194, 196
    in family wealth management, 213
    in legal opinion, 262–63, 273, 277
    in mining, 254
Starbucks, 62, 120
Supply chain management, 20, 31–33–34, 54, 62–65, 133, 135–36, 225, 283, 289, 291
Switzerland, 15, 17, 22, 61, 64, 121, 136, 159, 164, 167–68, 192, 194, 209, 214

Tax avoidance, 7, 13–15, 16, 283–84
    disclosure of tax avoidance schemes, 273–75
    in advance pricing agreements, 75, 81
    in art markets, 184, 190–94
    in beer and pharmaceuticals, 151
    in food, 55, 161, 164–65
    in legal opinion, 252, 263–67, 270–75
    in mining, 252
    in private equity, 122–24, 127, 132
    in tax transparency, 229, 231–32
    in tax treaties, 60–65
    in utilities markets, 41
Tax competition, 50, 54, 57–58, 61, 82, 257
Tax-efficient supply chain management, 20, 34, 54, 62–64, 144, 289
Tax evasion, 17, 133, 163, 166, 190–92, 196, 265
Tax havens, 34, 106, 121–23, 125, 159fn, 162–64, 166, 191, 225, 243
    See also *Secrecy jurisdictions*

Tax holidays 58, 247–48, 252–54
Tax Justice Network, 16, 121, 136, 159fn4,
  192fn10, 232
Tax transparency,
  expertise on, 222, 226, 229–33, 235–37
  legal affordances in, 220
  OECD and, 224–26, 229–38
  transfer pricing and, 232–36, 238
Tax treaties,
  expertise on, 56, 59, 62–63
  internalization advantages, 53–54, 62
  'treaty shopping', 50, 58, 60–62, 64
Technicization, 20, 221–22, 229–37
Transaction complexity, 10–13, 284
  in advance pricing agreements, 71
  in art markets, 183–84
  in beer and pharmaceuticals, 142–146
  in food, 159–60, 174
  in tax transparency, 223
  in utilities markets, 41–44
Transfer pricing, 19–20, 283
  in utilities markets, 34
  in advance pricing agreements, 69–74,
    80, 83
  in intangible capital, 99–100
  in private equity, 124
  in food, 155–58, 159–60, 162, 165–67,
    174–79
  in tax transparency, 232–36, 238
  in mining, 252, 255
Transnational,
  economic and legal order, 286–88
  epistemic community, 229
  policy community, 49, 55–56, 59, 6165
  social space, 286

Uber, 101–2, 104
Uganda, 58, 61
Ultra-High-Net-Worth Individuals, 12,
  16, 18, 214, 266, see also *Wealth
  management*
Uncertainty, 4, 17, 71–72, 143–45, 147,
  155, 187, 236, 245–55, 267, 287
  See also *Information asymmetries*
Utilities,
  legal affordances in, 30, 38
  water

Valuation processes, 3, 16–17, 22, 30,
  42–43, 49, 89, 119, 134, 159–60,
  178, 184, 251
Value, definition, 3–4
Value-Added Tax, 83, 101–2, 247
Veblen, Thorstein, 2–3, 184–85, 285
Veolia, 21, 35, 41–48

Walker, Richard, 92, 106
Water Services Regulatory Authority
  (U.K.), 37–41, 43–44
Wealth, definition of, 2–4
Wealth management,
  expertise, 201, 208, 212–13, 215, 218
  generational,
  legal affordances in, 202, 218
Weberian sociology, 8–10
World Bank Group, v, 10, 161, 256
World Economic Forum, 104

Zambia, 50–52, 54, 58, 61, 67, 246, 248
Zelizer, Viviana, 204, 288